CW00727155

coo 3.

GLOBAL CHANGE

Global Change

The Impact of Asia in the 21st Century

Edited by
Richard Thorpe and Stephen Little

First published 2001 by
PALGRAVE
Houndmills, Basingstoke, Hampshire RG21 6XS and
175 Fifth Avenue, New York, N.Y. 10010
Companies and representatives throughout the world

PALGRAVE is the new global academic imprint of
St. Martin's Press LLC Scholarly and Reference Division and
Palgrave Publishers Ltd (formerly Macmillan Press Ltd).

ISBN 0–333–92006–6

This book is printed on paper suitable for recycling and made from fully managed and sustained forest sources.

A catalogue record for this book is available from the British Library.

Library of Congress Cataloging-in-Publication Data

Global change: the impact of Asia in the twenty-first century/edited by Richard Thorpe & Stephen Little.
 p. cm.
 Papers presented at the Second Conference on Global Change held at Manchester Metropolitan University in 1998.
 ISBN 0–333–92006–6
 1. Asia—Relations—Foreign countries. 2. Asia—Economic Policy. 3. Asia—Economic conditions—20th century. I. Title: Impact of Asia in the twenty-first century. II. Thorpe, Richard. III. Little, Stephen.

DS33.3 .G54 2000
338.95—dc21

00–059181

10 9 8 7 6 5 4 3 2 1
10 09 08 07 06 05 04 03 02 01

Printed and bound in Great Britain by
Antony Rowe Ltd, Chippenham, Wiltshire

To
Tom Lupton
for his help
and inspiration
over the years

Contents

vii

Preface and Acknowledgements

This book is based on papers presented at the second Global Change Conference at Manchester Metropolitan University. The success of this second bi-annual conference was made possible only by the hard work of a large number of people who were involved in the conference, over a period of two years.

The Conference Planning Committee consisted of Tom Lupton, Tom Lowe, Frank McDonald, Richard Thorpe, Richard Warren, Patricia Rees and Steve Little. This group was ably supported by an administrative team of two people Chris Bagley and Barbara Cousins, who carried the event from its inception to its successful conclusion. The conference itself was grateful for the sponsorship of the Sefton Healthcare Group plc, who have continued to support this venture.

Between the conference and the completion of this book, the bulk of the secretarial work has fallen on Rachael Owen, Sarah Carr, Karen Fernandez and Mike Baker. We are most grateful for their patience and enthusiasm. Throughout this project we have had help and support from many others. For this we are grateful, but in particular thanks must go to Frank McDonald and Bruno LeBlanc. Frank McDonald put in a great deal of time and effort at the beginning of the planning stage of the conference, only to miss the event itself through absence abroad. Bruno LeBlanc acted as Rapporteur for the conference and made a gallant attempt to sum up the whole proceedings, an unenviable job, he did magnificently well. The editors and publishers wish to thank Financial Times Prentice Hall for Chapter 12 by Lawler and Ling. A revised version of this chapter can be found in International Economics, Hamid Seddighi and Kevin Lawler, to be published in 2001.

RICHARD THORPE
STEPHEN LITTLE

Notes on the Contributors

Jos Benders is a Senior Research Fellow at the Nijmegen Business School, a part of the Catholic University of Nijmegen, the Netherlands. Prior to joining the Nijmegen Business School in 1992, as a PhD student at the Department of Business Administration at Tilburg University, the Netherlands, Jos gained a fellowship to Indiana University at Bloomington, USA. Jos' research interests include the development and application of organization concepts, specifically those where there is a cross-national dimension. In addition he is involved in research into team-based working, and the history of cell-based manufacturing. Widely published in management journals, Jos has also authored a number of books including *Options: Work Design and Manufacturing Automation* (1993), *Useful but Unused; Group Work in Europe* (1999) (co-author) and *The Symbiosis of Work and Technology* (1995) (co-editor).

David H. Brown is a Senior Lecturer in the Department of Management Science and Chair of the Lancaster University China Group. Having completed his MA in Systems he worked for 10 years in industry as a consultant and technologist before joining the University. David has been Head of Department in Systems and Information Management and Director of the MSc in Information Management. His teaching and research interests are in the fields of strategy and systems, including their international context, and in recent years he has taken a special interest in the Far East, particularly China, where he has worked since 1996. The focus of this work often collaboratively undertaken has focused on management issues in State-Owned Enterprises (SOEs) and, Township and Village Enterprises (TVEs). He has published a wide range of articles and books, including *Advances in Chinese Industrial Studies* (editor with N. Campbell, 1900) and *Management Issues in China: Domestic Enterprises* (editor with R. Porter, 1900). In 1998 he was awarded a Professional Fellowship at Renmin University, China.

Ross Brown is a Research Fellow at the European Policies Research Centre at the University of Strathclyde in Glasgow, Scotland. His main research interests are foreign direct investment (FDI), regional economic development, supply chain linkages, inward investment agencies and cluster-based development strategies. He is currently undertaking research examining the role played by FDI in developing sectoral clusters in various European countries.

Christopher M. Dent is Senior Lecturer in Economics and European Studies at the University of Lincolnshire and Humberside. His research interests lie in the field of the EU's economic relations with East Asian countries and foreign economic policy, an area in which he has published widely. He has written a number of books, *The European Economy: The Global Context* (1997) and *The European Union and East Asia: A Economic Relationship Examined* (1999). He is currently working on a conceptualization of foreign economic policy with particular application to East Asian newly industrializing countries (NICs).

John H. Dunning has been researching into the economics of international direct investment and the multinational enterprise since the 1950s. He has authored, co-authored or edited 35 books on this subject and on industrial and regional economics. His latest monographs are a new edition of *American Investment in British Manufacturing Industry* (first published in 1958), *Alliance Capitalism and Global Business* (1997), and two edited books, *Globalization, Governments and International Business* (1997) and *Globalization, Trade and Foreign Direct Investment* (1998). He is Emeritus Professor of International Business at the University of Reading, UK, and State of New Jersey Professor of International Business at Rutgers University, New Jersey, USA. He is Chair of the Graduate Centre of International Business at the University of Reading, Senior Economic Advisor to the Director of the Division on Transnational Corporations and Investment of UNCTAD in Geneva, and Chair of a London-based economic consultancy, Economic Advisory Group Ltd, which specializes in research on international and regional economic issues. A *Festschrift*, edited by Peter Buckley and Mark Casson, was published in his honour in 1992. He is Chair of the Board of Editorial Advisors of the UNCTAD journal *Transnational Corporations*, and serves on several other editorial and advisory boards.

Jos Gamble is a Lecturer in Asia Pacific Business at the School of Management at Royal Holloway College (University of London). He has spent a total of six years working, studying and travelling in Asia, including four years in Shanghai. Between 1988 and 1990 he studied Chinese Language and Literature at Fudan University in Shanghai. He gained an MA and a PhD in Anthropology at SOAS (School of

Oriental and African Studies), University of London, his particular interest being the society and culture of the PRC. Jos worked for two years as a researcher for the School of Management at the University of Bath on a multidisciplinary project examining 'Manufacturing Organizations in the Asia Pacific' focusing on multinationals in the garment and electronics sectors.

Jeremy Howells has written and co-authored six books on research and innovation, most recently an edited book entitled *Innovation Systems in a Global Economy*, published by Cambridge University Press (1998). He has also published over 80 papers and reports on R&D and technological development. Jeremy has undertaken more focused management and development studies, funded by a range of public and private sector interests. These include studies for the UK Department of Trade and Industry (DTI), the Swedish Ministry of Industry and Trade, Industry Canada, the Japanese Ministry of International Trade and Industry (MITI) and the Ministry of Health and Welfare, regional development agencies, Training Enterprise Councils (TECs) and local authorities; in addition he has undertaken research for major international companies.

Andrew D. James is a Research Fellow at PREST (Policy Research in Engineering, Science and Technology), a research institute of the University of Manchester, UK. His principal research interests lie in company technology strategy and management, the internationalization of innovation at the level of the firm and the management of technology in mergers and acquisitions. He has a particular interest in the application of the innovation systems' perspective to the analysis of the innovation process and globalization, and was principal investigator on a study of Design Systems and Inward Investment funded by the UK Design Council.

Gerald Kaufman a graduate from Queen's College, Oxford University, was Assistant General Secretary of the Fabian Society before joining the political staff of the *Daily Mirror* in 1955, where he remained until 1964. He was Political Correspondent with the *New Statesman* from 1964 to 1965. In 1965 he became Parliamentary Press Liaison Officer to the Labour Party. He was elected to Parliament in 1970 and represents the Manchester constituency of Gorton (formerly Ardwick). Gerald has enjoyed a long and successful parliamentary career. He is Chairman of the House of Commons Select Committee on Culture, Media and Sport, a member of the Royal Commission on the Reform of the House of Lords and Chairman of the Booker Prize judges for 2000. Mr Kaufman has published *To Build the Promised Land* (1973), *How to be a Minister* (1980, rev. 1997), *My Life in the Silver Screen* (1985), *Inside the Promised Land* (1986) and *Meet me in St Louis* (1994).

Jürgen Krause is a PhD student whose main current area of research interest centres around the environmental impact made on international marketing strategies in SMEs. He has worked at the University of Applied Science in Bochum, Germany, and also as a Management Assistant for a German bank. He has published numerous articles on strategic marketing in Mittelstand firms and on developments in the German banking sector.

Hua Li is a PhD student in the International Business Unit at the Manchester Metropolitan University. She has experience of working for an export company in China, and is currently researching on the evaluation of the competitiveness advantages of industrial districts in China.

Kevin A. Lawler is a Reader in Industrial Economics at Sunderland Business School. He has published over 120 articles in professional journals and conferences. His research interests are focused on game theory modelling, transition economics and international economics. He is currently engaged in a major writing project in international economics.

Marcus C.H. Ling is a Research Fellow at Sunderland Business School. His current research interests include growth theory, internet economics and industrial economics. Dr Ling's recent work has focused on advertising economies, emerging economies and UK brewing.

Stephen Little formerly Senior Lecturer in the Department of Business Information Technology (BIT) at the Manchester Metropolitan University, is now at the Open University Business School. During 11 years in Australia based at Griffith University, Brisbane and the University of Wollongong, NSW, Stephen also held visiting fellowships to the Urban Research Programme at the Australian National University and the Fujitsu Centre for Managing Information Technology in Organisations at the Australian Graduate School of Management.

Frank McDonald is Head of the International Business Unit, Manchester Metropolitan University. He has been a Jean Monnet award holder to research the impact of EU integration on business activities.

He has research interests in the area of the impact of economic integration on business strategies and operations and assessing the importance of the development of industrial clusters in the internationalization process.

Patrick Minford has been Professor of Economics, Cardiff Business School, University of Wales at Cardiff since October 1997. From 1976 to 1997, he was Professor of Economics at Liverpool University. He was a member of the Monopolies and Mergers Commission between 1990 and 1996, and one of the HM Treasury's Panel of Forecasters ('6 wise men') from January 1993 to December 1996. For services to economics he was honoured with the award of CBE. He has authored a number of books and articles on exchange rates, unemployment, housing and macroeconomics.

Jonathan Morris is Distinguished Senior Research Fellow at Cardiff Business School, Cardiff University. Prior to this he was Professor of Management at Glamorgan University. His research interests are in organisation, management and work in Pacific Asian economies, particularly Japan and China. He has held six ESRC grants for research in this area, published over 60 papers and 4 books, including (edited) *Japan and the Global Economy* (1991) and (with M. Munday and B. Wilkinson) *Working for the Japanese* (1993).

Janet Morrison holds a BA in Political Science from the University of Virginia. She completed her MA at the University of Toronto, and obtained an LLB from the University of Newcastle-upon-Tyne. She is currently a Senior Lecturer and Programme Leader for International Business degrees in the Business School, University of Sunderland. Having studied in Japan, she has specialized in Japanese business and has written widely on the Japanese economy. More broadly, her teaching and research interests are in the area of international business and management, and she has written on the political and legal environment of international business.

Willem Noë obtained his MA degree at the University of Amsterdam, in macroeconomics and international economic relations. After a year at a Japanese securities firm in Amsterdam, he joined the Dutch Ministry of Economic Affairs in The Hague as a research economist. In 1991 he moved to the European Commission in Brussels, working first as a programme manager in DG-XII (Science, Research and Development) and later moving to DG-I to the Unit for the Analysis and Policy Planning, a small 'think-tank' unit which contributes to the study and implementation of comprehensive and coherent external policies. In 1996 he moved again to DG-III (Industry), the unit for industrial aspects of international trade relations. The focus of his work was to provide economic analysis on CEEC industries in the preparation for the future enlargement of the EU. A recent study in which he has been involved dealt with EU economic/industrial relations with Asia and the effects of the Asian crisis on EU industry.

Koji Okubayashi is Professor of the Graduate School of Business Administration at Kobe University, Japan. He graduated in 1966 from the School of Business Administration, Kobe University, receiving his MBA and Doctor's Degree from Kobe University. From 1968 to 1969 he was an Assistant in the Department of Economics, Momoyama-gakuin University, and from 1969 to 1975 Assistant Professor of the School of Business Administration, Kobe University, becoming a full Professor in 1986. His publications include *Organization for Humanistic Work* (Nihon rodo Kenkyu Kikou, 1986), *Human Resource Management in Transition Period* (Kyuo Keizaisha, 1995), *A New Paradigm of Loosely Structured Organization* (Bunshindo, 1995) and *Case Studies of Successful Personnel Management* (Chuo Keizaisha, 1994).

Vas Prabhu has specific responsibility for Research, Consultancy and External Developments and heads the four academic divisions of Strategic Management, Manufacturing and Operations Management, Marketing, and Human Resource Management at Newcastle Business School. His personal research interests and expertise lie in the area of World Class Manufacturing practices and performance. Under his direction, the 'Company Benchmarking' strand of the Raising Regional Competitiveness Project has just been completed. With over 25 years' experience in higher education, he has an in-depth knowledge of manufacturing on best practice and how to achieve it. He is responsible for the management of a number of consultancy-based centres that disseminate this knowledge throughout the region.

Hantang Qui is Senior Lecturer in International Business Strategy at the School of Business and Management, University of Greenwich, UK. In 1994 he came from China to Lancaster University where he was researching the strategic development of Chinese township and village enterprises. While in China, Hantang worked in the Management School of Fudan University in Shanghai. In addition to teaching and research duties at Fudan, he held various social and academic posts, such as chief editor of a management journal and secretary-general of a management association, where he developed extensive contracts with scholars, company managers and government officials in many parts of China. At present he travels frequently between the UK and China and maintains contacts with Chinese business circles. His research interests are in the areas of strategic management, international business and China-related management issues.

Marilyn Riley lectures in Manufacturing and Operations Management and Business Modelling at Newcastle Business School. She has a BSc in Operations Management from the University of Lancaster and is currently completing her PhD at Newcastle Business School. Her specialist field is the implementation of 'best practice' strategies in UK organizations. She is involved with the Newcastle Business School Best Practice Club and is involved in developing and delivering a wide variety of programmes at all levels to firms within the region.

Bob Ritchie is the Head of Business and Management Studies Department at the Manchester Metropolitan University and leads the Creativity, Enterprise and Innovation Research Group. In addition to researching within the area of Entrepeneurship and Innovation, he has published extensively in the fields of Risk Management and Information Management, publishing a number of international texts, journal articles and conference papers. His most recent publications include *Business Risk Management* and *Information Systems in Business*. The majority of these research activities have usually involved an international dimension. Bob is currently working with researchers in France, Israel, Cyprus and China, investigating the similarities and differences in the way they approach the support of entrepreneurship; risk and crises management; and effective supply chain management through relationship marketing.

Alexander Roy is a Research Fellow at the ESRC Centre for Research on Innovation and Competition (CRIC) in the University of Manchester. He is also a doctoral candidate at the Centre for Industrial Policy & Performance (CIPP) at the University of Leeds, supported by the ESRC in collaboration with The Foundation for Manufacturing and Industry. He holds an MA degree in Industrial & Labour Studies from the University of Leeds and a BCom degree in Commerce from the University of Birmingham. Prior to joining the MA programme at the University of Leeds, he worked on development issues for Oxfam Campaigns. His main research interests are innovation and foreign direct investment (FDI) in the service sector, especially with regard to the activities of Japanese multinationals. He has also taught extensively in the fields of economics and employee relations. His work has been published widely and has received awards from Routledge, the *Journal of Management Studies* and the University of Birmingham.

Hans Schmengler is Professor for International Marketing and Retail Marketing at Fachhochschule Bochum, University of Applied Sciences, Germany. He is co-ordinator for a number of projects, including the strengthening of relationships with universities in the USA (he is Guest Professor at Grand Canyon University in Phoenix, USA), and strategic marketing in the EU project NEUT (a project which aims at the practical positioning of business schools and universities in Romania and Bulgaria). His main research focuses on strategic marketing in Mittelstand firms, the sponsoring of sport and after-sales marketing. Professor Schmengler has published widely, particularly in the areas of after-sales marketing, and strategic and global marketing.

Xiaobai Shen is currently a consultant for China-related business in Edinburgh. She came to Britain in 1991 to take her doctorate in the University of Edinburgh, and worked as a research fellow in IMD (the International Institute for Management Development) in Lausanne, Switzerland. Her research covers a range of areas from technology development strategies for developing countries and national systems for innovation to enterprise development (as a learning and capability building process), joint ventures and cross-cultural management. Her recent publications include, *Casebook on General Management in Asia Pacific* (edited with Dominique Turpin) and *The Chinese Road to High Technology* (both 1999). In her previous career in China, Xiaobai Shen spent five years working in manufacturing industry during the Cultural Revolution. She was among the first to introduce modern management methods to China, teaching what she knew to young managers in Shanghai industries. She then moved to Beijing to take an MPhil in Science & Technology Policy at the Chinese Academy of Social Sciences, and worked for several years as a research fellow in the China Research Institute for Management Science.

David Smith is Reader in Strategic Management at University College Northampton, where he is the leader of the Strategic Management Research Group. Having worked for a Japanese multinational company, he taught for several years at the University of Derby, where he was MBA Course Director and actively involved in specialist management programmes for European companies, particularly in the aerospace and automotive industries. Dr Smith joined University College Northampton in 1997. He continues to teach on a variety of in-house management programmes. He is also actively involved in the supervision of doctoral students, researching a variety of aspects of international business. His current research interests include strategic alliances and strategic groups in the aerospace industry, foreign direct investment (FDI) in Europe and changing managerial practices and industry structures, the latter being undertaken in collaboration with Professor Peter Lawrence. He has published in a wide range of journals, including *European Business Review*, *Service Industries Journal*, *Journal of Management Development* and *International Journal of Operations and Production Management*.

Richard Thorpe is Professor in Management and Director of the Graduate Business School in the Faculty of Management and Business at the Manchester Metropolitan University. He is currently working on the development of a collaborate International MBA programme with schools in Paris and Prague, a programme related to economies in transition. Throughout the 1990s he worked and researched with colleagues in Britain, Spain, Hungary and the Czech Republic on projects with Central and Eastern Europe. He has published widely on aspects of management and development.

Giovanna Vertova works for the Istituto Affari Internazionali (IAI, Institute of International Affairs) in Rome and is a visiting Research Fellow in the International Business Unit at the Manchester Metropolitan University. She has researched extensively in the area of technological innovation and is currently investigating the role of socioeconomic networks in Italian industrial districts.

Tim Whitworth was a research student at the Staffordshire University, undertaking his empirical research in China as part of his Masters degree studies.

Barry Wilkinson is Professor of International Business at the University of Bath. Prior to that he worked at the University of Wales, Cardiff, and at the National University of Singapore. He is currently working with colleagues on the completion of a study of work organization and human resources management (HRM) under the new international division of labour in Pacific Asia. Previously, he researched and published on the diffusion of Japanese management systems, focusing on the social and political dimensions of Just-in-Time (JIT) and Total Quality Control (TQC) methods. He has also studied and published in the area of the impact of customer service initiatives on employees in British supermarkets. He is the author of *Labour and Industry in the Asia-Pacific* (1994), *The Japanization of British Industry* (Blackwell, with Nick Oliver, 1988) and *Working for the Japanese: The Economic and Social Consequences of Japanese Investment in Wales* (with Jon Morris and Max Munday, 1993).

Lee Zhuang is a Principal Lecturer in the Business School at Staffordshire University. He specializes in Strategic Management and has undertaken a number of studies into the development of business in China, including partnership arrangements with foreign enterprises.

List of Abbreviations and Acronyms

ABC	Activity-Based Accounting
ADD	Anti-Dumping Duties
AIDC	Aerospace Industry Development Corporation (Taiwan)
ANIC	Asian Newly Industrialized Country
APEC	Asia Pacific Economic Co-operation
ASEAN	Association of South East Asian Nations
ASEM	Asia-Europe Meeting
AVIC	Aviation Industries of China
BDI	British Direct Investment
BEZ	Beijing New-Tech Experimental Zone
BIS	Bank for International Settlements
BPR	Business Process Reengineering
BTM	Bell Telephone Manufacturing Company (Belgium)
C&W	Cable & Wireless
CAD	Computer-Aided Design
CAM	Computer-Aided Manufacture
CAR	capital adequacy regulations
CBI	Confederation of British Industry
CCP	Common Commercial Policy (EU)
CEE	Central and Eastern Europe
CEEC	Central and Eastern Europe Countries
CET	Common External Tariff (EU)
CFERT	China's Foreign Economic Relations and Trade
CIT	Centre for Information Technology (China)
CITC	China International Trust and Investment Corporation
CPC	Communist Party of China
CSCW	Computer-Supported Co-operative Research
CTV	colour television
DFI	Direct Foreign Investment
DTI	Department of Trade and Industry
DWTC	Daewoo Worthing Technical Centre
EAMP	East Asian Management Practice
EC	European Community
EDB	Economic Development Board (of Singapore)

EEC	European Economic Community
EFQM	European Framework for Quality Management
EIB	European Investment Bank
EIWU	Electrical Industry Workers' Union (Singapore)
EOQ	Economic Ordering Quantity
EQA	European Quality award
ERT	European Round Table (of Industrialists)
ESRC	Economic and Social Research Council
FDI	Foreign Direct Investment
FSU	Former Soviet Union
FTZ	Free Trade Zone (Malaysia)
G7	Group of Seven (Britain, France, Germany, USA, Japan, Italy, Canada)
GDP	gross domestic product
GSP	Generalized System of Preferences (EU)
HDD	hard disk drive
HDTV	high-definition TV
HEI	Higher Education Institute (Japan)
HHD	high human development
HRM	human resources management
IAD	International Automotive Design
ICOR	incremental capital – output ratio
ICT	information and communication technologies
IDF	Indigenous Defence Fighter (China)
IIP	investors in people
IME	Institute of Mechanical Engineers
IMF	International Monetary Fund
IPR	intellectual property rights
ISO	International Standards Organization
IT	information technology
IUKE	'Inside UK Enterprise' scheme
JADC	Japanese Aircraft Manufacturing Company
JAEC	Japanese Aero Engine Corporation
JDA	Japanese Defence Agency
JETRO	Japan External Trade Organization
JIT	job instruction training (TWI)
JIT	Just-In-Time
JMA	Japan Management Association
JMT	job methods training (TWI)
JSA	Japan Standards Association
JTR	job relations training (TWI)

JUSE	Union of Japanese Scientists and Engineers
JV	joint venture
KFP	Korean Fighter Project
LCD	liquid-crystal display
LDP	Liberal Democratic Party (Japan)
LED	light-emitting diode
LHD	low human development
LSI	large-scale integrated chip
LSO	loosely-structured organization (Japan)
M&A	merger and acquisition
MAS	Malayan Airline Systems
MFN	most favoured nation
MHD	medium human development
MITI	Ministry of International Trade and Industry (Japan)
MNE	multinational enterprise
MoF	Ministry of Finance (Japan)
MOFERT	Ministry of Foreign and Economic Relations and Trade (China)
MPT	Ministry of Posts and Telecommunications (China)
MRPI	Materials Requirement Planning I
MRPII	Materials Requirement Planning II
NAFTA	North America Free Trade Agreement
NAMC	Nippon Aircraft Manufacturing Company
NETC	Nissan European Technology Centre
NGO	non-governmental organization
NIC	newly industrializing country
NIESR	National Institute for Economic and Social Research
NMISA	Nissan Manufacturing Spain
NMUK	Nissan Manufacturing UK
NRD	Nissan Research and Development
NTB	non-tariff barrier
NTC	Nissan Technology Centre
NUMMI	New United Motor Manufacturing, Inc. (USA)
O and M	overhaul and maintenance
OECD	Organization for Economic Co-operation and Development
OEM	original equipment manufacture
OJT	on-the-job (training)
OLI	Ownership Location Internationalization
PCB	printed circuit board
PCBA	printed circuit board assembly

PDSS	public digital switching system
PIM	plastic injection moulding
PRC	People's Republic of China
PTA	Post and Telecommunications Agency
PTIC	Posts and Telecommunications Industrial Corporation (China)
QC	quality circle
R&D	research and development
SAIC	Shanghai Aviation Industrial Corporation
SAR	Special Administrative Region (Hong Kong)
SCAP	Supreme Commander of Allied Powers (Japan)
SEM	Single European Market
SEZ	Special Economic Zone (China)
SITC	Standard International Trade Classification
SME	small and medium-sized enterprise
SOE	state-owned enterprise
SOP	standard operating procedures (Toyota)
SPC	State Planning Commission (China)
SQC	statistical quality control
TEC	Training and Enterprise Council (UK)
TFP	total factor productivity
TNC	transnational corporation (Japan)
TPS	Toyota Production System
TQC	total quality control
TQM	total quality management
TVE	Township ands Village Enterprise
TWI	Training Within Industry (Toyota)
UN	United Nations
UNDP	United Nations Development Programme
USD	US dollar
VCR	video recorder
WTO	World Trade Organization
XAC	Xian Aircraft Corporation (China)

Introduction

Stephen Little and Richard Thorpe

BACKGROUND

This book is based on papers presented at the second conference on Global Change held at Manchester Metropolitan University in 1998. Its focus was on the role of Asia, both as a source of global paradigms and as region with the potential to inspire global strategies. The first conference, held in 1996 also produced a book (*Organizational Strategy and Technological Adaptation to Global Change*, McDonald and Thorpe, 1997). This identified the key issues in relation to global change and examined the role technology played in global change and its implications for organizations.

The 1996 conference examined the impact that the end of the Cold War had had and the emergence of the transitional economies of Eastern Europe and the former Soviet Union (FSU) as new players in a global economic system. The complexity of our world has become better appreciated following the removal of what Ohmae (1995) terms the 'bi-polar discipline' of the Cold War, a concept that served to obscure the differences within and between members of the Eastern and Western blocs and consigned the remainder of humanity to the disparagingly termed 'Third World'.

However, while globalization has increased the significance of intellectual capital as leveraged by information and communication technology, assumptions that a technically driven globalized economy can solve the remaining problems of differential development are being increasingly challenged. There is mounting evidence that economically marginal performers are being excluded from any influence over the priorities shaping the global economy. Rapid integration has brought together disparate national and regional interests and cultures and these have become increasingly interlinked within networked and globalized organizations. Information technologies have facilitated these changes through the reduction of transaction costs and the alteration of the relative advantages and economies of scale. This, in turn, has led to a complex layering of labour markets, both internal and external to the developed economies driving the process.

Framing the Conference

From the first Global Change conference the theme of the importance of East Asia emerged. At the time of its planning, the dramatic changes that have taken place in Asia were unanticipated, not least by the participants and individuals who selected Asia as the topic for the second conference, whose theme was Asia's impact in the twenty-first century. What resulted is reflected in the chapters contained in this book. The conference attracted a wide range of papers and discussion sessions covering the history of developments in Asia over the last 20 or 30 years, many measuring the changes in growth, but many also attempting to understand the processes of globalization and their effects. Papers were also presented that discussed and characterized local management thinking and local management practices in Asian countries, particularly from the perspective of Western companies working in Asia. However, there were also papers illustrating the learning that can be gained by Western organizations from Asian management practices.

Another feature of the conference was the variety of conceptual frameworks presented. There were papers offering classical economic analysis and organizational development perspectives, while some presented systems theory perspectives, and one even offered a Taoist perspective, for understanding not simply Asia, but the rest of the world! The richness of perspectives offered, it must be said, did not make for simplicity. The very different conceptual frameworks offered made it somewhat difficult for the wide range of academics present to converse with each other.

The main focus for the two days was on the current dynamics of the developments in the whole of Asia as they have emerged from the last 20 or 30 years. This period has seen a perceptible shift in the focus of growth in the world economy across the Pacific to the East Asian mainland. This broad context proved a helpful one as it avoided too close a focus on what might reasonably be claimed to be relatively short-term problems. This book therefore contains a range of chapters reflecting upon the complex consequences of the success of Japan and other Asian economies in transferring, transforming and re-exporting the socio-technical systems which drove the expansion of their economies. The responses of their erstwhile mentors have resulted in the rapid diffusion of product and process innovations in many different directions and the emergence of an incomplete but globalized world economy. Historical and cultural particularities from East and West ensure diversity and friction throughout an emerging global system that is often presented as a seamless technological artefact. For some time European and North American companies have sought to emulate aspects of Asian strategies and comparative advantage has been eroded as Asian methods, building on the Western industrial model, have been re-exported to the original industrial core of Europe and North America. Nuki (1998) shows that this in turn has engendered a response based on accelerating the product life cycle through the application of information and communication technologies (ICTs) at all stages of development and production. Recent events in the East Asian economies have undermined confidence in the idea of 'miracle economies'. Some acknowledgement of Krugman's (1996) views on the uncritical acceptance of high growth rates over relatively short periods from very low base levels is welcome. Unfortunately, the immediate impact in the West has been to reject out of hand the development strategies which delivered past growth even though the very different forms of crisis across the affected economies and their different responses reflect the diversity of these approaches within the region.

The emerging system of global production seems to have left the world divided into the 'triad' described by Ohmae (1990): three major regions of North East Asia, North America and Western Europe. Localities within these regions are restructuring rapidly in an attempt to obtain or ensure a continued prosperous place within them. Dunning (1993) has shown that the majority of direct foreign investment is within and between members of this triad.

Europe, North America and East Asia all contain the most advanced levels of economic development juxtaposed with developing economies. Each region therefore faces the challenge of supporting balanced growth in peripheral areas where available infrastructure and skills cannot support full integration into the global economy. There seems some degree of consensus that in the post-Cold War era difference and diversity were themselves resources, and Ohmae (1995) celebrates such variation as evidence of the need to pursue 'zebra strategies' which play to the relative strength of the most developed components of national economies in order to create regional linkages and synergies with the established global players.

The economic turbulence on the Western Pacific rim reflects the diversity of problems facing the participants in this network, but in many respects it is the success of their strategies which has brought these growing economies to the point at which a paradigm shift from a situation of catch-up to a position of sustained production of new technologies is now required. Some understanding of the dynamics of the strategies employed in East Asia has come through Kim's examination of the historical connection but significant difference between the *chaebol, zaibatsu* and *keiretsu* (Kim, 1996); further studies by Redding (1996) and Wong (1996) have added to understanding of Chinese business practices. At least part of the current crisis in East Asia is a reflection of the difference between the problems of technological leadership and those of catching-up with leading economies. Participation in the development of the intellectual resources necessary for this next stage requires direct integration into the emerging world system and a greater institutional alignment within and between regions.

In Part 1, 'Framing the Conference', the keynote speakers offered a variety of perspectives in relation to the current state of the East Asian economies.

Gerald Kaufman (Chapter 1) provided a politician's view of 'The Century of the Pacific Rim', emphasizing that the attention paid to the recent economic crisis in East Asia reflects to some extent the central role of this region in the world economy. In contrast, Patrick Minford (Chapter 2) analysed the current problems in Asian economies in terms of monetary mismanagement following the transfer of production and production technologies from the established manufacturing economies to the 'little dragons' and was not convinced that there were underlying technological drivers for the associated downturn in the global economy.

Peter Dicken provided a wide-ranging reflection on the often simplistic Western construction of a diverse region with complex relationships among its constituents. He considered the re-alignment following the removal of 'Cold War fault lines' and offered an alternative view of the regional impact of Japanese investments from that offered by Patrick Minford.

Willem Noë (Chapter 3) described the background and structure of 'Investing in Asia's Dynamism', a joint EC/UNCTAD report on EU direct investment aimed at both developing and developed regions of Asia. The European Union is particularly keen to encourage European investment into Asia's developing economies, with initiatives such as 'Asia Invest' aimed at smaller and medium-sized companies which may benefit from resource-sharing between European development and Asian manufacture. This latter programme is aimed at the same potential partners as those sought by the more developed Asian economies, and represents an attempt at cross-regional networking.

These chapters serve to raise as well as to frame a number of questions discussed at the conference.

THE DYNAMICS OF EAST–WEST EXCHANGE

Economies such as Korea, which have been highly successful during the catching-up phase of development, have shown that different socio-technical paradigms are needed to sustain an economy in the conditions of lower absolute growth encountered in relatively mature markets. Japan's earlier lead means that the debate over new economic strategies has intensified further since the collapse of the bubble economy, but consensus has not been achieved over exactly what changes should be made to the institutional structures which supported their post-war development. China, as the region's largest economy, has the advantage of size and continuing scope for the established high-growth paradigm. However, this size also increases the problems of regional differentials in development. The successful business networks of Hong Kong can only be developed so far into the wider hinterland before cultural and linguistic differences impede their further extension.

The Institutional Framework

In establishing the institutional framework for the conference, John Dunning (Chapter 4) contributed a substantial review of globalization and FDI in Asian developing countries which draws upon the enormous contribution he has made to the study and analysis of such patterns of investment over the past decades.

Janet Morrison (Chapter 6) addresses specific differences between Anglo-American and Japanese traditions of corporate governance and discusses how the fragmentation of the informal ties between companies and their main banks reflects both the institutional crisis in Japanese banking and the search for more effective monitoring within the framework of traditional values.

Christopher Dent (Chapter 5) analyses evolving forms and issues of governance affecting economic relations between the European Union and East Asia, particularly the growing influence of international institutions and the increasingly important role of multinational business interests.

The cost differentials of the emerging global production system have led developed economies to shift their focus towards the higher added value activities at the end of the production chain. Product differentiation and customer support are seen as the means of maintaining demand for goods and services in mature home markets. At the same time, across the system as a whole specific markets and specific technologies are at different points in the cycle of growth, maturity and decline. Maintaining a dominant role in this system means meeting the challenge of delivering continuous innovation at the cutting edge while ensuring effective diffusion of more mature technologies. The result of such efforts is the emergence of new forms of locational and functional differentiation across a globalized network of invention, innovation and implementation.

Locational decisions for the components of such a system are further complicated by differences within individual national states in both developed and developing regions. These may be at least as significant that those between them. Using 1991 statistics, Ohmae (1995) shows that China's national average *per capita* GDP of US$317 masks regional variations in GDP ranging from US$164 and 197 in Guizhou and Guangxi to US$1218 and 1527 in Beijing and Shanghai. While such differences may be most marked within economies undergoing rapid development, the logic of the current wave of technology-driven globalization has impacted on significant sectors of the developed economies themselves, giving rise to the concepts of 'sun-belt' and 'rust-belt'. Both Japan and Britain are finding that only specific geographical areas or economic sectors may benefit fully from integration into the global economy. Smaller local organizations and enterprises in particular may gain little. As with technology transfer premised on foreign direct investment (FDI), key resources may be diverted to the support of incoming capital, hampering local development initiatives. Inward investors may 'cherry-pick' demographically, establishing greenfield developments remote from existing competing companies. Such tactics allow them both the inducements offered by local authorities and a workforce whose age structure represents a significant cost advantage in itself. The resulting regional 'beauty contests' may result in supporting technologies, in particular the information and telecommunications infrastructure, optimized for these externally driven actors.

All sizes of organization, whether commercial, regulatory or voluntary, are increasingly being confronted with the need to operate across a multiplicity of boundaries – geographical, political and cultural – in order to function within the emerging global system. Delamaide (1994) mounts a case for the re-emergence of historical geographical and economic synergies across Europe since the end of arbitrary Cold War division. He offers a perspective on the pre-existing historical and cultural linkages which pre-date both the recent Cold War divisions and the emergence of the current nation states. In many areas such as the Baltic, these older linkages can be seen re-emerging in the pan-European context. The political geography underlying these connections goes back to the Hanseatic League or the Holy Roman Empire. Delamaide attributes the patterns of potential development across an enlarging European Community (EC) to a range of geo-historical connections. Elsewhere, he draws attention to the pivotal role of Turkey as a link between Europe and the Turkic republics of the FSU. Such cultural synergies offer a means of retaining regional coherence in the face of continuing expansion of regional entities such as the European Union.

Enduring cultural linkages, whether established through trade, migration or colonization can be identified throughout the emergent global system. In East Asia, as in Europe, the end of the Cold War has seen the admission of Cambodia to the Association of South East Asian Nations (ASEAN) and Vietnam to the Asia Pacific Economic Co-operation forum (APEC). The reassertion of Greater China in regions of former European and Japanese colonization has been of particular benefit to Taiwan, with some 35 000 enterprises now established on the mainland (China Intercontinental Press, 1997). Taiwan's connection to the Japanese economy means that Taiwanese inward investment to the PRC represents a layering of regional cross-influences and a transfer of a range of capabilities and traditions.

Taiwan has followed a classic route of state-sponsored development, particularly in the area of information technology (Tsai, 1993). Companies such as Tatung reflect the same Japanese colonial influence which produced the sprawling portfolios of the Korean *chaebols*. However, the mix of traditional Chinese business networks (Numazaki, 1996) with state-provided or state-sponsored infrastructure has produced a different outcome from both Korea and from Hong Kong, where the British colonial legacy was significant in terms of legal infrastructure as much as technical.

Both Ohmae (1995) and Delamaide (1994) mount arguments for the acknowledgement of complementary regional associations across national boundaries. However, both implicit and explicit in Ohmae's 'zebra strategy' is the view that national or even international regional government no longer has a significant role in development. While this is challenged by the evident success of some national government policies, even in the present period of crisis recovery, there are differences of opinion over which level of government – regional, national or transnational – is best equipped to deal with negotiations over a particular location's relationship to the wider economy.

Although linkages between the advanced areas of developing economies are creating new regions irrespective of national boundaries, few national governments are prepared to relinquish responsibility for the development of the state as a whole. While the assertion that national or even international regional government no longer has a significant role in development is increasingly being challenged, the differential development that has been entrenched through a dependence on a global infrastructure does threaten the legitimacy of the nation state. This is being driven by the priorities of the dominant developed economies. The development of co-operative economic mechanisms such as NAFTA and ASEAN suggest that there are means of achieving development which retain a role for national governments. However, the emergence of economic groupings as large as APEC, with the imminent addition of Russia, Vietnam and Peru, or the proposals for further expansion of the European Union, challenge the original coherence and logic of these associations.

Chains, Networks and Webs

The logic of a global production has led to the progressive relocation of basic manufacturing processes to the periphery, superseding the geographical separation of a periphery providing raw resources and a basic market from a core containing transformation processes and sophisticated markets. This process has been evident for many years, however, there is a consequent shift in focus in developed economies towards the end of the production chain where product differentiation and customer support can maintain demand for goods and services. This means that although the integration of this emergent system can be overstated, a system of connected markets and technologies at different points in the cycle of growth, maturity and decline cannot be described convincingly as a chain.

The metaphor of 'production chain' is being superseded by the idea of 'global production networks' in which R&D, routine manufacturing, final assembly and after-market support for products or services from a range of sectors may all be present in the same location. The redistribution of these activities during the product life cycle further undermines the traditional concepts of centre and periphery. The orderly transfer of these functions from core to periphery across the product life cycle described by Hirsch (1967) is replaced by an interpenetration of core and periphery in which market and raw materials source, production and consumption are co-located.

Modelling the Web

Information and communication technologies (ICTs) underpin the global system, they also offer opportunities for participation in the 'information economy' to peripheral areas. ICTs have enabled the disaggregation of the production chain into a network by locating each activity specifically at its point of greatest comparative advantage. The ability to disaggregate the intellectual capital required by the divergent stage of the design and development process from the convergent, focused discipline of the mass production process (see Jones, 1980) has been enhanced by the ability to control production lines from across national boundaries. The phenomenon of design activities located within the target market, with production located in the low-cost periphery, is already well recognized. Lipietz (1992) argues that the ability to separate production from consumption signals the end of the 'Fordist compromise' which drove the expansion of production on a base of strong domestic demand from the industrial work-force. Production workers remote from the destination market no longer need to be paid sufficiently well to consume the products of their own labour.

Castells (1996) offers a related paradigm of the 'network enterprise' which is composed of components from larger corporations, collaborating in specific spatial and temporal circumstances, while the main companies are still pursuing global strategies of direct competition. The framework of the network organization appears to offer an opportunity for contributions from smaller players through access to resources from within global networks. Inoue (1998) describes a 'virtual village' across part of Tokyo in which small enterprises are able to form and re-form alliances in order to provide high-technology services to larger companies. However, the additional accessibility and flexibility of advantage offered to smaller players is accompanied by the capability of larger firms to restructure in such a way that they can enter niche markets yet still draw on their wider resource base. Such firms may de-couple key business units, the better to target customers and markets traditionally served by much smaller firms.

The divisions within the emerging global economic system create additional problems which undermine the broader sustainability of its development. The newly industrializing countries (NICs) that are in the process of catching-up are engaged in a process in which development and growth are synonymous. They are sceptical of advice which suggests that they should adhere to higher standards than those applying at the equivalent stage in the development of the dominant established economies. Additionally, significant parts of the globe are excluded from this process of catch-up. Their difficulty lies in maintaining even relatively modest economic objectives. Exclusion from policy making processes or from influence over the emerging global production system reduces their ability to negotiate over the sustainable exploitation of the primary resources they have traditionally contributed to the global system. The issues reflect an emergent 'information apartheid' within the global economy and the spatial strategies facilitated through ICTs threaten any prospect of integrated development by allowing a 'cherry-picking' approach to both the human and physical resources of developing regions driven by external criteria.

Design Paradigms and Paradigm Shifts

A broad level of analysis is needed to account for the linkages described above and to examine regional economic activities in the context of the paradigm shift from catch-up based on rapid growth rates to technological leadership. A shift in the view of innovation and product life cycle to that of process life cycles, akin to double-loop learning (Argyris, 1983) is part of the required change. The repositioning of effort across the production network may better be understood from the perspective of the design philosophies and methods that have been applied to both product and processes during the last three decades. Galbraith (1977) staked the claim that information systems' design was in effect organization design. Information systems designers have in turn drawn heavily and effectively on a wide body of more general design research and theory.

In parallel to the development of organization theory through and beyond the framework of systems theory, design methodologies have reflected a changing understanding of the processes and the role of the participants and wider stakeholders in them. Scott (1992) argued that organization theory could be seen as developing from a closed rational systems view of classic management theory to an open natural systems view able to accommodate influences from the institutional and technical environments.

Jones (1980) presents design methods extant in the 1960s and 1970s, and relates them to a generic model of the design process. This model consists of three stages:

Divergent Search ⟶ Transformation ⟶ Convergence

The *divergent search* stage involves searching the possible solution space of a design problem. The ultimate objectives of a project are unstable and tentative, the problem boundary is unstable and undefined and evaluation is deferred. The aim is to increase uncertainty and widen the range of possibilities.

The *transformation* process is, in effect, the imposition on to the results of the divergent search of a pattern which will allow convergence to a single solution. At this stage objectives, briefs and boundaries are fixed, critical variables and constraints are recognized and the problem is divided into sub-problems for parallel or serial treatment. The freedom to change sub-goals and rapid evaluation of alternative choices is needed. Personal capabilities and orientation of the team are critical at this stage.

The *convergence* stage involves activities to reduce uncertainty. This stage requires a very different orientation. Here persistence and rigidity of mind become a virtue. Unforeseen sub-problems may prove critical at this stage and cause recycling to earlier stages, so it is dependent on the successful handling of the preceding stages. The models used to represent remaining alternatives become more detailed and concrete while the diligence of 'normal science' is used to arrive at a single satis-factory solution.

The received wisdom around this model is that the divergent stage involves the million-dollar decisions, while the convergent stage involves the thousand-dollar decisions.

This essentially linear model of design can be seen in the 'waterfall' model of information systems design (e.g. Birrell and Ould, 1985). Here the need for re-cycling indicated by Jones is accommodated between successive stages of development and refinement.

Considered in conjunction with generic production chains, such as that presented by Dicken (1998), the shifts of intellectual focus across the design stages suggest a paradox. It seems to run counter to the shift to the end of the chain in developed economies. However, the innova-tion of consumer-based added value services can involve significant divergent analysis, and the associated core technologies are likely to be retained by the most advanced players. The relative success of the NICs can then be seen as a highly effective entry at the convergent stage of the process. This involves efficient production utilizing mature tech-nologies. Arguably Japanese companies have developed considerable competence in the transformation stage with highly innovative prod-ucts derived from newer technologies. However, with some notable exceptions, these seem less proficient at the divergent stage which can be likened to the development of basic research strategies and fundamental innovation tracks. The relatively narrowly targeted strategies of Taiwanese firms have delivered world-class performance in key areas of information technology (IT). Dominance in motherboard design and fabrication, together with the manufacturing capability in the 'silicon forge' service provided to overseas designers requiring prototype chips, has allowed participation at key points in the production network. Once this level of performance was achieved, companies such as Acer were able to develop a more integrated presence as full-range manufacturers. In contrast, the evidence presented by Wilkinson *et al.* in Chapter 19 suggests that Malaysia, despite efforts to shift to transformative and divergent activities via the 'Multimedia Super Corridor' and related initiatives may still be stuck with the essentially convergent tasks of global commerce.

Just as views of organizational relationships have moved towards a network or web paradigm, so have models of the design process shifted to accommodate less linear and more situational views of design. The implications of a shift from a hierarchical to a network or web view of organizations is foreshadowed by Thompson (1967) in terms of coalition-formation across the organization, and by Mintzberg (1979) in the form of work constellations. Within design, the acknowledgement of design participation of users (e.g. Cross, 1972) also shifted models of the design process into less hierarchical and more situated paradigms.

Learning to be Global

Marvin (1988) describes the social learning curve associated with the introduction of new electrically-based technologies at the turn of the last century. Given the time taken for a general understanding of the appropriate use of the telephone to emerge, it is not surprising that a global consensus on the more recent generation of information and communication technologies underpinning the current wave of globalization is still to emerge. What is clear is that the necessary paradigm for the new global system will not emerge on its own.

Kaplinsky and Posthuma (1992) demonstrate the transferability of organizational technology in the form of Japanese manufacturing practice without high levels of capitalization. Marginal players – in this case, East African manufacturing companies – made significant improvements in their performance without substantial capital investment. The adoption of the organizational approaches utilized in Japan can transform efficiency and effectiveness in companies in developing economies without the supporting technology usually associated with it; the opportunity exploited was the gain from relatively capital-free reorganization. These gains were achieved through the use of intellectual resources which needed some consonance with cultural assumptions embedded within the imported techniques, but Kaplinsky and Posthuma argue that to be fully competitive with developed economies a similar level of capital resources is required.

If access to state-of-the-art technology is necessary for full participation in the global economy, access to such technology is no guarantee of its appropriate use. Sproull and Kiesler (1991) demonstrate that a process of organizational learning is needed to move beyond the technical effects of direct substitution of IT for manual processes. The transformative gains in effectiveness represented by the 'informated organization' (Zuboff, 1988) will come about in the globalized arena only through an understanding of the meaning of cultural interoperability at both pre-competitive and competitive stages of development (Kaye and Little, 1998). Vygotsky's 'zone of proximal development' (see Cole, 1985) offers a paradigm of how adjustment to a new consensual culture might be assisted. Actors, whether individuals or organizations, may be supported mutually by a scaffolding provided by institutionalized practices and structures, until the underlying values and assumptions are internalized. The use of activity theory in information systems development (Kutti, 1991) and the emphasis on group cognition in current computer-supported co-operative research (CSCW) provides some evidence of the practicality of the approach.

STRUCTURE OF THE BOOK

This book is divided into five main parts. Part 1 (Chapters 1–6) contains the keynote contributions and three other chapters dealing with the institutional framework which underlies both the difficulties and opportunities of the current situation. Part 2 (Chapters 7–10) deals with the diversity of mutual influences between East Asia and the remainder of the global economy, while Part 3 (Chapters 11–14) contains four chapters dealing with the influence of Western practices and investment resources on the East. Part 4 (Chapters 15–17) deals with north east Asia, specifically China, and Part 5 (Chapter 18–21) with South East Asia, Malaysia and Singapore.

Dealing with Diversity

The 'production web' metaphor is an attempt to capture the complexity and diversity of intra-and inter-firm linkages, and Part 2 examines the complex exchange of ideas between Asia and the rest of the global economy.

Koji Okubayashi contributes a study (Chapter 9) which reports on the findings of extensive research into the adjustment of Japanese management practices in Japanese affiliates in Germany and the UK. Two distinct approaches to adapting to external conditions have been observed, and these are described and discussed in relation to their impact in Japan and on the host economies.

Alexander Roy in Chapter 7 points out that while Japan's investment in the UK is the largest in Europe, it is predominantly directed to the service sector. The service sector is complex, and is not well integrated into theories of international investment. However, Roy suggests that the impact of financial and commercial services on the host economy requires careful investigation, since *a priori* impressions question whether the sectors can produce the benefits attributed to the manufacturing sector.

Jos Benders in Chapter 8 looks at one of the most influential Japanese manufacturing companies, Toyota, and considers the extent to which we can learn about the process of technology transfer and adaptation of systems from responses to the Toyota model.

Andrew James and Jeremy Howells in Chapter 10 examine the internationalization of product design and development through case studies of the activities of three Asian companies in the UK. Internationalization of innovative activities appears to be driven by both a desire to get closer to foreign customers, and a desire to access technological capabilities specific to national innovation systems.

West into East

Part 3 shows that the strength of economic linkages between Asia and the rest of the world is demonstrated by the return flow of influence.

Prabhu and Riley in Chapter 11 describe the results of an extensive survey into the adoption of East Asian management practices by UK companies which can be regarded as 'best-practice' organizations.

Hans Schmengler and Jürgen Krause in Chapter 13 report on the reaction of customers in the ASEAN countries to the service provided by German Mittelstand firms in the construction sector. They examine the balance between local subsidiaries and reliance on sales representation by agents.

Kevin Lawler and Marcus Ling in Chapter 12 examine the issue of British direct investment in China in the period since 1979. As the largest investment partner within the European Union, and with increasing government support for an Asian-oriented investment, British experience offers indications of best practice in penetration of the Chinese market.

North East Asia: China

China, as potentially the largest economy in the region, merits special attention in Part 4. The continuing economic reforms have presented a succession of challenges to the orientation of both domestic and foreign companies operating there.

Bob Richie, Lee Zhuang and Tim Whitworth in Chapter 14 provide an analysis of the reported experiences of companies engaging in joint venture enterprises in China in relation to managerial and operational issues.

Hua Li, Frank McDonald and Giovanna Vertova in Chapter 17 present a theoretical framework to explain the clustering process and its influence on domestic and international competitiveness. They provide a taxonomy of clusters and industrial districts illustrated by data from Shanghai and Beijing indicating that separate domestically and internationally oriented clusters are discernible.

David Brown and Hantang Qi in Chapter 15 explore the readiness of Chinese enterprises to meet the challenge presented by the continuing programme of economic reform. Both state and private enterprises are required to play their part, the former by increasing efficiency and shedding workers, the latter by continuing their dramatic growth and providing replacement employment opportunities. The difficulties of strategic implementation are illustrated by two case studies.

Xiaobei Shen in Chapter 16 compares the transformation of management in two telecommunication technology producers, one an established state-owned company, the other a more recent joint venture, and finds comparable difficulties in the development of appropriate technological capabilities.

South East Asia: Singapore, Malaysia

Part 5 addresses the problems of later entrants to the global manufacturing web. Ross Brown in Chapter 18 examines the role played by foreign direct investment (FDI) in the establishment of linkages in the electronics industry in Singapore. Both foreign investments and the development of indigenous local suppliers are dealt with. Barry Wilkinson *et al.* in Chapter 19 show that Malaysia's attempt to repeat Singapore's success in moving to higher-grade activities within a globalized electronics production chain has met with relatively limited success.

David Smith in Chapter 20 examines the growth of the aerospace industry in South East Asia. Both national government strategies and the development of strategic alliances by established Western companies have played a part in this. The growth of activity in the region represents a significant development in the world aerospace industry.

Hua Li and Frank McDonald in Chapter 20 conclude the book with a review of the main lessons to be learned for management from the Asian crisis of 1997–8. The chapter explores the various causes put forward to explain the crisis and provides an overview of the lessons that might be drawn.

References

Argyris, C. (1983) 'Action Science and Intervention', *Journal of Applied Behavioural Science*, 28(3), 115–40.
Birrell, N.D. and Ould M.A. (1985) *A Practical Handbook for Software Development*, Cambridge, Cambridge University Press.
Castells, M. (1996) *The Rise of the Network Society*, Oxford, Blackwell.
China Intercontinental Press (1997) *Questions and Answers Concerning the Taiwan Question and Reunification of China*, Beijing, China Intercontinental Press.
Cole, M. (1985) 'The Zone of Proximal Development: Where Culture and Cognition Create each Other', in J.V. Wertsch (ed.), *Culture Communication and Cognition: Vygotskian Perspectives*, Cambridge, Cambridge University Press.
Cross, N. (ed.) (1972) *Design Participation*, London, Academy Editions.
Delamaide, D. (1994) *The New Super-Regions of Europe*, New York, Penguin.
Dicken, P. (1998) *Global Shift: Transforming the World Economy*, 3rd edn, London, Paul Chapman.
Dunning, J.H. (1993) *Multinational Enterprises and the Global Economy*, Reading, MA, Addison-Wesley.
Galbraith, J. (1977) *Organization Design*, Englewood Cliffs, NJ, Addison-Wesley.
Hirsch, S. (1967) *Location of Industry and International Competitiveness*, Oxford, Clarendon.
Inoue, T. (1998) 'Small Businesses Flourish in Virtual Village', *Nikkei Weekly*, 26 January, p. 1.

Jones, J.C. (1980) *Design Methods: Seeds of Human Futures*, 2nd edn, Chichester, Wiley.

Kaplinsky, R. and Posthuma, A. (1994) *Easternisation: The Spread of Japanese Management Techniques to Developing Countries*, Ilford, Frank Cass.

Kaye, G.R. and Little, S.E. (1998) 'Setting Standards: Strategies for Building Global Business Systems', in F. McDonald and R. Thorpe, *Organizational Change and Strategic Adaptation to Global Change*, London, Macmillan.

Kim, E.M. (1996) 'The Industrial Organisation and Growth of the Korean Chaebol: Integrating Development and Organizational Theories', in G.G. Hamilton (ed.), *Asian Business Networks*, Berlin, de Gruyter.

Krugman, P. (1996) *Pop Internationalism*, Cambridge, MA, MIT Press.

Kutti, K. (1991) 'Activity Theory and its Applications to Information Systems Research Dan Development', in H.-E. Nissen, H.K. Klein and R. Hirschheim (eds), *Information Systems Research: Contemporary Approaches and Emergent Traditions*, Amsterdam, Elsevier.

Lipietz, A. (1992) *Towards a New Economic Order: Postfordism, Ecology and Democracy*, Cambridge, Polity Press.

Marvin, C. (1988) *When Old Technologies Were New: Thinking About Electric Communication in the Late Nineteenth Century*, New York, Oxford University Press.

McDonald, F. and Thorpe, R. (1997) *Organizational Strategy and Technological Adaptation to Global Change*, London, Macmillan.

Mintzberg, H. (1979) *The Structuring of Organizations: A Synthesis of the Research*, Englewood Cliffs, NJ, Prentice-Hall.

Nuki, T. (1998) 'Earlier and Faster – A New Trend of Japan's Production Strategy', in P. Bannerjee, R. Hackney, G. Dhillon and R. Jain, *Business Information Technology Management: Closing the International Divide*, New Delhi, Har Anand.

Numazaki, I. (1996) 'The Role of Personal Networks in the Making of Taiwan's *guanxiqiye* (related enterprises)', in G.G. Hamilton (ed.), *Asian Business Networks*, Berlin, deGruyter.

Ohmae, K. (1990) *The Borderless World: Power and Strategy in the Interlinked Economy*, London, Collins.

Ohmae, K. (1995) *The End of the Nation State: The Rise of Regional Economics*, New York, Free Press.

Redding, S.G. (1996) 'Weak Organisations and Strong Linkages: Managerial Ideology and Chinese Family Business Networks', in G.G. Hamilton (ed.), *Asian Business Networks*, Berlin, deGruyter.

Scott, W.R. (1992) *Organizations: Rational, Natural and Open Systems*, Englewood Cliffs, NJ, Prentice-Hall.

Sproull, L. and Kiesler S. (1991) *Connections: New Ways of Working in the Networked Organization*, Cambridge, MA, MIT Press.

Thompson, J. (1967) *Organizations in Action*, New York, McGraw-Hill.

Tsai, H.-J. (1993) 'An Evaluation of Spatial Aspects of IT Strategies in Taiwan', MSc dissertation, University of Wollongong, Wollongong.

Wong, S.-L. (1996) 'Chinese Entrepreneurs and Business Trust', in G.G. Hamilton (ed.), *Asian Business Networks*, Berlin, deGruyter.

Zuboff, S. (1988) *In the Age of the Smart Machine*, New York, Basic Books.

Part 1
Framing the Conference

1 The Century of the Pacific Rim

Gerald Kaufman

It was probably no accident that this Global Change conference, whose papers are included in this volume, was held immediately after the 1998 Europe–Asia Conference in London, or that it coincided with the alleged financial crisis in Japan, from which enormous waves and ripples have continued to spread.

The day before the conference, a newspaper carried the headline 'Asian Flu – will the developed world catch a cold?' That the Japanese economy going into a state of collapse could impact upon the entire rest of the world, developed and developing, dramatizes, in my view, not the failure but the success of the East Asian economies. The enormous headway that they have made is the only reason why we need to be worried. If they were pocket, local economies, it would not trouble us in the least. Indeed, the very fact that we had the Europe–Asia Conference – the first of its kind – in Britain demonstrates the enormous impact of the economies of East Asia on the rest of the world. I believe that this impact will stay, and indeed increase, as the years go by.

I first visited the region when, as a Minister of the Department of Industry 22 years ago, I went to South Korea and saw the huge investment in steel and ship building. At that time, the British steel industry was in serious difficulties owing to underinvestment and, where once we had been the world leader, our ship building industry had plummeted to about 1 per cent of the world's output. In South Korea, the investment was enormous and impressive, and there was an assumption that this would be enhanced by the use of underpaid labour, working far longer hours than in the West and with no trade unions as protection. Yet South Korea did develop into one of the 'tiger economies'. I also went to Japan, which of course had been ahead of South Korea in both steel and ship building investment. However, the Japanese had, most foolishly, invested in South Korean shipyards and steel mills which were, even then, outstripping their own because the investment was more modern and the labour cheaper. I also went to the Toyota motor car factory and there I saw a future which had not yet reached Britain, namely truly modern automobile manufacturing. In the production areas of the factories, scarcely a human being was to be seen – and this more than 20 years ago. Almost everything was done by robots, and the spaces were filled with bowls of flowers. Those human beings who worked on the conveyor belt were able to press a button and stop it at any time, and there was a permanent injection of workers' suggestions, of which many thousands were adopted over a year. To me, it was a humiliation to return to the then British Leyland factory at Heddington, where I saw a production line that petered out about half way through and which was extremely labour-intensive. The Far Eastern economies were way ahead of the economies which had developed first in the industrial revolution and its aftermath.

In the late 1980s, I went to China, and the contrast there was remarkable. The north of the country was characterized by slums and spittoons, the south (especially the special economic development zone of Shen Zien) by modern, gleaming cities – a Western atmosphere with East Asian industriousness. What I particularly noticed there was the huge amount of investment by Western industrial conglomerates, which of course was extremely attractive to them because pay in China was then very low and the availability of labour enormous. After I had visited those Western factories, of which Coca Cola is, inevitably, the most obvious example, I well understood the motivation of the Tiannamen Square massacre. That 'rising', it seemed clear to me, was put down not because the Chinese had lost face at the time of Gorbachov's visit, nor because there was an area of unruliness that needed to be contained, but as a demonstration to American investors of the safety of their investments – which have since, of course, increased greatly.

I also visited Thailand and Singapore in the earliest part of their development. In Singapore – an authoritarian, well disciplined state – I was fascinated to see that, of its non-oil exports, 19 per cent were then disk drives.

The technological revolution has, of course, been picked up in East Asia much more speedily than in the West. The achievements in East Asia are amazing, because they are not based on invention. Indeed, very little that the East Asian economies produce and export – to enormous profit – has actually been invented there. For example, the computer was invented in Manchester, but the Japanese and other East Asians have made billions out of it. The video tape was invented in Holland and pioneered by Philips of Eindhoven. However, it was a Japanese manufacturer who decided that there should be a standard video cassette the size of a paperback book – a design that has now flooded the world and that simply is not questioned. In fact, East Asian achievements have been based not on invention, but on development and on marketing.

There is a basic understanding in East Asia that because the price must be acceptable to the consumer, this must be the starting point, working backward to consumption. When I was at the Department of Industry, we commissioned a report on why the Japanese had destroyed the British motorcycle industry, which had at one time led the world, yet now scarcely exists at all, with practically the only British motorcycles available now being cherished, vintage specimens. The answer was that the British motorcycle industry worked forward from production to price, whereas the Japanese worked backward from price to production.

Above all, however, the reasons why these East Asian economies have been so successful are, first, education and, secondly, investment. Japan, South Korea and Hong Kong invest 20 per cent of their gross domestic product (GDP) in education, compared with 10 per cent in the USA, West Germany and the UK. The investment is predominantly – though, obviously, not overwhelmingly – in primary education. The idea is that is where everyone starts, and the new emphasis on primary education in this country is very belated. Even more important, however, in my opinion, is investment. I was in charge of British Leyland when we had to nationalize it because it was in such an incredible mess. We found that it was distributing more in dividends to shareholders than it was investing in new plant and in research – a mistake which has not been made in East Asia, in fact far from it; the so-called crisis which Japan has been going through stems directly from an investment boom in the late 1980s. This has resulted in overcapacity, which is why the Japanese Prime Minister was advised to cut taxes in order to stimulate purchasing power in Japan and thereby deal with the problematic surplus.

The situation was, however, the same in the rest of East Asia. Looking at the key years 1960 to 1985 in the region as a whole, investment as a percentage of GDP was up from 15 to 22 per cent. In Europe and the USA, investment as a percentage of real GDP was declining. Between those years, in a league table of growth in GDP in 118 countries, Taiwan was number 2, Hong Kong number 3, South Korea number 5, and Japan number 6. As a result of that, in a generation, the GDP of Hong Kong, Korea, Singapore and Taiwan (of which the last three were certainly regarded as potentially permanently poor relations) has come almost to equal that of the industrialized countries. Moreover, the *per capita* income of the billion people in the region has doubled in a decade.

Looking at more recent years, the developing economies of East Asia in the early 1990s showed an average real GDP growth of above 9 per cent, which is probably unparalleled by any group of comparable countries at any time since the industrial revolution. With all eyes on the problems and on events in Indonesia and Thailand, the forecasts in early 1998 were that, in Asia as a whole, there would be 7 per cent stable growth in GDP that year.

Japan is one of the two strongest economies in the world and, despite the current problems, its fundamental strengths remain intact. It has the third largest stock market in the world after London and New York, has overseas assets of £500 billion, owns half the world's savings, is the world's largest creditor nation and has an enormous trade surplus. No wonder, then, that there continues to be such concern about what is going on there.

After Japan is coming China. When I was there, I saw the beginnings of what was taking place, which is developing faster than might have been anticipated. Between 1978 and 1998, *per capita* income quadrupled. Millions were taken out of poverty, and was forecast that, by the year 2000, 50–60 per cent of the remaining rural poor would also be. In China, I talked to Chinese political and industrial leaders, who referred to countries outside China as 'the outside world', as through their own economy was somehow impervious. Now, however, the Chinese economy has been opened up and integrated with the rest of the world, with huge increases in external trade and foreign investment. Astonishingly, China's foreign exchange reserves are the second largest in the world. The economic reforms that are taking place as China moves from a command state economy to a market economy, including sacking half of the state employees – equal to the whole of the US workforce – will, in my view, have beneficial repercussions since, I believe, free markets cannot exist in a prison country. Since the economic reforms were started, the growth rates in China have been among the highest in the world, so that what was a very poor country at the end of the 1970s has now become much wealthier.

There has certainly been an East Asian economic miracle, but I believe that there is much more to come. India, a country noted for its poverty and ramshackle organization, has started to march forward, with economic reforms already bringing growth of 5–6 per cent, and I expect the miracle to spread to South Asia.

Looking at what has already happened in East Asia, what is beginning to happen in South Asia and, more widely, what is happening in New Zealand and in Chile (where major economic and industrial advances have been made), it is clear that the economic rim is taking over, with enormous growth in different ways all around the Pacific. Examples include the huge progress that is taking place in Vancouver, partly fuelled by the arrival of Chinese from Hong Kong, and on the west coast of the USA, with Microsoft and its competitors in Seattle, Silicon Valley in San Francisco and the computer-based industries of Los Angeles.

I believe that there is a great future for this country if we take advantage of the multimedia revolution, and I believe that this country can prosper, grow rich and remain influential. I also believe, however, that, just as the nineteenth century was the century of Europe, and the twentieth century has been the century of the USA, the twenty-first century will be the century of the Pacific Rim.

2 A Story of Monetary Mismanagement

Patrick Minford

This chapter builds on the perspective set in Chapter 1 by Gerald Kaufman, and develops it, looking at the process of globalization; the crisis which, I shall argue, is very largely one of monetary mismanagement; and, finally, lessons that the West can learn. The crisis mainly has lessons, in my view, for the Far East (on how to manage monetary systems in conditions of very rapid growth), the lessons for the West lying chiefly in the handling of, and reaction to, globalization.

Many factors underlie the modern global economy and many Westerners, particularly politicians, have focused on the trade explosion and the threat that it has posed to Western labour markets. There has been policy hysteria, with Ross Perot saying, 'We must have protection against this sort of unfair competition' and the late Sir Jimmy Goldsmith, a free marketeer, remarking, in an interesting juxtaposition of thought, 'Europe must be a free market, but not as far as international trade with the Far East is concerned. This is unfair competition.'

Others, meanwhile, notably Paul Krugman, have said that it is not trade that is causing the interesting changes in the West, the plight of unskilled workers, the rapid growth of inequalities, the sudden increase in skilled workers' wages and the rise in unemployment, particularly in the unskilled workforce. They have argued that only a tiny fraction of the West's gross domestic product (GDP) is represented by the rise in imports from the emerging Eastern market economies. Krugman has echoed the earlier words of Andrew Lock in his introduction to this conference, in which he pointed out that there was as much trade at the turn of the last century, without any problems of this type. Krugman, along with many other American economists, believes that the key cause is technology bias, through the computer causing a substitution of skilled workers for unskilled ones. It is said that the computer-led technology which started in the West has gradually been affecting technology everywhere else, and a good deal of evidence has been produced about the effect of technology on unskilled workers.

This debate has become heated, partly because it is a causal one (asking whether it is trade or technology that is causing these great upheavals in the world economy), and partly because it is a policy one (asking whether or not, if trade is the cause, we should adopt a protectionist approach). The implication widely drawn in this debate is that, if technology is the cause, there is not a case for protection, but that the unskilled workers must simply be retrained. In fact, there is no necessary correlation between the causal analysis and the policy debate. If the cause is trade, it does not imply that there should be protection and, equally, if it is technology, it does not imply that there should not be protection. It could in fact be argued, using international trade theory, that if technology is detrimentally affecting unskilled workers, one of the ways to help them is to introduce protection.

There are vast divergences in labour costs across countries, as illustrated by figures gathered by the Bureau of Labour Statistics in Washington, DC, expressing the costs of employing a worker as a fraction of those in the USA (see Table 2.1). (In 1995 China costs stood at about 5 per cent, and the 'Little Tigers' at around 30 per cent of US costs. Between these come Mexico, Poland and the Czech Republic. In 1995, Japan was very expensive and Germany was even more so, right at the top with massively expensive labour. The USA was very much in the middle, with surprisingly cheap labour costs.) These figures do not take account of technology, the implicit assumption being that this is not important because state-of-the-art technology is available anywhere.

Table 2.1   Total cost ($) per hour of production worker, 1995–9

	1995	1997	Feb. 1999 (est.)
Germany	185	155	160
France	124	99	106
Italy	96	92	101
US	100	100	100
UK	80	80	80
Japan	138	106	106
Korea	43	40	20
Taiwan	34	32	27
Hong Kong	28	30	28
Singapore	42	45	35
Mexico	9	10	10

Source: Bureau of Labour Statistics, Washington, DC.

There are, then, astonishing disparities in the costs of hiring an ordinary person per hour, including social charges.

As Gerald Kaufman observed, East Asia has done very little invention. It has, however, achieved a lot of innovation, in terms of product refinement. However, the 'little dragons' have not done an awful lot of innovation. What they have done is to attract considerable foreign capital and capitalized on the fact that they could produce, very much more cheaply, with state-of-the-art technology, products previously produced by the West. I believe that this is the main cause of the emerging market explosion.

Looking at the last few decades, de-industrialization has caused the share of GDP of basic manufacturers (i.e. those employing principally unskilled workers to perform low-tech, non-complex tasks) in the Northern hemisphere to fall, including in Japan, by approximately 1 per cent per annum over the period 1970–90. This represents a remarkable change from the situation between the end of the war and 1970, and is one of the new features of the globalized economy that is causing considerable concern. This has affected the West, too, with unskilled workers being left behind in the general rise in productivity and growth, and their employment collapsing. Between 1970 and 1990, there was a 4.2 per cent per annum contraction in the relative employment of unskilled versus skilled workers in the West and in the North, and a rise of 8 percentage points in the unemployment rate of unskilled workers in the Organization for Economic Co-operation and Development (OECD). Incidentally, the unemployment of skilled workers in the OECD also rose, by 3 percentage points, from a very low level – an interesting point that is often overlooked. Notwithstanding, living standards rose.

It is interesting that in the South (in respect of which available figures are less reliable), in contrast to what might be expected, the growth in the share of GDP devoted to basic manufacturing is, at 2 percentage points over 1970–90, in fact rather modest. There has also been a very large rise in the share of high-tech manufacturing suggesting, interestingly, that parts of the South (for example, South Korea and similar countries) are changing their strategy, and moving away from basic manufacturing. Looking at skilled and unskilled workers in the South, there seems to be quite a good rise in the wages of manufacturing workers, which is very natural for countries in the throes of industrialization. Indeed, in the South this is the age of the common man, who is coming out of subsistence agriculture, most often into manufacturing, and being paid serious money (though skilled workers are doing better still, much as in the North). There is a rise in unskilled employment relative to skilled employment, and unskilled workers are experiencing a rise in living standards.

A final, important fact is that the terms of trade of basic manufacturing (in which the South specializes) have collapsed relative to those of complex manufacturing and services (in which the West has competitive advantage), for example the products of the City of London and Hollywood. Over the period 1970–90, there has also been a very modest decline in the price of raw materials, including oil (perhaps a little surprisingly, given the oil crisis) reflecting the technological explosion in the West in terms of materials science. Looking at figures for the terms of trade of the South in basic manufacturing, their prime export, over recent decades, there was a collapse during the 1960s caused, in my view, by the entry of the 'Little Dragons' (for example, Singapore, Malaysia, and in particular South Korea) into world trade. There followed a period of relative stability in the terms of trade, until the mid-1980s, when there was another sudden decline, this time caused by the entry of China, with its massive expansion in manufacturing. There were, therefore, two major periods of very rapid expansion in the manufactures of developing countries, and I believe that one of the triggers of the current crisis is in fact a further wave of expansion. It is certainly interesting that in 1994 China felt it necessary to devalue by approximately 36 per cent, followed shortly afterwards by Japan, and now the most recent massive devaluations. It seems clear that some oversupply of manufactured products is developing.

These factors can now all be put together to try to explain what might be causing the West's problems. A fuller account of the analysis can be found in my paper with Jonathan Riley and Eric Nowell (1997). It seems to me highly unlikely that these problems could be caused by just one thing – be it the trade explosion or technology bias. Since most things that happen in the world have multiple causes, we took into account the full range of facts and constructed a model of the world economy, North and South – putting in, for example, constant returns to scale and competition in the world economy, and allowing, for instance, for technology to be different in the North and South, and for the North to have unemployment (since workers have some alternatives to having to work, that is benefits). We then used this model of the world economy to test the effect of trade, by applying an ongoing rise in productivity owing to inward capital investment in Southern manufacturing; the model predicted, not particularly surprisingly, de-industrialization, falling unskilled workers' wages and rising unemployment among unskilled workers for the North, and industrialization, rising wages and worsening terms of trade in the South. These were all the sorts of the things that had actually happened. Therefore, we began to think that trade could be the cause of the West's problems. However, while this would seem to be true if the model were used purely qualitatively, there was a misfit in quantitative terms between what we observed in wages, prices and volumes. There should have been very large volume changes for fairly modest relative price changes; however, there were not such volume changes.

When used to test the effect of technological bias alone, the model predicted that unskilled wages would fall and that the terms of trade would change. Unfortunately, though, the predicted outcome regarding industrialization did not tally with the situation in the real world. This makes sense because in the West, technology change causes there to be a lot of unskilled workers that become unemployed at the same factor prices as before. Those unskilled workers, of course, then bid down wages in order to get a job and that causes industrialization in the West. However, this obviously has not happened. So the main problem with the technological bias explanation taken on its own is that it does not account for de-industrialization in the West – in fact, quite the opposite.

We continued with the testing, looking at various factors, and juxtaposed what the model said would happen against what actually happened in the world economy over the last 20 years. A regression was run to ensure that each factor was weighted to fit the facts best. We found that there was total factor productivity (TFP) growth of just under 1 per cent per annum in the South, and a 1.5 per cent shift in the production functions of the North against unskilled workers owing to technological bias shift. The North experienced general productivity growth and rising social protection. A very important factor has been the raising of higher education participation rates which, by reducing unskilled labour supply, limits both the scale of unemployment and the shift against unskilled workers in wages in the North. It was this which contributed just under 0.5 per cent growth each year in the wages (and, therefore, living standards) of unskilled workers in the North, while the trade factor and the technology bias factor would each have caused a drop of about the same amount each year, by 0.5 per cent a year. Finally, there was Southern productivity growth in other sectors apart from basic manufacturing – for example, high-tech manufacturing and the non-traded sector; this also helped to defuse the crisis for unskilled workers in the North.

Turning to the crisis itself, what has happened in Asia is a collapse in the currency, which then triggered debt deflation. The 'little dragons' were all roaring away, growing at tremendous rates. Thailand was the first to feel the crisis but Japan laid the groundwork for the crisis by its response to what was called the 'bubble economy' in the early 1990s. The Japanese Central Bank governor socked the economy on the head with tight monetary policy, and precipitated a monetary collapse, the Yen appreciating out of sight. By 1995, the Central Bank realized the economy was in total crisis – the Yen had escalated, confidence was very low and the recession that resulted from this monetary contraction was not lifting – and so set the printing presses at the Bank of Japan going at full tilt, and thrust Yen at the foreign exchange market in an effort to stimulate monetary expansion. This did succeed, and in 1996 the situation was easing a little, and the country managed 3.5 per cent growth – a fact that people often forget. In 1997, however, the economy collapsed back into very anaemic growth. During the first half of that year, Japan seemed to be doing all right and then, just when the economy was beginning to pick up after numerous fiscal packages, the government brought in a rise in consumer taxes, as a result of the fiscal stabilization law. This knocked the economy and consumer confidence totally on the head, precipitating an economic decline in the latter half of 1997, a collapse in domestic demand. I had always told my students what a wise old guy Keynes was, but asserted that we should not need to use his very inefficient policies such as digging holes and filling them again because, thanks to him, we know how to manage a modern economy. Japan has, however, shown us how really to mismanage a modern economy! Indeed, we have rediscovered Keynes' liquidity trap, it being no longer possible to push interest rates down in Japan any further, because you cannot push on a string. Fiscal policy is now all that is left, and Japan is having to produce tax cuts to somehow get the consumer to spend.

Using our model, we simulated the effect on the world economy of the collapse of Asian 'tiger' imports by 10 per cent and a Japanese GDP contraction of about 3 per cent. The figures we got were as expected – reflecting a general contraction of world trade growth, heavily influenced by Japan itself. That one-off shock was offset by macroeconomic policy in the West and by action in Japan, and growth outside East Asia was reasonably unaffected until the most recent crisis.

It could be argued that the current crisis is similar to what happened in Mexico, where a comparable crisis of debt deflation was triggered in late 1994. While this led to a collapse in dollar terms of Mexican share prices, these are now almost back to where they were. In other words, perhaps there are the beginnings of normalization in a lot of these markets in the Far East.

To summarize, I believe that the Asian crisis was triggered by excess supply, owing to the underlying process of globalization and, especially, I believe, by Japanese monetary mismanagement. This mismanagement in Japan was followed by mismanagement in the 'tiger economies', which were roaring away but not looking at their banking systems. They did not put into place the things that world-weary ancient economies, such as ours, have learned about before and which people like the constitutionalist Walter Bagehot have told us to do – for example, having a lender of last resort, having prudential management and keeping an eye on prudential ratios in the economy. Thailand, for instance, was being covered with golf courses which were being financed by American, Japanese and German banks, in foreign currency, and yet no-one there had thought what would happen to all those loans if the peg went. This was a story of monetary mismanagement (not crony capitalism, which had nothing to do with the crisis) primarily in Japan, aided and abetted by bad prudential management in little 'tiger economies' that just never thought it could happen to them and that had not read any British history. They should have read Kindleberger's book[1], and then they'd never have got into this mess!

I believe that the Mexican example also tells us that we should not overreact to this situation, which can be reversed with global support, the International Monetary Fund (IMF) and openness in world markets (an important lesson of the inter-war period, when the Western world, panicking over unemployment, put up the shutters on world trade, which closed the world economy down).

To conclude, the West must remember two things. First, it must – because nobody else can at this point – offer the lender of last resort function at an international level (which, on the whole, it is doing). Secondly, it must keep markets open. The protectionist approach, as advocated by Ross Perot and Jimmy Goldsmith, is not the answer, but would simply destroy world trade generally. Nor is protection the answer to the West's or the North's many policy problems with unskilled workers. The answer is not the provision of benefits, either, because that just exacerbates unemployment. The answers are education and productivity.

QUESTIONS

Q: What do you think underlies the surprising figures on wage costs in Japan relative to those in the USA?

A: While higher education and productivity growth are vital to solving the West's problems, it is impossible to restructure an economy in which wages are totally out of line. With a flexible and open labour market, however, and wages kept within sight of those of backyard economies (such as Mexico and East Asia), it is possible to slow down sufficiently the process of losing older industries while building up new high-tech and service industries. Japan was starting to liberalize its service sector but when this crisis hit, together with terrible unemployment in the manufacturing sector, it reacted by just closing down reform. The first thing to do should be to become competitive and at least get the manufacturing sector going again. Combined with the right macroeconomic policies, this can help an economy back onto its feet. The answer, therefore, is that it is part of a policy mixture to get a modern economy back on its feet in a world full of cross-currents.

Q: What happened to the French economy to bring the figures in Table 2.1 from 124 to 99?
A: This is the same process going on in Europe as occurred in Japan. High unemployment (or the threat of this, as in the case of Japan), much of it concealed inside the big companies trying to be responsible, has led to currency depreciation by the continent. People often do not seem to have absorbed the fact that the Deutschmark has gone from 140 to the dollar in 1995 to around 185 to the dollar, in response to the same, continent-wide failure of a modern economy to deal with the challenges of unemployment posed by globalization. They have not drawn the necessary policy lessons until quite recently, and I think now what is happening is that they are bringing their currency down. Monetary union uncertainty is, from the point of view of continental politicians, a bonanza. It is causing a devaluation of the Euro before it even exists, which, from a policy viewpoint, is absolutely vital if they are to get a policy mixture on the continent that has any hope of avoiding disaster socially.

Q: With regard to labour costs, do you not think that while this is correct as far as it goes, in most modern economies labour costs are only a fraction of total costs (perhaps 10 or 20 per cent of GDP)? To what extent, then, does that still play an important role in being competitive at all?
A: This point is often made. The difficulty is that in a world of mobile capital, capital no longer becomes a domestic factor of production, it gets priced internationally. Therefore, if one strips out capital (since

countries can no longer rely on getting cheap capital domestically, to offset high labour costs), technology (which can be the same anywhere) and the raw material costs (which are also the same, because they are traded), land and labour are left. Land can be disregarded in this context because that really does represent such a tiny fraction and, in any case, tends to be very highly correlated with labour costs (since it is heavily used in non-traded goods).

Q: Why are knowledge and innovation, which are completely new variables, not taken into account at all?
A: Knowledge takes time to generate and it is not possible to generate enough in high-tech industries. There would need to be a massive boost from that sector to absorb the unemployed. Therefore, older knowledge in the modern world of globalization is going out the door to everybody else. So knowledge, too, becomes a common factor of production.

Q: If a country does not have the absorption capacity for technology, then surely it is not going to get the advantages of that technology?
A: No, but in the modern world, absorption capacity is created by hiring a big multinational. That is the story of China. This globalization is on the back of FDI, which brings in the knowledge. That is why the Welsh are so keen to get inward investment – because it brings in all sorts of knowledge on the back of the process. It is that which really is undermining the position of Germany. If we particularize it to Germany and the continent, the difficulty Germany has is that people in Poland and the Czech Republic are, on a conservative estimate, a tenth as expensive – probably as much as a twentieth in many cases. This is rather difficult to deal with in a world of capital mobility. I agree that, in principle, if a country could generate enough new knowledge on which it had a monopoly in the period when it had the monopoly on it, then that advantage could be used to cross-subsidize employees as part of the team. However, I do not think that it is a viable strategy for dealing with the large-scale unemployment problems of the modern world.

Q: Would you advocate fiscal policies to encourage and enhance R&D exposition in this country?
A: I would not. Although it is true that both R&D and education create productivity growth, there is a difference between the two. I believe there are ways in which the state can be moderately helpful in areas of education. For example, if as I would like to see, our higher education sector were sold off to the highest bidder, to enable the government to

subsidize critical areas. The only example of the state assisting in R&D that I can think of, is the American government's investment in defence, which has massively stimulated R&D, but which was unplanned and stimulated by the needs of war. On the whole, I believe that R&D should be left to the market.

Q: Is there a place in your model for demographics? Could it be that the very different distributions of the population across Southern and Northern Asia may relate to what you have been discovering?

A: My view is that demographics have little to do with the situation regarding the comparative advantages of the North and the South, but are connected to the macro situation in Japan. One of the difficulties of getting Japanese consumers to spend is that the government has, on the one hand, been warning them to save for their old age and, on the other, begging them to buy a few more gizmos to boost demand. In Germany, similarly, there has been great reluctance by consumers to spend in the present recovery because they have similar fears that they will not be supported by the state in their old age.

Note

1.　Kindleberger, C. (1996).

References

Kindleberger C. (1996) *Manias, Panics and Crashes: A History of Financial Crisis*, London, Macmillan.
Minford, P., Riley, J. and Nowell, E. (1997) 'Trade, Technology and Labour Markets in the World Economy 1970–90: A Computable General Questioning Analysis'; see also a forthcoming note of 'Corrigendum and Appendum' in the same journal, downloadable from my webpage <www.bigfoot.com/~ Patrick.Minford>. *Journal of Development Studies* (December).

3 Investing in Asia's Dynamism

Willem Noë

The study in this chapter, investigating Asian dynamism, was carried out in partnership with UNCTAD, in response to the need for analysis (recognized following the publication by the European Commission, in 1994, of *Towards a New Strategy for Asia*) to confirm the perception that the European Union was lagging behind (in particular, behind the USA and Japan) with regard to investment flows towards Asia. There were real concerns that the European Union might be missing out on growth benefits. Although the study concentrated mainly on EU investment in Asia, it was considered that there might be some benefit for Asia, too, since there were also very low flows from Asia to the European Union. The study was also used as background information for the first ASEAN meeting, which was held in Bangkok in 1996.

The study drew upon the strengths of the European Commission (the statistical office has excellent data on the EU's foreign direct investment (FDI) and expertise in the analysis of FDI) and of UNCTAD (with its excellent world foreign investment data). This joint work also gave out the important political message – to both the European member states and the less developed Asian countries – that FDI flows and problems should be addressed on a world level.

The report describes European FDI flows to South East Asia and Japan, suggests why EU FDI is lagging behind and concludes with some policy recommendations. Included in the report are also the proceedings of a conference held in Geneva following completion of the first draft of the report. At this conference, business people and policy makers discussed both the analysis and a survey asking firms involved in the European Round Table (a forum for especially large European firms investing in Asia) about investing in Asia and problems associated with this.

The study was finished at the end of 1996, but we believe that it is still relevant, particularly in the light of the Asian crisis. Although the data relates to 1993–4, it should be borne in mind that FDI data always lags a few years behind, so that no more than two years' further data at most would now be available.

The overall picture was that world FDI stock had risen fivefold over a period of 15 years (1980–94), in both developed countries and less developed countries. Within the group of less developed countries, however, it was a particularly small group that received the bulk of the FDI flows, and the stock of world FDI within the less developed countries was, during this period, one-third of world stock. These figures exclude intra-EU stocks and flows, which does in fact make a big difference.

At the same time, however, the stock of Asian FDI excluding Japan, rose ninefold – even faster than the overall world stock – and now accounts for approximately half of total stock in less developed countries. The Chinese factor plays a strong role in this. This development has been especially marked since the early 1990s, because until that time developed countries mainly invested in each other; they were both the key source for investment and the major host for FDI flows.

The European Union is the largest host and source region for FDI in the world, accounting for nearly half of world FDI stocks. Likewise, the outflows represent 45 per cent of world FDI outflows, although this share has been falling. The other players in the triad are the USA and Japan. These flows do include intra-EU stock, but this does not affect the position significantly. The European Union and USA vie for first place in stock, each with a share of about 30 per cent. The members of the triad are still the major investors in Asia, although the share of each fell in the period 1985–94. The triad deserves a separate mention as a major FDI destination in the region, but it is also very noticeable that its presence has been low and is falling further, now accounting for less than 20 per cent of stocks and flows in China.

A lot of investment is going to Taiwan and Hong Kong, and much seems currently to go to countries with a major ethnic Chinese population (75 per cent of FDI flows in China coming from countries with a predominantly ethnic Chinese population). There are, in fact, some very severe statistical problems with the FDI inflows and outflows to China, since a large part of the outflows are actually flows from China to Hong Kong and back (since FDI receives special treatment). It is estimated that this increases total FDI inward flows from China by as much as one-third. It is well known that Japan has a very low inward FDI, the European Union being the main investor, holding about one-third of stocks.

Between 1980 and 1993, the share of inward FDI stock in Asia fell for each of the triad members, and now accounts in total for less than 50 per cent of the total stocks in Asia. The European Union has the smallest share of FDI stock of the triad members in the region as a whole, and indeed in nearly every individual Asian country. Consistently, the European Union has a lower FDI presence in stocks and flows. Most of that FDI is concentrated within Asia – on chemicals, petroleum and services, which together account for about 70 per cent of the FDI presence. The build-up is similar to that of the USA, whereas Japan is more spread out in a number of other sectors. It is also noticeable that there is very little FDI in textiles, metallurgy, electronics and automobiles, except in China, where companies such as Volkswagen have been investing. The absence of investment in electronics and automobiles is especially noticeable, the reason being that these are sectors that build on regional networks in which the European Union lacks a presence. It is increasingly hard for EU companies to enter these markets, in which the USA and Japan either are already, or are becoming, well established.

From an EU perspective, the less developed countries' share of outward FDI has always been lower than that of the triad members. Again, the share of Asia in outward EU FDI, both in stocks and flow, has been lower than that of the USA and Japan. That share (particularly to Asia) has been increasing a little recently, and according to the latest data (that from the statistical office) there has been an increase in flows. Around 5 per cent of total extra EU flows has been going to Asia, and this has stayed at 5 per cent. There is, therefore, no real upward trend so far, which leads us to the conclusion that although Asia has certainly received more attention in terms of investment, there is still a missing link in the triad in terms of investment flows from the EU to Asia – and, indeed, vice versa.

All this leads to a number of questions. Why does the European Union lag behind in investment flows towards Asia? Does the European Union have higher FDI barriers than elsewhere? Does Asia erect higher barriers to EU, compared to Japanese and US, investors? If it does, is the discrimination deliberate, or effective (in terms of some barriers tending to hit harder on EU firms because of their different structural characteristics, for example, of the EU flows or of the Asian economy itself)?

For the European Union, there were, at the time of the study, several demands and projects closer to home, such as the 1992 Single Market project, which provided a huge attraction for FDI both within and outside of the Union (the Single Market having a clear effect – now well established through recent studies – on attracting FDI), and the attention given to Central East European (CEE) countries (in which the European Union is a major investor) after 1989.

There was also, certainly for small and medium-sized enterprises (SMEs), a certain unfamiliarity with what was happening in Asia, together with a belated recognition of the fact that Asia was growing up fast and had gone through a liberalization wave in terms of FDI, especially in the 1980s. In addition, there was an underestimation of growth potential in Asia, particularly in the case of SMEs, because large companies usually have access to better information.

There were also some historical factors, including Japan and the USA having longer and deeper trade links with Asia through being part of the region. For example, Japan and the USA participate in APEC and other regional fora where the European Union is not present, heightening their awareness of, and enabling them to have a say in, what is happening in Asia.

A further interesting point was that the European Union relied more on exports to Asia than on FDI as a vehicle to get its products to the markets. It is usually through local sales that EU firms work in developed countries, but in Asia in particular, the situation is reversed. Another factor was the Asian preference for minority participation in firms, which was not seen as problematic by the Japanese, whilst EU firms, who tend to dislike having to give up control of assets, preferred a majority participation. Yet another factor was the targeting by Asian governments of certain sectors which seemed to have more Japanese and US firms. For instance, the electronic sector in South Korea attracted some US and Japanese firms, but not EU firms.

All this means that transaction costs with Asia are higher for the European Union. Transaction costs can be seen as a form of fixed costs which hit harder on EU manufacturing firms than their often larger US or Japanese counterparts. There is also a lower level of government support in EU member states. The USA, for instance, with its Department of Commerce, usually plays a more active role in supporting and providing information for its firms. Japan hosts or supports a number of government or semi-government institutes with Asian connections. Other institutes actively support firms – particularly SMEs – in entering Asian markets, while most of the EU governments do not.

In summary, it can be said that while the effective burden of transaction costs was higher for EU firms, there was certainly no deliberate discrimination; this disadvantage was really the effect of a neglect so far in trade and investment which, being cumulative, builds up the competitive disadvantage.

In terms of policy changes, the European Commission is looking to establish a framework of uniform and clear multilateral rules, especially at World Trade Organization (WTO) level, to support investment in general. The OECD's multilateral agreement on investment has for the moment run into serious difficulties and we believe that the WTO is in fact a more appropriate forum for a multilateral FDI framework. As noted above, the European Commission produced *Towards a New Strategy for Asia* in 1994. This supported a whole host of programmes to stimulate EU FDI to Asia, including the development of ASEAN, which figures as an informal forum for discussion. Many business oriented initiatives were also introduced following the publication of this strategy, including exchange programmes for students, managers and government policy makers; programmes for technical corporations, for example on intellectual property rights; and business-to-business corporation investment. Many of these programmes have been built up in partnership with business, including investment partner schemes, European business 'infocentres' and the Asia Invest Programme, a major initiative, with a significant budget for five years. SMEs are a particular focus for the supply of information for market research, organization of 'round tables' and part-financing of business meetings. It is hoped that this will result in an increase in FDI flows between the European Union and Asia, in both directions. To a certain extent, these flows have already been increasing, including from SMEs.

We feel very strongly that the crisis in Asia will not lower the long-term growth prospects of FDI. In fact, I personally believe that it could even strengthen them, FDI remaining very attractive and EU firms being positive about the European Commission's developments. I have been looking at the effects of the Asian crisis on EU sectoral developments and have noted that there has indeed been a host of new EU acquisitions in Asia and that Asian firms are also actively seeking investment from Europe, in line with their strategy to diversify away from Japanese and US investors.

To turn finally to South Asia, we do not have yet a competitive disadvantage in India, and investment regulations have apparently now been eased. India is again much more open to FDI, and here the EU firms are much more on a level playing field with Japanese and US firms in terms of investment stocks. We are therefore certain to try to stimulate investment in South Asia.

QUESTIONS

Q: What would your figures on FDI look like if you took the UK and the Netherlands out of the aggregate?
A: Those countries, certainly, are major investors. Indeed, the UK is usually by far the biggest investor. I do not have exact figures available, but I would imagine that about one-third to a half would be chopped off those investment flows.

Q: Do you have records on success rates for foreign investment, indicating whether, as some survey results suggest, Asian investments are more successful than US or European ones?
A: There might be some data on profitability in the report but I cannot be sure since that reflects the profitability of the investment itself. UNCTAD may be a source of such data, in the form of the *World Investment Report*.

4 Globalization and FDI in Asian Developing Countries

John H. Dunning

INTRODUCTION

This chapter seeks to do three main things. First it examines the extent to which Asian developing countries have participated in the trend towards a globalizing world economy over the past two decades or so. Second, it looks more specifically at the ways in which one of the main engines of globalization – inbound investment by foreign institutions and individuals in Asia and outbound investment by Asian multinational enterprises (MNEs) and individuals – have contributed towards a deepening economic interdependence between Asian countries and the rest of the world. Third, it presents some recently published data on trends of European foreign direct investment (FDI) in Asian developing countries, and of how some 310 leading MNEs and international experts, view future corporate investment priorities between 1996 and 2001.[1]

Where possible, we shall adopt a threefold classification of Asian developing countries, which corresponds to that used by the UNDP[2] – high human development (HHD), medium human development (MHD) and low human development (LHD) countries. The *Human Development Index*, compiled by the UNDP, while incorporating gross domestic product GDP *per capita*, also embraces other variables, such as life expectancy and adult literacy. A list of the Asian countries assigned to each group is set out in the Appendix (p. 62). We are aware that there are other criteria for classifying Asian developing countries, apart from their stage of human development. For example, in some situations, size is a critical variable; and, where appropriate, we shall distinguish between small and medium-to-large Asian countries.

The contents of this chapter will be mainly descriptive, and no formal econometric analysis of the data will be undertaken. However, we will attempt to relate our statistical findings to the main body of extant theory; and also offer some additional hypotheses of our own.

GLOBALIZATION AND DEVELOPING COUNTRIES

Our interpretation of the term 'globalization', and of how it differs from 'internationalization', is contained in a quotation by Anthony McGrew in McGrew and Lewis (1992).

> Globalization refers to the multiplicity of linkages and interconnections between the states and societies which make up the present world system. It describes the process by which events, decisions, and activities in one part of the world come to have significant consequences for individuals and communities in quite distant parts of the globe. Globalization has two distinct phenomena: scope (or stretching) and intensity (or deepening). On the one hand, it defines a set of processes which embrace most of the globe or which operate world-wide: the concept therefore has a spatial connotation. On the other hand it also implies an intensification on the levels of interaction, interconnectedness or interdependence between the states and societies which constitute the world community. Accordingly, alongside the stretching goes a deepening of global processes. (p. 23)

In short, then, globalization is leading to the structural transformation of firms and nations, and is creating new relationships and new dependencies. Sometimes, the transformation takes place at a regional level: much of the integrated production networks of MNEs is so focused. Sometimes, it occurs at a global level. For example, the contemporary global financial system is one in which national markets throughout the world, though physically separate, operate as if they are in the same place (Stopford and Strange, 1991). One scholar has put it even more dramatically by averring that global financial integration is 'the end of geography'.[3]

The main causes of globalization are well known. I shall focus on just two. The first is the pressure on firms – by consumers and competitors alike – to continually innovate new products and upgrade the quality and/or reduce the price of existing goods and services. Escalating costs of R&D, coupled with ever-shortening product life cycles, are compelling firms to curtail the scope of their value added activities and to search for wider markets. To effectively and speedily exploit core competencies, firms are finding they need to combine these with the core competencies of other firms, and those of governments. Hence, the emergence of strategic alliances and networks which, together with FDI, are the main instruments fashioning deep economic interdependence.

The second cause of globalization is the renaissance of market-supporting policies pursued by national governments, and the growth of market-led regional integration. In the last five years alone, more than 30 countries have abandoned central planning as the main mode of allocating scarce resources, while over 80 have liberalized their inward FDI policies. The privatization of state-owned enterprises (SOEs), the liberalization and deregulation of markets – especially for services – and the removal of a bevy of structural distortions, have all worked to stimulate cross-border corporate integration, both within MNEs and between independent firms, or groups of firms.

In this presentation, I will consider just eight indices of globalization and Table 4.1 sets out how these vary between the three groups of Asian developing economies, other developing countries, developed countries and all countries. These indices are:

(1) Trade as a percentage of GDP, 1995
(2) Changes in (1), 1980–95
(3) Share of world exports of 'fast-growth' products, 1995
(4) Changes in (3), 1980–95
(5) Inward plus outward direct investment stock as a percentage of GDP, 1995
(6) Changes in (3), 1980–95
(7) Inward plus outward foreign portfolio investment as a percentage of GDP, 1994–5
(8) Use of international communications media, 1994.

The findings of Table 4.1 are self-evident. Briefly highlighted they are:

• Asian economies are *more globalized than other developing economies*, and enjoy a larger share of the exports of 'fast-growth' products to the OECD. As might be expected, smaller Asian countries tend to be more globalized than their larger counterparts.
• The propensity of Asian economies to be *more deeply integrated into a global economy* tends to increase as economic development proceeds. As other research (Dunning, 1981, 1986; Dunning and Narula, 1996) has shown, there is a GNP per capita threshold before a country is able to attract substantial amounts of inward direct investment and another threshold before it engages in outward direct investment. These thresholds are also seen to vary with the size, industrial structure and general economic environment of the developing countries but, as identified in Table 4.1, only Group 1

Table 4.1 Indices of globalization of Asian economies, 1980–95

	Trade				Foreign investment				International communications	
	% of GDP (1995)	Change% (1980–95)	% of growth trade	Change% of growth trade	FDI as % of GDP (1995)	Change% (1980–95)	FPI as % of GDP (1995)	Change M&As (1990/1–1995/6)	Int. tel. calls (1994)	Internet users (1994)
1. Asian developing economies	46.9	83.8	378.4	NA	43.4	456.8	23.0	635.2	32.9	16.6
a. Group 1	162.0	53.6	596.4	47.3	34.5	122.3	35.9	431.2	97.2	49.6
b. Group 2	180.8	252.8	522.1	233.1	27.3	253.2	14.9	296.2	1.2	0.2
c. Group 3	39.2	45.2	175.0	64.1	11.4	1074.4	1.5	3352.0	0.4	0.0
2. Latin American economies	27.2	–0.2	122.1	72.6	18.0	168.4	4.1	209.8	NA	NA
3. African economies	NA	NA	–47.7	NA	NA	NA	NA	689.5	NA	NA
a. Sub-Sahara	NA	NA	–29.3	NA	NA	NA	NA	1202.8	1.4	NA
b. Other	50.7	3.1	4.6	NA	8.0	384.9	NA	306.3	NA	NA

46

Table 4.1 (cont'd)

	Trade				Foreign investment				International communications	
	% of GDP (1995)	Change% (1980–95)	% of growth trade	Change% of growth trade	FDI as % of GDP (1995)	Change% (1980–95)	FPI as % of GDP (1995)	Change M&As (1990/1–1995/6)	Int. tel. calls (1994)	Internet users (1994)
4. All developing economies	41.4	5.6	88.2	NA	19.7	404.3	10.6	365.2	2.5	1.5
5. All developed economies	35.6	–1.1	186.8	NA	20.5	81.1	39.3	84.7	35.1	232.2
6. All economies	37.3	–0.3	157.8	NA	20.4	120.0	33.8	108.7	0.7	60.9
7. Smaller Asian economies	162.0	53.6	596.4	NA	34.5	122.3	35.9	431.2	97.2	49.6
8. Larger Asian economies	110.0	149.0	348.6	NA	19.4	663.8	8.2	1824.1	0.8	0.1

Note: NA = Not available.
Sources: World Investment Report (1997); World Economic Forum; *The World Competitiveness Report* (1997); *UNDP Human Development Report* (1997); IMF, *Balance of Payments Statistics* (1987, 1997).

and a handful of Group 2 Latin American countries are experiencing 'balanced' globalization – by which we mean that they are (a) sharing in export growth of dynamic products, (b) are engaging in outward as well as inward and outward FDI and merger and acquisition activity and (c) making good use of international communications facilities.

- Almost certainly part of the more outward-looking stance of Asian (and other developing countries) reflects a trend towards *regionalization*, rather than globalization. Thus, for example, it is estimated (UNCTAD, 1997) that 75 per cent of all inward direct investment in Asian developing countries between 1990 and 1995 originated from elsewhere in Asia. On the other hand, it is clear that Asian developing countries are gaining an increasing share of world *outward* FDI as their own firms take a more global perspective on the sourcing of products such as footwear, clothing, consumer electronics, semiconductors, toys, computer software and some kinds of technology; and as they seek to make inroads into European and US markets.
- There is some suggestion that an increasing proportion of *cross-border strategic alliances* are now involving Asian firms. According to a survey of Booz, Allen and Hamilton (1997), the average value of a cross-border strategic alliance concluded by Japanese and other Asian firms was four times greater than that of US firms in the mid-1990s; while approaching two-thirds of developing Asia is viewed by the leading western MNEs as offering the best prospects for new forms of cross-border collaboration, for acquiring complementary technological and other skills and for exploiting new markets.

What are the main explanations for the facts just described? We might highlight just three. The first is the increased liberalization of markets in Asian developing countries, a more positive attitude to the inbound investment and a growing belief that, to be competitive in international markets, the leading Asian firms need to engage in outward direct investment. Almost certainly, one important contributor to the current economic crises in the Far East is the imprudent haste at which both firms and governments of Asian developing countries have tried to 'catch-up' with their Western counterparts.

The second factor is the growing competition among firms – and particularly MNEs from industrialized countries – both to protect existing and to exploit new markets, and to be more cost-effective in their global sourcing and production strategies. This has fostered a new international division of labour; and, because of their favourable real

costs, and investment incentives offered by their governments relative
to those of their competitors, Asian developing countries have gained
the lion's share of new FDI and inward strategic alliance over the last
decade.[4]

The third factor is the forceful yet market-friendly development
strategies pursued by governments of Asian developing countries
which, in the main, have been consistent with the tenets of globalization
(and increasingly so over the last decade). However, again, through
zealous and incautious expansionist macroeconomic policies and the
fostering of easy credit by the financial sector, Asian governments may
well have contributed towards the economic downturn and growing
indebtedness of their economies.

FOREIGN INVESTMENT AND THE DEEPENING
INTERDEPENDENCE OF THE ASIAN ECONOMIES

One of the key attributes of a deepening economic dependence, or
interdependence, of a country with the rest of the world is the extent to
which that country is invested in by foreign institutions and individuals,
and/or the extent to which its own institutions and individuals invest in
other countries.

In this section we shall primarily concentrate on FDI as a globalizing
vehicle. The growth of inbound foreign portfolio investment (FPI)
mirrors the strength and vitality of the local capital market, and the
confidence with which foreign institutions view the local economy, while
outbound FPI normally reflects the availability of locally generated
savings, and the perceived opportunities for investing in foreign countries; we shall briefly consider this variable as well.

The significance of inbound and outbound foreign investment to the
three groups of Asian economies, and the 'balance' between the two
over the last two decades,[5] highlights four main points:

- As a proportion of their GDP, the combined inward and outward
  and direct stock of Asian developing countries rise from 3.6 per cent
  in 1980 to 20.2 per cent in 1995. The corresponding increases for
  South, East and South East Asian developing countries were 4.6
  per cent and 22.1 per cent. These rates of increase are somewhat
  greater than those for South America (6.8 per cent and 20.1 per
  cent) and North Africa (3.5 per cent and 10.8 per cent) but not (and
  rather surprisingly, as it is usually perceived to be marginalized in

the globalization process) for Sub-Saharan Africa (3.2 per cent and 24.0 per cent).

- The most pronounced trends towards globalization have occurred in China and Asian developing countries – the significance of inbound FDI has increased the most in China and to a slightly less extent Vietnam, Nepal and Myanmar. At the same time, Hong Kong, Taiwan, and Korea have each moved along their investment development paths to become important outward investors. It is also noteworthy that an increasing proportion of Asia outward direct investment has been directed to advanced industrial countries, outside Asia (Dunning, Narula and Van Hoesel, 1997); and, in part at least, has been geared to gaining access to new resources and markets rather than to exploiting a particular competitive advantage of the investing firms.

- While, until the mid-1980s, most of new FDI in and by Asian developing countries took the form of greenfield investment, in the last decade the share in global mergers and acquisitions (M&As) accounted for by these countries has risen sharply. In 1990, for example, the total value of these M&As involving South, East and South East Asian firms as buyers or sellers was 4.9 per cent; by 1995 this figure had risen to 11.8 per cent. However, in both years, 65 per cent of the Asian firms' sales and 87 per cent of the purchasing Asian firms were from China and Group 1 countries.

- Since the early 1980s there has been a huge increase in inbound portfolio investment into Asian developing countries – particularly in bonds and notes. In 1985–6 such countries accounted for 1.5 per cent of global inbound FPI; by 1994–5 this proportion had risen to 4.7 per cent. Corresponding figures for outbound FPI from Asian developing countries were 0.7 per cent and 3.2 per cent. In 1989–90 FPI into Asia was still only 7.1 per cent of FDI, by 1994–5 this proportion had risen to 41.4 per cent. Partly the increase, which again was strongly concentrated in China and Group 1 countries, reflects the development of the capital markets in these countries. As a ratio of GDP, the market value of Asian domestic capital markets was 1.2 in 1995–6, three times the average for all developing countries.

What are the explanations for these facts? In terms of Dunning's OLI paradigm of international ownership, location, internationalization, production (Dunning, 1993) the marked increase in inbound FDI reflects the rising locational advantages of Asian in relation to other developing countries and/or a greater propensity of foreign direct investors to internalize the markets for their competitive (i.e. owner-ship-specific) advantages. The opening up of several markets into which FDI had been previously restricted (e.g. in Korea) and the gradual upgrading of indigenous but location-bound created assets (especially skilled labour, the institutional framework and techno-logical infrastructure) needed by foreign firms to exploit their own particular core competencies explains much of the growth of inward FDI. At the same time, Asian firms have come to evolve their own unique competitive advantages which, together with rising domestic wage rates and encouragement, both from the banking system and their home governments, explain the upsurge in outbound investment over the last decade.

Of course, the opening up of the PRC to inbound FDI was perhaps the greatest stimulus to that country's entry into the global market economy. In 1996, that country accounted for 31.5 per cent of the Asian inbound FDI stake of the leading Asian outward investors. Hong Kong was responsible for 49.4 per cent of all such investment and Singapore and Taiwan another 28.6 per cent between them. How-ever, it is estimated that more than two-thirds of that investment went to mainland China – i.e. was symptomatic of a trend towards regional-ization rather than globalization.

Whether one prefers Ozawa's 'stages of economic development' (Ozawa, 1992, 1996) or our own 'investment development path' explanation of the dynamics of FDI in and out of developing countries, the deepening of the structural integration between Asian economies and the rest of the world and the continual upgrading of indigenous resources facilitated by both inward and outward FDI have exhibited an entirely predictable pattern over the last two decades.

Moreover, in explaining why Asian developing countries – be they in Groups 1, 2 or 3 – have generally recorded higher levels of FDI than those of other developing countries – particularly in the last decade – one finds the more export and market oriented approach of Asian governments, a more entrepreneurial culture and the Confucian ethic of the Asian people, and a greater quality control and a consensus approach to decision taking by Asian firms, have all helped these economies to embrace the challenges and opportunities of the global economy more easily than their counterparts in Africa and Latin America.

While recent economic events will most certainly slow down the pace of globalization in East Asian countries in the near future,[6] the demands on Asian firms to become even more competitive in their home and foreign markets is likely to become even more pressing. And though outbound FDI is likely to be curtailed, and some expansion plans shelved,[7] it is also likely that the depreciating currency of several Asian countries (notably Malaysia, Hong Kong, Korea and Indonesia) will lead to more inbound FDI – particularly from Europe and the USA – including some acquisitions of, or alliances with, Asian firms now facing financial difficulties. In the longer run however, we anticipate a renewed upgrading in the resources and capabilities of the Asian 'tigers', particularly in sectors in which, if they are to be internationally competitive, their firms also need to be part of a global network of valued added activities.[8]

EUROPEAN FDI IN DEVELOPING ASIAN ECONOMIES

With these thoughts in mind let me now turn to consider recent, and likely future, trends of European FDI in Asia. In doing so I shall rely very heavily on a 1996 European Commission/UNCTAD report,[9] a 1997 UNCTAD/Invest in France/Arthur Anderson study[10] and a 1997 study by the European Round Table of Industrialists.[11]

Table 4.2 sets out some data on FDI by EU countries in selected Asian countries between 1980 and 1993, compared to that of other triad investors. This reveals that, over this period, the EU's stock of all FDI in the named Asian countries fell from 16.4 per cent to 12.9 per cent, but that this mainly reflected a rise in non-triad (mostly intra-Asian) FDI in the region. In the case of Group 1 and most Group 2 countries for which data is available, the increase in the European stake more or less kept pace with that of the US and Japanese stake. However, in China, Europe – and to a lesser extent the USA – MNEs have lagged well behind their Asian counterparts and this pulled down the share of all EU FDI in Asia quite considerably.

When one looks at individual Asian countries, one sees the share of European FDI, relative to that of US and Japanese FDI, being the highest in Singapore and Malaysia, countries in which the UK and/or other European investors have long had cultural, ethnic, political or economic links. By contrast in the Philippines, and Thailand, the USA has a larger than average stake, while the Japanese presence is seen to be most marked in Indonesia and Korea, and that of mainland China is concentrated in Hong Kong and Taiwan. Again this picture is largely consistent with traditional FDI theory. What, however, is perhaps

Table 4.2 FDI by the triad in developing Asia, 1980–93 (million dollars and percentage)

| | Stocks | | | | | | Flows | | | |
| | 1980 | | 1985 | | 1993 | | 1985–7 | | 1990–3 | |
	Value	Share of total FDI	Value	Share of total FDI	Value	Share of total FDI	Value	Share of total FDI	Value	Share of total FDI
Hong Kong										
European Union	NA	NA	182	12.4	647	12.3	33	17.2	17	12.5
Japan	NA	NA	308	21.0	1 788	34.1	84	44.2	67	49.5
USA	NA	NA	788	53.7	1 474	28.1	80	42.2	15	10.7
Triad total	NA	NA	1 278	87.2	3 910	74.6	197	103.6	99	72.8
All countries	NA	NA	1 466	100.0	5 244	100.0	190	100.0	135	100.0
Korea, Republic of										
European Union	123	6.6	241	6.6	2 220	19.8	31	7.4	360	34.8
Japan	1 026	55.0	1 002	52.3	4 466	39.8	224	53.6	226	21.8
USA	491	26.3	1 073	29.5	3 259	29.1	120	28.7	333	32.2
Triad total	1 640	87.9	3 216	88.5	9 945	88.7	375	89.6	919	88.8
All countries	1 866	100.0	3 634	100.0	11 209	100.0	419	100.0	1 034	100.0
Singapore										
European Union	1 342	39.6	2 040	30.4	5 271	26.9	147	16.5	342	16.3
Japan	567	16.7	1 600	23.9	6 167	31.5	355	39.8	489	23.3
USA	1 001	29.6	2 440	36.4	6 851	35.0	268	30.0	572	27.3
Triad total	2 910	85.9	6 081	90.7	18 289	93.4	771	86.2	1 404	66.9
All countries	3 387	100.0	6 708	100.0	19 581	100.0	894	100.0	2 098	100.0
Malaysia										
European Union	1 720	26.6	2 264	26.6	5 842	17.1	84	10.3	837	15.2
Japan	1 135	17.6	1 602	18.8	7 435	21.8	284	34.7	1 142	20.7

USA	413	6.4	604	7.1	3 586	10.5	65	7.9	709	12.9
Triad total	3 268	50.6	4 470	52.5	16 864	49.5	144	17.6	2 688	48.8
All countries	6 462	100	8 510	100	34 091	100	818	100.0	5 508	100
Group 1										
Countries Total										
European Union	3 185	27.2	4 727	23.3	13 980	19.9	295	12.7	1 556	17.7
Japan	2 728	23.3	4 512	22.2	19 856	28.3	947	40.8	1 924	21.9
USA	1 905	16.3	4 905	24.1	15 170	21.6	533	23.0	1 629	18.6
Triad total	7 818	66.7	15 045	74.0	49 008	69.9	1 487	64.1	5 110	58.2
All countries	11 715	100.0	20 318	100.0	70 125	100.0	2 321	100.0	8 775	100.0
Indonesia										
European Union	851	8.3	2 672	17.4	9 967	14.7	269	25.7	1 205	13.4
Japan	3 462	33.7	5 009	32.6	13 937	20.6	329	31.4	1 379	15.3
USA	437	4.3	974	6.3	3 701	5.5	123	11.7	450	5.0
Triad total	4 750	46.2	8 655	56.4	27 605	40.8	721	68.8	3 034	33.7
All countries	10 274	100.0	15 353	100.0	67 625	100.0	1 047	100.0	8 999	100.0
Phillippines										
European Union	114	9.3	349	13.5	748	17.1	15	12.3	71	21.7
Japan	206	16.8	362	14.0	890	20.3	12	9.5	111	33.7
USA	669	54.6	1 461	56.6	1 937	44.1	79	65.2	55	16.7
Triad total	988	80.7	2 172	84.2	3 576	81.5	105	87.1	237	72.1
All countries	1 225	100.0	2 580	100.0	4 389	100.0	121	100.0	329	100.0
Thailand										
European Union	156	15.9	350	15.8	1 484	10.7	24	9.2	210	10.3
Japan	285	29.0	622	28.0	4 579	32.9	100	38.5	602	29.4
USA	322	32.8	721	32.5	2 412	17.3	69	26.7	311	15.2
Triad total	762	77.7	1 693	76.2	8 476	60.9	193	74.4	1 122	54.8
All countries	981	100.0	2 221	100.0	13 918	100.0	259	100.0	2 050	100.0
China										
European Union	300	13.6	584	8.3	2 018	3.5	113	5.5	300	2.6
Japan	128	5.8	502	7.2	4 288	7.5	245	12.0	782	6.7
USA	372	16.9	1 106	15.8	4 680	8.2	312	15.2	830	7.1
Triad total	800	36.3	2 192	31.2	10 986	19.2	670	32.7	1 911	16.4

Table 4.2 (*cont'd*)

| | Stocks | | | | | | Flows | | | |
| | 1980 | | 1985 | | 1993 | | 1985–7 | | 1990–3 | |
	Value	Share of total FDI	Value	Share of total FDI	Value	Share of total FDI	Value	Share of total FDI	Value	Share of total FDI
All countries	2 202	100.0	7 015	100.0	57 172	100.0	2 048	100	11 631	100.0
Group 2 Countries Total										
European Union	1 421	9.7	3 955	14.6	14 217	9.9	421	12.1	3 501	10.5
Japan	4 081	27.8	6 495	23.9	23 694	16.6	686	19.7	5 316	15.9
USA	1 800	12.3	4 262	15.7	12 730	8.9	583	16.8	3 686	11.0
Triad total	7 300	49.7	14 712	54.1	50 643	35.4	1 689	48.6	12 502	37.3
All countries	14 682	100.0	27 169	100.0	143 104	100.0	3 475	100	33 473	100.0

Note: NA = Not available.
Source: UNCTAD, Division on Transtional Corporations and Investment, FDI database.

a little surprising is the increase in the share of the European Union since the 1980s in countries with strong US or Japanese connections – e.g. the Philippines and Korea – and a decrease in their relative participation in countries in which they have strong historical ties – Singapore and Malaysia. It would seem, then, there has been some convergence in the geographical origin of triad FDI in the Asian countries over the last decade, which is paralleling the trend in other parts of the world – the USA and Europe.

Part of the explanation for these changing shares of EU FDI is that while the pre-1980s patterns of FDI strongly reflected the competitive advantages, psychic ties and natural resource needs of the investing countries, in more recent years most FDI has been in sectors in which competitive advantages tend to be more firm than *country*-specific, and in which large MNEs from each of the triad countries are well represented. The auto, chemical, electronics, clothing and footwear and telecommunications industries are cases in point. It is our belief that both the geographical origin and the industrial structures of inbound investment – particularly in Group 1 Asian developing countries – will continue to converge,[12] and reflect as much the degree of multinationality or strategies of the investing firms as their countries of origin.

Other data on the sales of foreign affiliates in Asia and exports to Asia from the three triad countries or regions suggest that, in 1993, EU firms exported slightly more to Asia than their Asian subsidiaries produced and sold. This was in contrast to the rest of the world, where the main modality of servicing foreign customers was through FDI rather than exports. In the case of US and Japanese firms, too, the relative significance of deep integration was higher in other regions than developing Asia.

Economists usually distinguish between different kinds of trade and FDI according to their *natural resource* and/or *created-asset* intensity.[13] UNCTAD[14] has compiled data on the percentage shares of developing Asia in world manufacturing, FDI stock and manufactured exports of the European Union, Japan and the USA by industry groups in 1985 and 1993. This shows quite clearly the growing importance of capital and technology-intensive trade and investment, relative to more traditional natural resource and labour-seeking FDI. It also shows that relative to their share of all manufacturing FDI that of EU MNEs in technology-/capital-intensive FDI has increased the most, and that their 'revealed' comparative advantage[15] in both these kinds of FDI is higher than that for the USA and Japan.

Turning now to surveys of European business and their attitudes towards investing in Asia, we would make two points:

(1) The *regulatory environment* in most Asian countries – and particularly in smaller Group 1 countries – is perceived to compare reasonably favourably with that in other developing countries, particularly in respect of alliance formation and investment protection. Of the 10 countries, Singapore, Hong Kong, Republic of Korea, Malaysia, Thailand, Taiwan, Philippines, Indonesia, China and India, identified by the World Economic Forum (1995, 1997), Korea was ranked the least liberal in its attitudes towards FDI. In another 1997 survey conducted by the European Round Table of Industrialists[16] (which embraced a rather different sample of developing countries) most of the Asian developing countries were classified as being 'quite open' in 1996 and/or were opening up to FDI at above-average speed (see Figure 4.1).

(2) Of the transaction cost-related barriers to FDI in Asia, set out in Table 4.3, those related to bureaucracy, corruption and lobbying

		Still partly closed	Degree of openness achieved, end-1996*			
			Moderately open	Moderately open to private investment, some delays and cost remain	Quite open →	Very open
Speed of opening, 1993–6*	Countries of the very fast track of opening, 1993–6		China India Egypt Nigeria		Brazil, Indonesia Kenya, Korea Mexico, Turkey Thailand	Ecuador
	Countries opening with a high average speed	Vietnam		Pakistan Zimbabwe	Ghana Malaysia Philippines Taiwan	Argentina Tunisia
	Countries opening with somewhat lower speed, 1993–6	Iran	Syria	Bangladesh	Colombia Saudi Arabia Sri Lanka	Guatemala
Categories of openness: Potential addition to the inflow of FDI if remaining impediments were to be fully removed (FDI in percentage points of gross fixed capital formation, for illustration only)		>6	5–6	4–5	3–4	1–3

Figure 4.1   Investment conditions, speed of opening in 1993–6 and degree of openness reached at end 1996

Note: *The higher up in this chart a country is placed, the higher was the speed of opening observed in 1993–6; the further to the right, the more open a country has become at the end-1996.

were the ones most frequently mentioned by an opinion survey of some 300 businessmen conducted by the World Economic Forum (1995, 1997). These were again most marked in Group 2 Asian countries. Including developed countries in our analysis, it is clear that, as countries move along their investment development paths, the transaction cost-related barriers to inbound FDI fall. Table 4.3 also shows that relative to other developing countries, Asian countries do well on all counts identified except with respect to the quality of their local capital markets. In particular, they were perceived to have a particularly good telecommunications and technological infrastructures and their governments were thought to be more transparent at successfully communicating their intentions.

The 1997 Invest in France/DATAR/Arthur Andersen report compares the perceptions of some 310 MNE executives and international experts about past and future FDI intentions. This shows that, over the past five years, and among developing regions, Asian countries have been ranked the highest by all groups of foreign investors. Even more impressive, it is anticipated that over the next five years developing Asia will have a higher priority for new FDI than either Western Europe and North America.[17] As might be expected, Asian and Japanese MNEs grade the developing Asian region higher than do their US or Western Europe counterparts; however, it is the Western-based firms which are most upgrading their investment expectations in Asia.

The data examined suggest that historically speaking – and with a few major exceptions – Western European MNEs have generally underestimated the growth potential of the dynamic Asian economies. Partly this is most certainly due to the greater 'psychic' distance between Europe and many Asian countries than as between Japan and the USA and these countries and the fact that, in engaging in low-cost production outside their home countries, European MNEs have preferred to use neighbouring regions (e.g. Southern Europe and North Africa) rather than most distant locations. Partly, too, European MNEs are (or perceive they are) at a competitive disadvantage in supplying goods to Asian markets *vis à vis* their Japanese or Asian counterparts. More recently, the 'benign' neglect[18] of Asia by European MNEs has been exacerbated by the further liberalization of trade and FDI in the European Union and by the partial renaissance of the market economy in Central and Eastern Europe.

Table 4.3 Transaction cost-related barriers to FDI in Asian developing countries[a]

Economy	Cultural barriers * (A)	Country image * (B)	State control (C)	Transpa- rency * (D)	Bureau- cracy * (E)	Corrup- tion * (F)	Lobbying (G)	Distri- bution system * (I)	Tele- commu- nications (J)	Techno- logical infrastruc. (K)	Labour Regulation * (L)	Overall assess- ment (M)
Group 1												
Singapore	8.5	9.0	7.1	7.4	7.6	9.4	7.8	9.2	9.3	8.6	3.2	7.9
Hong Kong	8.5	8.6	9.0	6.4	7.0	6.9	6.5	8.2	9.3	6.3	8.2	7.7
Korea (Rep.)	4.9	5.8	4.6	3.1	2.5	4.6	5.3	3.5	7.4	5.5	8.0	4.8
Thailand	6.6	7.4	5.1	2.9	4.1	2.6	3.7	5.5	4.9	4.3	6.9	4.9
Malaysia	6.7	8.4	5.7	6.1	5.5	4.8	4.9	7.3	7.2	5.3	7.9	5.8
Taiwan	8.5	6.7	NA	4.6	4.0	4.4	NA	6.2	NA	NA	4.9	NA
Group 2												
Indonesia	7.3	6.2	4.4	4.2	3.6	2.3	3.6	4.5	5.9	4.0	5.8	4.6
Philippines	8.8	6.4	4.7	4.8	2.8	2.0	3.6	3.9	3.7	3.1	5.6	4.1
China	6.7	7.8	4.1	5.8	1.8	2.5	4.5	3.7	5.3	2.7	5.0	4.2
Group 3												
India	7.4	4.1	4.0	2.7	2.7	1.9	3.9	3.3	4.0	3.8	2.8	4.1
Other Asia	8.0	3.9	5.9	2.6	3.0	2.4	4.1	5.8	6.3	6.3	7.2	5.6
Average, 11 Asian economies	7.6	5.7	4.6	4.0	2.8	2.2	3.9	4.2	5.0	4.0	5.9	4.5

	(A)	(B)	(C)	(D)	(E)	(F)	(G)	(H)	(I)	(J)	(K)	(L)
Developed countries[b]	7.3	6.7	6.1	5.0	3.9	7.0	4.5	7.4	7.8	6.5	4.9	6.3
Developing countries and countries in transition[c]	8.0	5.2	5.1	3.5	2.5	2.7	4.2	4.8	4.9	3.5	4.8	4.6

Notes: NA = Not available.

a Survey results are scaled from 0 (least favourable to FDI) to 10 (most favourable to FDI) in terms of the items (A)–(L) below.

* Indicates 1997 data.

(A) National culture is closed (0)/open (10) towards foreign cultures
(B) Image of your country abroad is distorted (0)/reflects reality accurately (10)
(C) State control of enterprises distorts (0)/does not distort (10) fair competition in your country
(D) The government does not often communicate its intentions successfully (0)/is transparent towards citizens (10)
(E) Bureaucracy hinders (0)/does not hinder (10) business development
(F) Improper practices (such as bribing or corruption) prevail (0)/do not prevail (10) in the public sphere
(G) Lobbying by special interest groups distorts (0)/does not distort (10) government decision making
(H) Distribution systems are generally inefficient (0)/efficient (10)
(I) Telecommunications infrastructure does not meet (0)/meets business requirements very well (10)
(J) Technological infrastructure is developed slower (0)/faster (10) than in your competitor countries
(K) Average assessment according to criteria (A)–(K)
(L) Labour regulations are (0) to restrictive/ (10) are flexible enough

b Average for Australia, Canada, France, Germany, Italy, Switzerland, UK and USA
c Average for Argentina, Brazil, Chile, Colombia, Czech Republic, Egypt, Hungary, Mexico, Peru, Poland, Russia and Venezuela

Source: World Economic Forum (1995, 1997).

While the increased attention now being given by European MNEs to Asia suggests some reprioritization of their geographical preferences – as witnessed, for example, by a sharp increase in approved new projects by European investors in India, and an increasing number of bilateral and tax treaties concluded between EU member states and Asian countries in the first half of the 1990s[19] – it is too early to judge whether, over the next decade or so, they can make substantial inroads to markets already largely secured by Asian and US MNEs. Perhaps the best opportunities lie in the penetration of the giant Chinese and Indian markets and of the newly emerging economies of the Indian sub-continent, (including Myanmar).[20] For historical and cultural reasons India, perhaps, offers the greatest opportunities; although relative to other Western investors, the European presence in Malaysia and Indonesia has always been quite strong. Clearly, too, more needs to be done in creating additional new and closer Asia–European trade, technology and FDI networks, particularly in the light of closer trans-Pacific links likely to follow as APEC gets up steam. It is here, in particular, that the European Commission and the European Investment Bank (EIB) can provide useful institutional support and financial help, particularly to small firms as they seek both to evaluate and exploit opportunities for FDI, and for alliance formation between European and Asian firms.

CONCLUSIONS

This chapter has demonstrated that many Asian developing countries are at the forefront of the globalization process; and that the more advanced of these are becoming important outward investors, not only elsewhere in Asia but in industrialized Western nations. It has further shown that inbound FDI is playing an increasingly important role in helping Asian developing economies to upgrade their economic structures in tune with the demands of the international market place; and to help them gain access to foreign resources and markets (UNCTAD, 1997). In this connection, the recent export performance of US manufacturing subsidiaries in Asia is most impressive.[21] The emergence and growth of domestic capital markets has also facilitated the inflow of FPI[22] which has further stimulated both investment and exports by indigenous firms.

A final section of the chapter showed that, except in Asian countries which have close historical and cultural ties, European FDI in developing Asian countries has lagged behind that of other countries. This is partly because European investors have given Asia a lower invest-ment priority than other regions, and partly because other Asian and US MNEs had already gained an export foothold in these markets. On the other hand, since 1993 there has been a slight shift in the geography of new European FDI (notably from the UK) towards developing Asia, and according to the European industrialists' survey, this shift is likely to accelerate over the next five years.

Finally, while the events of 1998 will undoubtedly slow down the globalization process of the Asian economies – and particularly out-bound FDI by their MNEs – we do not anticipate this will lead to a major shift in the economic philosophy or outward-looking stance of these countries. We would agree with *The Economist* (1998) that the remedy for the current bout of Asian 'economic flu' lies in more prudent monetary and fiscal policies, a further liberalization of domestic finan-cial systems, stricter bank regulation and supervision and exchange rate flexibility. In turn, these reforms, coupled with a continuation of market facilitating macro-organizational strategies, should lead to leaner, fitter and more stable Asian economies, and even more compet-itive Asian MNEs. It is this – as much as any short-term repercussions of the crisis – which the Western industrialized nations should be most concerned about. And one way they may be able to capitalize on the current weakness of Asian currencies is for their own corporations to gain a further foothold (via FDI and alliance formation) in what, after all remains, and is likely to remain one of the most dynamic growth regions in the world.

Appendix: Countries Associated with High, Medium and Low Human Development Categories

High Human Development (HHD)
Hong Kong
Singapore
Korea, Republic
Brunei Darussalam
Thailand
Malaysia
Taiwan

Medium Human Development (MHD)
Sri Lanka
Philippines
Indonesia
China
Vietnam

Low Human Development (LHD)
Myanmar
India
Pakistan
Cambodia
Nepal
Bangladesh

Notes

1. This survey was conducted in 1996, well before the economic events of 1997–8.
2. United Nations Development Programme.
3. O'Brien (1992), quoted in Kobrin (1993).
4. See especially the Appendixes in UNCTAD (1997).
5. Collated from *World Investment Report* (1997); *World Economic Forum; The World Competitiveness Report* (1997); *UNDP Human Development Report* (1997); IMF, *Balance of Payments Statistics* (1987, 1997).
6. Both indirectly and as a result of the rippling effects these events have on the rest of the world. For example, in December 1997, the IMF revised downwards its projections for world economic growth (GDP) by 1 percentage point in 1997 and 0.8 percentage point in 1998, with particular sharp reductions for the Asian economies of 3.8 per cent for Korea, 5.4 per cent for Indonesia and 7.0 per cent for Thailand (IMF survey, 1998).
7. For example, in December 1997 and January 1998, a number of Korean MNEs including Hyundai and Samsung Electronics announced they were postponing or shelving expansion plans for their UK subsidiaries.
8. At the same time it is possible that the ownership and/or control structure of Asian globalization might change; and that Western firms may play a more important role than they have done up to now.
9. *Investing in Asia's Dynamism, European Union Direct Investment in Asia*.
10. *International Investment: Towards the Year 2001*.
11. *Investment in the Developing World*.
12. At least a two-or even three-digit SIC level. However, within these industries, the principle of comparative advantage still holds good and different countries tend to specialize in the production of different kinds of products.
13. The former is sometimes referred to as Heckscher–Ohlin (H–O) trade, and the latter as Schumpeterian (S) trade.
14. Division on Transnational Corporations and Investment, FDI database; UNCTAD trade statistics database.
15. Obtained by dividing the share of a particular type of FDI or exports by the share of all FDI and exports.
16. The European Industrialists' survey (1997) excluded Singapore and Hong Kong from the Asian developing countries, but included Bangladesh, Vietnam, Pakistan and Sri Lanka.
17. This survey was undertaken between June and October 1996.
18. An expression of European the Commission (UNCTAD, 1997), p. 59.
19. According to the European Commission (UNCTAD, 1997), pp. 64–5. survey, by November 1994, 109 such tax treaties and 103 investment treaties had been concluded.
20. In December 1996, EU countries accounted for 40 per cent of the (approved) FDI stocks (Mason, 1997).
21. In 1993, for example, US manufacturing subsidiaries in Asian developing countries exported 69.9 per cent of their sales. The corresponding proportion for Latin American subsidiaries was 41 per cent, for African subsidiaries 50.4 per cent and for subsidiaries in all countries 51.1 per cent (US Department of Commerce, 1995).

22.   Between 1983–9 and 1990–5 the annual average flows of inward portfolio investment to Asian countries increased nearly eight times (from $1840 million to $14512 million). However, due primarily to substantial privatization schemes in Brazil, Mexico and Argentina, and in Central Europe, the inflow of portfolio capital to other developing countries over the same period of time was twenty-eightfold (from $8719 million to $20048 million).

References

Booz, Allen and Hamilton (1997) *Cross Border Alliances in the Age of Collaboration*, Los Angeles, Booz, Allen and Hamilton, Study for Invest in France Mission/Arthur Andersen/DATAR, *International Investment: Towards the Year 2001*, New York and Geneva, UN.

Dunning, J.H. (1981) 'Explaining the International Development Path of Countries: Towards a Dynamic or Developmental Approach', *Weltwirtschaftliches Archiv*, 119, 30–64.

Dunning, J.H. (1986) 'The Investment Development Cycle Revisited,' *Weltwirtschaftliches Archiv*, 122, 667–77.

Dunning, J.H. (1993) *Multinational Enterprises and the Global Economy*, Reading, MA, Addison-Wesley.

Dunning, J.H. and Narula, R. (eds), (1996) *Foreign Direct Investment and Governments*, London and New York, Routledge.

Dunning, J.H., Narula, R. and Van Hoesel, R. (1997) 'Explaining the New Wave of Outward FDI from Developing Countries', Occasional Paper, 2/96-013, Maastricht, MERIT.

Economist The (1998) 'Keeping the Hot Money Out', *The Economist*, 24 January, 85–6.

European Round Table of Industrialists (ERT) (1997) *Investment in the Developing World*, Brussels, ERT.

Fry, M.J. (1993) *Foreign Direct Investment in South East Asia*, Singapore, Institute of South East Singapore.

IMF (1998) 'Interim Assessment Revises Global Growth Projections Downwards', *IMF Survey*, 27(1), 12 January, 1–4.

Invest in France Mission/DATAR/Arthur Andersen (1997) *International Investment: Towards the Year 2001*, New York and Geneva, UN.

Kobrin, S.J. (1993) 'Beyond Geography: Inter-Firm Networks and the Structural Integration of the Global Economy', Working Paper, 93–10, Philadelphia, William H. Wurston Center for International Management Studies, The Wharton School.

Mason, M. (1997) *Foreign Direct Investment in Burma/Myanmar. Trends, Determinants and Prospects*, New Haven, Yale University, mimeo.

McGrew, A.G. and Lewis, P.G. (1992) *Global Politics: Globalization and the Nation State*, Cambridge, Polity Press.

O'Brien, R. (1992) *Global Financial Integration: The End of Geography*, London: Pinter.

Ozawa, T. (1992) 'Foreign Direct Investment and Economic Development', *Transnational Corporations*, 1(1), 27–54.

Ozawa, T. (1996) 'Japan: The Macro-IDP, Meso IDPs and the Technology Development Path' in J.H. Dunning and R. Narula (eds), *Foreign Direct Investment and Governments*, London and New York, Routledge.

Stopford, J. and Strange S. (1991) *Rural States, Rural Firms*, Cambridge, Cambridge University Press.

UNCTAD (1997) *World Investment Report: Transnational Corporations, Market Structure and Competition Policy*, New York and Geneva, UN.

UNDP (1997) *Human Development Report 1997*, Oxford, Oxford University Press.

US Department of Commerce (1995) *US Direct Investments Abroad: Provisional Results, 1993*, Washington, DC, US Department of Commerce.

World Economic Forum (1995) *World Competitiveness Report 1995*, Geneva, IMD and World Economic Forum.

World Economic Forum (1997) *World Competitiveness Report 1997*, Geneva, IMD and World Economic Forum.

5 The European Union and East Asia: Geoeconomics, Economic Diplomacy and Crisis Management

Christopher M. Dent

INTRODUCTION

The economic relationship between the European Union and East Asia has become an important structural feature of the world economy. Together with North America, these three regions constitute the so called 'triad' that collectively dominates international trade, production, investment, finance and technological development. This chapter places the EU–East Asia economic relationship in the geoeconomic context of triadic relations, and in particular considers the EU's strategizing in response to the possible 'Pacific Century' scenario (see Chapter 1 in this volume). The development of the European Union's economic diplomacy with East Asian states is highly relevant here, both at the bilateral and inter-regional levels, and this too is examined. A key theme running through this chapter also concerns the impact of the East Asian financial crisis, and we shall conclude by discussing what scope exists for both regions to conduct joint 'crisis-management' exercises.

THE GEOECONOMICS OF THE EU–EAST ASIA RELATIONSHIP

Setting the Geoeconomic Context

The significance of the EU–East Asia economic relationship emerged as part of the new global order of the 1990s, where the end of the Cold War heralded a shift from politico–ideological competition to economic competition between different trade 'blocs'. While the reference to 'blocs' is now increasingly contested, the switch of emphasis from geopolitics to geoeconomics nevertheless remains centred on the world's economic superpowers – the USA, the European Union and Japan. During the early 1990s in particular, there was much analysis and speculation concerning the triadic struggle for industrial supremacy (Hart, 1992; Albert, 1993). This continues to be relevant, although globalization has somewhat obscured the battle-lines between the triadic powers through 'insider' FDI projects, international strategic alliances and other transnationalized economic linkages. The advance of global economic interdependence has rather made triadic co-operation more expedient, especially where mutual policy or business objectives exist. Upholding the multilateral trading system is a case in point.

In this geoeconomic context, both competition and co-operation are functional expressions of maintaining economic security, this being generally defined as safeguarding the current and future prosperity of the home territory (e.g. nation state) or regional alliance of territories (e.g. the European Union) to which the former belongs. These can refer to actions undertaken at the bilateral level and also those aimed at upholding economic security at the multilateral or systemic level. Each theoretical tradition within the discipline of international political economy offers its own perspective here. Neo-realists would argue that preserving economic security in an anarchical inter-state system requires governments to exercise 'power politics', and thus inter-state competition rather than co-operation has greater salience. This contrasts with the neo-liberal institutionalist view which proposes that both state and non-state actors enter into co-operative ventures with others to achieve mutually beneficial economic security outcomes. Global interdependence, they would contend, makes this more imperative and hence multilateral co-operative regimes are seen as integral to the international economic security architecture. Marxists stress how the developed countries, in pursuing economic security objectives, seek to maintain the core–periphery divide in the world economy as a means to reinforce their dominant position. In a similar vein, reformists broaden the scope of economic security to include not just trade and investment, but also environment, drug trafficking, economic migration, nuclear proliferation and other 'new' security issues.

East Asia's dynamic industrialization has posed both a significant economic security threat and an opportunity to the European Union. On the one hand, the Union faces potential economic marginalization in an anticipated 'Pacific Century' (CEC, 1995a, 1995b). Trans-pacific linkages were already strong before the creation of APEC in 1989 which augmented them further.[1] On the other hand, East Asia represents a source of new prosperity and engine of global economic growth. However, East Asia's recent financial crisis brought a new geoeconomic context to the Euro–Asian relationship. By November 1998, a great deal of debate had been generated on whether East Asia's troubles would precipitate a global-scale crisis. Furthermore, many commentators were predicting the demise of the 'Asian way', or East Asian developmental statist model: US policy makers,[2] the IMF[3] and free market protagonists such as *The Economist* magazine (Phillips and Higgott, 1998). Some even prophesied that a second 'American Century' was imminent (Zuckerman, 1998), or that a new bipolarity would emerge in the crisis' aftermath (Lehmann, 1998). Moreover, as Belo (1998: 434) argued, the USA saw the crisis as an opportunity to 'achieve what it has been trying to push over the last decade, with little success: the free market transformation of economic systems that are best described as state-assisted capitalist formations'.[4] It also used its structural power via multilateral institutions like the IMF to realize key foreign economic policy objectives in East Asia, namely secure better market access for American producers in the region and thus reduce the burgeoning US trade deficit.

Although neo-liberalism made significant ideological advances in Western Europe during the 1990s, the European 'communitarian' social market model still prevailed in many key EU member states such as Germany and France by the end of the decade. This helps explain why the EU as a whole has been far less triumphalist over the East Asian crisis, and also why many European politicians believe that the crisis only underscores the need for greater market re-regulation rather than further deregulation – the elixir generally prescribed by their American counterparts. Meanwhile, the European Union has had to come to terms with at least a temporarily deflated East Asia (Bridges, 1998). If this situation persists, the longer-term geoeconomic balance of power could well revert to the transatlantic axis. If the crisis proves only to be a short- or medium-term setback to East Asia's dynamic economic development, then the Union's geoeconomic motives for further prioritizing its relations with the region remain strong. It will at this point be useful to consider the most recent trends in EU–East Asia trade and investment.

The Dynamics and Statics of EU–East Asia Economic Exchange

The East Asia states have been the European Union's most dynamic trading partners over recent decades. In 1960, East Asia accounted for just 6.4 per cent of extra-EU imports and 7.4 per cent of extra-EU exports. By 1980, these shares had risen to 11.7 per cent and 8.4 per cent, and by 1997 to 26.9 per cent and 20.2 per cent, respectively (*Eurostats*). Japan and China have become major EU trading partners: they represent two of the top three extra-regional traders with the European Union, the other being the USA. Furthermore, Korea, Taiwan and Hong Kong are now individually comparable trade partners to Canada and Australasia for the European Union. The Union's trade significance to East Asia has remained relatively static since the 1970s (*IMF Directory of Trade Statistics*). While North America has had a similar experience, its shares of East Asian trade remain generally much higher than Europe's. Meanwhile, East Asia's intra-regional trade has grown substantially in recent years, rising from about 25 per cent in the early 1970s to around 40 per cent by 1997.

With respect to balances of trade, *Eurostat* data on EU–East Asia trade (1975–97) show that East Asia has maintained a substantial trade surplus against the European Union since 1975. In 1997, this stood at ECU 33.8 billion – a peak of ECU 51.5 billion being achieved in 1991. However, if both Japan and China are removed from the equation,[5] then the European Union would itself enjoy a ECU 10.3 billion surplus with the other East Asian states in 1997. In the technological balance of trade, there has also been a general shift in favour of East Asia. While the Union retains a clear competitive advantage in chemicals, East Asian states have made significant advances in other key sectors (Table 5.1). China not only despatches large volumes of low-tech exports (e.g. clothing, footwear and toys) to Europe, but also a growing quantity of higher-tech products (e.g. electrical machinery, telecoms and audio-visual goods). The latter similarly applies to East Asia's newly industrialized countries (NICs) whose exports to the European Union have become increasingly technology-intensive. Meanwhile, Japan continues to receive relatively lower-tech imports from the European Union in return for its higher-tech exports sent to the Single European Market (SEM).

East Asia's techno–industrial convergence with the European Union naturally intensifies the competitive threat it poses to European business. However, this convergence also offers important commercial opportunities for EU firms. The growth of European FDI in East Asia can, for example, be partly attributed to the region's techno–industrial advances that have enabled EU firms to retain competitive advantage in key production operations, and furthermore expand into nearby dynamic markets (CEC, 1996a). In addition, the improving techno–industrial

Table 5.1 EU–East Asian trade: sectoral analysis, 1997 (ECU million)

	Japan		China		NIC group[1]	
	EU imports	EU exports	EU imports	EU exports	EU imports	EU exports
Food, livestock, drink + tobacco	1 806	3 818	91	3 216	924	259
Crude materials, fuels + energy	1 341	2 002	346	1 068	1 357	387
Chemicals	1 957	8 406	3 949	5 785	1 841	1 369
Organic chemicals	975	1 528	1 455	1 511	708	355
Medicinal/ pharmaceuticals	73	1 387	736	1 785	338	289
Plastics	538	1 646	829	427	84	274
Machinery + transport equip.	11 197	40 162	38 994	43 604	14 165	9 929
Power generating mach. + equip.	736	3 063	2 089	465	369	1 014
Specialized industrial machinery	555	5 149	1 845	1 506	111	2 342
Metalworking machinery	515	323	1 155	1 221	237	79

General industrial mach. + equip.	1 253	872	3 301	1 361	692	1 673
Office machines and computers	17 324	1 956	7 997	1 672	2 582	169
Telecoms and audio-visual	1 710	5 012	5 303	4 262	919	2 633
Electrical machinery	10 581	10 124	8 726	1 749	3 164	1 236
Road vehicles	3 565	3 893	13 862	5 842	150	994
Other transport equip.	1 543	814	2 478	302	413	150
Other manufactures	19 150	20 204	10 396	10 730	22 929	2 473
Textiles	199	1 788	1 835	593	857	1 254
Iron and steel	186	1 849	289	162	219	400
Clothing and footwear	5 997	1 877	130	2 031	7 490	41
Manufactures of metals	279	1 670	1 611	731	556	1 575
Miscellaneous manufactures	3 708	1 976	2 964	1 594	5 565	184

Note: 1. Korea, Taiwan, Hong Kong, Singapore, Malaysia, Thailand.
Source: Eurostat.

capabilities of East Asian firms has provided EU firms with a new source of strategic alliance partners, with Korea's *chaebol* multinationals[6] being particularly relevant here.

To what extent, though, has European business exploited these new commercial opportunities? Table 5.2 indicates that the EU's shares of inward FDI in most East Asian locations have risen over the 1980–96 period, most notably in the Association of Southeast Asian Nations (ASEAN) group[7] where the stock of EU investment had accumulated to $66.2 billion. However, EU firms still lag well behind their American and Japanese counterparts by comparison. Furthermore, by 1996 the European Union accounted for only 4.4 per cent of the inward FDI stock in China – the most dynamic and significant FDI location in the region.[8] Overall, then, the EU's share of East Asia's inward FDI stock has actually fallen over the period from 16.4 per cent to 12.8 per cent. Thus, as with trade, the Union's general position as an East Asian inward FDI partner has remained relatively static.

Table 5.2   Cumulative stocks of FDI in developing East Asia, by triadic source, 1980, 1985, 1993 and 1996

	Value (US$ million)				Share of FDI (per cent)			
	1980	**1985**	**1993**	**1996**	**1980**	**1985**	**1993**	**1996**
ASEAN-5[1]								
EU	4 183	7 675	23 313	66 249	18.7	21.7	16.7	25.3
Japan	5 655	9 195	33 009	56 855	25.3	26.0	23.6	21.7
USA	2 842	6 200	18 488	31 335	12.7	17.5	13.2	11.9
Triad	12 678	23 071	74 810	154 439	56.8	65.2	53.5	58.9
World	22 329	35 372	139 604	262 322				
China[2]								
EU	300	1 551	6 430	17 351	13.6	6.7	2.9	4.4
Japan	128	2 140	9 257	21 289	5.8	9.2	4.2	5.4
USA	372	3 046	14 897	28 378	16.9	13.1	6.7	7.2
Triad	800	6 737	30 584	67 018	36.3	29.0	19.2	17.0
World	2 202	23 204	222 234	396 196				
Hong Kong[3]								
EU	–	182	647	542	–	12.4	12.3	13.8
Japan	–	308	1 788	1 312	–	21.0	34.1	33.4
USA	–	788	1 474	1 104	–	53.7	28.1	28.1
Triad	–	1 278	3 910	2 958	–	87.2	74.6	75.3
World	–	1 466	5 244	3 928				
Korea[4]								
EU	123	241	2 220	4 021	6.6	6.6	19.8	22.8

Japan	1 026	1 902	4 466	5 567	55.0	52.3	39.8	31.5
USA	491	1 073	3 259	5 091	26.3	29.5	29.1	28.8
Triad	1 640	3 216	9 945	14 679	87.9	88.5	88.7	83.1
World	1 866	3 634	11 209	17 669				
Taiwan								
EU	–	376	1 648	2 293	–	7.3	9.3	9.3
Japan	–	1 182	5 056	6 571	–	22.9	28.6	26.6
USA	–	1 932	4 716	6 386	–	37.4	26.6	25.8
Triad	–	3 490	11 420	5 250	–	67.3	64.5	61.7
World	–	5 160	17 705	24 722				
Total								
EU	4 779	9 434	34 258	90 456	16.4	17.9	8.7	12.8
Japan	7 313	14 272	53 576	91 760	25.1	27.1	13.5	13.0
USA	4 657	13 031	42 834	72 481	16.0	24.7	10.8	10.3
Triad	16 748	36 737	130 668	254 697	57.5	69.7	48.1	36.1
World	29 115	52 645	395 996	705 004				

Notes: 1. Indonesia, Malaysia, Philippines, Singapore and Thailand.
2. 1980, 1985 and 1996 figures are 1984, 1987 and 1995 data, respectively; all figures based on approved FDI flows.
3. Secondary sector only and 1985 figures are 1984 data.
4. 1980 and 1985 figures are 1981 and 1986 data, respectively.
Source: UNCTAD, Division on Transnational Corporations and Investment database.
– = data not available.

Meanwhile, there have been some important developments regarding East Asian FDI in Europe (UNCTAD, 1997). Japan is by far the largest East Asian investor in the region with $113.0 billion of FDI stock by 1996. Although the level of Japanese FDI in the USA is much higher at $248.3 billion, the European Union's share of Japan's outward FDI total rose from 11.6 per cent to 19.2 per cent over the 1981–96 period, overtaking Asia's share along the way (JETRO – Stock of Outward FDI from Japan by Geographic Destination, 1981, 1996). While contributing much smaller levels of FDI in Europe, investment from East Asian NIC sources has also been on the increase. Korea is East Asia's second largest 'greenfield' investor in Europe with a $2,104 million FDI stock by 1996. This, though, could soon be dwarfed depending on whether LG and Hyundai maintain their respective multi-billion dollar investment projects already initiated in the UK.[9] As data on the stock of outward FDI from Korea by geographic destination 1987–96 (Bank of Korea; UNCTAD database) shows, Europe's share of outward Korean FDI rose sharply from 2.5 per cent in 1987 to 15.3 per cent by 1996, yet this remained well below that for other triad regions, with North America's share at 31.5 per cent and East Asia's 44.0 per cent. Singaporean FDI in Europe, at $3,930 million in 1995, was actually higher than Korean FDI in Europe but has received less public attention owing to this being mostly acquisitional in nature. Moreover, Singaporean firms have not embarked on the same ambitious FDI projects that their Korean counterparts undertook from the mid-1990s onwards.

ECONOMIC DIPLOMACY

We can define 'economic diplomacy' as the means and parameters within which trade, investment and any other international economic relations are conducted between representative agents. From one perspective, economic diplomacy concerns the use of defensive and promotive policy measures by the protagonist. Defensive measures are generally derived from the application of commercial policy instruments, whereas promotive measures typically originate from trade and economic co-operation accords but also commercial policy concessions. Another important perspective on economic diplomacy concerns its negotiatory engagement at the bilateral or multilateral level, where conflict resolution may be the prime issue (e.g. settling a WTO disputes case) which thus hopefully leads to promotive outcomes, although defensive motivations for negotiation may also prevail (e.g. the containment of a competitive threat).

In its supranational form, the European Union began to function as an effective protagonist of economic diplomacy on the world stage from around the early 1970s onwards. Its Common Commercial Policy (CCP) was formally established in 1968 with the completion of the customs union arrangement between the original EEC6 member states.[10] Although supranational policy competence has been granted to the European Commission on external trade, the Union's economic diplomacy is forged within a complex, multi-level system of governance where various actors exert their own influence. These include other EU institutions, national governments, firms, industrial associations, NGOs and other stakeholding constituents.

Economic diplomacy is conducted at bilateral, plurilateral, interregional and multilateral levels. The European Union has signed numerous bilateral trade agreements with East Asian countries,[11] and engages with them within multilateral regimes like the WTO. In the CCP's hierarchy of preferences, the East Asian states are positioned as follows:

- *Japan*: 'most favoured nation' (MFN) trade relations
- *China and ASEAN*: beneficiaries of the EU's Generalized System of Preferences (GSP) scheme which confers tariff concessions in both industrial and agricultural product lines
- *Korea, Singapore, Hong Kong*: recent GSP beneficiaries until they 'graduated' in May 1998, now MFN trade relations
- *Taiwan*: 'informal' trade relations with the European Union given Taiwan's contested sovereignty dispute with China.

While China and ASEAN continue to enjoy EU tariff concessions through the GSP scheme, like other East Asian states they have had to contend with a relatively wide application of EU anti-dumping duties (ADDs) on their products. Over 1985–97, these attracted 46.8 per cent of all EU anti-dumping investigations. Up until the early 1990s, East Asian producers were also subject to a wide range of quantitative restrictions in both 'sensitive' sectors (e.g. agriculture, textiles, clothing) and those where concentrated penetrations in EU markets had been achieved (e.g. consumer electronics, automobiles). Far from creating a 'Fortress Europe', the SEM helped eradicate, reduce or rationalize these restrictions as part of augmenting the SEM's own integrity.[12] This coincided with a switch from a defensive to a more promotive EU economic diplomacy towards East Asia, a response to the new geoeconomic realities already discussed. Under this new approach, the Union sought new accords with the East Asian states and introduced its 'New Asia Strategy' in 1994 to provide a more coherent basis for developing relations. The Union's economic diplomacy with each East Asian partner nevertheless continues to evolve in its own distinct manner, and these are now considered.

EU–Japan

The path of EU–Japan economic diplomacy has been the longest and most problematic. Japan's ascendant economic superpower status and substantial competitive threat to a broad range of European industries has presented a serious challenge to the Union since the 1960s. By the 1980s, Japan's growing trade surplus with both the Union and the USA had become a highly politicized issue, and helped bring triadic relations to the fore. The G7 Plaza Accord of 1985, in which Japan agreed to revalue the Yen, was an important step forward in easing trilateral competitive friction and promoting trilateral co-operation.[13] Within the GATT–WTO framework, the Union and Japan have also worked with the USA at pushing forward the new multilateral trade agenda. The trilateral context to EU–Japan economic diplomacy can also be extended to the 'two-against-one' coalitions. The USA has often requested the Union's support when seeking to broaden *'gaiatsu'* (foreign pressure) against Japan in trade or FDI-related negotiations.[14] In the Uruguay Round of GATT, both the USA and Japan led an alliance that cajoled the Union into further liberalizing its agriculture trade regime. Although not explored to great effect, an EU–Japan coalition to counteract the excesses of US unilateralism has occasionally been deployed.

With the emergence of the new post-Cold War global order, the triadic powers signed bilateral 'Declarations' between themselves beginning with the USA–EU accord of 1990, its EU–Japan equivalent in 1991 and finally a Japan–USA agreement in 1992. The EU–Japan Declaration helped redress the trilateral imbalance of relations somewhat, while smoothing the path for more cordial economic relations in the 1990s. Like the USA, the Union has taken an active interest, and even peripheral participation in Japan's 'deregulation programme' of the 1990s, especially where the country's structural impediments to import have been targeted. Over the decade, the EU experienced a marked growth in its exports to Japan[15] which can be partly attributed to more fervent national and EU-level export promotion campaigns.[16] However, Japan remains a prime focus of the EU's Market Access Strategy (CEC, 1996b) with many sectoral imbalances still persisting, thus presenting ongoing challenges to EU–Japan economic diplomacy (CEC, 1995c, 1996b).

EU–China

Economic relations between China and the Union initially evolved out of strong geopolitical imperatives. West Europe was a strategic source of advanced capital, technology and imports for China. However, the basis of a more formalized China–EU economic diplomacy was established with the advent of Deng Xiaoping's rule. In 1978, the first EU–China trade agreement was signed, followed in 1985 by a upgrading trade and co-operation agreement. By the early 1990s, China had become a significant trading partner for the Union, and also a substantial target of EU defensive trade measures. Although many of these have now been removed, China is still subject to the largest number of ADDs imposed on any EU trading partner[17] (32 definitive duties in November 1998) and all three of the Union's quantitative restrictions on third country imports.[18] Moreover, China's relatively high tariff levels, regular breaches of intellectual property rights (IPR) and other numerous trade-related problems, together with its growing trade status, have made the Union keen advocates of the country's accession into the WTO (CEC, 1995d, 1998a). This has become the central focus of EU–China economic diplomacy as the Union, along with the USA, are effectively the gatekeepers of China's entry into the multilateral trade order. While the Union intends to use the WTO as another channel through which to pursue its trade disputes with Beijing, it also must consider the geoeconomic significance of China's new role that its imminent WTO membership will bring (Casadio, 1996).

EU–ASEAN

There are two main features of EU–ASEAN economic diplomacy that make it distinctive. The first relates to the strong post-colonial links between the two regional groups and the second to the inter-regional dimension of this diplomacy. In 1980, the signing of the ASEAN–EC Co-operation Agreement established the initial framework from which a variety of joint policy initiatives and business contact groups have emerged. These have increased as Southeast Asia's industrialization process has created a firmer basis for economic and policy co-operation, and hence an evolution away from the 'donor–recipient' character of early EU–ASEAN economic relations. However, endeavours to move beyond the politico–institutional framework of the 1980 Agreement (CEC, 1996c) have been hampered by bilateral disputes. These include Portugal's quarrel with Indonesia over human rights abuses in East Timor. More recently, the formal process of ASEAN–EU relations was stalled in November 1997 after the Union contested Myanmar's legitimacy to acquire observer status in EU–ASEAN Joint Co-operation Committee meetings owing to its own human rights record.[19] Notwithstanding this politico–institutional débâcle, ASEAN–EU business contact networks continued to interact as usual.

EU–Hong Kong and EU–Taiwan

The Union's economic diplomacy with Hong Kong also has a post-colonial dimension, and moreover hinges upon that of Hong Kong's relations with the UK, its former colonial master. However, attempts have already been made by the European Commission to establish a more resolute EU-level basis for developing economic relations with the new Special Administrative Region (SAR) of China (CEC, 1997).

Although the SAR's main foreign policy competencies are governed from Beijing, it still retains its own currency and the ability to function as a separate customs authority. This enables Hong Kong's trading partners to conduct bilateral and multilateral economic relations with the SAR until 2047, the date by which complete sovereignty is returned to the PRC.

Developments in the joint governance of Hong Kong between the SAR government and Beijing are being closely observed by Taiwan. The contested sovereignty of the island between the incumbent Kuomintang (Taiwan's National Party) government and Beijing has meant that Taiwan's economic diplomacy with most third countries is conducted at an informal level. Here, the role of business representatives has been an integral part of the economic diplomacy equation. This relates to the quasi-diplomatic functions performed by various EU business associations in Taiwan, and similarly those performed by 'non-official' Taiwanese trade offices dispersed around EU capitals. In addition, informal and low-level commercial talks between Taiwan and the Union have been convened on an annual basis since the early 1980s. Taiwan's growing commercial importance and accession negotiations to join the WTO[20] has necessitated the Union affording greater priority to developing its economic diplomacy with the island state.

EU–Korea

Up until the mid-1990s, Korea–EU economic diplomacy was primarily concerned with managing various trade disputes. From the Union's perspective, these derived from Korea's ardent neo-mercantilist practices, such as aggressive state-assisted exporting and strategic protectionism. From a Korean perspective, these stemmed from Europe's industrial and entrepreneurial inertia in adapting to new competitive realities. Tensions eased with the formalizing of Korea–EU economic diplomacy once democratic reform in the country had become reasonably embedded. The Korea–EU Trade and Co-operation Agreement was signed in 1996 (CEC, 1996d), the same year Korea entered the OECD, and thus into internationally recognized advanced industrial statehood. Commercial disputes still remain a key feature of Korea–EU economic relations[21] but considerable success has been achieved at developing their co-operative aspect. Developments in EU–Korea FDI relations have played an important part in this respect, as has Korea's techno–industrial convergence with Europe. Furthermore, Korea could play an important advocacy role for the Union in its relations with the Asia Pacific.

The Asia–Europe Meetings (ASEM)

The Asia–Europe Meeting (ASEM) 'dialogue framework' represents the most important development in EU–East Asia relations to date, providing an inter-regional dimension to promotive economic diplomacy. Established in March 1996 by the first ASEM summit held at Bangkok, it seeks to promote the economic, political and cultural aspects of these relations (CEC, 1996f). However, it is ASEM's economic aspect that dominates and is centred on two 'Action Plans' (trade facilitation and investment promotion) and the work of the ASEM Business Forum. Bilateral economic diplomacy between the Union and its East Asian trade partners is also generally reinforced by the ASEM process, with many of its initiatives being pursued through existing bilateral links. While ASEM provides an important new fora for Euro–Asian business networking and a means to establish some congruency in selected administrative procedures (e.g. customs, standards and certification), we must reserve judgement on whether it will progress beyond its current largely symbolic value (Dent, 1998a).

CRISIS MANAGEMENT

The above analysis has detailed the general shift from defensive to promotive economic diplomacy that was apparent between the European Union and East Asian states by the mid-1990s. However, the new co-operative culture has been tested by the rigours exerted by the 1997–8 East Asian financial crisis. At the bilateral level, commercial tensions have arisen from two main sources. First, East Asian producers have exported more aggressively to EU and other international markets in an endeavour to compensate for the domestic market and financial constraints imposed by crisis conditions. Secondly, the weak macroeconomic position of many East Asian states caused a significant fall in demand for EU exports in late 1997–early 1998, particularly in non-essential, luxury good sectors (CEC, 1998b).

At the multilateral level, the Union had to come to terms with the contagion of the East Asian financial crisis within the world economy. Europe's own stock markets had experienced significant downturns over the latter half of 1998, although towards the end of this period a recovery was evident. However, by this time the threat of a crisis-induced global recession had not disappeared, thus underscoring the need for both the Union and East Asia to undertake joint 'crisis-management' exercises. This touched on a wider issue, namely to what extent both regional powers could assume greater responsibility for co-managing the international economic system in the post-hegemonic era. Whether the Union and East Asia's major states (i.e. Japan, China, Korea) could take such a lead without the USA is, though, highly questionable. The USA remains the world's 'default' hegemon, and East Asian states still look to America for leadership and initiative in times of global economic instability.[22]

The ASEM is the most obvious framework through which any Euro–Asian initiatives for establishing a 'global stability pact' or similar could emerge. However, the Second ASEM summit held in London in April 1998 demonstrated the general failure to deliver an effective joint policy response to the East Asian financial crisis. EU leaders were prepared to offer very little in either financial or technical support, agreeing to establish an Asia–Europe Trust Fund of ECU 30.9 million to fund the provision of technical assistance for those East Asian financial sectors in most difficulty. No new policy framework was established to deal with potential crisis-induced problems that might affect EU–East Asia economic relations.[23] Moreover, the Union is likely to remain too preoccupied and committed to its own financial project – economic and monetary union – to provide resources elsewhere, despite the fact that many European banks were highly exposed to the East Asian financial crisis.[24] The next real opportunity for the ASEM process to contribute was at the Seoul 2000 summit.

However, it is too early to judge the wider effectiveness of the ASEM in dealing with such matters in the future. It is still in its formative years and the Euro–Asian socialization process between regional business representative and policy making communities on the 'ASEM scale' has only just begun. We must also remember that APEC began in a similarly modest fashion. Furthermore, given the crisis-related tensions in trans-pacific economic relations discussed earlier, together with the certain commonalties between the EU 'communitarian' social market model and East Asia's developmental state model, there exists an important opportunity for fortifying the Euro–Asian axis. As suggested earlier, the Union has much to gain geoeconomically from demonstrating what a dependable economic partner it can be to East Asia during such uncertain and unstable times.

CONCLUSION: FUTURE PROSPECTS FOR THE EU–EAST ASIA ECONOMIC RELATIONSHIP

The future salience of the EU–East Asia economic relationship is contingent upon a variety of factors. For much of 1998, the bilateral and systemic impacts of East Asia's financial troubles have dominated the discussion of this issue. However, the longer-term legacy of the crisis on Euro–Asian relations remains far from clear. The evolution of the trans-pacific economic relationship, the path of respective regionalisms in Europe and East Asia, the EU and East Asian state participation in the WTO's new trade agenda, the maturing of the ASEM process and future business networking between EU and East Asian firms represent other important determinants that should also be considered on roughly equal terms. Furthermore, the momentum behind East Asia's dynamic industrialization may have been simply stalled by the crisis, thus implying that the region's future geoeconomic significance to the Union has not been diminished. It is even conceivable that the post-crisis restructuring of the most affected economies could leave them much stronger than before.

Moreover, most of the fundamentals that produced the initial East Asian economic miracle are still intact – e.g. human resource development, fervent entrepreneurship and business network flexibilities. European business and policy makers should therefore be circumspect in ascribing peripheral geoeconomic importance to East Asia as the early twenty-first century unfolds.

Notes

1. In 1982, trans-pacific trade overtook transatlantic trade flows for the first time.
2. These included Charlene Barchevsky (US Trade Representative) and Jeffrey Garten (Under-Secretary of State for Commerce).
3. The IMF's Managing Director, Michel Camdessus, saw East Asia's troubles as a 'blessing in disguise' in that they would eventually eradicate 'crony capitalism' and further liberalize the region's markets.
4. Belo (1998) further defines developmental statist practices as 'the complex of protectionism, mercantilism, industrial policy and activist state intervention in the economy'.
5. In 1997, Japan and China's trade surpluses with the Union were ECU 23.2 billion and ECU 20.9 billion, respectively.

6. Korea's *chaebol* are large conglomerated companies that dominate the Korean economy. The four largest *chaebol* are Samsung, Hyundai, LG and Daewoo. These all have major FDI interests in Europe (Dent and Randerson, 1996).
7. Brunei, Indonesia, Laos, Malaysia, Myanmar, the Philippines, Singapore, Thailand and Vietnam.
8. The relatively low combined 'triad' figure can be attributed to the very high level of Hong Kong and Taiwanese FDI in China. Hong Kong accounted for 59.0 per cent of the inward FDI stock in China by 1995.
9. These refer to LG's $2.6 billion project in South Wales and Hyundai's similar $3.7 billion electronics production complex investment in Scotland.
10. The management of the common external tariff (CET), a defining feature of customs unions, made this expedient.
11. Indeed, the 1970 EC–Japan Trade Agreement was the first significant EU-level trade accord to be signed with a third country.
12. This was to avoid the internal market distortions that national-level trade restrictions on third-country imports would cause to the SEM arrangement. See Hanson (1998) for further analysis of the 'Fortress Europe' issue.
13. A core objective of the Trilateral Commission established in the early 1970s. However, the Commission's work largely centred on issues of high politics (e.g. politico–military security) rather than economics. See also Brzezinski, 1973).
14. The Union has denied the USA this support, as demonstrated in the 1998 US–Japan autos and auto-parts dispute. Strange (1995) has been an advocate of this resistance.
15. Over the 1992–97 period, the value of EU exports to Japan rose by 62.3 per cent from ECU 22.2 billion to 36.0 billion.
16. Such as the UK's 'Priority Japan' and France's 'Le Japon: C'est Possible' campaigns. The European Commission 'Gateway to Japan' (1993–6) and a more ambitious exercise launched in March 1997 becoming part of the wider Japan EXPROM programme.
17. Over the 1985–97 period, Chinese imports attracted 13.8 per cent of all EU anti-dumping investigations.
18. These relate to Chinese imports of toys, ceramic tableware and footwear.
19. Myanmar joined ASEAN in early 1997, along with Laos.
20. Completed in the summer of 1997.
21. For Korea, this particularly relates to the Union's application of ADDs on Korean goods. Meanwhile, the Union's commercial disputes with Korea centre on the country's 'internal' barriers to international trade (Dent, 1998b).
22. For example, the international community looked in unison to the US Federal Bank chief, Alan Greenspan, in Autumn 1998 to reduce American interest rates as a means to buoy up the crisis-inflicted world economy.
23. Policy makers and banking representatives from the Union and East Asia have worked in a largely ad hoc manner with the IMF in addressing the crisis.

24.   According to the Bank for International Settlement (BIS), by June 1997 European banks held $365 billion in loans outstanding to Asian banks and companies, compared to $275 billion for American banks and $45 billion for Japanese banks.

References

Albert, M. (1993) *Capitalism Against Capitalism*, London, Whurr.
Belo, W. (1998) 'East Asia: On the Eve of the Great Transformation?', *Review of International Political Economy*, 5(3), 424–44.
Bridges, B. (1998) 'Coping with Contagion: Europe and the Asian Economic Crisis', *Working Paper*, 78, Lingnan College Centre for Asian Pacific Studies.
Brzezinski, Z. (1973) 'US Foreign Policy: The Search for Focus', *Foreign Affairs*, 51(4), 708–23.
Casadio, G.P. (1996) 'China's Role in World Trade and its Re-entry to the GATT: A European View', in H.-C. de Bettignies (ed.), *Business Transformation in China*, London, International Thomson Business Press.
Commission of the European Communities (CEC) (1995a) 'Free Trade Areas: An Appraisal', SEC(95) 322 Final, Brussels.
Commission of the European Communities (CEC) (1995b) 'Background Note on APEC', Brussels.
Commission of the European Communities (CEC) (1995c) 'Europe and Japan: The Next Steps', COM(95) 73 Final, Brussels.
Commission of the European Communities (CEC) (1995d) 'A Long-Term Policy for China–Europe Relations', COM(95) 279 Final, Brussels.
Commission of the European Communities (CEC) (1996a) 'Investing in Asia's Dynamism: EU Direct'.
Commission of the European Communities (CEC) (1996b) 'Summary of Market Access Problems in Japan', Brussels.
Commission of the European Communities (CEC) (1996c) 'Creating a New Dynamic in EU–ASEAN Relations', Brussels.
Commission of the European Communities (CEC) (1996d) 'Framework Agreement for Trade and Co-operation between the European Community and its Member States, on the one hand, and the Republic of Korea, on the other', Brussels.
Commission of the European Communities (CEC) (1996f) 'Regarding the Asia–Europe Meeting (ASEM) to be held in Bangkok on 1–2 March 1996', COM(96) 4 Final, Brussels.
Commission of the European Communities (CEC) (1997) 'The European Union and Hong Kong: Beyond 1997', COM(97) 171 Final, Brussels.
Commission of the European Communities (CEC) (1998a) 'Building a Comprehensive Partnership with China', COM(98) 181 Final.
Commission of the European Communities (CEC) (1998b) 'Crisis in Asia: Effects on EU Industry', DG3 Background Note, 18 February 1998.
Dent, C.M. (1998a) 'The ASEM: Managing the New Framework of the EU's Economic Relations with East Asia', *Pacific Affairs*, 70(4), 495–516.

Dent, C.M. (1998b) 'New Interdependencies in Korea–EU Trade Relations', *Journal of Contemporary Asia*, 28(1), 336–89.

Dent, C.M. and Randerson, C. (1996) 'Korean Foreign Direct Investment In Europe: The Determining Forces', *The Pacific Review*, 9(4), 531–52.

Hanson, B.T. (1998) 'What Happened to Fortress Europe?: External Trade Policy Liberalisation in the European Union', *International Organisation*, 52(1), 55–85.

Hart, J. (1992) *Rival Capitalists*, Ithaca, Cornell University Press.

Lehmann, J.-P. (1998) 'European and Asian Policies on Trade and Investment: Past Perspectives – Future Prospects', paper given at the *Beyond Liberalisation: Making Economic Policy in Europe and the Asia-Pacific* Conference, 15–16 October, European University Institute, Florence.

Phillips, N. and Higgott, R. (1998) 'The Limits of Global Liberalisation: Lessons from Asia and Latin America', paper given at the *Beyond Liberalisation: Making Economic Policy in Europe and the Asia-Pacific* Conference, 15–16 October, European University Institute, Florence.

Strange, S. (1995) 'European Business in Japan: A Policy Crossroads?', *Journal of Common Market Studies*, 33, 1–25.

UNCTAD (1997) *Sharing Asia's Dynamism: Asian Direct Investment in the European Union*, Geneva, United Nations.

Zuckerman, M. (1998) 'A Second American Century', *Foreign Affairs*, 77(3), 18–31.

6 Corporate Governance: Global Issues and Japanese Perspectives

Janet Morrison

INTRODUCTION

Corporate governance has tended to be seen in terms of contrasting national 'systems', engaged in a Darwinist-like contest to decide which is the best, the assumption being that only the 'fittest' will survive in global competition. On examination, these systems consist of a web of relationships both internal and external to companies, which have evolved in particular national environments, each with its own distinctive history and culture. In any national context, there is wide circle of stakeholder relationships, with varying degrees of proximity to the company's activities. Investors, managers, employee workforce, consumers, suppliers and the investing public generally has expectations of the company. Inevitably, some of these expectations conflict, and corporate governance necessarily involves choices impinging on the various constituencies. The question, 'What is the company for?' elicits a range of responses, reflecting the varying patterns of national corporate structures and values. The 'Anglo–American' system, first on the scene, is a legacy of liberalism and democracy, of which it has been said, 'in American society the individual is king. Not the nation, not the government, not the producers, not the merchants, but the individual – and especially the individual consumer – is sovereign' (Miller, 1997: 39). Without undue fear of oversimplification, the classic American stance is suspicious of big business, big banks and strong central government. Mechanisms for accountability of management loom large, just as checks and balances are central to the federal system of government.

The spectacular successes of the post-war Japanese economy cast alarm across the boardrooms of corporate America, as Japanese manufacturing companies in particular made inroads into product markets which American companies had dominated. Prominent studies of the Japanese company, and of Japanese society generally, from the 1970s onwards, revealed that the company in Japan has traditionally had a wider societal dimension, encompassing wider issues than the finance oriented and market oriented approaches of the American model (Nakane, 1970; Clark, 1979; Johnson, 1982; Abegglen and Stalk, 1985). These and other studies brought to the fore questions of whether corporate behaviour was culturally 'imbedded', whether the Japanese company was unique to Japanese national culture. Alternatively, there was the possibility that the Japanese might simply have found better ways of solving the familiar problems of control and accountability – ways which could be transported to non-Japanese environments, and from which lessons could be learned (Dore, 1987). A wide-ranging debate on mechanisms of corporate governance has ensued, fuelled in large measure by greater investor awareness and activism in both America and Europe. Various national systems have come under the spotlight, and comparative research has resulted. In particular, the USA, Britain, Germany and Japan have featured, Japan most often being likened to Germany (Roe, 1993; Kester, 1997; Mayer, 1997). A comparative study on MNCs confirms that national differences still persist, and that cultural factors are inescapable, although its authors prefer 'national' to 'cultural' and do not attempt to analyse the relevant national differences. (Pauly and Reich, 1997).

Corporate governance in Japan, as the research cited above has shown, does reflect cultural norms and values but, it will be argued here, these have not been static and immutable, as is often portrayed: they have evolved in particular economic and political contexts over a long period of time, as have other national systems Moreover, they continue to evolve. For Western observers it has been tempting to reach for simplistic 'cultural' explanations of national differences, when in fact a multiplicity of factors have been at work. It is in the context of this changing environment over time that corporate governance must be viewed, an approach which has only been touched on in survey studies of comparative corporate governance.

THE COMPANY IN JAPANESE SOCIETY

Like its Western counterpart, the Japanese company is an entity recognized in law as a separate 'person', with its own liabilities, rights to own property and to make contracts. It is thus legally separate from its shareholders, who are the legal owners. Control is effectively delegated to the management, who are overseen by a board of directors, who represent the shareholders. A summary of legal structure of the company, however, gives little indication of the realities behind the corporate form. The company in Japan is seen as a 'social unit made up of the people who work full-time in it' (Dore, 1987: 54). Abegglen and Stalk (1989: 233) put it this way: 'The essence of the Japanese company is the people who compose it'. These are admittedly broad-brush categories. As a tool of analysis, Ronald Dore contrasts the 'company law model' with the 'community model'. In the former, the key players are the management and shareholders, whose relationship is adversarial, rather than one of trust. In the community model, the emphasis is on the people who make up the company, and who have a long-term vested interest in its success. In this model, he says (1987: 54), the shareholders are 'like customers, ... one group of outsiders'. Of course, theoretically this is incorrect: in Japan as elsewhere they are the legal owners, but this view reflects the social importance of the Japanese company as a community. Indeed, Abegglen and Stalk (1985: 233) say that the personnel are 'to a considerable degree the owners of the company'.

A closely related question is, 'What is the company for?' If its aim is to serve society, as Japanese companies typically depict their mission, how does this manifest itself in the ways the company goes about its business? After all, it may be argued, a company must make profits to survive, whether it takes a short-term view of maximizing shareholder value, or whether it sees itself as having a wider social mission. In terms of financial goals, Japanese companies have traditionally prioritized growth in market share, continued employment and high profitability (Sherman and Babcock, 1997: 275). Western managers, on the other hand, take a keener interest in total shareholder returns, a priority often accused of being short-termism, and harmful to long-term performance. Japanese companies, while in for the long haul, have been accused of paying too little attention to shareholder interests, in favour of the firm's employees, to the detriment of the overall financial health of the company. But, as Kester (1991: 76) has pointed out, stake-holders' interests do not fall into clear and distinct categories, but overlap, forming a 'coalition of stakeholders', who hold a mixture of long-term and short-term claims. Japanese managers are therefore 'agents of the entire coalition of stakeholders' (Kester, 1991: 79).

Poor investments, declining profitability and falling share prices in the 1990s called into question the ways in which Japanese companies have been run, with the inevitable focus on managements, and the ways in which they are monitored. There are both internal and external monitoring mechanisms, both formal and informal means. Banks have traditionally played a key role in supervision, but as companies have moved away from debt financing to equity financing, the role of banks in corporate governance has diminished, a factor which has repercussions for corporate oversight generally, re-focusing attention on other monitoring bodies. To list them briefly, they are: the board of directors, and especially outside directors; the statutory auditor; *keiretsu* partners who, like banks, are corporate shareholders; individual shareholders, who in Japan to date have had little say; the government and the Bank of Japan. Not all of these, of course, are of equal importance, but it is hoped to sketch out the role of each of these monitors, together with changes which are occurring and indicated for the future. It is unclear what outcomes will emerge from the current 'governance recession' in Japan (Sherman and Babcock, 1997: 273), especially in the context of economic downturn and ailing financial institutions. It is hoped here to elucidate Japanese perspectives, along with comparative perspectives, on some of the major issues.

THE JAPANESE COMPANY AS SHAPED BY HISTORICAL EVENTS

The growth of the great capitalist enterprises of Europe and North America in the latter half of the nineteenth and early twentieth century was paralleled by Japanese industrial development in the same period, but it would be a mistake to assume that similar entrepreneurial forces were driving industrialization. The turning point which marked the birth of modern Japan was the Meiji Restoration of 1868. The term 'restoration' here is a misnomer, disguising what was in effect a revolution – economic, political and social. Japan had been a feudal society, virtually isolated throughout the Tokugawa era (1603–1868), nominally under the sovereignty of a powerless Emperor. A weak central government proved unable to control powerful local clans, and also unable to stand up to the Western powers who established 'treaty ports' along Japan's coast. That government was removed in a *coup d'état*, by a coalition of clan leaders who charged themselves with bringing modernization to a backward Japan, acutely conscious of a need to catch up with Western powers. The Meiji oligarchs were successful in (1) stripping away the feudal structures which stifled economic development and social mobility and (2) exploiting the ideological potential of imperial 'restoration' for a programme of nation-building, which effectively amounted to economic nationalism.

Japan's industrial revolution, then, dates from the Meiji era, and was driven by a combination of government policy and private enterprise (Nakamura, 1983: 59). This partnership has become characteristic of Japanese economic development, most notably in the post-Second World War period. Tokugawa Japan had been a thoroughly feudal, agrarian economy, imbued with the Confucian precepts of both social hierarchy and of the community as family. There were thriving merchant houses in the Tokugawa era, some of them, such as Mitsui, ancestors of modern companies. These were family-based businesses, which had no separate legal identity, and their owners, of course, did not enjoy limited liability. Despite the limitations of the social order and the difficulties raising capital, they did possess entrepreneurial spirit and profit motivation. But they were firmly part of a Confucian world picture, hardly an incipient bourgeoisie in the Western sense, with its ethos of self-interested individualism. The Confucian value system dictated 'the need to be benevolent as well as self-interested' (Dore, 1987: 181). It is in these merchant houses that we find the cultural roots of the familism associated with the Japanese company, based on relational ties rather than legal contractual ties, a key theme in Japanese corporate culture.

From 1867 the joint stock company was recognized as a legal entity, and was much promoted by the Meiji leaders as a vehicle for rapid industrial development, as being 'modern and Western' (Clark, 1979: 31). The corporate *form* thus became established in advance of the *content* of modernization, in a pattern similar to that of Germany, but the reverse of the British pattern. (Nakamura, 1983: 66–8). This has been called 'capitalism from the top down', (Nakamura, 1983: 104) and at its vanguard was a banking system, facilitating industrial development. New manufacturing and commercial enterprises opted for incorporation, with banks subscribing for shares and also lending money directly to the companies (there were 143 banks by 1882, Clark, 1979: 32). This established a pattern that has continued, more or less uninterrupted, to the present.

While the bankers were often former merchants (Nakamura, 1983: 105) the highly educated class of warrior-bureaucrats (former samurai of aristocratic origin) were key figures in industrialization, and formed the backbone of Japan's new managerial elite. It was this elite of new managers who, when faced with a volatile labour market, adopted the ideal of *familism* in their companies. The offering of lifetime employment, with wages based on seniority, was a pragmatic response to the problems of acquiring and keeping a skilled, stable and loyal workforce.

The Role of the State

The role of the state was a key factor in Japanese economic development in this early period. While the 'opening up' of Japan led to an interest in Western liberalism, the basic assumption of liberalism, that of the inherent value of the individual, was never embraced. To the classic liberal, the state represented an interference with the market, whereas the Japanese view has been that 'wealth was defined... not as a relationship between individual and market, but in terms of social productivity' (Najita, 1993: 24). Industrial policy was thus seen as the responsibility of the state.

The 'state' in these formative years was, in effect, the bureaucracy, established by the Meiji oligarchs, themselves 'warrior-bureaucrats'. The government was the Cabinet formed by the oligarchs themselves, who were officially 'advisors to the Emperor'. Wishing to cloak their rule with Western constitutional forms, they promulgated the Meiji Constitution in 1889 and, later, legal codes based on French and German models. While the Meiji Constitution provided for an elected assembly (based on very restricted suffrage), its role was advisory only. Movements for wider political participation gave rise to political parties which naturally pressed for representative government, and party government did feature in the late nineteenth and early twentieth centuries. But, except for some brief 'flowerings' of democracy, the Japanese state resisted democratic pressure until democratization was imposed by the Post-Second World War American Occupation. The state was looked on as the institutional embodiment of the nation, legitimated by ancient imperial links, not by the democratically expressed will of the people.

The *Zaibatsu*

Capitalism 'from the top down' was the basis of Meiji industrial policy. A feature of Japanese corporate structure which has its roots in the Meiji Era is the *zaibatsu*, or 'financial clique', so named because these conglomerates were built around banks. The Meiji government encouraged these concentrations by offering subsidies to selected entrepreneurs, who went on to form huge empires, such as Mitsui and Mitsubishi, consisting of a holding company with numerous subsidiaries engaged in a range of industries – and, in particular, the heavy industries. About a dozen conglomerates controlled 'about 80 per cent of the nation's industrial, commercial, and financial enterprises'

(Kawai, 1960: 148). Far from being feudalistic structures, as they are sometimes portrayed, the *zaibatsu* represented Japan's new capitalist dynamism, and became the powerhouses of industrialization and technological development. They flourished in the period of party governments, through their close ties with politicians and bureaucrats. But by the 1930s, democratic reforms went into reverse, with the ascendency of the ultra-nationalist and military forces which came to dominate the state. A totalitarian state was anathema to the interests of big business, and business leaders clashed with the country's new nationalist leadership (Rafferty, 1995: 70). While the Meiji era saw the emergence of Japan's first national industrial policy, Japan had been far from a statist society. On the contrary, factionalism amongst the country's leaders was endemic (Ramseyer and Rosenbluth, 1995). The Meiji oligarchs left no stable political institutions in place, relying on personal leadership, which gave way to fragmented authority structures, leaving the country vulnerable to military takeover, against which the vaguely worded Meiji Constitution provided no effective safeguards.

The legacy of the Occupation and the *Keiretsu*

Japan's defeat in the Second World War, which left some two-thirds of the country's industrial base destroyed, presented the American Occupation authorities (officially, SCAP, the Supreme Commander of Allied Powers) with an opportunity to re-mould the country along liberal democratic lines. A new democratic constitution was hurriedly introduced, incorporating individual rights and democratic sovereignty, with the legislature as the supreme law making power (the Emperor was reduced to a figurehead). The bureaucracy, significantly, was left intact, to facilitate administration of the country. The *zaibatsu*, which were felt to be 'the evil genius' behind the war machine (Kawai, 1960: 153) were to be dismantled, making way for economic democratization. There were two major laws introduced: an Anti-Monopoly Law, along the lines of American anti-trust legislation and a 'Deconcentration' Law, providing for the break-up of existing conglomerates and banning holding companies in future. SCAP did not wish to go in for widescale compulsory dissolution of companies, preferring 'voluntary' dissolution. The indomitable head of Mitsubishi, Koyata Iwasaki, held out against SCAP, asserting that Mitsubishi had done nothing wrong, but was pressurized into dissolution in the end (Rafferty, 1995: 73). In all, some 83 holding companies were broken up, Mitsui and Mitsubishi being broken up into 240 separate companies (Kawai, 1960: 148).

Within 10 years these groups, comprising Japan's corporate elite, had re-formed informally. The Occupation had failed to appreciate that merely breaking up the formal arrangements did not affect the informal ties, which remained intact. In the Japanese context, the associational ties had always been more significant than formal legal structures. The new groupings, or *keiretsu*, are loose groupings, characterized by cross-holding shares, typically grouped around a main bank. As with its predecessors, the modern *keiretsu*, however, is more accurately depicted 'not as a particular pattern among specific sets of firms but as an overall process in which arms'-length markets are replaced by intercorporate cooperation' (Gerlach, 1992: 82). These relationships, as Gerlach (1992: 94) has pointed out, form an 'underlying continuity', independent of formal structures. Now, over 50 years on, as part of a policy of liberalization, the legal ban on holding companies has been lifted, by revision to the Anti-Monopoly Law, effective from December 1997 (*Asahi Shimbun*, 9 December 1997). A number of provisos has been added, to prevent excessive concentration. The amended law, while increasing the range of formal legal options for corporate control, must be seen in the context of the enduring informal relationships which pervade Japanesse business culture.

MANAGEMENT: THE ETHOS OF SERVICE

The key players in determining how a company is run are its senior managers. In Japan they are almost inevitably long-standing servants of the company, and often descendants of the founder. The Chief Executive Officer in a Japanese company is the President, who takes ultimate responsibility for decisions, in the 'symbolic assumption of guilt' if something goes badly wrong (Clark, 1979: 125). Scandals involving unauthorized, and sometimes illegal, transactions, usually end in a spate of resignations at the top. The office of Chairman is separate, unlike the custom in America, and the Chairman is likely to be a figurehead, often a retired President. While the Japanese company seems to have an array of hierarchical ranks, decision making is usually seen as a collective process. The notion of consensus decision making is possibly over-emphasized in some writing about Japan, and may seem difficult to reconcile with the hierarchy typical of Japanese organizations. The harmony which the company maintains on the surface may conceal considerable turbulence underneath the surface, well away from the public gaze. The Japanese system has been called an 'egalitarian hierarchy' (Yoshimura and Anderson, 1997: 186). The lifetime employment system, coupled with age seniority, has contributed to a sense of community. With little risk of takeover in the Japanese system, and weak monitoring by boards of directors, management can become complacent and entrenched, in which case it usually requires a crisis to shake things up.

There are numerous companies, including large ones, that are still run by autocratic presidents, in many cases related to the founding family, nepotism and gerontocracy are not uncommon accusations. In Matsushita Electric, the consumer electricals giant, when Akio Tanii resigned as President, taking responsibility in the wake of a 50 billion yen scandal in 1993, an outsider, Yorishita Morishita was brought in and announced new management methods (Rafferty, 1995: 178). Three years later, Masayaki Matsushita, a grandson of the founder and son of the Chairman, Masaharu Matsushita, was appointed vice-president, and it is expected that he is destined to take over the presidency, supplanting the incumbent outsider president. The Chairman, now aged 80, had married the founder's daughter and took over the family name, a practice which is said to blend meritocracy with hereditary succession (*Asahi Shimbun*, 19 July 1997, *Financial Times*, 18 July 1997).

Executives in Western companies generally receive remuneration packages a great deal more generous than their Japanese counterparts. Directors' remuneration and terms – and accountability – have become high-profile issues in corporate governance. Stock options have been a favoured method of remuneration in America, where they are seen as an incentive towards improved corporate performance (although there are 're-pricing' and other devices to reduce the downside) (Monks and Minow, 1996: 240). Outright share ownership, as well as share options, can be incentives, offering the employee a financial stake in the company. Heretofore, companies in Japan have been able to offer shares, but not share options. The Commercial Code has now been amended to allow for stock options and for redemption of shares (*Yomiuri Shimbun*, 19 May 1997). Further to its comments on the new flexibility in remuneration, the newspaper observes that shareholders' meetings and boards of directors are important areas of corporate governance which are due for reform.

THE MONITORING ROLE OF *KEIRETSU*

Keiretsu ties have played a key role in Japanese corporate governance, and are unique to the Japanese system. The *keiretsu* group is made up of a web of interlocking shareholding, which involves companies holding shares in each other. The most important of these interlocks has traditionally been with the main bank, although companies borrow from other banks in addition. The interlocking of shareholding is not confined to *keiretsu* ties, and for some years these ties have been loosening, as companies see themselves free to form other advantageous links, often between supplier and customer. The practice of cross-holding of shares is seen as important to establish an enduring relationship in what the Japanese call 'stable shareholding arrangements' (Sheard, 1994: 311; Jones and Tsuru, 1997). The shareholding company effectively becomes an 'insider', with a long-term commitment, and supportive of the incumbent management. Such a shareholder is therefore a protection against the hostile takeover. By contrast, in the Anglo–American system, which is much more market oriented, the takeover is a tool against inefficient management. Such a tool, however, is a fairly blunt instrument: it can remove bad management only after the damage has been done, it cannot prevent managerial disasters. The market is, however, an external monitor, and as such is arguably more effective than internal monitoring, which is based ultimately on trust and self-discipline. This divergence of outlook represents one of the most profound differences between the Japanese and Anglo–American models of corporate governance.

In the typical Japanese listed company about 70 per cent of its shares are held by other companies, mainly in small parcels, and these will be companies with which there are transactional relations (Sheard, 1994: 312). Most importantly, financial institutions inevitably feature in the top shareholder positions, although a bank is limited in law to a 5 per cent holding. While a company may have numerous dispersed individual shareholders (a listed company has on average 12 910 shareholders), a coalition of the largest 20 or so shareholders could theoretically control the firm, constituting a 'latent corporate control coalition' (Sheard, 1994: 318).

This cross-ownership is linked to relational contracting, based on loose, long-term, firm-specific investments, as in the case of a supplier and assembler in the motor industry. (Gilson and Roe, 1993: 884). This model of contracting relies above all on the parties' good intentions, in an 'open-ended relational contract' (Gilson and Roe, 1993: 885), based on mutual trust, rather than on detailed, legally enforceable written agreements, as in the classical contracting model. As has been pointed out, while Japan adopted a Western-style legal system, the Japanese have not been amenable to reliance on legal remedies, even when they exist, or to the 'reducing' of relationships to a bundle of legal rights and obligations. Partly, this has been deliberately fostered by governments and, arguably, the situation is gradually changing, as individuals are turning more to pursuing legal causes of action through the courts, but this has been, and still is, very much the exception (Upham, 1987).

Of course, there is no guarantee of future good faith in relational contracting, and therefore no barrier to opportunism. However, the cross-holding of shares reduces the risk of opportunism, which would occur in classical arm's-length contracting. In the Japanese model control of a portion of equity in this way conveys governance rights, and also reduces opportunism. The owner of equity, in other words, has the incentive to monitor. 'Multiple relationships – stockholder and creditor, stockholder and supplier – increase the incentives to intervene' (Gilson and Roe, 1993: 888). But, of course, this is internal monitoring, and the cynic might argue that internal monitoring equals weak monitoring. What is to stop parties reaching for a cosy arrangement based on, 'I won't monitor you if you won't monitor me.'? What, if anything, is there to prevent 'co-operative shirking'? (Gilson and Roe, 1993: 891). Gilson and Roe conclude that intense product market competition is the answer. Each party is dependent on the other, and both parties suffer if the relationship does not succeed.

This 'mutual monitoring' (Kester, 1997: 233) relies heavily on communication and information-sharing between the organizations. Interaction between individual managers helps to establish the trust which is vital in a 'web of enduring personal relationships' (Kester, 1997: 232). Transfers of management are common, possibly involving a seat on the board of directors. While they are looked on as 'outside' directors, these equity-holding stakeholders with multiple relational ties are in a position to intervene directly in the management of the company if the need arises. In an example cited by Kester, Nissan Motor's long-term collaboration with Fuji Heavy Industries led to a '*de facto* takeover' by Nissan, from a position of holding only 4 per cent of Fuji's stock, plus representation on Fuji's board. This was achieved without financial re-structuring or any shares changing hands amongst Fuji's major shareholders (Kester, 1997: 235). By contrast, the American T. Boone Pickens acquired a 20 per cent holding in Koito Manufacturing, a major supplier to Toyota, which had a smaller holding in Koito and also seats on its board. Such was the Toyota influence that the American intruder could not obtain a seat on the board, despite being the company's largest shareholder, and eventually sold his shares (Rafferty, 1995: 78).

THE MONITORING ROLE OF THE MAIN BANK

The most important interlock has traditionally been the company's 'main bank', and it is significant, too, that the company's shareholding in the bank commonly exceeds the bank's holding in the company (Sheard, 1996: 314). Moreover, the company relies on a main securities company to oversee trading in its stock, to provide a 'watchdog' role for it in the market (Sheard, 1996: 321), and to warn of any risks of takeover.

The board is also likely to have representation from the company's main bank, both as lender and shareholder, although there is now much less reliance on banks and on debt financing. This is largely because of the perilous financial state of banks generally in Japan, which have not recovered from accumulated bad-debt problems after the collapse of the 'bubble economy' at the end of the 1980s. Traditionally a bank's monitoring has been carried out on behalf of other bank lenders and shareholders (Jones and Tsuru, 1997), usually via representation on the board. The effectiveness of the bank as monitor, it has been argued by Gilson and Roe, is not to improve 'normal' corporate governance, but to react in cases of crisis, coming up with managerial and financial re-structuring, if necessary (Gilson and Roe, 1993: 880). They go on to say that, 'the Japanese main bank has served thus far primarily as a crisis manager, allocator of capital, and gatekeeper to bankruptcy' (Gilson and Roe, 1993: 881). By displacing inefficient management of poor-performing companies by direct intervention, the main bank substituted for the market mechanism in the Anglo–American system, but not totally. The system allowed managers relative freedom from outside pressure, except in crisis situations. Roe and Gilson conclude that, 'Avoiding bank intervention gives both management and employees an incentive for team performance' (1993: 881). In the past, it has not been uncommon for a bank to rescue a client company in financial distress (Hoshi, Kashyapand Scharf Stern, 1990; Shibakawa, 1994). But the banks can no longer afford to extend financial lifelines. As an example, when Yamaichi Securities, one of the four major securities firms, failed in November 1997, it had been expected that Fuji Bank would step in to prop it up, but the bank declined.

THE JAPANESE BOARD OF DIRECTORS

The banks and other key corporate shareholders have traditionally left management a great deal of latitude in running the company. In the

Japanese Commercial Code, as in most jurisdictions' company law, the shareholders as owners elect the board of directors to represent their interests, and the management is accountable to the board. The shareholders' only other 'voice' is the general meeting. Although the outward forms are similar to Western systems generally, Japanese boards and managements are distinctly different in composition and processes.

The board of a large Japanese company could well have 30 or more members, which is more than double the size of the average American board (Monks and Minow, 1996: 169). Its members are mainly long-time employees of the company, who have risen through the ranks to managerial level. The directors owe a duty of good faith to the company, (Art. 254, Commercial Code, cited in Oda, 1992: 287), as well as a duty of care and skill, to act as a 'good manager' (Art. 644, Civil Code, quoted in Oda, 1992: 287). Two or more directors are appointed as 'representative' directors, indicating their authority to commit the firm legally. These directors are, however, obliged to seek board approval for their transactions. Other directors who habitually leave management to the representative directors can be legally liable for any mismanagement of the business (Judgment of the Supreme Court, 22 May 1973, cited in Oda, 1992: 288).

While not recognized in law, there are in practice several ranks of directors, representing particular departments and divisions (Clark, 1979: 100). Their main interests are naturally with the particular group of employees they represent, and with whom they have worked for many years – a reflection of Japan's lifetime employment system, although the system itself is now weakening. It would be fair to say that they are not well placed to take a critical overview of the company, nor would they be naturally inclined to take a critical view of senior management, to whom they habitually defer. Even though there is no statutory duty towards employees in Japanese company law (Clark, 1979: 103), the interests of employees predominate over the interests of smaller shareholders, who are not represented. The interests of the many small, dispersed shareholders are more likely to be served by the use of independent 'non-executive' directors, a practice which has become the norm in America. In Japan, such directors are a rarity.

As has been mentioned, there might be two or three outside directors, such as a retired bank manager from the company's main bank, or directors from associated companies. Also likely to feature are the 'amakudari', retired civil servants 'descended from heaven', from ministries with which the company has dealings. While these are termed 'outside' directors, they are not independent, if we take that term to refer to directors who have no ties with the company except their seat on the board (Monks and Minow, 1996: 193). In a survey of 40 major Japanese companies reported in August 1997, only 17 firms had outside directors, and most of these were not independent but from members of the *keiretsu*. The accompanying interviews showed widespread sceptism of outsiders, despite their acknowledged value in ensuring transparency of management in other countries. Typical is a quote from the Bank of Tokyo–Mitsubishi: 'It is doubtful whether outsiders would be able to make timely and appropriate judgments' (*Yomiuri Shimbun*, 8 August 1997).

The case of Sony Corporation is an interesting example. Until 1998, it had a board of 38 members, whose meetings had become empty, rubber-stamping exercises. At a stroke, it reduced its board from 38 to 10 members, allowing the demoted directors to retain their pay and executive privileges. The firm at present has three non-employee directors, in a move that it feels is a step closer to the 'global standard of management'. Still, their role is looked on as one of 'friendly adviser rather than "monitors" representing Sony shareholders' (*Asahi Shimbun*, 21 July 1997).

THE STATUTORY AUDITORS

In the survey reported in *Yomuiri Shimbun* cited above, a number of the company officers interviewed said that the statutory auditors 'serve the purpose of keeping the management in check' (*Yomiuri Shimbun*, 8 August 1997). This certainly is the intention of the legislation, but the reality is that the auditor, like the directors, is more than likely to be supportive of management and disinclined to 'rock the boat'. Auditors are often ex-employees or ex-directors who, after a gap of five years, are deemed to be 'independent'. Auditing requirements vary with the size of company: the larger the company, the more onerous the requirements. The Commercial Code was strengthened in 1974 and 1981 to give powers to the auditors to look into the legality of directors' activities. They are required to report any directors' activity which is against the law or in breach of the company's own articles, and they may themselves call a board meeting if necessary (Oda, 1992: 292–3). These powers of auditors go beyond the financial affairs of the company, and place on them wider duties in respect of positive monitoring of directors. The difficulty is that, despite the intention to establish auditors as independent, they are still likely to be on the side of management.

THE INDIVIDUAL SHAREHOLDER

What attracts the individual investor to a Japanese company? Dividend income is likely to be taken, even though the company is cash-rich. Watching the shares grow in value may be satisfying, but the trend in stock prices in Japan was downward throughout the 1990s. The shareholder has little voice in the company's affairs. There is the right to speak at the annual general meeting, an annual 'set-piece' occasion which the company is required by law to hold. In theory, there should be full disclosure of information to shareholders, who are free to use their votes accordingly at the meetings, the reality is that managers are not forthcoming with company information, and do not welcome shareholder participation.

Company managements fear the long general meeting, in which they are made to answer for their activities. So compelling is the urge to keep the general meeting short and free from embarrassment that companies pay *sokaiya*, corporate racketeers, to go along and 'deter' awkward questions. *Sokaiya* themselves usually use as a bargaining counter their 'inside' knowledge of the company which, unless suitably rewarded, they will divulge. Of annual general meetings in 1997, 93 per cent of listed companies (1927 firms) held their meetings on the same day (a device to get round possible *sokaiya* disruption); and the average duration was 29 minutes (*Yomiuri Shimbun*, 29 October 1997).

Payments to *sokaiya* are illegal, in contravention of the Commercial Code, but despite efforts to wipe them out they have stubbornly persisted. In 1997, one racketeer, Ryuichi Koike made deals with the four big securities firms – Nomura, Yamaichi, Daiwa and Nikko – reaping a total of 700 million Yen in illegal payments. He also netted 11.7 billion Yen in illegal loans from Dai-ichi-Kangyo Bank. As a result 36 executives of the five firms were arrested, and in all, 77 senior company officials resigned, 'to take responsibility' (*Yomiuri Shimbun*, 25 December 1997). Numerous other companies have become embroiled in illegal dealings with *sokaiya*, which have come to light: Mitsubishi, Hitachi, and Toshiba, to name some of the more spectacular. Many, including Mitsubishi, have claimed that payoffs were made by employees independently, and that senior managers were unaware. Given the huge sums involved, however, this is highly unlikely (*Yomiuri Shimbun*, 29 October 1997). While increasing penalties is a logical way to attempt to stamp out such corruption, the causes are deeply rooted in Japan's corporate culture. Traditionally, managers have relied on personal links with bureaucrats, politicians and other influential figures. Gifts and favours, while useful to keep relations on a favourable footing, mean that just about every company will have 'something to hide', which the *sokaiya* have become adept at exploiting.

In the cases of illegal payoffs, a number of normally passive shareholders are exercising rights under recent revisions to the law. While they are relatively few in number, they have created a disproportionate stir in Japan's corporate boardrooms. The Commercial Code was revised in 1993 to allow the holder of 1000 shares to sue the company for damages. 1996 saw 188 such lawsuits (*Asahi Shimbun*, 15 October 1997); other high-profile cases involved Dai-ichi-Kangyo Bank, Nomura Securities and Yamaichi Securities; there are also suits against directors alleged to be responsible. The claim against DKB alone is for 7.5 billion yen. Apart from the money involved, the unfavourable publicity is damaging for Japan's corporate community generally. Japan's ruling Liberal Democratic Party (LDP) and the country's Federation of Economic Organizations (*Keidanren*) favour restrictions to shareholders' legal actions (*Asahi Shimbun*, 6 October 1997). In particular, they favour the 'internalizing' of complaints by a procedure for channeling them to auditors, thus avoiding the risk of shareholder litigation. For the shareholder – to whom, after all, managements are meant to be responsible – the curtailment of the right of litigation would be a retrograde step, especially as both the auditors and the shareholders' meetings have proved to be ineffective monitors.

MONITORING THE MONITORS

Japan's spectacular economic growth in the post-war period was guided by an industrial policy, orchestrated by the bureaucracy. In his book, *MITI and the Japanese Miracle* (1982), Chalmers Johnson described the role of MITI (Ministry of International Trade and Industry), as well as that of the Ministry of Finance, from 1925 to 1975. His argument is that the Japanese 'miracle' was based on the 'capitalist developmental state', which meant the bureaucracy above all. This position is now seen as extreme, as more recent research suggests interactive relationships among bureaucrats, politicians and industrialists, rather than domination by the bureaucracy (Argy and Stein, 1997; Ramseyer and Rosenbluth, 1995). This latter view, I would suggest, is more in keeping with the country's historical precedents. MITI and the Ministry of Finance, often bitter rivals over policy, have exerted controls in a number of ways. 'Administrative guidance' – which amounts to administrative legislation – has been one method of regulating company structures, products and markets. But, above all, the control of credit through the Ministry of Finance has been an effective tool to control corporate activities.

While state regulation has been a feature of economic life in Japan, regulatory authority is in fact fragmented (Sherman and Babcock, 1997: 268). The Ministry of Finance is in charge of monitoring of corporate compliance with securities law through its divisions, such as the Securities and Exchange Surveillance Committee. Banks and brokerages are subject to inspection by the Ministry of Finance which, in theory, should perform an external monitoring function. It is well known, however, that 'cosy' relationships, as they are called in the press, exist between ministry officials, politicians and companies, effectively nullifying the formal inspection procedures. It is not surprising that the corruption scandals connected with banks and brokerages, often involving discretionary dealing for 'preferred' clients (which is illegal), go unchecked in official inspections. The Bank of Japan, nominally under the Ministry of Finance, has been looked on as a final guarantor of weak financial institutions, in a 'convoy' system. This protective system is now falling apart: it is now accepted by the government that fundamental reform of the banking system, and its monitoring, must be undertaken to restore confidence in the sector, both at home and abroad. Failures of weak, uncompetitive institutions are inevitable, as evidenced by the failure of a regional commercial bank, as well as the failure of a major securities firm, Yamaichi Securities. In the latter case, much of the business was picked up by the American firm, Merrill Lynch, in what is perhaps a sign of the times. Of course, more astute monitoring might have pointed out the weaknesses before it was too late. The *Washington Post* commented, in an editorial entitled, 'Goodbye Japan, Inc.', 'The 'cooperative' spirit too often gave way to coziness, cronyism and corruption. Spreading the pain became synonymous for covering up bad business decisions and protecting failure' (*Washington Post*, 25 November 1997).

Liberalization of markets has been taking place in Japan for some years, largely as a result of US pressure. Financial deregulation has been under way since 1997, also aimed at opening up markets, in the hope that more competition and greater transparency will lead to improved performance. But opening up markets inevitably carries risks – and fears. Weakened banks have necessarily imposed a credit squeeze which has led, in turn, to increased numbers of bankruptcies and rising unemployment. Major companies find their 'no-redundancy' policies stretched to breaking point, and are no longer able to pay the large bonuses and generous perks that workforces have become accustomed to, thus breaking implicit contracts. Business relationships, both intra-firm and inter-firm, are therefore under strain. The government is expected to devise plans for economic recovery and reform of the banking system while, at the same time, causing minimal damage to the LDP's traditional friends in business and banking.

CONCLUSION

Capitalism 'from the top down' has been the well established pattern in Japan dating, as has been shown, from the country's earliest period of industrialization. But the theme has not been one of state capitalism: it has rather been one of private enterprise guided by industrial policy. This pattern reflects a view of the company as the creator of social wealth, which contrasts markedly with the individualist assumptions underlying Western capitalist systems. In the community model of the company, in which implicit contracting prevails, corporate governance relies mainly on internal and informal monitoring of management. But, as I have described, the result has been to pay little heed to investor value, and it is in this respect that Japanese companies are now seen as weak. The global investor looking for assurances of sound corporate governance will find few internal or external monitoring mechanisms designed to keep managements on their toes. The outward forms are there in most cases, but the monitoring functions of, for example, boards and shareholder meetings are generally mere formalities. In the past, the more effective monitoring has been the function of the main bank, but this role is now fading fast, and companies are now having to adjust to the realities of market forces. The challenge will be to adjust to global changes while maintaining the traditional values which have been the source of the nation's economic strength.

References

Abegglen, J.C. and Stalk, Jr, G. (1985) *Kaisha, the Japanese Corporation*, New York, Basic Books.

Argy, V. and Stein, L. (1997) *The Japanese Economy*, London, Macmillan.

Clark, R. (1979) *The Japanese Company*, London, Yale University Press.

Dore, R. (1987) *Taking Japan Seriously*, London, The Athlone Press.

Gerlach, M.L. (1992) 'Twilight of the *Keiretsu*?', *Journal of Japanese Studies*, 18(1), 79–118.

Gilson, R.J. and Roe, M.J. (1993) 'Understanding the Japanese *Keiretsu*: Overlaps Between Corporate Governance and Industrial Organization', *Yale Law Journal*, 102, 871–906.

Hoshi, T., Kashyap, A. and Scharfstein, D. (1990) 'The Role of Banks in Reducing the Costs of Financial Distress in Japan', *Journal of Financial Economics*, 27, 67–88.

Johnson, C. (1982) *MITI and the Japanese Miracle*, Stanford, CA, Stanford University Press.

Jones, R.S. and Tsuru, K. (1997) 'Japan Corporate Goverance: A System in Evolution', *OECD Observer*, 204 (February–March), 40–1.

Kawai, K. (1960) *Japan's American Interlude*, Chicago, University of Chicago Press.

Kester, W.C. (1997) 'Governance, Contracting, and Investment Horizons: A Look at Japan and Germany', in D. Chew (ed.), *Studies in International Corporate Finance and Governance Systems*, New York, Oxford University Press, 227–42.

Mayer, C. (1997) 'Corporate Governance, Competition, and Performance', *Journal of Law and Society*, (1), March, 152–76.

Miller, C. (1997) 'Is the American Corporate Governance System Fatally Flawed?', in D. Chew (ed.), *Studies in International Corporate Finance and Governance Systems*, New York, Oxford University Press, 38–45.

Monks, R.A.G. and Minow, N. (1996) *Watching the Watchers: Corporate Governance in the 21st Century*, Cambridge, MA, Blackwell.

Najita, T. (1993) 'Japan's Industrial Revolution in Perspective', in M. Miyoshi and H.D. Harootinian (eds), *Japan in the World*, Durham, NC, Duke University Press.

Nakamura, T. (1983) *Economic Growth in Prewar Japan*, trans R.A. Feldman, New Haven, Yale University Press.

Nakane, C. (1970) *Japanese Society*, Berkeley, CA, University of California Press.

Oda, H. (1992) *Japanese Law*, London, Butterworths.

Pauly, L.W. and Reich, S. (1997) 'National Structures and Multinational Corporate Behavior: Enduring Differences in the Age of Globalization', *International Organization*, 51(1) (Winter), 1–30.

Rafferty, K. (1995) *Inside Japan's Powerhouses*, London, Weidenfeld & Nicolson.

Ramseyer, M. and Rosenbluth, F. (1995) *The Politics of Oligarchy*, Cambridge, Cambridge University Press.

Roe, M.J. (1993) 'Some Differences in Corporate Structure in Germany, Japan, and the United States', *Yale Law Journal* 102, 1928–2003.

Sheard, P. (1994) 'Interlocking Shareholdings and Corporate Governance', in M. Aoki and R. Dore (eds), *The Japanese Firm*, Oxford, Oxford University Press, 310–49.

Sherman, H.D. and Babcock, B.A. (1997) 'Redressing Structural Imbalances in Japanese Corporate Governance', in D. Chew (ed.), *Studies in International Corporate Finance and Corporate Governance Systems*, Oxford, Oxford University Press, 267–77.

Shibakawa, R. (1994) 'Corporate Governance, Cost of Capital and Financial Distress', *Hitotsubashi Journal of Commerce and Management*, 29, 1–14.

Upham, F. (1987) *Law and Social Change in Postwar Japan*, Cambridge, MA, Harvard University Press.

Yoshimura, N. and Anderson, P. (1997) *Inside the Kaisha: Demystifying Japanese Business Behavior*, Boston, MA, Harvard Business School Press.

Newspapers

Asahi Shimbun
Financial Times
Washington Post
Yomiuri Shimbun

Part 2
Diversity

7 Theories of Japanese Multinational Investment: Critical Comments from the UK Perspective*

Alexander Roy

INTRODUCTION

Since the early 1980s, foreign direct investment (FDI) by transnational corporations (TNCs) has grown at a much faster rate than either world output or global trade. As a result, TNCs have come to be seen by many as the central drivers of 'globalization' (Dunning, 1996). Moreover, a number of European governments have come to regard the attraction of inward investment as a strategy for securing employment and increasing international economic competitiveness. Investment from Japan has been perceived as particularly beneficial, with the operations of Japanese TNCs believed to epitomize 'best practice', generating positive spillover benefits for host economies. This has been a dominant view in the UK, where consecutive governments have been keen to attract investment from all countries, and, as Table 7.1 shows, have managed to secure the largest share of Japanese FDI in the European Union.

Table 7.1   Japanese FDI stocks in the European Union, up to 1995 (US$ million)[a]

European Union total (US$ million) 92 203				
Of which (per cent)				
UK	Netherlands	Belgium/Luxembourg	Germany	France
40.0	22.8	10.6	9.4	8.3
Spain	Ireland	Italy	Austria	Portugal
3.3	2.2	2.2	0.6	0.6

Note: [a] Denmark, Finland and Sweden are excluded because their FDI stock is less than US$100 million.
Source: UNCTAD (1996), Table II.2.

However, there are weaknesses in the current theoretical and empirical treatment of Japanese investment within the advanced economies that undermine some of the assumptions behind current policies. This chapter is a conceptual treatment of these issues, which underpins an ongoing empirical research project regarding Japanese financial sector FDI in the UK. The first section outlines the general situation regarding Japanese FDI into the UK. The second section critiques extant theories of FDI as they relate to Japanese transnationals. The third section focuses upon the service sector, highlighting the importance of Japanese financial services to the UK economy. In light of this, the literature on transnational banking is reviewed as it relates to the case of Japan. The final section draws some preliminary conclusions and discusses some important issues for future research.

JAPANESE FDI AND THE UK ECONOMY

FDI has increased twentyfold since the 1960s, much faster than either world trade or output, such that the global stock of FDI totalled US$2730 billion by 1995 (UN, 1996). The UK has been central in this process, with absolute levels of both inward and outward FDI second only in the world to the USA. By the end of 1995, the stock of inward investment received by the UK totalled £159 million, and the UK had invested over £165 million abroad (CSO data, UN, 1996). The three primary investors into the UK have been the USA, Japan and Germany (Cm 2867, 1995). As Table 7.1 showed, the UK is the most popular location for Japanese investment in the European Union. In absolute terms, however, the USA has been by far the dominant investor, accounting for nearly a third of all FDI. Japan, by contrast, provides a far smaller share of investment, and even this proportion had declined by the first half of the 1990s to only 2.9 per cent of the direct inflows (FM&I, 1996).

The composition of inward investment into the UK has been dominated by the non-manufacturing sector, with manufacturing accounting for only 30 per cent of FDI (FM&I, 1996). Contrary to popular perception, Japanese investment in the UK, as Table 7.2 shows, has also concentrated in the service sector, especially finance, commerce and real estate.

It is commonly argued that the simple reason why the UK has attracted the most Japanese investment in Europe has been the English language, together with a legal and cultural affinity with Japan

Table 7.2   Sectoral distribution of Japanese FDI in the UK, 1981–94

Sector	Cumulative FDI flows (per cent)
Total (US$ million)	19 170
Primary sector	1.1
Mining	1.1
Manufacturing sector	23.7
Foodstuffs	0.6
Textiles	1.3
Chemicals	0.7
Iron and steel/non-ferrous metals	0.4
Machinery	1.8
Electronic industry	10.1
Transport equipment	7.3
Other	1.6
Service sector	75.3
Construction	0.8
Commerce	12.2
Finance and insurance	31.7
Transportation	0.3
Real estate	20.6
Other	9.7

Source: UNCTAD (1996).

(Auerbach, 1989; Julius, 1990). Other factors found to be important are, the greater deregulation of the UK financial services market, the freedom from exchange controls for TNCs and the welcoming attitude of the UK government since 1979, when compared to other EU countries (Julius, 1990; Strange, 1993).

In terms of the initial decision to locate within the Union, though, access to the Single European Market (SEM) has been a key factor. During the late 1980s and early 1990s, the appreciation of the yen and trade frictions with Europe – spurring the fear of a 'Fortress Europe' post-1992 – were also important incentives for European investment (Cleeve, 1997; Dunning, 1985; Ford and Strange, 1998; PACEC, 1995). Low wage costs are rarely cited by Japanese firms as a reason for location within the European Union, and indeed the Union has over-taken the lower-wage economies of South East Asia as the second largest recipient of Japanese FDI, behind the relatively high-wage US economy (though this trend has reversed during the 1990s, MoF in

MITI, 1998). Nonetheless, Japanese *manufacturing* investment within the Union has been drawn to relatively low-wage areas, such as the government 'assisted regions' in the UK (Ford and Strange, 1998; Morris, Munday and Wilkinson, 1993). The final notable feature of Japanese FDI into Europe has been a preference for greenfield investment and 100 per cent ownership, at nearly two-thirds of FDI, compared to joint ventures and mergers and acquisitions (JETRO, 1997a).

THEORIES OF FDI AND THE JAPANESE FIRM

The traditional explanation for international production was that differential global interest rates encouraged capital to undertake 'portfolio' investment. As a result, capital scarcity in the less developed countries returned higher interest rates than the capital-abundant advanced nations, leading to investment flowing from the developed to the developing world (often following colonial lines). After the Second World War, however, this international division of labour broke down and FDI flows rapidly became concentrated within the developed world and in certain industrial sectors (Dicken, 1998). Hymer (1976: 27–8) in the late 1950s, was the first to critique traditional macroeconomic accounts, arguing that the 'theory of international operations is part of the theory of the firm'. As a result of his work (see Yamin, 1991), two competing microeconomic theories of the transnational firm have developed – the orthodox, transaction costs approach, which emphasizes an efficiency dynamic, and the radical alternative, which sees market power and distributional considerations as central.

Transaction Costs Theory and Japanese TNCs

Although inspired by Hymer, the first principles of transaction costs (or 'internalization') theory are derived from the seminal work of Coase (1937). Coase argued that the existence of a firm meant that internal administrative co-ordination must offer distinct advantages over the use of the external price mechanism. Otherwise the situation would represent a Pareto-inefficiency and the firm would be competed out of existence. In Williamson's (1975) terms, using the market incurs 'transaction costs' that may potentially be reduced by co-ordinating activities within firms. Internalization theorists argue that this analysis implies that it then becomes possible to develop firm-specific competitive advantages over and above other firms.

Operating in international markets, as Hymer originally observed, involves even higher transaction costs than in domestic markets, because of differences in business environment, culture, laws, regulations, and so on. This gives domestic firms an intrinsic advantage over foreign firms. As such, firms in possession of competitive advantages would logically prefer to license or franchise these advantages to foreign companies if they wished to exploit them overseas, in order to avoid their intrinsic disadvantage. But the 'market' for competitive advantages is argued to be particularly imperfect, especially in the cases of intangible assets and technology. 'Arm's-length' transactions (such as licensing and franchising) diminish control over proprietary assets, and may allow the licence to 'opportunistically' appropriate an undue share of the returns to the asset. Logically, these transaction costs are compounded when arm's-length markets are international, for the same reasons as for other markets. Therefore, despite the higher transaction costs of international operations, firms may still find it relatively more profitable to directly invest in overseas operations, effectively 'internalizing' the external international market (for example, Buckley and Casson, 1976; Hennart, 1991).[1]

The competitive advantage of Japanese firms is argued to be their ability to produce higher-quality goods at a lower price than their Western rivals. This is believed to be underpinned by innovative internal organization, especially production methods and human resource management (HRM). 'Lean production' methods are believed to increase flexibility and efficiency, reduce inventories and improve product quality in comparison to traditional mass-production techniques. The Japanese employment system of seniority-based lifetime employment internalizes the external labour market, while enterprise unions provide a company-specific collective 'voice' for workers. Despite its apparent contradiction of orthodox Western notions of efficiency, which are based upon cost minimization and external flexibility, the Japanese system is argued to have a strong microeconomic rationale. The incidence of labour 'exit' almost disappears, significantly reducing the recruitment and training costs resulting from labour turnover. The incentives for opportunistic behaviour are similarly diminished, resulting in information-sharing, greater internal flexibility – and, as a result, higher productivity (Freeman, 1984; Womack, Jones and Roos, 1990).

From the perspective of internalization theory, the competitive advantage of Japanese goods does not, in itself, provide a rationale for FDI, as exporting should – once relative transport costs have been taken into account – be just as profitable. Recent decades, however, have seen the market for Japanese imports rendered highly 'imperfect' by the imposition – or the threat – of tariff and non-tariff barriers (NTBs) in the European Union and the USA (see Auerbach, 1989). More recently, an increasing need to adapt products to more sophisticated consumer markets is argued to enforce a strategy of 'global localization' by TNCs (for example, Oliver, Morris and Wilkinson, 1992). Thus it is argued that it has been necessary for Japanese companies to invest in Europe in order to gain access to, and then subsequently to expand sales within, the SEM. Moreover, the organizational advantages believed to underpin Japanese production are intangible assets, and therefore not easily amenable to being licensed overseas, implying the need for FDI.

In this vein, internalization theory casts Japanese TNCs as promoters of global efficiency and welfare, by replacing 'natural' market imperfections with more efficient internal coordination (Hennart, 1991). Consumers benefit because of the provision of better and cheaper products, while productivity in host countries is increased through the use of more efficient techniques. This in turn acts as both a demonstration of best practice and a competitive spur to incumbent local companies, further boosting economic performance.

Weaknesses

This perspective, however, has important conceptual and empirical weaknesses. Research has found that many of the widely held perceptions regarding Japanese companies and Japan's economy do not stand up to close scrutiny. First, though the 'three-treasures' model of HRM (lifetime employment, seniority-based wages and promotion and enterprise unionism) applies to both blue-collar and white-collar workers, this is only within large firms in certain sectors, while women are effectively excluded. As a result, only around 20 per cent of the total workforce actually experience so-called 'Japanese' employment relations, casting doubt upon the overriding efficiency imperative of the system (Moore, 1987). Some Japanese scholars (for example, Koike, 1984) have argued that this labour market 'dualism' is economically rational, as large Japanese firms provide regular employment and seniority wages to those workers who have acquired a wide range of firm-specific skills, whilst denying them to those that have not. However, the work of Jacoby (1979) suggests that this simple efficiency rationale is unable to explain the historical development of internal labour markets that was observed in Japan. Jacoby notes that internal labour markets were introduced only when profitability was threatened by the backward-sloping labour supply curve (the substitution of leisure for work at higher wage levels) of the Japanese craft guilds (the *oyakata*). There was, in fact, a greater microeconomic rationale for applying the system to semiskilled (non-*oyakata*) workers, but this did not occur until after the Second World War – alongside the introduction of enterprise unionism – to counter the rise of powerful, and often radical, independent unions (also Moore, 1987). Hence, despite its post hoc efficiency rationalization, the protection of profitability in the face of shifting power relations was the prime dynamic in the development of the Japanese employment system.[2]

Similarly with 'Japanese' production methods, research has found that their diffusion has been highly uneven, with only a few manufacturers (such as Toyota) serving as corporate exemplars. Moreover, critics have argued that 'Toyotaism' is primarily a method of work intensification that extends, rather than replaces, the logics of Western scientific management (Dohse, Jürgens and Malsch, 1985), while requiring more standardized product runs than supposedly inflexible Fordist mass production (see Coffey, 1995a, 1995b). Furthermore, the idea that 'Fordism' should be taken as a benchmark is in itself problematic, as the concept overgeneralizes and idealizes the similarly complex and contradictory reality of production modes in the West (even within the Ford company itself, see Elger and Smith, 1994).

The corollary is that most companies in Japan operate neither 'Japanese' production nor HRM systems. Moore (1987) claims that employee relations within Japan's small and medium-sized enterprises (SMEs) – which account for approximately 75 per cent of employment and encompass the greater part of the service sector (Whittaker, 1990) – are not essentially different from those found in other industrialized countries: no long-term employment guarantees, performance-based market wages rather than seniority pay and only limited, and weak, union coverage. Further, much of the employment in services and SMEs has been 'feminized', owing to the exclusion of women from the 'regular' workforce (that is, those experiencing 'Japanese' employment), allowing management to pay lower wages for equivalent work.

Given that over two-thirds of FDI from Japanese companies is within the service sector, as Table 7.3 shows, and that there is a greater predominance of transnational SMEs from Japan than among Western TNCs (Dicken, 1998), it is not clear how far the expansion of Japanese FDI can be explained by the internalization of organizational advantages.

Table 7.3   Sectoral distribution of Japanese outward FDI, 1981–95

Per cent of cumulative flows	Primary (per cent)	Manufacturing (per cent)	Services (per cent)
UK (1981–94)	1.1	23.7	75.3
Europe (to 1994)	2.6	23.2	74.2
World (to 1995)	4.8	28.7	64.9

Sources: MoF in AJEI (1994); UNCTAD (1996).

Although the large service sector companies, such as the general trading companies (*sogo shosha*), banks and securities houses – that have characterized much of Japan's internationalization – *do* operate 'Japanese' employment practices, these have not been transferred overseas. They are coming under increasing pressure for change within Japan itself (author's research amongst the financial sector in the UK; Scher, 1997).

Japanese 'Transnational Monopoly Capitalism'

Radical economists have utilized a very different conception of the firm on which to base their theories of TNCs. They criticize the conceptual foundations of Coasian transaction cost economics, by reference to Marglin's (1976) work on the transition – during the UK Industrial Revolution – from the 'putting-out' system towards hierarchically organized factories. Marglin argues that though the 'internalization' of production in factories increased output for a given level of costs, the gains were secured by increasing inputs – especially labour – and thus the net effect upon *productive* efficiency (the ratio of inputs to outputs) was indeterminate. Moreover, since workers at the time exhibited a backward-sloping labour supply curve, the resultant increase in working time reduced workers' utility, even if incomes rose. Therefore, Marglin contends, though factory production was *profitable* for capitalists, this does not necessarily mean that it was also efficient, either in technical or Pareto terms. Since the logic of Pareto-optimality means that people will not freely choose to be made worse off, this suggests that the world is not characterized by 'voluntary exchange'. Given that Coase's analysis is built from just such a Pareto-framework, radicals dismiss the efficiency dynamic that drives the internalization argument.

As such, any conjecture that the expansion of transnationals *logically* represents a Pareto-gain can no longer be sustained. Radicals argue that TNCs are powerful economic entities that, in a non-voluntary exchange world, are in the position to pursue their strategic interests regardless of the interests of less powerful actors. Given that the central dynamic of the TNC is the pursuit of global profits, rather than efficiency *per se*, this means that the net impact of FDI may be neither Pareto-optimal nor technically efficient (for example, Sugden, 1991). Tomlinson (1998) extends this argument specifically to the actions of Japanese TNCs, that while Japan's transnationals have expanded aggressively abroad to their own advantage, this has in itself been the root cause of the extended slump experienced by the domestic Japanese economy since the early 1990s.

It was again Hymer (1976) who first noted that transnational production was primarily a feature of oligopolistic sectors. He argued that FDI represented a method for national firms to exploit *monopolistic* advantages overseas, and thereby defend or increase their market power *vis-à-vis* competitors. In the case of Japanese firms, it has been argued that a key cause of economic power is the existence of oligopolistic domestic industrial groups (the so-called *keiretsu*). Hymer's argument was developed more fully by Knickerbocker's (1973) theory of oligopolistic reaction, which posited that TNCs would match their competitors' every move in order to maintain their market share. Indeed, 'follow-the-leader' strategies have been extremely important in the service sector, resulting in high-level service activities clustering in a small number of 'world cities' (Friedmann, 1986). Such 'herding' behaviour would also appear to be a marked feature of Japan's financial sector investment into Europe (see Arora, 1995).

In oligopolistic international markets, TNCs recognize that any attempt to drive out their rivals will provoke mutually destructive retaliatory price-cutting. Cowling and Sugden (1987) argue that, as a result, rivalry comes to co-exist with tacit collusion, implying quasi-monopoly outcomes on an international scale. Furthermore, Sugden (1991) asserts that the national segmentation of international workforces and the high potential mobility of capital allows TNCs to 'divide and rule' their workers, thereby increasing the proportion of returns appropriated by capital instead of labour (in Marxist terminology, TNCs are in a better position to increase the rate of exploitation than national firms). The result, radicals argue, is the tendency for TNCs to seek out the lowest global labour costs, 'deindustrializing' the advanced economies, with eventual global stagnationist tendencies (Cowling and Sugden, 1987), as illustrated by the 'hollowing out' and subsequent slowdown of the Japanese economy (Tomlinson, 1998).

Weaknesses

Japan's overseas investment has indeed shown a tendency to relocate manufacturing in Southeast Asia and certain areas within the European Union, such as the UK's assisted regions, where wages are relatively low and labour is weak (Taylor, 1993; JETRO, 1997b). Also, workers within Japanese transplants are commonly instilled with the need to match Japanese productivity levels if plants are to continue in operation (for example, Garrahan and Stewart, 1992), suggesting at least a weak form of a 'divide and rule' strategy.

However, the transnational monopoly capitalism emphasis on minimizing labour costs is unable to explain the 1980s' trend *away* from investment in the low-wage Asian countries towards the advanced economies. This is largely owing to the key importance of the service sector in Japanese FDI, which is not easily accommodated by monopoly capital theory (see below). Nonetheless, the dominant recipient of *manufacturing* FDI is still the relatively high-wage US economy, whilst the second largest host to manufacturers within Europe has been Germany, with higher labour costs than Japan itself (Eltis, 1997). This suggests that factors other than low wage costs, such as market access and appropriately skilled labour, are more important to much of Japan's FDI. Neither is it clear that Japan's TNCs have engaged in international oligopolistic collusion, given the aggressiveness with which Japanese manufacturers and financial institutions have competed against their Western counterparts, often on the basis of price. For example, Mason (1997) describes how Japanese incursion into European auto, electronics and banking markets provoked EU protectionism after lobbying by incumbent firms.

It has also been argued that Japanese subsidiaries have maintained '*keiretsu*' relationships in the West (see Gittelman and Graham, 1994, on the USA and Europe; and Smith and Elger, 1997, on the UK), suggesting notions of collusive behaviour and concentrations of economic power. However, as Scher (1997) notes, the common English usage of the term '*keiretsu*' (even by many Japanese authors) is misleading, as it wrongly conflates two very distinct relationships.

In Japanese, *keiretsu* means 'affiliated companies' and applies only to *vertically* grouped companies (for example, the intricate inter-firm supply networks witnessed in Japan's auto industry). Such linkages are essentially power relationships.[3] They can be easily understood by the monopoly capitalism approach in a similar way to international subcontracting relationships, which are viewed as a method of extending *de facto* strategic power without expanding formal ownership. By contrast, the horizontal groups of major corporations, typically centred around a bank and a trading firm (such as Mitsui), are known as *kigyo shudan* in Japanese. These relationships involve strategic co-operation amongst relative equals, with minimal formal cross-ownership. Although some authors argue that these relationships are designed to gain functional advantages, the historical reality is that these relationships arose as a pragmatic response to the break up of the monopolistic *zaibatsu* conglomerates by the post-Second World War US authorities. While the formal holding company structures of the *zaibatsu* were ostensibly removed, traditional ties within the groups remained intact, held together by informal cultural relationships (symbolized by small cross-shareholdings, see Scher, 1997). The monopoly capitalism approach has difficulty conceptualizing such structures, as it essentially views the existence (or absence) of competition as being a static function of the number of firms in an industry. In the Japanese case, oligopoly has been maintained over time, despite large firm numbers relative to other advanced industrial economies.

Nevertheless, *keiretsu* and *kigyo shudan* relationships are coming under increasing strain within Japan, owing to the extended post-'bubble' recession, and the increasingly international outlook of Japan's more successful corporations (for example Scher, 1997). These relationships are even more nebulous and fragile outside Japan, not least because the use of indigenous management undermines the cultural 'glue' that is crucial in holding these informal relationships together. Research by the author in the UK, for instance, reveals that business relationships between Japan's UK-based financial institutions and Japanese corporations are relatively insignificant, and are generally diminishing in importance. For Japan's financial TNCs, a key problem has been that, despite the internationally oligopolistic structure of the sector, they have been increasingly unable to cope with severe competition from non-Japanese institutions.

Internationalization of the Circuits of Capital

The dynamic of competition in co-existence with market power is better encapsulated by the theory of the internationalization of the circuits of capital. This classical approach, typified by Jenkins (1987), argues that the need for capital to continually expand in order to reproduce itself[4] has the inherent tendency for this expansion to reach an international scale. The act of expansion results in capitals coming into competition with one another, resulting in oligopolistic rivalry at the same time as particular capitals (namely firms) are growing larger. This has been seen with the emergence of Japanese TNCs, which have grown to compete aggressively with their US and European counterparts. Noting this, Jenkins (1987) argues that a key problem with the monopoly capital approach is its reliance on Baran and Sweezy's (1966) description of the hegemonic global position of US TNCs and, as such, it has now become outdated.

The approach also emphasizes that distinct circuits of capital exist, and that these have internationalized during different historical periods. The circuit of commodity capital was the first to become internationalized, with the development of world trade. This was followed by the circuit of money capital, in the form of international portfolio investment. Only since the Second World War has the circuit of productive capital internationalized significantly, with the growth of FDI in international production (Palloix, 1975). However, the approach does not encompass the even more recent large-scale growth of service sector FDI, nor the important role service sector internationalization has played in facilitating the international expansion of all three circuits of capital (Dicken, 1998). This has been largely because of Marx's explicit dismissal of services as non-productive, arguing that they do not generate surplus value (see Riddle, 1986). Where the approach has incorporated the service sector, this has generally been under the rubric of 'post-Fordism' (for example, Tickell, 1992) which, it was argued above, suffers from a number of conceptual weaknesses. Finally, as a macroeconomic theory, the circuits of capital approach cannot explain the micro-level variations that have distinguished Japanese FDI from that of other countries (Dicken, 1998).

The 'Japanese Model'

The tendency to homogenize patterns of FDI, in the search for 'general' theories, has been argued by some Japanese academics to impose an undue Western perspective upon Japan's internationalization experience. They argue that the Japanese experience is sufficiently unique to warrant a Japan-specific model (for example, Kojima, 1978).

The Japanese model thus developed posits that Japan's overseas investments have been primarily determined by dynamic comparative advantage (drawing upon the Hecksher–Ohlin–Samuelson (H–O–S) factor endowments model – for example, Ohlin, (1967). From this perspective, Japanese development saw, first labour-intensive industries (such as textiles), and later heavy industry and chemicals, gradually transferred to Japan's more labour- and resource-abundant Asian neighbours, as Japanese wages rose, and resources and land became scarce (Ozawa, 1991). Kojima (1978) argues that this allowed both home and host economies to restructure, the latter developing an industrial base while Japan concentrated upon more knowledge-intensive assembly production. But Japan's very success in mass-producing higher value added goods, such as electronics and vehicles, has continued to force up domestic wage levels and the value of the Yen, while generating a huge current account surplus and trade frictions with other advanced economies. This has seen overseas production increasingly directed towards North America and Europe as well as Southeast Asia, initially to overcome trade barriers, but also because the high Yen means that production in the West has become relatively inexpensive. Both Ozawa (1991) and Yoshitomi (1996) have argued that, far from the 'hollowing out' of the Japanese economy that some Westerners perceive (for example, Tomlinson, 1998), this allows domestic companies to concentrate on the highest value added manufacturing, such as hi-tech component production, and to develop the 'flexible automation' systems needed to produce the highly differentiated goods desired by modern consumers. In this light – in explicit contrast to the monopolistic expansion of Western TNCs – Japanese FDI is seen as fostering national economic specialization, thereby increasing global efficiency and welfare through trade on the basis of comparative advantage.

Weaknesses

Unfortunately, despite the specific focus upon Japan, there are a number of empirical shortcomings with the 'Japanese' model. Ozawa (1991), for instance, like many Western observers, places an undue emphasis upon unique Japanese production methods because he overstates the importance of the auto industry to Japanese investment. He similarly uses the 'flexible automation' concept in an unreflective manner, overemphasizing the importance of consumer goods relative to intra-firm trade, producer goods and, more importantly, services. Fundamentally, the Japanese model still remains wedded to manufacturing, when it has been *non*-manufacturing that has really distinguished Japan's FDI. Indeed, the assertion that Japanese manufacturing investment in Europe has now exceeded that in the lower-cost Asian economies is in fact false. Although Japan's *total* FDI stock in Europe is now greater than that in Asia, this is only because of far larger quantities of *non*-manufacturing investment, while, as Table 7.4a shows, Asia's manufacturing stock remains larger. Indeed, as Table 7.4b illustrates, this pattern was consolidated during the first half of the 1990s, with flows of manufacturing investment being increasingly directed *back* towards Asia, especially into China. Further, unlike non-manufacturing FDI in Asia, which includes a relatively high proportion of resource-securing primary investments, non-manufacturing FDI in Europe has been almost exclusively in the service sector (see Table 7.3). Therefore, it would seem that any rounded understanding of Japanese FDI in the advanced economies, such as the UK, needs to have an adequate conception of service sector investment.

Table 7.4   Japanese FDI

(a)   Japanese FDI, by region and by sector, stocks up to 1994 (US$ million)

	North America	Europe	Asia	Latin America	Rest of the World
Manufacturing	54 514	19 372	28 350	7 277	5 599
Non-manufacturing	130 354	64 265	38 167	42 640	32 017
Total	184 868	83 637	66 517	49 917	37 616

Source: MoF, in AJEI (1994).

(b)   Trends in Japanese manufacturing FDI flows, by region, 1989–95 (percentage growth rate)

Financial year	1989	1992	1993	1994	1995
USA	0.4	–31.9	6.7	13.3	53.9
Europe	99.7	–21.9	–2.9	–9.1	7.5
Asia	35.9	6.0	17.9	41.6	55.5
China	1.8	110.4	112.0	34.5	87.9
World	18.0	–18.3	10.7	23.8	35.1

Source: MoF and JETRO, in JETRO (1997b), Table 9.

SERVICE SECTOR FDI

Services do not fit easily into the existing theories of international investment, which were originally developed with regard to the stra-tegic decisions by (usually US) manufacturing firms over whether to export or whether to invest overseas. The nature of many services, as intangibles, means they are not easily tradable. As a result, exporting is not a viable strategy, and therefore foreign direct investment is necessary if overseas markets are to be supplied (Dicken, 1998). However, there has not, thus far, been any real attempt to integrate the theory of services into the extant theories of international production. Indeed, as Hashimoto (1991: 10) argues, services are 'a useful functioning' realized over the course of time (compare goods that exist at a particular point in time). As such, they do not fit easily into the essentially static frameworks of the internalization and radical theories outlined above. By contrast, while dynamic approaches, such as the circuits of capital approach, can theoretically incorporate a process-based theory of services, as noted above, their Marxist foundations have resulted in a tendency to explicitly dismiss services as non-productive. None of these approaches, therefore, sit comfortably with the increasingly dominant proportion of employment and output accounted for by the service sector, or with the growing importance of services to economic growth.

As a result, there has been the tendency to use Dunning's (1989) flexible 'eclectic paradigm' of international production in order to conceptualize service sector FDI. This framework attempts to synthesize existing theories by arguing that FDI occurs only if, first, a firm possesses 'ownership-specific advantages' (whether competitive or monopolistic); then the host economy needs to have 'location-specific advantages' over and above the firm's home country and other potential host nations; finally, FDI is undertaken if 'internalization' is the most transaction-cost-efficient method of overseas expansion (see Dunning, 1993, who abbreviates the paradigm's variables to OLI).

Dunning (1991: 125) concedes that his approach 'is not (and has never purported to be)' a general theory of the TNC, but rather represents a 'methodology and . . . a generic set of variables which contain the ingredients necessary for any specific explanation of particular types of foreign value-added activity'. However, there are two criticisms that can be made of this standpoint. First, the fact that the OLI variables apply – albeit with varying degrees of importance – to all forms of FDI is largely a truism. There is the risk that researchers adopting the paradigm (especially within a deductive-research approach) will concentrate solely or largely upon the OLI variables, to the neglect of extraneous factors that may also be important. Insofar as this occurs, the framework essentially becomes deterministic.[5] This may be particularly problematic with regard to services, because the current lack of empirical understanding of the sector means that it is not possible to rule out the existence of 'x' factors that may not be observed in other sectors. This is particularly relevant to Japanese services, which have received very little research attention despite (or perhaps because of) the considerable interest generated by Japan's manufacturing sector.

Second, Dunning's approach has philosophical parallels with the development of Williamson's 'new institutionalism'. In a similar manner to Williamson, Dunning attempts to avoid the restrictive theoretical straitjacket of orthodox neoclassical economics, incorporating disparate social and geographical factors into his framework. Nonetheless, there remains a central philosophical emphasis upon efficiency as the key economic dynamic. While Dunning accepts that TNCs possess economic power and may wield this to their own advantage, in contrast to the radical approaches, the overriding characteristic of Dunning's economic world is one of efficiency rather than fiat. This mirrors the differences between the socially grounded old institutionalism and Williamson's efficiency-driven new institutionalism (Hodgson, 1998).[6] Moreover, as both Casson (1987) and Sugden (1991) have pointed out, this is theoretically inconsistent and contradictory. Dunning's retention of internalization as a central concept requires the existence of a voluntary-exchange world, which he explicitly rejects with his acceptance of TNCs' economic power.

Theories of Transnational Banking

Since the Second World War, Japanese investment flows into Europe have become dominated by the financial services sector, which accounts for nearly half of all service sector FDI, and over one-third of investment in total (AJEI, 1994). The UK has been the most favoured host within Europe to Japan's financial services, mainly due to the City of London's status as Europe's (if not the world's) premier international financial centre.[7] Financial sector expansion was led by Japan's banks, closely followed by the securities houses. Japan's insurance and other financial companies expanded overseas only more recently, mainly during Japanese boom in the mid-1980s to early-1990s (see Arora, 1995). In the process, Japan's banks and other financial service TNCs have grown into some of the largest players in the sector (Hawawini and Schill, 1994). For example, despite their recent difficulties, Japanese banks still comprise seven of the world's 25 biggest banks, more than from any other country (*The Banker*, July 1998).

Because of the long history of international banking, in contrast to the service sector in general, a literature on banking FDI has emerged. This literature emphasizes that trade in finance is heavily constrained because of the need to establish proximity to clients, together with greater national regulatory restrictions than in comparison with the manufacturing sector. The result is that exporting is far less significant than FDI in the internationalization of finance.

As such, it is typically argued that – drawing from Hymer – the precondition for FDI is that a bank must possess some ownership advantage in order to be able to compete in a foreign market. Grubel (1977), for instance, argues that banks have followed their clients overseas, exploiting the advantage accruing from their existing personal relationships and the information they already hold about their clients' businesses. Grubel uses Kindleberger to posit that this is essentially 'defensive' in nature, since it aims to protect market share from foreign competitors. Arora (1995: 208) notes that this 'following clients' hypothesis has become a 'cornerstone' of international banking theory, endorsed by '[p]ractically every author on the subject',[8] and he finds marked 'herding' behaviour in his econometric study of the expansion of Japanese banks into Europe.

However, in the case of the UK, this would be to overlook the fact that Japan's main banks' originally invested in London back in the 1950s and 1960s. Even much of the subsequent expansion of investment in London occurred during the 1970s and mid-1980s (JETRO, 1996). As such, FDI by the banks *led* Japanese manufacturing, where significant European investment did not occur until the later 1980s (MoF in Dicken, Tickell and Yeung, 1997). This suggests a far more proactive strategy by the banks than simply 'following clients'. It has been claimed that Japan's trading companies (the *sogo shosha*) facilitated the internationalization of the Japanese economy (for example, Dicken, Tickell and Yeung, 1997). It is likewise plausible that the early overseas expansion of Japan's banks was designed to encourage investment by the manufacturing sector, thereby allowing further growth of the banks themselves to meet the demand thus created.[9]

Gray and Gray (1981) argued that the nature of financial regulation (at the time they were writing) meant that banks were effectively guaranteed a minimum profit level, but that overall profit was also constrained by national capital adequacy regulations (CAR). This gave banks the motivation to 'escape' into unregulated supranational markets. The opportunity to operate at higher levels of capital gearing meant the banks could increase their *absolute* profit levels, despite the lower marginal returns generated in the more competitive conditions of supranational markets.[10] This helps to explain London's pre-eminence as an international financial centre, being both key to the supranational

Euro markets as well an important market in its own right, together with relatively liberal financial and inward investment regulations.

This superficially appears to be a useful way of explaining Japanese FDI, given the heavily regulated nature of Japan's financial sector. But Japanese regulations have historically been extended to overseas affiliates, even in supranational markets. Moreover, the environment has changed significantly since Gray and Gray were writing in 1981. Whilst Japan, in line with other advanced economies, has progressively reduced its financial regulation (with Japan's 'Big Bang' currently – albeit very slowly – underway), there has also been the establishment of some degree of supranational regulation (Iwama, 1995). This process of regulatory convergence and globalizing markets suggests that the escape motivation will now be of diminished importance to financial sector FDI. Indeed, in Japan's case, Iwama (1995: 106) argues that the supranational Basle capital adequacy requirements were essentially an Anglo–American protectionist measure, 'introduced in order to put a brake on the aggressive entry of Japanese banks'. Similarly, Mason (1997) describes how the European Union's single financial market was designed in the late 1980s – despite resistance from the UK – to favour the interests of European over non-European institutions, primarily because it was felt at the time that Japanese institutions would come to dominate the EU market.

It was argued that the lower cost of capital in Japan gave its banks an unfair advantage in international markets. There are problems with this argument, however, not least because of significant measurement difficulties regarding international comparisons of the cost of capital. Iwama (1995) suggests that instead it has been Japanese shareholders' acceptance of *low profitability* that has permitted more favourable spreads.[11] Iwama points out that overseas affiliates in fact raise most of their funds (often in dollars) on the international market at international rates, irrespective of the cost of capital in Japan.

Iwama also argues that this latter situation undermines the related argument that financial sector internationalization has been driven by the need to channel Japan's current account surplus overseas. The recycling of these funds comprises only a minor source of funding for overseas affiliates, and indeed there is a noticeable pattern of affiliates *borrowing* short in order to finance long-term lending.

In sum, the literature suggests that there are various reasons for banks to become transnational but, in the Japanese case, the key is that this internationalization has been an *active* expansionary strategy, not simply the passive outcome of macroeconomic forces. This strategy appears to have favoured growth over profitability, partly owing to Japan's 'late-starter' status, and as such has parallels with the internationalization of Japanese manufacturing. However, it is not clear that the motives for transnationality have been the same for both sectors, nor which sector (if either) has been the leader and which the follower.

Further, whilst the orthodox FDI literature has generally been sanguine about the global efficiency-enhancing properties of manufacturing transnationals, this does not appear to be the consensus regarding transnational finance. Gray and Gray (1981), for example, argue that while transnational banks convey similar efficiency benefits to other TNCs, these are on a far smaller scale. In the case of Japanese banks, given their severe 'bad-debt' problems, it is not at all clear what efficiency benefits they are currently in a position to transfer. Indeed, the occurrence of bank (and other financial sector) failures, and the extensive consolidation and retrenchment of Japanese banks' overseas operations, means that at the present time there is the risk of significant *negative* impacts upon host economies.[12]

Moreover, it is also argued that banking FDI is intimately linked to endemic instability in financial markets (for example, Grubel, 1977). Whereas the concerns of early commentators were upon the oil crises and Third World debt, successive financial shocks during the 1990s, particularly in Japan, Southeast Asia and Russia, highlight the continued importance of these issues as the context for theoretical and empirical research (Kregel, 1998).

CONCLUSIONS

Our current understanding of Japanese inward investment has been shaped by the extant theories and research on TNCs. However, these theories concentrate upon the manufacturing sector, when in fact it is services that have dominated Japanese investment. Although there exists a literature on transnational banking this, like the manufacturing sector theories, currently suffers from a number of weaknesses when applied specifically to Japanese FDI. Moreover, in contrast to manufacturing there has been little systematic empirical research into the impact of service sector investment upon host economies. Given the attention of policy makers towards Japanese investment, particularly in the UK, it is important that academic debates are as comprehensive as possible. There is the risk that the assumptions underpinning current policies may not be correct, because of their basis upon only part of the picture.

There remains an urgent need for further research into services and service sector FDI if our understanding is to keep pace with global change.

Notes

*Funding from the Economic and Social Research Council (ESRC) in collaboration with The Institute for Manufacturing is gratefully acknowledged. Particular thanks go to Professor Peter Nolan, Dr Kathy O'Donnell and Hugo Radice for useful comments regarding an earlier version of this chapter, as well as the feedback received from participants of the 1998 Global Change conference in Manchester. The usual caveats apply.

1. Despite the foundation of internalization upon the 'new institutionalism' of Coase and Williamson – ostensibly a critique of neoclassical economics – it can be considered as philosophically analogous to the orthodox neoclassical theory of FDI (this is well illustrated by Hennart, 1991).
2. This interpretation is rejected by some Japanologists and sociologists, who argue that enterprise unionism is the logical extension of the group oriented, non-conflictual nature of Japanese society, and that it was the radical unions that were anomalous. (The author is grateful to Ronald Dore for making this point.)
3. This assertion is rejected by some authors. Dore (1983), for example, sees these relationships as founded upon Japan's trust-based culture, while Flath (1996) takes the opposite stance, and regards these relationships as a rational way of minimizing the transaction costs of 'opportunism'.
4. Formally, this is the Marxist idea that:

    $$M - C \ldots P \ldots C' - M'$$

    where M = money capital; C = commodity capital; P = productive capital and where

    $$M' > M; C' > C; P' > P$$

    is the necessary condition for capital to successfully reproduce itself.

5. Note that this is not a criticism of the paradigm *per se*, but of the ways in which the paradigm may be used.
6. Though within FDI theory the distinction is somewhat more complicated since, as argued above, orthodox internalization theory draws very strongly on Williamson itself.
7. The concentration of Japanese service sector investment in world cities, such as London, has important regional implications that are typically overlooked by the literature on Japanese manufacturing, which tends to see inward FDI as important in regenerating declining industrial regions (for example, Morris, Munday and Wilkinson, 1993, regarding the UK).

As Dicken, Tickell and Yeung (1997) argue, while this may be true, there is a danger of overemphasizing the importance of this effect, and misdirecting the attention of policy makers (see Roy, 1998b).

8. Though Kindleberger (1983) himself has in fact argued that banks can lead *or* follow international business, depending upon historical economic circumstances.

9. For example, the regional representative offices of Japanese banks in the UK have been found to encourage investment by manufacturers in the offices' localities in order to increase regionally based business (see Roy, 1998).

10. This rationale sits more easily with the radical approaches, given their emphasis upon absolute profits, than neoclassical approaches, which emphasize marginal profit*ability*.

11. The acceptance of low profitability itself has many roots, including the prevalence of corporate cross-shareholdings and the concomitantly underdeveloped nature of the Japanese capital market, together with the compensatingly high capital gains exhibited by shares during Japan's 'bubble' economy.

12. The City of London has not yet been severely affected by these changes, because of Japanese banks' tendency when consolidating their European operations to do so solely in London. Nevertheless, owing to bankruptcy or complete retrenchment, there have been several Japanese withdrawals from London over the last three years (author's research).

References

AJEI. (1994) *Britain and Japan 1994/5 – An Economic Briefing*, 3rd edn, London, AJEI.

Arora, D. (1995) *Japanese Financial Institutions in Europe: International Competitiveness of Japanese Banks and Securities Companies*, Amsterdam, North-Holland.

Auerbach, P. (1989) 'Multinationals and the British Economy' in F. Green (ed.), *The Restructuring of the UK Economy*, Brighton, Wheatsheaf, 263–78.

Baran, P.A. and Sweezy P.M. (1966) *Monopoly Capital an Essay on the American economic and social order*, New York, Monthly Press.

Buckley, P.J. and Casson, M.C. (1976) *The Future of the Multinational Enterprise*, London, Macmillan.

Casson, M.C. (1987) *The Firm and the Market*, Oxford, Blackwell.

Cleeve, E. (1997) 'The Motives for Joint Ventures: A Transaction Costs Analysis of Japanese MNEs in the UK', *Scottish Journal of Political Economy*, 44(1), 31–43.

Cm 2867 (1995) *Competitiveness: Forging Ahead*, London, HMSO.

Coase, R.H. (1937) 'The Nature of the Firm', *Economica*, 4, 386–405.

Coffey, D. (1995a) 'Rethinking Rover: The Just-in-time Experience', *CIPP Bulletin*, 7, 5–7.

Coffey, D. (1995b) 'Turning Virtue into Vice: Does "Lean" Make Sense?', *CIPP Bulletin*, 7, 10–12.

Cowling, K. and Sugden, R. (1987) *Transnational Monopoly Capitalism*, Brighton, Wheatsheaf.

Daniels, P.W. (1993) *Service Industries in the World Economy*, Oxford, Blackwell.

Dicken, P. (1998) *Global Shift: Transforming the World Economy*, 3rd edn, London, Paul Chapman.

Dicken, P., Tickell, A. and Yeung, H. (1997) 'Putting Japanese Investment in Europe in its Place', *Area*, 29(3), 200–12.

Dohse, K., Jürgens, U. and Malsch, T. (1985) 'From "Fordism" to "Toyotaism"?', *Politics and Society*, 14(2), 115–46.

Dore, R. (1983) 'Goodwill and the Spirit of Market Capitalism', *The British Journal of Sociology*, 34(4), 459–82.

Dunning, J.H. (1985) *Japanese Participation in British Industry*, London, Croom Helm.

Dunning, J.H. (1989) 'Transnational Corporations and the Growth of Services: Some Conceptual and Theoretical Issues', *UNCTC Current Studies, Series A No. 9*, New York, United Nations.

Dunning, J.H. (1991) 'The Eclectic Paradigm of International Production: A Personal Perspective', in C.N. Pitelis and R. Sugden (eds), *The Nature of the Transnational Firm*, London, Routledge, 117–36.

Dunning, J.H. (1993) Multinational Enterprises and the Global Economy, Reading, MA, Addison-Wesley.

Dunning, J.H. (1996) 'Globalisation, Foreign Direct Investment and Economic Development', *Economics and Business Education*, 2(14), 46–51.

Elger, T. and Smith, C. (1994) 'Introduction' in T. Elger and C. Smith (eds), *Global Japanization: The Transnational Transformation of the Labour Process*, London, Routledge, 1–24.

Eltis, W. (1997) 'The British Economy: The Most Competitive in Europe?', *Euro – Japanese Journal*, 4(1), 26–32.

Flath, D. (1996) 'The Keiretsu Puzzle', *Journal of the Japanese and International Economies*, 10(2), 101–21.

FM&I, (1996) 'UK Inward Direct Investment', *FM&I Brief*, September, pp. 9–11.

Ford, S. and Strange, R. (1998) 'The Locational Determinants of Japanese Manufacturing Investment Within Europe', paper presented at the AIB Conference, Vienna, 8–10 October.

Freeman, R.B. (1984) 'De-mystifying the Japanese Labor Markets', in M. Aoki (ed.), *The Economic Analysis of the Japanese Firm*, Amsterdam, North-Holland, 125–9.

Friedmann, J. (1986) 'The World City Hypothesis', *Development and Change*, 17(1), 69–83.

Garrahan, P. and Stewart, P. (1992) *The Nissan Enigma: Flexibility at Work in a Local Economy*, London, Mansell.

Gittelman, M. and Graham, E. (1994) 'The Performance and Structure of Japanese Affiliates in the European Community', in M. Mason and D. Encarnation (eds), *Does Ownership Matter? Japanese Multinationals in Europe*, Oxford, Clarendon Press, 127–58.

Gray, J.M. and Gray, H.P. (1981) 'The Multinational Bank: A Financial MNC?', *Journal of Banking and Finance*, 5, 33–63.

Grubel, H.G. (1977) 'A Theory of Multinational Banking', *Banca Nazionale del Lavoro Quarterly Review*, 123, 349–63.

Hashimoto, Y. (1991) 'The Concept of Service and Definition of "Servicialization"', *The Economic Review of Shiga University*, 273–4, 41–70.

Hawawini, G. and Schill, M. (1994) 'The Japanese Presence in the European Financial Services Sector', in M. Mason and D. Encarnation (eds), *Does Ownership Matter? Japanese Multinationals in Europe*, Oxford, Clarendon Press, 235–87.

Hennart, J.-F. (1991) 'The Transaction Cost Theory of the Multinational Enterprise' in C.N. Pitelis and R. Sugden (eds), *The Nature of the Transnational Firm*, London, Routledge, 81–116.

Hodgson, G.M. (1998) 'The Approach of Institutional Economics', *Journal of Economic Literature*, 36, 166–92.

Hymer, S. (1976) *The International Operations of National Firms: A Study of Direct Foreign Investment*, Cambridge, MA, MIT Press.

Jacoby, S. (1979) 'The Origins of Internal Labour Markets in Japan', *Industrial Relations*, 18, 184–96.

Jenkins, R. (1987) *Transnational Corporations and Uneven Development: The Internationalisation of Capital and the Third World*, London, Methuen.

JETRO (1996) *Directory of Japanese Affiliated Companies in the EU: 1996–97*, Tokyo, JETRO.

JETRO (1997a) *Directory of Japanese Affiliated Companies in the EU: 1997–98*, Tokyo, JETRO.

JETRO (1997b) *JETRO White Paper on Foreign Direct Investment 1997*, Tokyo, JETRO.

Julius, D. (1990) *Global Companies and Public Policy: The Growing Challenge of Foreign Direct Investment*, London, Chatham House Papers Pinter.

Knickerbocker, F.T. (1973) *Oligopolistic Reaction and the Multinational Enterprise*, Boston, MA, Harvard University Press.

Koike, K. (1984) 'Skill Formation Systems in the US and Japan: A Comparative Study', in M. Aoki (ed), *The Economic Analysis of the Japanese Firm*, Amsterdam, North-Holland, 47–75.

Kojima, K. (1978) *Direct Foreign Investment: A Japanese Model of Multinational Business Operations*, London, Croom Helm.

Kregel, J.A. (1998) 'Yes, "It" Did Happen Again – A Minsky Crisis Happened in Asia', *Working Paper*, 234, presented at the Eighth Annual Hyman P. Minsky Conference on Financial Structure, 23–4 April.

Marglin, S.A. (1976) 'What Do Bosses Do? The Origins and Functions of Hierarchy in Capitalist Production', in A. Gorz (ed), *The Division of Labour: The Labour Process and Class-Struggle in Modern Capitalism*, Brighton, Harvester, 13–54.

Mason, M. (1997) *Europe and the Japanese Challenge: The Regulation of Multinationals in Comparative Perspective*, Oxford, Oxford University Press.

MITI (1998) 'Charts and Tables Relating to Japanese Direct Investment Abroad: January 1997' <http://www.jef.or.jp/news/ab/index.html> 7/1/98 15:14:58.

Moore, J.B. (1987) 'Japanese Industrial Relations', *Labour and Industry*, 1(1), 140–55.

Morris, J., Munday, M. and Wilkinson, B. (1993) *Working for the Japanese: The Economic and Social Consequences of Japanese Investment in Wales*, London, Athlone Press.

Nolan, P. (1994) 'Fordism and post-Fordism', in P. Arestis and M. Sawyer (eds), *The Elgar Companion to Radical Political Economy*, Aldershot, Edward Elgar, 162–6.

Ohlin, B. (1967) *Interregional and International Trade*, rev. edn, London, Oxford University Press.

Oliver, N., Morris, J. and Wilkinson, B. (1992) 'The Impact of Japanese Manufacturing Investment on European Industry', in S. Young and J. Hamill (eds), *Europe and the Multinationals: Issues and Responses for the 1990s*, Aldershot, Edward Elgar, 185–202.

Ozawa, T. (1991) 'Japanese Multinationals and 1992', in B. Bürgenmeier and J.L. Mucchielli (eds), *Multinationals and Europe 1992: Strategies for the Future*, London, Routledge, 135–54.

PACEC (1995) *Assessment of the Wider Effects of Foreign Direct Investment in Manufacturing in the UK*, London, DTI.

Palloix, C. (1975) 'The Internationalization of Capital and the Circuit of Social Capital', in H. Radice (ed), *International Firms and Modern Imperialism*, Harmondsworth, Penguin, Ch. 3.

Riddle, D.I. (1986) *Service-Led Growth: The Role of the Service Sector in World Development*, New York, Praeger.

Roy, A. (1998) 'Japanese Financial Sector FDI. Outside London: Foreign Services and Regional Development', paper presented to the EIBA Annual Conference, Jerusalem, 13–15 December.

Scher, M.J. (1997) *Japanese Interfirm Networks and their Main Banks*, Basingstoke, Macmillan.

Smith, C. and Elger, T. (1997) 'New Town, New Capital, New Workplace? The Impact of the Employment Relations of Japanese Inward Investors in a West Midlands New Town', paper presented to the EMOT Conference, Malaga, 9–12 January.

Strange, R. (1993) *Japanese Manufacturing Investment in Europe: Its Impact on the UK Economy*, London, Routledge.

Sugden, R. (1991) 'The Importance of Distributional Considerations', in C.N. Pitelis and R. Sugden (eds), *The Nature of the Transnational Firm*, London, Routledge, 168–93.

Taylor, J. (1993) 'An Analysis of the Factors Determining the Geographical Distribution of Japanese Manufacturing Investment in the UK, 1984–91', *Urban Studies*, 30(7), 1209–24.

Tickell, A.T. (1992) *The Social Regulation of Banking: Restructuring Foreign Banks in Manchester and London*, unpublished PhD thesis, School of Geography, University of Manchester.

Tomlinson, P. (1998) 'The Japanese Crisis – A Case of Strategic Failure?', in G. Fontana, C. Forde, E. Jenkins, K. Petrick, A. Roy, G. Slater and D. Spencer (eds), *Third Annual Postgraduate Economics Conference: Conference Papers*, Leeds, Leeds University Business School.

UN (1996) *World Investment Report 1996: Investment, Trade and International Policy Arrangements*, New York, UN.

UNCTAD (1996) *Sharing Asia's Dynamism: Asian Direct Investment in the European Union*, New York and Geneva, UN.

Whittaker, D.H. (1990) 'The End of Japanese-Style Employment?', *Work, Employment and Society*, 4(3), 321–47.

Williamson, O.E. (1975) *Markets and Hierarchies: Analysis and Anti-Trust Implications – A Study in the Economics of Internal Organisation*, New York, Free Press.

Womack, J.P., Jones, D.T. and Roos, D. (1990) *The Machine that Changed the World: Based on the Massachusetts Institute of Technology Five-million-dollar Five-year study on the Future of the Automobile*, New York, Rawson.

Yamin, M. (1991) 'A Reassessment of Hymer's Contribution to the Theory of the Transnational Corporation', in C.N. Pitelis and R. Sugden, (eds), *The Nature of the Transnational Firm*, London, Routledge, 64–80.

Yoshitomi, M. (1996) 'On the Changing International Competitiveness of Japanese Manufacturing Since 1985', *Oxford Review of Economic Policy*, 12(3), 61–73.

8 Learning from Learning at Toyota*

Jos Benders

INTRODUCTION

In the second half of the 1970s the interest in 'Japanese management' gained momentum Japanese firms started outperforming their American and European rivals with such highly visible products as consumer electronics and passenger cars. Short study trips were made and extensive academic research was undertaken, impressions and data were collected, analysed and communicated, primarily to a practitioners' audience. Although many factors were mentioned to explain the success, only part of those could directly be influenced by managers, and the term 'Japanese management' subsumes these. Publications started appearing, which shaped different actors' understandings of the Japanese success – and, more importantly, the potential to become successful by drawing on, or even imitating that success. Could successful practices, techniques and/or concepts be transferred from Japan? When practitioners started applying their insights, their experiences could be evaluated, leading to enhanced understanding and further reshaping of knowledge about 'Japanese management'. Selective interpretations, practical experiences and publications from various sources and quality shape and reshape our collective understanding of 'Japanese management' on a continuous basis. Such processes have taken place in the case of 'Total Quality Management' (TQM) in the USA (Hackman and Wageman, 1995) and 'lean production' in Germany (Ortmann, 1995). Such fashionable concepts constitute a strategic problem for managers: what, if anything, can be learned from them? Should managers simply follow the flock out of fear of lagging behind their competitors or reject such ideas as mere fads which will soon fade away?

Below I give a brief description of the historical development of the Toyota Production System or 'TPS'. Toyota is chosen because much of what has become known as 'Japanese' manufacturing, management and personnel practices was applied or even pioneered in this particular firm. The company's outstanding performance record made it

132

a model for other companies, and the exemplar of 'Japanese management'. Managers can learn how Toyota learned and 'transferred' insights
from others, including non-Japanese organizations. This entails lessons
for using insights from sources and concepts prescribing particular lines
of action.

THE EVOLUTION OF THE TOYOTA PRODUCTION SYSTEM

In 1937, Kiichiro Toyoda (1894–1952) founded Toyota Motors. Thirty
five years earlier, his father Sakichi (1867–1930) had invented a loom
which stopped automatically when threads broke. This meant raw
material would not go lost nor would imperfect fabric be produced
after a thread broke. Secondly, operators no longer had to monitor
every single loom continuously, one operator could monitor several
looms simultaneously. The idea that machines stop automatically when
abnormalities occur is called *jidoka* in Japanese, and has been translated as 'autonomation' in English. In a company brochure, *jidoka* is
presented as one of the two fundamental pillars of the TPS (Toyota,
1992), 'Just-In-Time' being the other.

Apart from the production advantage, the *jidoka* principle turned
out to be important for another reason: it allowed Sakichi to found two
firms, Toyoda Spinning and Weaving in 1918 and Toyoda Automatic
Loom in 1926. The looms produced by the last firm were so successful,
that in 1929 Sakichi sold the patent to the British firm Platt Brothers
and gave the revenues to his son Kiichiro to start experimenting with
cars (Cusumano, 1985).

The start in the 1930s proved troublesome. The Japanese domestic
market was small and dominated by Ford and General Motors, which
had factories in Japan. In addition, all knowledge about building cars
had to be built up. Having visited factories in the UK and USA Kiichiro
decided that this was feasible, because he could draw on other sources
of knowledge, Japanese engineers and academics, and utilize the
experience with precision machinery built up in Toyoda Automatic
Loom. Furthermore, machines could be bought abroad and then
duplicated in Japan. At the time, the star case of automobile manufacturing was Ford. Over the years, Ford had pioneered and developed
the assembly line. Large and highly specialized machines were another
essential component of Ford's mass production system. This was
studied carefully in Japan; however, Kiichiro realized that a mass-
production system would not be suitable: the required investment was

far too large for the small volume production with which Toyoda wanted to start. Only after the Japanese government proclaimed a protectionistic law in 1936 was the Toyota Motor Company founded and production started at an assembly plant at Kariya. In November 1938, the production of trucks began in the new Koromo plant.

JUST-IN-TIME

The development of what was to become the TPS really got off the ground only after the end of the Second World War. Whereas all other Japanese car manufacturers turned to Western competitors for technical assistance, Toyota decided to move on its own (Kawahara, 1997). The engineer Taiichi Ohno is generally seen as the genius behind it and its inventor – or perhaps 'developer' is a better word. Ohno had started his career at Toyoda Spinning and Weaving, whose main competitor was a firm called Nichibo. A benchmarking study showed that the considerably more productive Nichibo differed from Toyoda in three important ways:

> Toyoda had separate buildings by process steps; Nichibo had adopted the line layout along the process flow. Toyoda moved yarns in large lots; Nichibo conveyed them in small lots. Toyoda had emphasized skills of rework (yarn tying) at the downstream step; Nichibo had emphasized making good yarns at the upstream and eliminating rework at the downstream. (Fujimoto, 1998: 33)

From this comparison, Ohno gained three insights which would prove to be essential for the later development of the TPS:

1. organize along product flows rather than by functions
2. make small rather than large batches
3. try to prevent the occurrence of defects by solving the problems that cause them (rather than only repairing defects).

After Toyoda Spinning and Weaving was absorbed by Toyota in 1943, Ohno realized these principles might lead to substantial productivity increases in car manufacturing as well. On the first principle, he wrote: 'establishing a continuous flow is basic' (Ohno, 1988: 33).

In the Koromo plant 'flow production' was already being tried. Instead of following Ford's example and installing special-purpose, high-volume machines, it was decided to use 'adjustable' machines that could produce a large range of products. These were installed on movable boards to facilitate layout changes. From the design phase, the idea was to achieve 'flow production', yet putting it into practice proved difficult, an experience that engineers in the contemporary Japanese aircraft industry shared (Wada, 1995). In September 1945, when the American authorities gave approval to resuming car production, the experiments were continued. This offered new career opportunities at Toyota to engineers who had been employed by the aircraft industry, and knowledge transfer from the aircraft to the automotive industry was possible.

Unfortunately, the equipment was outdated and there was hardly money to buy new machines. As a consequence, innovations had to come from new ways of organizing rather than from more sophisticated machinery. With Ohno's appointment as manager of the engine shop of the Koromo plant in 1947, the TPS could be developed. However, he was soon elected as a union official and served in this capacity until March 1948.

Ohno started changing the layout. In parts production, the so-called 'functional layout' was common: similar machines are placed together, and the parts-in-process are transported from one group to the next to undergo different operations. In final assembly, such flow or line production had already become well known with Ford's conveyor belt as the exemplary case. Ohno decided to apply the same idea in parts production, which had never happened at Ford (Ohno, 1988: 103). Initially, the machines were placed in the form of an 'L', but as of 1949, the 'U-form' became the preferred alternative. This U-form has also become known as a 'horseshoe cell' (Figure 8.1). Like a line, the U-form allows continuous and uninterrupted production. An additional advantage is that workers can operate several work stations simultaneously, and that the number of work stations per workers can be varied with fluctuations in the demanded production volume. Multi-machine processing requires workers capable of handling different kinds of machines, which requires adequate instruction and training, and that work is not machine-bound: if workers have to monitor and tend a machine on a continuous basis, multi-machine operation is not possible. Here *jidoka* comes in the play: machines stop automatically, and the necessity to stay with a machine constantly is lifted.

The principle of adjusting the number of workers to the workload is called '*shojinka*'. The short distances between work stations makes *shojinka* possible. In Figure 8.1, three workers operate 10 work stations:

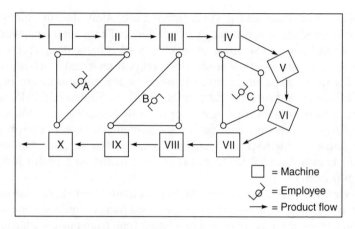

Figure 8.1   The horseshoe or U–form cell
Source: J. Benders. Used by permission.

worker A works stations I, II and X, worker B takes care of III, VIII and IX and worker C has the remaining stations under control. When production increases, a fourth worker can be added, which involves a reassignment of work stations to workers.

Toyota mentions 'Just-In-Time' (JIT), as the second pillar of the TPS. This pillar's invention, and even its name, are attributed to Kiichiro Toyoda, who as early as 1937 had ordered that no more parts were to be produced than the assembly department needed (Fujimoto, 1998: 34). But when production volumes rose, he decided that is was no longer necessary to follow this rule and it was abolished. As a result, work-in-process came to pile up. When Ohno joined Toyota Motors in 1943 he realized immediately that the problem was caused by the co-ordination between production phases, but it took him five years to come up with the solution: reverse the flow of information (Cusumano, 1985: 270–1). Instead of 'pushing' products through the factory from raw material to finished product, products had to be 'pulled' out of the factory. In other words, a work station was to ask the previous work station to supply it with work-in-process only at the moment and in the quantity that it was needed. An order for the final product leads to a need for its constituent parts and hence an order for them. This way, intermediate stocks could be reduced drastically, which fits in with Toyota's philosophy to eliminate any form of waste or '*muda*'.

Ohno had read about this pull or 'supermarket system' in a Japanese newspaper after the war. It had been applied by American plane constructors during the Second World War, who had been inspired by a supermarket. The supermarket system had two advantages. Clients themselves take the desired quantity of the desired product at the moment of their choice off the shelves. Secondly, the empty shelves signalled immediately what had to be replenished. Ohno thought it could be applied at Toyota, and started experimenting in 1948. Yet when monetary reforms caused the so-called 'Dodge recession' in 1948–9, daily operational problems absorbed his attention: shortness of supplies and unreliable deliveries. It wasn't until 1953 that the means to realize the supermarket idea were introduced: the so-called '*kanban*'. These are cards which were sent to previous work stations to order parts. The *kanban* can be seen as the main means of communication of the JIT system. In 1954, the supermarket system was first implemented, but it took years to perfect. When the new Motomachi factory opened in 1959, *kanban* were used factory-wide. In 1962, they were implemented at all Toyota factories, and three years later *kanban* was also used for order with suppliers.

In the process of creating the JIT system, new problems surfaced. One consequence of eliminating buffers is that the system becomes very sensitive to any kind of disturbance of regular production conditions, whether these are caused by defect parts or fluctuations on the workload. Reducing or even eliminating buffers was one way of fighting *muda*, and had the additional advantage that defects would show up immediately so that the causes could be solved right away. In the conventional system with its large buffers, operators could simply take a correct product and throw away the defect one. The cause of the defects would not be looked for, nor corrected. At Toyota, however, continuous improvement means looking for the root problem and eliminating that (see below).

The problem of uneven workloads was aggravated by the variety of models that had to be produced. Different models lead to different work types. Production came to be planned in such a way that the workload was distributed as evenly as possible, for which the term *heijunka* is used. As of the late 1950s, monthly sales orders came to be used to draw up the daily production schedule. All models were produced every day, rather than completing the entire monthly demand for a particular model in one row, and then starting with the production of the next one.

An important impediment to implementing JIT were the so-called 'set-up times', the time it takes to change tools or dies when other parts have to be produced. This could take up to three hours for particularly heavy tools or dies. As a result, it was uneconomical to change tools frequently: incurring considerable downtime and hence loss of production. The conventional logic held that an optimal batch size could be calculated by taking, among other factors, a given set-up time into account. The longer this set-up time, the larger the optimal batch size. By using the so-called 'Formula of Camp' the 'Economic Ordering Quantity' (EOQ) could be calculated. Ohno challenged this logic by trying to reduce the set-up time, so that small batches could be produced economically and the level of intermediate stocks and associated costs reduced. Again, the inspiration had been found in the USA: on a trip in the mid-1950s, Ohno bought presses with rapid change-over features. Ohno wondered why Western manufacturers nevertheless still needed a considerable amount of time to change dies, and found the answer in the apparently unquestioned, prevalent habit of producing in large batches. In 1955, an external consultant named Shigeo Shingo was hired for this purpose. Shingo's goal were 'single set-up times': they had to be reduced to less than 10 minutes so that a single digit sufficed to give the set-up time measured in minutes (Cusumano, 1985: 286). Shingo's 'Single Minute Exchange of Die' method involved often very simple adaptions to existing machines – for instance, replacing bolts which need manual tightening by click devices which can be quickly attached (Shingo, 1983). Over the years continuous improvement reduced set-up times drastically. As an example, Ohno (1988: 39) mentions a reduction from several hours in the 1940s via 15 minutes in the 1950s to three minutes around 1970. The ultimate goal was to make batch sizes of just one, so that intermediate stocks could be completely eliminated.

STANDARDIZATION AND IMPROVEMENT

As described above, some key notions that later became essential elements of the TPS were formulated very early. This also holds for standardization and continuous improvement. At Toyoda Spinning and Weaving, experience workers had gradually been called away for military service. Their places were taken by men and women without any factory experienced or training. By standardizing and simplifying all operations, and by describing them as 'standard operating procedures' (SOPs), newcomers could easily be taught how the work had to be done. Right after his transfer to Toyota Motor in 1943, Ohno started applying SOPs there as well.

The first thing I did was standardization of jobs. The shop floor of those days was controlled by foremen–craftsmen. Division managers and section managers could not control the shop floor, and they were always making excuse for production delay. So we first made manuals of standard operation procedures and posted them above the work stations so that supervisors could see if the workers were following the standard operations at a glance. Also, I told the shop floor operators to revise the standard operating procedures continuously. (Fujimoto, 1998: 36)

In 1948, Ohno's policy on standard procedures were officially approved, which opened the way for their diffusion within the company.

One effect of placing the SOPs above work stations was that a supervisor could easily check whether the job had been done correctly. Such visualization is another much-followed recipe at Toyota, '*andon*' being another example, the 'traffic lights' placed at work stations. Green signals indicate that everything is going well, orange stands for minor problems that can be solved without stopping the line and red means that the line has to be stopped and all workers are expected to help solve the problem. *Andon* allows all workers to see whether production is going smoothly.

The SOPs were bundled in handbooks, and some were visualized and displayed above work stations, so that every worker could see at one glance how a particular job had to be done. Again, Ohno's earlier experience played a vital role here: he states that he realized the importance of having people write the procedures themselves when his boss at Toyoda Spinning and Weaving asked him to prepare standard work methods sometime in 1937–8:

It was a difficult project...A proper work procedure...cannot be written from a desk. It must be tried and revised many times in the production plant. Furthermore, it must be a procedure that anyone can understand at first sight. (Ohno, 1988: 20)

In Ohno's view, workers themselves had to suggest improvements as they were specialists at their own work, and best capable of improving it. Involving workers in continuous improvement became to be seen as an important means to improve Toyota's competitive position. Once a particular way of working was established and laid down in a SOP, a better way of working was sought and if found, a new SOP would replace the old one. As part of the Scientific Management movement which had come over from the USA at the beginning of the century, time-and-motion studies had quickly gained popularity in Japan (Conti and Warner, 1993). Such studies, however, were normally carried out by specialists, who devised improved ways of working which were prescribed to workers. Ohno stressed that workers themselves should make improvement suggestions, but it was May 1951 before the 'Creative Idea Suggestion System' was put into effect. This was shortly after the Toyota directors Eiji Toyoda and Shoichi Saito had returned from study trips to Ford's production plants in the USA. Both had noted Ford's Suggestion System, which also stressed the importance of shop-floor employee as providers of improvement suggestions. Although pre-war factory regulations at Toyota already mentioned 'the creative spirit' and rewards for improvement suggestions, the first programme to stimulate this was installed only in 1949 and confined to specialists (technicians and engineers). Ohno's stress on shopfloor employees as sources of improvements was institutionalized only two years later with the 'Creative Idea Suggestion System'. According to company statistics it was not till 1969 that the average number of suggestions per employee per year was higher than one (Yasuda, 1991).

Also in 1951, a large-scale training programme called 'Training within Industry' (TWI) had been introduced. Again, the source of inspiration lay in the USA where TWI had been developed and widely applied in order to stimulate (wartime) production. TWI consisted of 'three standardized training programmes for supervisors and fore-men'. The first, Job Instruction Training (JIT), taught supervisors the importance of proper training of their workforce and how to provide this training. The second, Job Methods Training (JMT), focused on how to generate and implement ideas for improvement. The third, Job Relations Training (JTR), was a course in 'supervisor–worker relations and leadership' (Robinson and Schroeder, 1993). A key principle for diffusing TWI was the 'multiplier effect': the standard method was taught to supervisory personnel who were to train others to use the method. In the courses the importance of establishing and later adhering to standards, 'learning by doing' as a means of instruction and continuous improvement were stressed. TWI was widely taught after the end of the war, often sponsored by the US government. Japan was no exception to this rule, and as of 1948 TWI was introduced via various channels. Toyota was among the earliest companies to adopt TWI, and a former managing director credited TWI as an important means for soliciting suggestions and creating an improvement climate (Robinson and Schroeder, 1993: 51–2). Consistent with TWI, in 1955 improvement activities were incorporated in the foreman's job description at Toyota.

The topic of 'quality control' is closely related to continuous improvement. Again, much of the inspiration came from the USA, and via the widespread application of quality control in Japan. The Americans W. Edwards Deming (1900–7) and Joseph Juran gained the status of quality gurus. Yet the diffusion of various quality initiatives involved considerably more than these individuals' contributions. As part of the measures to revitalize the Japanese economy, the General Headquarters of the Supreme Commander for the Allied Powers (SCAP) organized seminars on management practices, including quality control. Before and during the war there had been quality initiatives, but the quality movement gained momentum only through various promotional activities after the Japanese defeat in August 1945. Three Japanese management associations started offering educational programmes in 1946, although the scale of these efforts seems to have remained limited until 1949:

- Japan Management Association or 'JMA' (founded in 1942)
- Japan Standards Association or 'JSA' (founded in 1945)
- Union of Japanese Scientist and Engineers or 'JUSE' (founded in 1946).

In 1949 and 1950, the Civil Communications Section of the General Headquarters organized management seminars to improve the deplorable state of the post-war communications system: there were many breakdowns owing to the poor quality of various components manufactured in Japan. In 1950, W. Edwards Deming visited Japan as adviser on sampling to the General Headquarters. The JUSE director invited him to give a series of lectures in statistical quality control (the same he had given in the USA during wartime). A year later, Deming gave additional courses in Japan. Notes from the first course were published in Japanese, and Deming donated the royalties to JUSE. In return, JUSE decided to fund two prizes: the Deming Prize and the Deming Implementation Prize. Deming stressed the statistical techniques to control quality. Another American adviser, Joseph Juran, visited Japan in 1954 on the invitation of JUSE's managing director who had read Juran's *Quality Control Handbook* (first published in 1951). Juran's lectures were attended by senior managers, which proved instrumental for the diffusion of quality control in Japan. Where Deming had stressed the technical side, Juran focused on managerial aspects. Statistical quality control (SQC) had to become 'company-wide' or total quality control (TQC) (Nonaka, 1995).

Toyota was rather late in adopting TQC. Only after its arch-rival Nissan had won the prestigious Deming Prize in 1960 was TQC formally introduced. In 1965, Toyota managed to win this award, and started stimulating its application with suppliers.

CONCLUSION

The formation of the TPS took roughly somewhat more than three decades, from Kiichiro's first orientation on automobile manufacturing to a manufacturing system with distinctive features. The early realization that the small domestic market made simply copying Ford's mass production system infeasible, and that an alternative needed to be found, was instrumental. Kiichiro Toyoda himself may have first thought of the ideal of 'Just-In-Time' production, but he never succeeded in realizing or even approaching it. Taiichi Ohno deserves the credit for pursuing this goal zealously, and ultimately creating a production system which became a hallmark of competitiveness and thus a model for others to follow.

Yet the development of the TPS was by no means a grand design. In the first place, developing an alternative way of producing cars was hampered and at the same time necessitated by scarcity of financial resources and of technical knowledge, besides the already mentioned limited market. Had the market been large and resources sufficient, the TPS might never have come into existence. Secondly, whereas 'Just-In-Time' may have been invented by Kiichiro Toyoda (he developed the idea even before the war), Ohno may have taken up the thread when he read about American aircraft manufacturers. In retrospect it may matter little who first invented it, but clearly there was no grand design. In the third place, throughout the development of the TPS its contributors actively looked at other manufacturers, industries and publications for ideas and techniques that could be transferred to Toyota's factories. With the possible exceptions of *kanban, jidoka* and *heijunka*, practically all essential elements of the TPS were copied from elsewhere. Small batches, the product-focused layout, eliminating the source of defects and the need for SOPs came from a Japanese textile firm, whereas the supermarket system, set-up time reduction and continuous-improvement schemes were all based on American experience, although it must be conceded that some of these elements may have been 'invented' independently from each other in approximately the same period, and that some ideas drew from a common knowledge base. The latter may hold for the emphasis on SOPs and continuous improvement, which during the Second World War were stressed by both the American TWI programme and Ohno. Perhaps surprisingly, the formal incorporation of quality control at Toyota took place when the basics of the TPS were already in place, and it took even more years before the continuous-improvement schemes led to substantial numbers of improvement suggestions.

Furthermore, the development was on a trial-and-error basis. Some tracks proved to be dead alleys, and at some instances the solutions brought new problems with them. The latter can also be created by external changes. In fact, what has been described above can be seen as the 'classic TPS'. In line with the idea of continuous improvement, Toyota keeps making changes to its production system (Benders, 1996).

The TPS can be seen as the ultimate result of an enduring pursuit of a vision, into which existing techniques were incorporated and which may have developed over time. The persistence with which the vision was pursued was important in selecting what could be learned from others. Here seems to lie a contrast to the reception of knowledge on 'Japanese' management in at least some Western countries. For instance, quality circles (QCs) were embraced eagerly at the beginning of the 1980s because they were seen and certainly propagated as an important explanation for the Japanese success. Precisely because of this, bandwagon effects coincided with their uncritical adoption, leading to their massive abandonment a few years later. In retrospect, this has been explained because they were often not attuned to the adopting organizations' ways of working and structures (Hill, 1995).

The gamut of labels under which various aspects of 'Japanese management' over the years have been propagated indicates that there is a continual market for them. To be successful on this market, advocates must convince potential adopters of the desirability and at the same the possibility of adopting their ideas. These advocates must deploy a range of rhetorical tactics for this purpose, among which are stressing performance improvements and the universal applicability of their ideas beyond their original environment. Their goal is not to give an accurate academic representation of the pros and cons, but to sell their product. Obviously, the extent to which such rhetorical tactics are used varies, but the point here is that such writers have influenced practitioners' understanding of what 'Japanese management' is all about and what they can learn from it. From the evolution of the TPS the lesson can be drawn that solutions are solutions only when they fit the problem(s) organizations face. A vision on the organization's future can act as the criterion against which to judge what ideas should be adopted, and which ones not. In addition, one can learn from Toyota that complete production systems can never be totally copied, but elements (practices or techniques) can be incorporated and embedded into one's own productive system. Reflection on how that can be done remains difficult, and must be carried out locally.

Note

*The author is indebted to Saskia Ijszenga and Patrick Vermeulen for their comments on earlier drafts of this chapter.

References

Benders, J. (1996) 'Leaving Lean? Recent Changes in the Production Organization of Some Japanese Car Plants', *Economic and Industrial Democracy*, 17(1), 9–38.

Conti, R. and Warner, M. (1993) 'Taylorism, New Technology and Just-In-Time Systems in Japanese Manufacturing', *New Technology, Work and Employment*, 8(1), 31–42.

Cusumano, M.A. (1985) *The Japanese Automobile Industry; Technology & Management at Nissan and Toyota*, Cambridge, MA and London: Harvard University Press.

Fujimoto, T. (1998) 'Reinterpreting the Resource-Capability View of the Firm: A Case of the Development–Production System of the Japanese Auto Makers', in A.D. Chandler, P. Hagstrom and O. Solvell (eds), *The Dynamic Firm: The Role of Technology, Strategy, Organization, and Regions*, Oxford, Oxford University Press, 15–44.

Hackman, J.R. and Wageman, R. (1995) 'Total Quality Management: Empirical, Conceptual and Practical Issues', *Administrative Science Quarterly*, 40(2), 304–42.

Hill, S. (1995) 'From Quality Circles to Total Quality Management', in A. Wilkinson and H. Willmott (eds), *Making Quality Critical; New Perspectives on Organizational Change*, London, Routledge.

Kawahara, A. (1997) *The Origin of Competitive Strength; Fifty Years of the Auto Industry in Japan and the US*. Tokyo, Kawahara Akira.

Nonaka, I. (1995)'A History of Quality Control in Japan', in J.M. Juran (ed.), *A History of Managing for Quality: The Evolution, Trends and Future Directions for Quality*, Milwaukee, ASQC Press.

Ohno, T. (1988), *The Toyota Production System; Beyond Large-Scale Production*, Cambridge, Productivity Press.

Ortmann, G. (1995) *Formen der Produktion; Organisation und Rekursivität*, Opladen, Westdeutscher Verlag.

Robinson, A.G. and Schroeder, D.M. (1993) 'Training, Continuous Improvement, and Human Relations: The US TWI Programs and the Japanese Management Style', *California Management Review*, 35(2), 35–57.

Shingo, S. (1983) *A Revolution in Manufacturing: the SMED System*, Stamford: Productivity Press.

Toyota (1992) *Toyota Production System*, Tokyo, Toyota.

Wada, K. (1995) 'The Emergence of the "Flow Production" Method in Japan', in H. Shiori and K. Wada (eds), *Fordism Transformed. The Development of Production Methods in the Automobile Industry*, Oxford, Oxford University Press.

Yasuda, Y. (1991) *40 Years, 20 Million Ideas – The Toyota Suggestion System*, Cambridge and Norwalk, Productivity Press.

9 The Japanese Style of Management of Japanese Affiliates in Germany and the UK*

Koji Okubayashi

RESEARCH THEME AND RESEARCH METHOD

Research Theme

The effort of Japanese corporations based abroad trying to implement 'Japanese management' and compete with local companies has been studied for a long time. The central issue is how to define 'Japanese management' in such Japanese corporations. In the post-war period of rapid economic growth, the seniority wage system, lifetime employment and enterprise unions were commonly regarded as the basic indicators of 'Japanese management'; however, it is difficult to find such overseas affiliates implementing the 'three sacred pillars'. At the same time, one may not take it for granted that Japanese affiliates generally follow the management style of the local companies. Our primary research theme is to clarify how the management of Japanese affiliates differs from that of local companies and from the typical 'Japanese management' approach of their Japanese headquarters.

The indexes of 'Japanese management' had to be defined before conducting the investigation of affiliates. We define the characteristics of 'Japanese management' and various management systems derived from that concept as the 'loosely-structured organization' (LSO). The LSO embodies organic shop organization and flat management organization and includes the following systems: the team work system, multi-skilled workers, QC circles information-sharing system, qualification systems and the like. The LSO has become prominent in Japan since the 1980s, along with the adoption of micro-electronic technology. It has become a basic characteristic of a new

'Japanese management', as has already been described by our project team (Okubayashi, 1995). The issue here is to clarify to what extent the LSO has been adopted outside Japan, especially in Germany and the UK. The concept of LSO signifies not just the structure of a corporation, but also the corresponding production systems and the human resources management (HRM) programmes. LSO is a form of corporate organization which fits multi-products mid-scale production systems and includes new salary systems and education and training systems on the premise that it facilitates employees in becoming multi-skilled workers and technicians. Therefore, when we attempt to clarify to what extent the Japanese affiliates in Europe adopt 'Japanese management' (consisting of LSO), it is necessary to investigate not only the basic organizational structure but also technology systems, production systems, work organization, the structure of management organization and HRM systems as components of LSO. LSO is a concept which integrates the diverse aspects of the corporation.

Companies Investigated

The author stayed in Europe for a period of six months (April–September 1994) to conduct the interviews with Japanese affiliates. The author was based at the Wissenschäftliche Hochschule für Unternehmensführung-Koblenz from April until June 1994, while Japanese affiliates in Germany were interviewed. The companies chosen for the interview belong to the electronics industry, which was chosen:

- first, because electronics companies open more affiliates in Europe among the Japanese manufacturers
- secondly, the Japanese electronics affiliates demonstrate a high competitive edge in the European market and achieve good performance by maintaining Japanese management
- thirdly, the management of the electronics industry has not been researched as much as that of the automobile industry – one may say that the electronics industry is an untapped area.

A total of nine companies were interviewed; these consisted of manufacturers of VTRs, TVs, stereo sets, semiconductors, copy machines and TV parts. From June to September 1994, the author was based at the School of Management, Imperial College, London. In the UK Japanese companies in a number of industries have opened manufacturing affiliates, but the companies investigated were limited to the electronics and automobile industries, including their R&D centre. These industries were chosen:

- first, to enable this research to compare the electronics industry in Germany with that in the UK
- secondly, because the investigation of the automobile industry would demonstrate the distinctive features of the electronics industry
- thirdly, the inclusion of the R&D centres would enable us to understand the corporate strategy of such Japanese companies.

The companies investigated consisted of factories of automobile, TV, VTR, copy machine, air-conditioner, semiconductor, TV parts and stereo set manufacturers. Six of the companies investigated have factories both in the UK and Germany, so the differences between Germany and the UK could be examined.

Research Method

The Japanese Chambers of Commerce of Düsseldorf and London assisted with the selection of the companies investigated. The questionnaire (Appendix 2, p. 171) was mailed to the companies in advance. After the plant tour, an interview based on the questionnaire was conducted. Some data associated with the questionnaires has not been disclosed owing to confidentiality. The questionnaires were fine-tuned during the interviews and were found to be effective in clarifying the actual practices of Japanese affiliates outside Japan.

One interview was conducted at each company, each lasting at least three hours, some taking eight–nine hours from beginning to end, including a meal. It was worthwhile to have the opportunity to get to know Japanese employees working abroad, including their experiences of problems.

The interviewee was sometimes the head of the Japanese affiliate or his Japanese subordinate working for it. When information is obtained from the Japanese, the 'Japanese management' which the Japanese perceive can be understood. However, it is not possible to understand how the local employees regard the 'Japanese management'. The author had opportunities to speak to some local people working as head of the affiliate and attempted to get the features of 'Japanese management' through their perception.

This chapter does not describe the details of each company case, but presents the 'Japanese management' adopted by the Japanese electronics and automobile affiliates from the overall impressions of the interviews from Germany and the UK. Exact sources of specific information have not been disclosed because of confidentiality agreements made prior to the interviews.

Hypothesis on the Investigation

As already explained, the questionnaire was prepared in advance. As you can appreciate from the length of the interviews, the information obtained diverged from the questionnaire. In order to maintain consistency across such divergences it is necessary to have some certain hypotheses.

Socio–technical systems was used as the basic theory for the interviews. The basic concept of a socio–technical system is that an optimal combination of technical system and social system increases production efficiency and simultaneously satisfies the people who work under such an optimally combined system (Emesy and Thorsrud, 1976). However, while socio–technical systems theory was applied to this research, the theme of the research was not to look for the optimal combination of the currently ongoing system in the Japanese affiliates, but to clarify what social system has formed under the circumstances in which a technical system designed in Japan had been transplanted. This is similar to tracing technology transfer. When the Japanese technical system is transferred to Germany and UK, the pivotal question is whether each of the local social systems can comply with the Japanese technical system, or whether the Japanese social system is also transplanted.

Therefore, the interview asked not only to what extent systems from the 'Japanese management' model were introduced, but also how the technical systems were designed and utilized. The author attempts to clarify the features of the management of the Japanese affiliates, taking into account the inter-relationship of such factors as management environment, production method (technical system), organization structure and HRM. The aforementioned framework is the same as that of the project team for the LSO. By applying the same framework to the investigation on the Japanese affiliates outside Japan, the author intends to search for the 'Japanese' features of management. In other words, the concrete research theme is to discuss the universality of the LSO.

REASONS FOR LOCAL PRODUCTION IN EUROPE

In giving reasons for the local production of electronic equipment such as TVs and VTRs in Germany and/or the UK, many companies cited the principle of 'production-close-to-market'. Germany has the highest labour cost among the European countries, but the situation is different from the usual one in which production goes to sites in developing countries on account of lower labour costs. Behind the behaviour of Japanese affiliates in Europe lies the thinking that it is best to undertake production of products which meet the needs of European consumers within Europe.

Secondly, from the late 1980s, the tendency of the Yen to appreciate drove many Japanese companies to reassess the EU market. The integration of the EU market in 1992 also prompted Japanese companies to enter European markets. Though the high tariff barrier of the European Union was a major reason for the increasing number of Japanese companies moving to Europe, they constructed their production sites in Germany and the UK with the intention of covering markets in East Europe, the Middle East and Africa from the European Union. For example, air-conditioners are produced in Scotland to target the large markets surrounding the Union.

A third reason is the globalization strategies of Japanese companies, which require the construction of European production sites. The underlying triadic doctrine developed with the rapid expansion of international productions by Japanese companies. This doctrine divides the global market into America, Europe and Asia, and requires bases in each which function independently of each other. Company strategies placed the independent bases for European headquarters, R&D, production and marketing in the European market, centered on the EU market, which is independent from America and Asia. The triadic doctrine of the globalized companies required them to have production bases in Europe. Under this doctrine Europe is assigned as the production base for semiconductors and such maturing products as TVs, VTRs and stereo sets.

The fourth reason reflects the triadic doctrine that each area should pursue autonomous business development. For example, originally the basic specification for TVs was designed by headquarters in Japan, the affiliate was assigned to assemble its parts according to the specification. However, by the 1990s each factory had its own design department which had begun to be managed separately from other plants. The fact that Japanese companies opened their own basic research centres and development centres in Europe is evidence of the trend towards autonomy, under the triadic doctrine that products meeting consumers' needs are designed, developed and manufactured by way of the autonomous business units.

This raises the question: what production system is designed by Japanese companies under this strategy?

PRODUCTION SYSTEM

The first point to consider is that most machines and equipment were designed and made in Japan when factories in Germany and UK started up. Even in the case of joint venture start-ups, though existing buildings continue to be utilized, former machines and equipment were replaced with those made in Japan and their technical systems were brought from Japan. The main reason for installing Japan-made machines with almost no change was the difficulty in procuring machines in compliance with the Japanese requirement standards. For example, in the case of semiconductor production, adequate clean-room technology was not available in Europe. State-of-the-art designs were completed in Japan and the entire line of machines and equipment were shipped from Japan to be placed in factories in Europe. This meant the transfer of complete manufacturing machines. In terms of the socio–technical system, all of the technical systems were designed in Japan. However, there was one case in which machines available in Europe were deployed for some of the system by partly adjusting the Japanese specification. Such a case is rather limited and does not involve the introduction of a European technology system to the Japanese affiliates.

The 'localization' of technical systems in Japanese affiliates is not as simple as that of personnel management, even in Europe. The automobile industry represents a single-product mass-production system and the electronic industry represents a multi-product small-volume production system. All of the three Japanese automobile companies in the UK produce only two or three types of car. The mixed production line system which assembles several types of car on the same production line, often evident in the Japanese mother factories, is very rarely seen in Japanese affiliates in the UK. However, if we take into account detail variations such as the position of a handle or body colour as indicators of 'multi-product', these Japanese automobile affiliates can be said to be in the category of a multi-production system.

In contrast to the auto industry, more than 100 types of TV are manufactured in the Japanese affiliates. More than 140 variations of TV are assembled in one Japanese factory, taking account of combinations of the cathode ray tube size, types of broadcasting system and colour of the TV.

One Japanese affiliate in the electronics industry produces TVs and VTRs under the same management organization within the same factory site. Manufacture of copy machines is also based on a multi-product mass-production system. Therefore, it can be concluded that among the Japanese affiliates the production system of the electronics industry is dominated by the multi-product mass-production system. What types of organization do they apply for that production system?

WORK ORGANIZATION

The first impression which the author gained on the factory tour of many Japanese affiliates was that there are more *notice boards on which pictures, graphs and slogans* are put than in their European counterparts. Many figures as well as pictures show visibly the roles and job contents of each operator at each stage of production process. These figures help visitors to understand the production process, but also help the operators at the shop floor to understand their roles and duties in relation to the operators around them. These figures and pictures explain easily the targets of production, their rate of accomplishment and trends of production efficiency at their shop. Through this 'visual management', workers can obtain information on production and changes of production condition visually and share it with their colleagues and supervisors. Visual management is one of the devices for information-sharing which is often practised in the Japanese style of management. They can naturally understand through these figures what is happening at their shop without the effort of reading in-plant newspapers.

Visual management is one of the devices for sharing information about personnel among workers and managers when information on the notice board extends to personnel affairs. Some plants, for example, put pictures of their workers showing who works in which place, and some others indicate who is absent today and who is on a training course. When a worker looks at these notice boards, he/she can easily understand what roles he/she has to play in the production process and with whom he/she has to cooperate. This kind of information will promote intimate human relations to simulate improvement of product quality, or *kaizen* activities.

However, some Japanese companies operating in Germany face problems in introducing this visual management where the philosophy of individualism is traditionally supported by the culture, including workers. One Japanese company, for example, had to move the notice-board which showed who is absent and who is on long-term leave among workers at shop floors from the shop floor to their room foremens'. Many workers protested against the disclosure of personal affairs such as absenteeism and long-term leave to their colleagues. Such complaints are rare in Japanese companies in the UK. The practices of information-sharing thus have some limitations concerning the content of the information shared among people in the company, depending on the host-country culture.

The second point of the international comparison is the question of whether *the task is assigned to each worker or to a team*. In Japan, task assignment is usually based on a team of a section or sub-section. The practice of task assignment based on teams became especially popular owing to the introduction of microelectronics technology. Multi-skilled training and job rotation which are elementary characteristics of 'organic organization' are promoted in the team-based work organization.

However, at Japanese companies in Germany, each job is usually assigned to each worker, not to a team. The elementary contents of each job are standardized and objectively defined by the development of collective bargaining and training system outside each company. The multi-skilled worker and job rotation may disturb the principle of the rigid job boundary of each job and sometimes conflicts with the concept of the standardized job. Further the practices of multi-skilling without a corresponding wage increase, common in Japan is not readily accepted by German workers.

However, it is not true that job rotation is not used at all by Japanese companies in Germany. TV assembly workers, for example, agreed to move to new jobs in security in the same factory as an alternative to being discharged by the Japanese company owing to reduced production. Workers will easily agree to change their job or transfer to another job when they have little alternative employment opportunity in the local area. Japanese companies in Germany plan to establish the practices of multi-skilling and job rotation to increase the flexibility of production, which cannot be introduced easily and quickly into German companies.

Japanese companies in the UK also tried to introduce practices of multi-skilling and job rotation. Some Japanese companies in the UK have been successful in establishing these personnel management practices under the presence of trade unions in the 10 years since they started manufacturing. They said that it was easier in the UK than in Germany to implant elementary practices of personnel management from their mother plant in Japan.

The third point of the international comparison to identify the Japanese characteristics of Japanese affiliates in Europe is to establish whether they introduced QCs in their factory. Generally speaking, it seems to be very difficult to introduce QCs in Germany where individualism as a principle of behaviour dominates the shopfloor atmosphere. A Japanese manager frankly related how he tried in vain to introduce quality control activities in Germany for three years. Many Japanese managers in Germany said that the establishment of QCs there is a future target.

However, one Japanese company succeeded in introducing QCs in its factory in Germany. It provided a Japanese specialist to lead quality control activities and *Kaizen* and prepared a manual to implant QCs in foreign factories. It sent some German workers who won a competition in quality activities in their factory to the international contest held in the Japanese headquarters. The improvement of a production procedure of the factory was reported to be highly appreciated by the Japanese headquarters. Japanese factories in Europe, as members of the Japanese multinational company which organized the world-wide quality control contest, are very keen to succeed with these activities in their host countries. It seems to be expected that Japanese companies in Europe will succeed in promoting QCs in their plants in Europe.

The fourth point of comparative analysis concerns *absenteeism* as one of the indications of work attitude. Many Japanese managers often complain of the large number of absent workers, including sick leave, which is easy to ask for with documentation from a doctor in Germany. Approximately 20 per cent of employees were absent owing to sickness leave, paid vacation and absenteeism in some Japanese companies. The Japanese manager in Germany may feel that German absenteeism is very high compared with its counterpart in Japan based on his own experience of no more than 50 per cent of annual paid vacation being utilized for its own purpose in Japan. Despite the astonishment of Japanese managers, this is quite rational behaviour by workers, since many forms of paid leave are guaranteed with collective agreement in Germany.

As a device to reduce high absenteeism, one Japanese company in Germany tried to include number of absences owing to personal reasons into indexes of personal appraisal after agreement with the works council. As a result, the absence rate has gone down rapidly. Some workers continued to work without absence owing to personal reasons and almost without using annual paid vacation, some German engineers accomplished their task within an indicated deadline without demanding payment for overtime work, according to a Japanese manager. Therefore, some people in Germany can work as hard as Japanese workers.

However, high absenteeism does not indicate low intensity of work. Many Japanese managers acknowledged that both German and English employees, including white-collar workers, do their job quite intensively. Some Japanese managers realized that German workers accomplished the same number of tasks with shorter working hours than their Japanese counterparts. However, annual labour productivity of the factory as a whole might be felt to be low by Japanese managers owing to long paid vacations and the shorter total amount of annual work hours per workers than in the Japanese case.

In the final analysis, it can be said that the work organization of Japanese affiliates in Germany and in the UK is mechanistic in the sense that standardized and fragmented jobs are assigned to each worker instead of a team. However, with the introduction of multiskilling, job rotation and QCs, the work organization of Japanese affiliates is moving towards that of an organic organization owing to the increased flexibility of the production process. Therefore, the work organization of Japanese affiliates is, at this moment, in a transition stage from a mechanistic to an organic model.

MANAGEMENT ORGANIZATION

'Management organization' in this chapter means organization of managers above sub-section head, the relations of managers between departments and work organization among staff departments at the headquarters. When we look into the offices of production management, design, sales, personnel and so on in Japanese affiliates in Germany and the UK, we usually find these departments are concentrated into *one big office*, except for the President's room. This type of office layout is common practice in Japan and often referred to as the 'one big room' or the 'see-through office'. The typical case of the 'one big room' is where a factory manager stays in the centre of the big room so he can view all of the room and employees. This type of office layout, although quite popular in Japan, seems strange from the viewpoint of European managers, who usually expect to have their own room as a department or section leader.

When a Japanese affiliate started as a joint venture between a German or English and Japanese company, and therefore when many managers are local ones, their offices could not be quickly changed into one big room. Therefore some Japanese affiliates agreed to give department managers a personal room. It seems to be natural that German or English managers, having made a lot of effort to reach a higher social stratification through higher education, should demand a personal room as a status symbol to show some differences from rank-and-file, blue-collar or white-collar workers. None the less, Japanese affiliates in Germany and UK adopt the one big room, because managers in one big room can easily communicate with other employees and managers in different sections in order to share background information, although Japanese managers recognize that some white-collar employees are dissatisfied with this practice.

A second point of the difference in offices between Europe and Japan is that local as well as Japanese managers wear the *same or almost the same uniform* as that of blue-collar workers. This practice is usually termed 'single-status'. All of the employees including white- and blue-collar, rank-and-file workers and managers have lunch provided by the cafeteria, sitting side by side. There is no special canteen for white-collar employees or managers, except for visitors; there is no special parking area for white-collar employees. In the newer electronics and automobile factories, the colour of walls is standardized between the office and the factory: the principle of single-status in Japanese affiliates is applied even to the physical environment in the office and the factory. These examples of single-status practices are received positively by blue-collar workers, although some white-collar employees are not satisfied. They are also very effective in promoting a feeling of unity among employees as well as a feeling of 'belongingness' towards their company.

The third point is that engineers themselves also accept the idea of *single-status among employees*. Generally speaking, engineers who graduated from a university usually demand advantageous treatment, both in Germany and the UK. They invest a lot of money and energy to become graduate engineers and demand treatment comparable with their educational investment once they reach their profession. Therefore a rigid stratification of engineer, technician and workers is established. Engineers mainly engage in designing efficient machines or in developing new products, and technicians do the job of preparing and maintaining the machines. The engineers define their job as 'creative work' in their office far from the shopfloor.

However, engineers in Japan are required to visit the shopfloor often in order to be familiar with the daily practices of operators at the shopfloor level. These attitudes and philosophy of Japanese engineers are termed '*Gembashugi*' which is even taught in universities. The Japanese engineers are expected to design efficient machines with the objective of easy operation and to give detailed information to the machine operators; this can be easily achieved in the culture of single-status. The physical closeness between engineering department and shop floor also explains other aspects of '*Gembashugi*'. '*Gembashugi*' is always practised in Japanese affiliates in Germany and the UK. Engineering departments of recently established factories of Japanese affiliates are usually located very close to the shopfloor. The engineering department of a Japanese TV factory, for example, is located within the same building as the assembly shop. Engineers of a Japanese affiliate often visit the shop floor to improve the machinery and production system after watching its operation. Direct observation reveals that '*Gembashugi*' is an element of the Japanese style of management usually transplanted into Japanese affiliates in Germany and the UK. This is one of the main reasons why the quality of products and effectiveness of production is maintained in Japanese affiliates in Europe.

Fifth, Japanese affiliates in Germany and the UK usually have a *simple management hierarchy* reflected in a management ladder such as President, department manager, section head, sub-section chief, foreman and finally rank-and-file workers. This management ladder eliminates deputy department manager, assistant department manager, assistant section head, etc, which are usually used in Japanese companies. In that sense, the management organization of Japanese affiliates is simple and flat. There are many reasons for this simplicity. One may be that European factories are not as large as their Japanese counterparts. Another may be that engineering and sales functions are usually carried out by Japanese headquarters or other Japanese affiliates in Europe. Therefore, the management organization of Japanese affiliates' factories resembles Japanese companies producing small types of products in large volume.

The development of managers in Japanese affiliates is usually done by the *internal promotion system*. The key managers or executives of Japanese affiliates are usually recruited by head-hunting local managers from the same industry. The key local manager usually decides to recruit other managers and employees. The vacant positions of managers are as a principle filled by internal promotion of local employees, which is a popular practice in the Japanese style of management.

Judging from the observations mentioned above, the author concludes that many practices of Japanese management organization are already applied in Japanese affiliates in Germany and the UK. However the principle of individualism of European managers cannot easily be 'Japanized' even though Japanese affiliates promote information-sharing among managers. Managers below departmental heads insist on carrying out their own duties by defining their job demarcation as a profession and do not like to take group responsibility for their company as a whole, although directors often voice their opinion outside their own professional territory. These managers prefer to take a narrowly defined view of their own responsibility, sharing information with other managers rather than their company as a whole.

PERSONNEL MANAGEMENT

Employment

One of the elementary factors of successful 'Japanese management' in foreign countries is its acceptance by local employees including white- as well as blue-collar workers. However, the acceptance of 'Japanese management' depends not only on how much Japanese affiliates adapt to local management practices, but also on how successfully they can select employees who will accept 'Japanese management' practices. In other words, Japanese affiliates can apply 'Japanese management' practices to the local employees without much trouble if they can hire employees who can easily follow Japanese practices.

We can identify two groups of Japanese affiliates, depending on their employment policies. The first group consists of companies which declare the acceptance by employees of Japanese practices as a *criterion of employment*. These intend to hire only applicants who clearly accept 'Japanese management' practices which reflect the main philosophy of Japanese headquarters – group production, job rotation, multi-skilling, etc. – at the recruiting examination. Applicants who insist on individualism as the principle of their work activities will not be selected by these Japanese affiliates. When a Japanese affiliate starts an operation as a joint venture, it usually discharges all of the former local employees and rehires only employees who declare their acceptance of the Japanese way of working. Employees who have accepted Japanese practices at the hiring point can quickly become accustomed to the Japanese way of working after their induction training. This approach has been common among Japanese affiliates starting their operation from the latter half of the 1980s.

Generally speaking, Japanese affiliates usually hire a local personnel manager who is in charge of all of the aspects of its personnel management. The degree to which he or she understands the spirit and mechanism of 'Japanese management' determines the success of implanting it. Many local personnel managers interviewed by the author were sceptical about their native practices of personnel management and had studied Japanese management as an alternative before they joined the Japanese affiliate; they were therefore commited to the application of Japanese practices as much as possible in the affiliates.

The other group of Japanese affiliates do not stick to Japanese practices or philosophy of management. They intend to hire local employees only on the basis of their *skill and knowledge necessary for the jobs*, without any explanation of the philosophy of their company at the interview. Although only a small group, it shows that there are some Japanese affiliates following the hiring practices of the host countries. These Japanese affiliates do not intend to rigidly apply the original Japanese practice of management to their local factories.

Education and Training

It is well known that Japanese companies provide well established, in-house training to both blue- and white-collar employees. Japanese affiliates also emphasize the importance of on-the-job training (OJT) for local workers. Japanese skilled workers may be dispatched from the Japanese mother plant to work as advisers for the improvement of local workers' skills. In other cases, local leaders receive OJT in the Japanese mother plant and then teach new skills and know-how to local operators. This type of OJT promotes the easy transfer of operators' skills from the Japanese mother plant to local workers in affiliates in Europe.

Japanese training managers often observe that foreign workers receiving training in Japanese mother plants do not transfer the skill and knowledge they obtained on their Japanese training course to other local employees. It may be that individualistic workers, who are accustomed to keeping things to themselves, do not like to release valuable information to their colleagues at the same level. However, many Japanese managers in the Japanese affiliates reported that the local workers who receive additional training in Japanese mother plants will often teach their skills to their subordinate workers once they are given a leader's position in their local plant. They sometimes write a special manual about aspects of the work procedure and behaviour which would not be so clearly recognized by Japanese workers. A Japanese manager said that he could understand work procedure and tacit knowledge of the operations which were made explicit by OJT teaching by senior workers. Therefore the OJT of local workers in Japanese mother plants contributes both to transfer of Japanese skills to local workers and to making the operational skill of Japanese workers more objective.

The education of white-collar employees in Japanese affiliates cannot be accomplished only by OJT. In the UK, for example, white-collar employees who want to obtain knowledge and skill in professions like finance, marketing and design have to attend a business school or part-time university course. When they request such professional training their managers usually permit them to attend. The companies accept the training expense as a kind of social cost for building professional workers, since some employees move to other companies after finishing their education. Japanese companies would not easily accept such a social cost.

Wages

All of the Japanese affiliates interviewed by the author in Germany and UK determined wage rates via job classification. The wage rates of companies belonging to an employers' association in their local area are usually determined by collective agreement in that area. The wage rates of companies not belonging to employers' associations are determined by the company itself, taking into consideration relevant local collective agreements. Japanese affiliates do not usually apply the seniority principle to the wages of their employees nor do they apply the principle of annual wage increases which is usual in Japan. Nor do they give large bonuses to their employees. Instead, they provide two or three weeks' worth of wages to their employees at the end of the financial year. Therefore we conclude that Japanese affiliates do not usually implement the seniority wage system adopted by Japanese mother plants.

The main way for workers to increase their wages is to climb up the ladder which determines the wage rate of each qualification. Young workers would improve their wages by complementing their qualification with training within and outside their company. Under these conditions the wages of young workers seem to increase until the age of

30, which looks like a seniority wage system. However, because these increases are based not on their seniority but on the improvement of their qualification, this principle differs fundamentally from that of a seniority wage system.

Wage rate differences are an important aspect of wage systems and provide financial incentives to employees. However, it is very difficult to obtain realistic data about these, because wage levels for each class of job are usually confidential. The author therefore tried to gain an impression from Japanese managers concerning wage rate differentials in Germany and the UK compared with those of their Japanese counterparts. Many Japanese personnel managers replied that wage rate differentials among blue-collar workers in Germany and UK were very close to the Japanese ratios, but salary differentials among directors, managers and white-collar workers were much larger than those of Japanese companies. They stated that the salary differentials among white-collar employees, including managers and executives, are also much bigger than those of Japanese companies.

Judging by this information, wage differentials of employees in Germany and the UK based on job classification are larger than those of Japanese companies. We can easily imagine that white-collar employees compete with each other for higher position within their organization and higher social status, more discretion and a higher salary in both European countries. The absolute level of wages seems to be an important factor in determining the country and location for FDI. Some Japanese affiliates invested more in Scotland than in England owing to cheaper wages. However, some Japanese affiliates built a new semiconductor plant in Germany where the general wage level is the highest in Europe. The wage level of a country, therefore, cannot be said to be the most important factor for deciding the place for FDI. In the case of semiconductor manufacturing, the proportion of wage in total production cost seems to be small owing to the large fixed cost of facilities.

In assembly industries such as TV and videotape recorder production, the wage level and skill level of workers may play an important role in determining the location of FDI. It sometimes happens that FDI moves to a new place owing to the wage level differentials between assembly workers for belt-conveyer lines. Annual wages for these in 1994 were around £6500–7500 in Wales, £7500 in England and £6000–7000 in Scotland; consequently, some Japanese affiliates intend to make new investments in Scotland. However, the differentials between labour cost per unit of product and wage in the UK seem to be smaller than those in Japan because of the smaller amount of fringe benefits.

Merit Rating

It is often said that the introduction of a merit rating programme is very difficult in the USA and Europe because of strong opposition from trade unions. From the unions' standpoint, the practice of merit rating stimulates competition among workers and, therefore, undermines the solidarity of trade union members. Truly objective evaluations of performance of each worker in different jobs cannot be established easily enough to prevent nepotism among evaluators.

However, some Japanese affiliates adopted merit rating plans in Germany and the UK. As mentioned already, one Japanese affiliate in Germany included absenteeism as an evaluating item for merit rating with the agreement of work councils; this merit rating contributed to a reduction of absenteeism among the employees. A Japanese affiliate in the UK also introduced a merit rating system with employees themselves agreeing the ratings. We could not identify how many Japanese affiliates applied the merit rating system in Germany and the UK, but our attention was attracted to the use of the system by some Japanese affiliates, despite lack of favour among trade union members.

Job Description

Japanese organizations are often said to differ from those of Western countries in the clarity and concreteness of job content. Job content in Western countries is clearly defined to make an employment contract. Therefore when a manager requests some additional activities outside the job content, the worker usually demands additional payment.

In contrast, job content in Japan can be flexible depending on the worker who carries out the job, and standard job contents are officially written in ambiguous words. It may not be effective for an organization as a whole to define rigid boundaries for each job when workers often change their job by a job rotation system and accomplish their task by a team: a worker would be criticized by his colleagues if he or she insisted on limited job content based rigidly on the job description.

The author asked the Japanese affiliates whether they have rigid job descriptions in Germany and the UK. A research centre of Japanese companies in the UK replied that it did not intentionally prepare job descriptions. The tasks for each employee were assigned by the director of that centre, and employees had to be very flexible depending on the projects assigned. Remuneration for each employee was determined not by job description but by consultation between each employee and his or her project leader. The director did not intend to use job descriptions for determining remuneration in order to avoid problems in negotiations between employees and the director.

For Japanese companies planning to introduce Japanese work organization in foreign countries, the rigid job descriptions of the host country, established through negotiations between trade unions and companies, is an obstacle to change. Japanese affiliates integrated many categories at the shopfloor level into two groups of job. Some other Japanese affiliates were able to reduce the number of job categories by restructuring the organization at the start of a joint venture. This strategy, to integrate many jobs into a few categories of job group, was successful at NUMMI (New United Motor Manufacturing, Inc.) in the USA. With reduced categories, they implemented the flexible utilization of employees by job rotation or transfer without negotiation as employment conditions of the new job. Japanese managers reported that young employees successfully adapted to new categories of the job while some older workers had difficulty in working with the new job contents, which contained several former jobs. The compromise between the Japanese idea of ambiguous job content and the concept of rigid job content in European countries resulted in grouping a few categories of jobs. These innovations in work organization by Japanese affiliates in the UK may lead to changes in the traditional principles of job demarcation.

In Germany, however, it seems difficult for a company to introduce a new classification of jobs because, generally speaking, the contents of a new job have to be established by consensus among the representatives of employers and trade unions and specialists of occupations representing the public who are independent of each company. The training and education required and the remuneration for each job are usually determined on the basis of a standardized job content. Japanese affiliates cannot introduce a new job category outside these standardized job descriptions in each local area. This is also one of the main reasons why Japanese affiliates feel it is more difficult to apply QC activity and work teams to German industry than in the UK.

INDUSTRIAL RELATIONS

Japanese managers were concerned about their relations with local trade unions in host countries where they planned investment, especially in industrialized countries in the 1960s and 1970s. One of the main reasons was the historical fact that trade unions in Japan were first recognized by law after the Second World War and that the enterprise unionism of Japan differs from the craft unionism and industrial unionism of Western countries. However, these worries have been mitigated by the success of Toshiba's dealings with trade unions at NUMMI. Nevertheless, Japanese companies still prefer to avoid any troubles with trade unions – or, at best, not to bargain with them in host countries.

One example of successful dealing with trade unions by Japanese affiliates in the UK is the case of Toshiba UK, who successfully established a Japanese style of management after starting a joint venture with Philips. The main characteristics were, first, a 'single-union' agreement and, second, the 'non-strike' clause in their collective agreement.

The 'single-union' clause means that the company will bargain with only one trade union which represents several trade unions within the company. Under this clause, the company can save the time and energy of bargaining several times. Toshiba's success with an agreement to a 'single-union' clause indicates that new trade union and management relations can be possible even in the traditional atmosphere of industrial relations in the UK.

The 'non-strike' clause means that the trade unions and the management do not rely on strikes but on arbitration outside the company when they cannot reach agreement. This presupposes a labour court, which does not exist in Japan. These single-union and non-strike clauses of Japanese affiliates contribute to peaceful industrial relations in the UK where industrial relations seem to be more antagonistic than in Japan.

One of the mechanisms of peaceful industrial relations in Japan is the labour–management consultation system. This system reaches consensus between employees and management by regular meetings or repetitive consultations which do not presuppose strikes. Representatives of employees in this system can understand the situation of their company within the industry through information provided by the management at the consulting table. The frank and sometimes confidential exchange of company information and employees' opinions promotes mutual understanding between the two parties.

Almost the same functions as a labour–management consultation system can be carried out by the Works Councils of Japanese affiliates in Germany. Works Councils are required by law in companies employing more than 50 employees, which is not the case in Japan. Japanese affiliates try to perform the same function in Works Councils as in labour–management consultation.

The stance and activities of the employees' representatives on the Works Council towards the management are an important factor in peaceful industrial relations in Japanese affiliates in Germany. As far as the author could determine, some representatives of the Works Council are trade union members, but the proportion is small at present. It was not the case that these representatives acted with direction from trade unions, nor did they stimulate an antagonistic atmosphere at the Works Council. The trade unions' influence in Works Councils seems to be small in Japanese affiliates. The management usually attributes a positive role to the Works Council as an effective communication channel for mutual understanding between employees and management.

A peaceful Works Council does not necessarily mean that Japanese affiliates can successfully deal with trade unions as a whole, however. Most of the Japanese affiliates visited by the author were located on so-called 'green sites' remote from the influence of trade unions. At a 'green site', the price of land is cheap and workers tend not to have affiliations with trade unions which might oppose the management. This may not reflect the importance of trade unions in determining the location of FDI, but it is the fact that many Japanese affiliates have settled in 'green sites.'

The 'green site' locations of Japanese affiliates does not mean that their employees do not belong to any trade unions. A Japanese manager of one Japanese affiliate in Germany said that about 10–20 per cent of employees were trade union members, and some representatives on the shopfloor were union members. However, trade union members cannot dominate the opinions of the employees when trade union density is at such a low level. A representative of a local trade union sometimes comes to the employees' meeting of a Japanese affiliate, but it is a polite formality so the opinions of local trade unions do not lead the opinions of employees at the moment. Consequently from my impression of the attitudes of personnel managers interviewed, managers of Japanese affiliates seem to be confident when dealing with trade unions in the UK and Germany.

ROLES OF JAPANESE PERSONNEL

Despite the process of localization of personnel, some Japanese managers and employees are still working in Japanese affiliates in Germany and the UK. What positions within the organizations are occupied by

Japanese? What roles do Japanese personnel play in the process of localization of management at Japanese affiliates?

The number of Japanese personnel was smaller than the author expected, although the degree of localization varies depending on management strategy and the year of foundation. The number of Japanese personnel is usually reduced drastically after the establishment of a plant. However, when new products or new facilities are introduced in the plant, so-called 'supporters' from Japan increase, although the managers of the plant do their best to keep their number as small as possible.

On the other hand, the Japanese managers have to consider what positions should be left to Japanese as a minimum requirement. Many of the Japanese managers interviewed replied that the positions of President, financial department manager and a staff position in the production technology department should be for Japanese personnel where a Japanese mother company held 100 per cent of stock of the company. A Japanese engineer would be indispensable for communicating precise technological problems and requirements to a Japanese mother factory. The engineer should not necessarily be a production manager, but would have to be familiar with all aspects of the production technology. Other positions besides these three should be localized to local employees of the host country. Consequently, Japanese personnel do not usually take the position of managers but of assistants to line managers.

When the number of supporters increases or communication in English or German does not work effectively, unofficial line organization by these Japanese personnel sometimes develops. A Japanese affiliate calls this informal organization 'shadow management'. This 'shadow management' would disappear through the localization process, but might be necessary until the establishment of the production system. One of the Japanese affiliates has a local President; this company succeeds in living with its host community owing to a high development of localization. It is expected that most Japanese affiliates will attempt a high degree of localization as there are benefits in the localization of top management, besides providing both financial and moral incentives to local managers.

First, a local President can easily obtain information about political, as well as economic affairs, in the local area through a personal network. Economic affairs cannot be clearly separate from political affairs – as indicated, for example, by the political consultation about international trade between the US and Japanese governments. A local

President can quickly respond to economic changes by understanding political trends in the local area. He can bridge the gap between the local political world and the Japanese economic world. A Japanese President of a Japanese affiliate can hardly build a personal network with local politicians even if he speaks English or German fluently.

Second, a local President is sometimes a leader of the economic world in the local area. He often considers the development of his Japanese affiliate equal to the economic development of the community. Therefore, a local President helps Japanese affiliates to live with the host community. The localization of the managers of Japanese affiliates promotes the implanting of 'Japanese management' in host countries.

CONCLUSIONS

This chapter has described what aspects of, and how much, the Japanese style of management is practised in some Japanese affiliates in the automobile, electronics and semiconductor industries in Germany and the UK through interviews with their managers. Based on these interviews and the author's impressions from the factory visits, the following points can be summarized:

(1) Technological determinism of the social system cannot be applied to Japanese affiliates without any preconditions. Their work organization and way of work are somewhat different from those of the mother plant in Japan despite the fact that most of their facilities are designed and produced in Japan.
(2) The so-called 'three sacred pillars' of traditional Japanese management (seniority wage system, lifetime employment and enterprise union) hardly exist in the Japanese affiliates researched in Germany and the UK.
(3) Team work, multi-skilled workers, QCs and information-sharing, which are among the main characteristic of the 'loosely-structured organization' under the new style of 'Japanese management', are practised, or have at least been tried to be introduced, by some Japanese affiliates.
(4) The new style of 'Japanese management' is more easily accepted in the UK where the sense of community is more common than in Germany, where the idea of individualism is dominant in social life.

(5) There are two groups of Japanese affiliates. One makes the effort to introduce almost the same practices of management as the mother plant in Japan, by selecting employees who can accept group work and by training them in the Japanese way of working. These companies often clearly express their basic policy such as the 'Toyotaism' and the 'Canon' way of production. The other intends to adapt their way of management to each set of local practices. They do not stick to their original way of management in Japan.

(6) Some Japanese affiliates which have made a long effort to apply the Japanese practices of management to their local plant, or which use quite new facilities within local industries, can apply some practices of personnel management characteristic of the 'loosely-structured organization'.

(7) The establishment of these practices of new-style 'Japanese management' in the local plants of Japanese affiliates can be possible only within the plant, and cannot spread over other plants in the same local area. The spread of the Japanese practices of management to other plants in the host country will require some changes in social institutions such as the training and educational system, industrial relations, etc., which exist outside the control of the company.

Appendix 1: List of Japanese Affiliates Interviewed in Germany and the UK

Japanese Manufacturing Companies Interviewed in Germany, 1994

Matsushita Video Manufacturing GmbH
Star Micronics Manufacturing Deutschland GmbH
Canon Giessen GmbH
Denon Consumer Electronics GmbH
Alps Electric Europa GmbH
Mitsubishi Semiconductor Europe GmbH
Develop Dr. Eisbein GmbH & Co.
Hitachi Semicondector (Europe) GmbH
Sanyo Industries Deutschland GmbH

List of German Companies Interviewed, 1994

Electro-Recycling-Nord GmbH
Denkhaus Logistik GmbH

Japanese Companies Interviewed in Great Britain, 1994

Fujitsu Europe
Toyota Moter Manufacturing (UK) Ltd
Nissan Motor Manufacturing (UK) Ltd
Canon Research Centre Europe Ltd
Honda of the UK Manufacturing Ltd
Sony Manufacturing Company UK
Sanyo Industries (UK) Ltd
Panasonic Matsushita Electric (UK) Ltd
ALPS Electric (UK) Ltd
NEC Semiconductor (UK) Ltd
Hitachi Consumer Products (UK) Ltd
Heysham 2 Power Station
Mitsubishi Electric UK
Apricot Computer Ltd
AIWA (UK) Ltd
Toshiba Consumer Products (UK) Ltd

Appendix 2: Research Items About Japanese Companies in Europe

1 Locating in Europe

(1) Has the company been established as a joint concern or a wholly invested company?
(2) Does the company use the existing facilities as they are or build new facilities?
(3) Does the company take account of policies about tariffs in the EU market?
(4) What are the competitive advantages attributable to locating in Europe?
(5) Is the company invited to locate there by the local government?

2 Role of the Factory

(1) Does the factory produce only for the EU market or other markets?
(2) Does the factory produce only one category of product or several categories of product?
(3) Does the factory only manufacture products or also design products?
(4) What is the company's future expansion plan?

3 Extent of Autonomy the Business Unit Has

(1) Does the company have some product development functions?
(2) To what extent is the company closely related with dealers in local area?
(3) Does the company have discretion to procure machines and equipments?
(4) To what extent is the company allowed to invest in the local market at its own discretion?
(5) Does the company pay a royalty to its headquarters?
(6) How does the company decide an intra-company transfer price?
(7) What division does the company place a R&D function in?
(8) What division coordinates the business of several business units?

4 Relations to Companies the Company has been Dealing With

(1) Does the company give some technical assistance to suppliers or develop products with them?
(2) Is the relation between the company and suppliers short-term or long-term?
(3) Is the company closely related with affiliated companies in Japan?

5 Layout of the Factory

(1) Who designed the layout of the factory and where is it designed?
(2) Does the company procure machines and equipment in the host country or import them from Japan?

6 Production System

(1) Is the production system a single-product and mass-production system or a multi-product and mass-production system?
(2) Is the production system a one-way system or a network system?

7 Work Organization of Blue-collar Workers (at Shopfloor Level)

(1) Does the factory assign a group of jobs to a work group (*han*, block, team-work) or one job to each worker?
(2) Does the factory put job rotation into practice? And who decides it, the personnel department or each supervisor?
(3) Does the factory intend to cultivate multi-skilled workers? And to what extent can it cultivate them?
(4) Does the factory implement some group activities (e.g. sports club activities)?

8 Attitudes of Workers Towards Work

(1) What percentage is the absenteeism rate in the company?
(2) Does a suggestion system work with success in the company?
(3) What kind of practices does the company introduce to improve the quality of work?
(4) Are QC and *Kaizen* (activities for improvement) implemented now in the company?
(5) Are 5S activities implemented now in the factory?

9 Work Organization of White-collar Workers (at Office Level)

(1) Are many people working together in one big room?
(2) Does each manager have his or her own office?
(3) Do employees help to work one another within the section, or does each employee perform his or her own duty? (How does the layout of desks influence division of labour among them?)
(4) Is the management ladder from president to section head in the company flatter than that of typical Japanese companies?
(5) To what extent does a salary gap among levels of management ladder exist?
(6) Does the company transfer employees among functions or fix employees in one section to specialize?
(7) Do directors often propose something beyond their own sections?
(8) Do employees have loyalty to the company?

(9)   Has the company ever experienced any headhunting?
(10) Does each section tend to hold information for itself or to transfer information to other sections horizontally and vertically?
(11) Is there any overtime work without overtime payment?

10   Engineers

(1)   Does the company recruit engineers on a local level or a nation-wide level?
(2)   Does the company have single-status practices? And do its employees wear a uniform?
(3)   Is the production engineer's office room located near to a shopfloor?
(4)   Does the engineer have an individual office or work together with other employees in one big room?

11   Information-sharing

(1)   Can employees understand the meaning of each process of production with visual management aids?
(2)   Can they understand the target and outcome of each production process?
(3)   Do employees have a meeting in every group, and do all department managers have a meeting together?
(4)   Does the factory have some meetings at which factory manager and a representative of employees or all employees attend together?
(5)   Is a handbook for employees printed?
(6)   Are some notices about goals or slogans posted on the wall in order to enable all employees working in the factory to find them?
(7)   Does the company send employees many times to Japan?

12   Philosophy

(1)   Does the company have some formalized manuals such as 'Canon-Way', 'Toyota-Way', 'Honda-Way'?
(2)   Is a notice about the company's philosophy posted on a board on the shopfloor?

13   Criteria of Recruitment

(1)   Does the company prefer employees promoted within the company or mid-career applicants who have worked at other companies?
(2)   Does the company choose applicants who agree to work in the Japanese way or have high ability?
(3)   Is the separation rate of the employees above the local average or below it?
(4)   Does the company take into account the local market or the national market for recruitment?
(5)   Does the company use a headhunter?

14 Groups of Jobs and Hierarchies of Management

(1) How many jobs does the company have?
(2) Is the wage rate gap within a job big or small?
(3) How many hierarchical levels are there within a job group?

15 Wages

(1) How much is the wage rate of the lowest job?
(2) What is the job title and wage rate of the job in which the largest number of employees engage?
(3) What are the job titles of those who do not belong to trade unions?
(4) How much is the difference between labour cost and wages?

16 Merit Rating

(1) How often is merit rating implemented in the company?
(2) What is the attendance rate of employees of the company?
(3) Is a signature by a manager necessary for merit rating?
(4) Is there any complaint about appraisals?

17 Job Description

(1) Is the content of job description rigid or obscure?
(2) Is the job description utilized in merit rating?

18 Education and Training

(1) What is the level of education just after employment?
(2) How often does the company use off-the-job training outside the company?
(3) How many employees apply for an MBA course?

19 Role of Japanese Employees

(1) What kind of job is a Japanese employee responsible for?
(2) In what kind of job do Japanese employees work as assistants?
(3) Do Japanese employees compose 'shadow management'?
(4) What language is used formally in the company?
(5) What positions remain for Japanese employees after localization of management?

20 Trade Unions

(1) Does the company have a trade union?
(2) What percentage of employees in the company join the union(s)?
(3) Does the company have any employee representative system?
(4) Does the company have a collective agreement?

174   *Japanese Affiliates in Germany and the UK*

Note

*The author would like to take this opportunity to express appreciation to the companies and their people who kindly participated in the investigation, and to the Chambers of Commerce in Düsseldorf and London for their help. The author also appreciates the frank and open contributions of company employees interviewed.

References

Emery, E. and Thorsrud, F. (1976) *Democracy at Work: The Report of the Norwegian Industrial Democracy Programme*, Leiden, Martinus Nijhoff Social Science Division, 4–6.
Okubayashi, K. (1995) 'Japanese Effects of New Technology on Organization and Work', *Zeitschrift für Betriebswirtshaft*, Ergänzungsheft, 4–1995.

10 Global Companies and Local Markets: The Internationalization of Product Design and Development Activities*

Andrew D. James and Jeremy Howells

INTRODUCTION

The focus of this chapter is on the internationalization of the product design and development activities of multinational enterprises.[1] In particular, the analysis centres on East Asian firms and the implications that the internationalization of their innovative activities might have for the international transfer of management practices and technological knowledge. Drawing on case studies of the UK product design and development activities of one Japanese company (Nissan) and two South Korean companies (Daewoo Automotive and Samsung Electronics), factors influencing the internationalization of their product design and development activities are studied. It is argued that the internationalization of innovative activities can be seen to have been driven, on the one hand, by a desire to get closer to the customer in locally differentiated markets and, on the other, by a need to access technological capabilities specific to particular national innovation systems. The implications for the transfer of management practices and technological knowledge depends on the market orientation and technology strategy of the individual company. These are likely to influence the type of innovative activities they conduct overseas, the factors that influence their location decisions and their impact on the innovation system of the host nation.

It should be acknowledged that design and development represents one aspect of the production and exploitation of new knowledge in a company. Internationalization of other activities that contribute to knowledge production and exploitation can be seen in the growing

175

trend amongst companies to establish overseas centres focused on applied research (Turner, Ray and Hayward, 1997). This chapter therefore considers key issues that arise in relation to the internationalization of a certain sub-set of innovative activities – namely, product design and development. In the next section the persistence of local differences in markets and technological activity despite trends towards economic globalization is discussed. The chapter then goes on to explore the growing internationalization of the innovation process within large firms. This is followed by the analysis of case studies of UK product design and development in three East Asian companies and how these fit into their international business activities. A number of themes emerging from these case studies are discussed before finally some tentative conclusions from this research study to date are presented.

Inevitably, the financial crisis that struck Asia in 1998 will have implications for the international activities of East Asian companies; already, planned investments in the UK have been delayed or cancelled. Given that the study on which this chapter is based was completed before the events of 1998, we cannot comment directly on these matters from our case study material. Nevertheless, an understanding of the factors that have influenced the internationalization of their innovative activities may contribute to an assessment of the robustness of such investments and their contribution to the UK economy.

LOCAL DIFFERENCES IN MARKETS AND TECHNOLOGICAL ACTIVITY

Notions of economic and cultural globalization have become common currency in popular discourse and policy debates. Nevertheless, it remains the case that, in important respects, technological activity and market requirements continue to be locationally differentiated. Market requirements and customer tastes continue to differ as a consequence of, among other things, differences in national regulations and economic institutions as well as harder to define national variations in culture and life style.

Important differences also persist in national innovative capabilities, and the reasons for these differences have been the focus of the national innovation systems' approach associated with, among others, Freeman (1988) and Carlsson (1995). The national innovation systems' approach pays particular attention to those institutions and relationships located within the borders of a nation state which interact in the production, diffusion and use of new knowledge. In particular, it has focused on the similarities and differences between national innovation systems and the extent and manner in which these differences explain variations in national economic and innovative performance. The research on national innovation systems emphasizes the importance to the innovation system of both formal institutions and relationships, but also informal activities and structures, including processes of network formation, communication patterns between firms and policy makers and informal knowledge trading. These innovation systems may be sectorally specific, with different patterns of interaction between the sectors in a national context. At the same time, the sectoral systems, although rooted within national boundaries, can also spill over national territories as well. This is, in part, because scientific and technological activity is increasingly international in its creation and dissemination, but also reflects the existence of multinational enterprises which are increasingly configuring and co-ordinating their technology on a global level.

It is emphasized here that the distinctive characteristics of national innovation systems provide multinational enterprises with an incentive to disperse their research, design and development facilities. Internationalization of their innovative activities allows multinationals access to technological capabilities that are specific to particular national innovation systems which they can then integrate at the corporate level (Chesnais, 1992). Equally, it allows companies to get closer to customers and users. This suggests that the particular characteristics of national innovation systems may have a growing influence on the decisions of multinational companies regarding investment and divestment and their strategies regarding the location of research, design and development, production and other activities. Reich (1991) argues that the scientific and human resource endowments of countries are likely to be of growing importance to the prosperity of individual states because they may confer advantages in attracting and retaining innovative and high value added activities. In the same vein, Chesnais (1992) observes that, if the most fundamental resource in the modern economy is knowledge and the most important process is learning, then we might expect that the locational advantages of a country will be increasingly related to knowledge-intensiveness, the capacity to participate actively in the production of technology and the possession of agglomeration economies which bring together the complementary assets needed for successful innovation. This is a very different perspective to the traditional policy concerns about the attractiveness of a particular location to multinational investment. These have focused on labour costs, the availability of direct subsidies from national governments, access to large and/or high income markets, quality of communications infrastructure and the like.

Learning and knowledge interaction still remain highly geographically bounded within national innovation systems. Learning is predominantly a social activity which involves person-embodied acquisition patterns rooted in direct, localized learning and experience. As such, learning at a distance is constrained (although not impossible, Crook, 1994) especially where it requires a high tacit knowledge component where 'social presence' associated with face-to-face contact is important (Howells, 1995). Within a national innovation system, a company can gain new knowledge through collaboration with other firms in the same industry or sector (horizontal collaboration) or via collaboration backwards with suppliers, or forwards with firms further up the production or marketing chain. New knowledge can also be gained through intermediaries, such as design and technical consultancies, that undertake specific design, prototyping or test services. Lundvall (1992) emphasizes the importance of this 'learning by interacting' in the context of user–producer relationships. The importance of such informal learning and tacit knowledge in technological development in the process equipment technology, particularly scientific instruments, machine tools and advanced manufacturing technologies, is well known. Certainly, the work of Von Hippel has illustrated the importance of the user's practical experiences in using scientific instruments, and the tacit knowledge gained from this, as a valuable input to instrument makers in their further refinement and development of their products (Von Hippel, 1989). Equally, getting 'close to the customer' has been an important theme in the innovative activities of firms across a range of sectors (Macdonald, 1995).

At the same time, internationalization of innovative activities presents opportunities for the transfer of management practices and technological knowledge between national innovation systems. This may involve the transfer of technological knowledge embedded in the national innovation system of the host country back to the multinational's home country. Such technological knowledge generated by and embedded in the national innovation system may include understanding of user requirements, general technological capabilities and capabilities in specific product areas as well as harder to specify creative ideas and practical experience generated through formal and informal learning processes (Howells, 1998). Such transfers of technological knowledge have prompted concerns about scientific 'hollowing out'. By this is meant the danger that foreign companies merely transfer scientific knowledge to the home country, where commercialization takes place with minimal benefit to the host economy. Certainly, there may be substantial costs attached to inward investment if it means, as is sometimes argued, that the national innovation system simply becomes an appendage of foreign innovation systems and such linkages are used mainly to support production elsewhere in the world (Walker, 1993).

However, it may equally be the case that the internationalization of innovative activities may present opportunities for the transfer of technological knowledge and management practices from the home nation of the multinational to the host country. Attracting innovative activities may help strengthen national innovative capabilities and help avoid the 'branch-plant economy' syndrome sometimes argued to be associated with inward investment. It may also provide opportunities for learning where the management practices of the inward investor are in some way superior to those used in the host economy.

Clearly, local differences in markets and technological activity persist. Equally, though, at least in some sectors, the international transfer of management practices and technological knowledge between national innovation systems may cause sectoral innovation systems to spill over national boundaries.

THE INTERNATIONALIZATION OF THE INNOVATION PROCESS

Historically, most international companies have tended to undertake the majority of their innovative activities within their home national innovation system (Patel, 1995). Indeed, despite an increase in the internationalization of innovative activity, the great bulk of innovative activity continues to be concentrated in multinationals' home countries. The proportion of R&D activity undertaken by multinationals outside their home countries remains quite small – or, in the case of Japan, negligible.[2] Similarly, Lorenz (1995) argues that, just as most multinationals' cutting-edge R&D is located in the home country, so the design and development of advanced new products occurs in the home country with most foreign design work consisting mainly of local or regional adaptation of those products.

This reflects the locational rigidity of innovative activities (Howells, 1990). Much of the existing spatial pattern of R&D in industry has changed very little since its initial establishment and this has resulted in a highly static spatial pattern of existing research laboratories. Possible factors behind this low locational mobility of existing innovative activities may be seen in work by Gibbs *et al*. (1985) who found that not only were research operations extremely cost-insensitive in terms of location but companies were particularly concerned about losing key research staff if they decided to move their research laboratories elsewhere. This geographical rigidity is heightened by the fact that in existing companies new R&D units are frequently located at, or near to, existing corporate research establishments to maintain good research communication flows. The benefits of research concentration include the benefits of economies of scale and scope associated with larger R&D operations (Scherer, 1970); minimum efficient size associated with indivisibilities of certain scientific instruments, facilities or specialist staff; good internal communication links within the R&D function (Allen, 1977); increased security over in-house research and reducing the risk of competitor copying or 'leapfrogging' in key research fields (Pearce, 1989) and the ability to create a well established dense local innovation network with higher education institutes (HEIs), contract research companies and other support agencies and related institutions.

Notwithstanding the historic locational rigidity of innovative activities, an increasingly large number of companies in the electronics, pharmaceuticals and automotive sectors, among others, are establishing global R&D networks (Howells, 1990). Developments in information and communication technologies are undoubtedly changing the structure and nature of research and design facilities operating abroad (Howells, 1995). The advent of telematics has increased the scope for the internationalization of innovative activities by multinational enterprises and the world-wide sourcing of technological knowledge (De Meyer, 1993). The growth in external research and technical links with both customers and suppliers has led to the acknowledgement by many companies that they need to locate specialized research and technical teams to engage in collaboration and also act as 'listening posts' in key technical 'hot-spots' around the world. Thus, Japan has been a growing centre for materials research for European and US companies. Such moves are also evident in growing collaborative links with overseas universities by major multinational corporations. Consequently, manufacturers may gain competitive advantage by upgrading the capabilities of their foreign factories through adding some form of research or product design and development activity (Taggart, 1997).

In addition, there have been managerial and organizational changes in the structure and operation of research and design activities within multinational companies. The first of these has been the appearance and development of overseas design and research units taking a lead role in a particular scientific field or product area. The second issue is that of more general managerial restructuring and refocusing. Many multinational corporations have sought to sharpen up their operations by devolving power down to divisional or business-unit level. This has affected how research and design is structured within these companies. Thus, some have got rid of their centralized corporate research and design facilities altogether, while others have introduced more complex patterns of restructuring.

These more complex patterns reflect attempts to achieve a trade-off between the benefits of globalization and proximity. Despite the availability and use of the latest information and communications technologies it does appear to be the case, at least in certain circumstances, that effective management of innovation – and, in particular, new product development – still requires close physical proximity between those involved in the various stages of design and development and those involved in other functions of the firm, such as production engineering, marketing and sales. Such changes, of course, do not mean that multinationals will necessarily choose their home country as the location for such activities but instead may lead to product mandates and greater autonomy for subsidiaries in local or regional markets. What is evident from this discussion is that many of these recent changes are leading to the growth and increasing complexity of multinationals' product design and development operations over time, associated in turn with a direct increase in the number and dispersion of design and development sites.

Clearly, the market orientation and technology strategy of a multinational company are likely to influence the type of innovative activity it conducts overseas and the factors that influence its decisions on where to locate such activities (Behrman and Fischer, 1980; Hood and Young, 1982; Howells, 1990). The distinction between 'home-base-augmenting' and 'home-base-exploiting' activities has been used to categorize these foreign R&D sites. The transfer of managerial practices and technological knowledge is likely to differ between them. The objective of a 'home-base-augmenting' site is to absorb knowledge from the local scientific community, creating new knowledge and transferring it *to* the company's central R&D site. To maximize the impact of the local site there is likely to be an emphasis on ensuring its active participation in the local community. This may involve the exchange of its researchers with local university laboratories (which may lead to a two-way transfer of technological knowledge between foreign company and host community). It may also include exchanges with home-base R&D activities to promote technology transfer to the company's central R&D site. In contrast, the objective of a 'home-base-exploiting' site is to commercialize knowledge by transferring it *from* the company's home base to the foreign site and from there to local manufacturing and marketing. To maximize the impact of the local site there is an emphasis on developing strong relationships with home-base R&D activities. The local site will also seek to develop good relations with its local manufacturing and marketing activities.

This dichotomy, while useful, does not do justice to the variety of types of international innovative activities that exist and the consequent flows involved (see, for example, Erdilek and Wolf, 1997). Thus, Behrman and Fischer (1980) identify three groups of multinationals, what they call home-market firms, host-market firms and world-market firms. Each tends to have rather different R&D patterns and we might also expect to see differences in their overseas product design and development activities, the factors influencing their decision on where to locate such activities and their impact on the host economy (see Table 10.1 for a summary).

Table 10.1   A typology of multinationals and their innovative activities

Market orientation	R&D activities	Product design/ development activities	Factors in location of product design / development activities
Home market	Little overseas R&D support laboratory	Adaptation of parent company technology to local markets	Market to be served
Host market	Locally integrated laboratories	Product innovation and development for local markets	Market to be served and local product design/ development capabilities
World market	International interdependent research laboratories	Product innovation and development for global markets	Local product design/ development capabilities

Sources: Adapted from Behrman and Fischer (1980); Hood and Young (1982).

- Starting with *home-market orientated* companies, it might be expected that their overseas product design and development activities will be limited to the adaptation of parent company technology and designs to local market needs. The location of overseas product design and development activities will be driven primarily by the market to be served and these overseas activities will assume only a subsidiary role in the product development activities of the parent firm. Their impact on the host economy in terms of the transfer of technological knowledge and creation of new local capabilities is likely to limited.

- In the case of *host-market orientated* companies, product design and development activities are likely to be more extensive with local centres engaged in product innovation and development for the specific needs of local markets and customers. The location of product design and development activities will be driven by the market to be served and access to local skills, capabilities and resources. Their impact on the host economy may well be significant with the development of new localized capabilities and some potential opportunities for learning from the management practices of the parent.

- Finally, in the case of *world-market orientated* companies, foreign product design and development activities are likely to be extensive and engaged in product innovation and development for global markets. The location of product design and development activities will be driven by the company's global production network and determined by the availability and distribution of skills, resources, and capabilities around the world. Product design and development activities serve global markets through a single global manufacturing network. The impact of local product design and development activities may be significant with research and design centres acting as 'centres of excellence' for the company world-wide and providing the focus for capability generation and technology transfer across the whole company.

Case Studies: Nissan, Daewoo Motor Company and Samsung Electronics

The typology set out in the previous section suggests that we might expect to see considerable organizational variety in the product design and development activities of multinational enterprises and the factors that influence their location decisions. In this section we present case studies of the UK product design and development activities of three companies: one Japanese (Nissan) and two South Korean (Daewoo Automotive and Samsung Electronics).[3] The UK is the location for the greatest concentration of Japanese R&D facilities in Europe and approximately one-third of all such European facilities are based in the UK. A survey in 1995 of the European operations of Japanese manufacturing companies found that 32 out of the 217 Japanese manufacturing operations in the UK surveyed undertook design activities of some kind (15 per cent). These companies include Hitachi, Nissan and Sony (JETRO, 1996). Turner, Ray and Hayward (1997) detailed the research, design and development activities of some 30 Japanese firms in the UK and found that they were engaged in a spectrum of activities from fundamental research at one end to product design and development at the other. The three case studies illustrate some of the drivers behind the internationalization of the innovative activities of East Asian companies and the character of the design and product development activities undertaken by the companies in the UK.

Nissan European Technology Centre (NETC)

Established in 1933, Nissan is a leading global automobile company manufacturing in Europe, North America, Africa, South America and South East Asia as well as its home country of Japan. Nissan led Japanese inward investment in motor manufacturing in the UK with its 1984 decision to open a plant in Sunderland. The plant, which opened in 1986, is now a major manufacturer of cars for the UK market and for export to Europe and Japan.

There has been a gradual evolution of design and development activities within Nissan which is reflected in both its global organization and the changing nature of design and development activities in the UK/Europe. At first, Nissan had designed, developed and manufactured cars in Japan and then exported them for sale in Europe. Gradually, the company's European activities evolved through the export of knock-down kits of parts from Japan for assembly overseas until it established overseas manufacturing plants such as Nissan Manufacturing UK (NMUK) in Sunderland in 1986 and NMISA in Spain, both with a high degree of local parts' content (Nakamura, 1997). NETC was established in 1988 as a design and development company separate from the Sunderland manufacturing plant. NETC began by sharing responsibility with technical centres in Japan and the USA, designing and developing cars made in European plants (Howells and Wood, 1993). NETC's main product design and development roles are the development of vehicles which satisfy the European market and customers; creating local designs to suit the European manufacturing plants and supporting on-going local production; and the development of components and systems with the company's European suppliers. Nissan's strategy is based on its concept of 'Globalization': production and sourcing decisions are based on markets and customer tastes, job share and global rational supply of parts. Nissan has three main development centres which are responsible for product design and development: NTC (Nissan Technology Centre), an 8000-employee facility located in Japan; NRD (Nissan Research and Development) located in Detroit, USA, employing 500 staff; and, NETC, with 380 employees in Europe. In addition, a small design unit (50 employees) was established when the Sunderland plant was built and this continues to have responsibility for testing and current model development.

Product design and development in Nissan, as in other car manufacturers, has to balance the need to satisfy local customer preferences, while maintaining an economic production volume. In an effort to do this within limited resources, Nissan is seeking to integrate product design and development activity on a global basis. This involves efforts to design globally common vehicle platforms and fundamental body structures and this requires strong integration within Nissan's global product design and development organizations. The main responsibility for co-ordinating platform design rests with Nissan's technical centre in Japan. NETC's role is to establish the best use of European technology for Nissan cars produced and marketed in Europe. In particular, NETC's responsibilities are component and system development with European suppliers; feeding these requirements into the global basic platform design; local adaptation of design specifications; and the suitable adaptation of European components, including off-the-shelf components (Nakamura, 1997). NETC is competing with Nissan's centres in the USA and Japan for future product development activity. Efficiency is seen to be a key factor in investment decisions. The USA has the advantage of being a single market rather than 13 different markets, as in Europe, and there are also more Japanese supporting suppliers' transplants in the USA than in Europe. NETC believes that if it can develop products better and more efficiently then it will be well placed to get future development work. Indeed, with integrated development, the key question becomes how design and development work is to be shared between Europe and Japan.

One of the key relationships for NETC is with its suppliers. Suppliers play an important and growing role in Nissan's product design and development activities through simultaneous engineering. Indeed, the decision to locate NETC at Cranfield, close to the core of the UK automotive supplier industry in the Midlands, reflects the weight given to developing long-term relationships. Automotive suppliers are now recognized by motor manufacturers as key members of the design team. This is not only because they supply 70 per cent of the final product and can input ideas to keep costs down but also because they ought to know more about emerging technologies and customer expectations of their products. The challenge to Nissan is to change the view of their suppliers with regard to their role in new product development. NETC also has an important role in accessing external sources of information to feed into the product development process. Customer reaction to current products is assessed through independently run surveys and Nissan seek to judge future customer requirements through clinics and testing.

In Nissan's view, the UK's strengths as a location for design and development activities relate to the infrastructure that exists in the form of professional organizations like the Institute of Mechanical Engineers (IME), world-renowned universities, and the perception of London as a major centre of style and fashion. In terms of weaknesses, from the Japanese there is the perception that the UK is isolated in Europe.

Daewoo Motor Company

The South Korean Daewoo Group, formed 30 years ago, is a diversified conglomerate with interests in construction, ship building, motor vehicle and component manufacturing, heavy industry and machinery, electronics and consumer goods, telecommunications equipment, textiles and financial services. With sales of over £38 billion, 25 domestic companies, 253 overseas subsidiaries and over 210 000 employees, Daewoo Group was ranked the 31st largest company in the world by *Fortune* magazine before the Asian financial crisis. The Group's automotive division, Daewoo Motor Company, is midway through a major development programme which was designed to make it one of the world's top 10 vehicle manufacturers by the year 2000. Through joint ventures and international acquisitions, Daewoo Motor Company has sought to develop an international vehicle production capability, with car plants being developed in India, Vietnam, China, Iran, the Philippines, Indonesia, Uzbekistan, the Czech Republic, Romania and Poland as well as its established vehicle plants in South Korea. Supporting these production plants, Daewoo Motor Company has three technical centres in South Korea (Pupyoung), Germany (Munich) and the UK (Worthing).

Daewoo established its Worthing Technical Centre (DWTC) through the acquisition of the assets of IAD (International Automotive Design) Ltd in 1994. IAD, a leading independent design house with wide experience with a variety of automotive manufacturers, had gone into receivership in 1993. Acquisition was seen by Daewoo as an ideal opportunity to acquire key skills and expertise as part of an industrial design strategy focused on gaining access to design capabilities and local design knowledge to design cars for European and other markets. The role of DWTC is to provide R&D and product development support on a world-wide basis as part of Daewoo's 'globalization' strategy and in particular to support the company's plants in Poland, Romania, the Czech Republic and Uzbekistan. Since acquisition, the number of staff employed at the DWTC had grown from 170 to 850 staff in 1997. Daewoo expanded its facilities to include a greenfield, purpose-built engineering design facility costing over £30 million and the company is making efforts to enhance communication between its three technical centres and establish better links with automotive-related institutions, including universities.

Samsung Electronics

Samsung Electronics, part of the South Korean Samsung Group, was established in 1969. The company is a leading producer of semiconductor memory chips and also manufactures consumer goods including televisions, refrigerators and microwave ovens. Samsung's design division was established in 1971 and was moved to Seoul, away from the main factory, in 1988 in order to attract qualified personnel. There are 40 corporate staff in a total design division of 250 with a budget of $126 million for the three years from 1996. Samsung's design strategy aims to establish a design culture throughout the company as part of its corporate goal of 'quality rather than quantity'. The company has established design teams in Palo Alto (California), Tokyo and London, plus a newer centre in China. It also uses the services of foreign design consultants for audio products in Japan, multimedia in the USA and general home appliances in Europe.

Over the last 10 years Samsung has established a number of factories in Europe with the object of localizing manufacturing, product specification and design as part of its wider strategy to implement a new global configuration (Cho, 1997). Many products, however, are still specified and manufactured in South Korea. European design activities are located within the European marketing centre in Samsung's European headquarters and include modification of products for the European market as well as more fundamental product design work. The designs produced may be manufactured in Europe or South Korea. The headquarters moved to London from Germany, with the design centre being relocated from Frankfurt to London in September 1995. This was part of a major reorganization by Samsung aimed at re-focusing on Europe as a whole rather than its historical country-by-country approach. The headquarters oversees 12 European subsidiaries and provides co-ordination, logistics, marketing, product planning, specification and design.

The design centre consists of a Design Manager (a UK national), a Korean Deputy Design Director, two industrial designers and one graphic designer and two Korean designers-in-residence. The design centre was deliberately located next to the marketing department, reflecting Samsung's aim to understand the Europe-wide market, to create appropriate product design strategies and to identify opportunities for innovation in product technology, shape and features. This is part of a wider feeling within the company that while in the past Samsung was good at imitation, it now needs its own brand identity. In turn, however, this has caused some tensions. In particular, the desire of Samsung's headquarters to develop a global image for the company has been felt by some to conflict with a localized market-specific design focus. This is reflected in the design centre's limited independence, with long-term product planning determined in South Korea and projects allocated from there. The UK group tries to identify opportunities but only occasionally influences policy.

With regard to the location decision, Samsung's headquarters relocated to Britain because of the UK's flexible labour laws, the English language and culture clashes with the Germans. Samsung also sees the UK as having a very good skills base with more design consultancies with international clients than in other parts of Europe, other in-house teams to recruit from and a renowned educational infrastructure. However, this does not appear to have been the key factor in the location decision and there is a feeling in parts of Samsung that the UK may not be the best location for its design activities. In the words of one former design manager, it is perceived as being 'between the USA and Europe' rather than being pan-European.

DISCUSSION

These case studies illustrate a number of points about the internation-alization of the product design and development activities of multina-tional enterprises and, in particular, the activities of the UK design and development centres of some East Asian companies. Some of the most important issues are discussed here.

Organizational Variety

What is clear from these case studies is that the UK-based design and product development activities of East Asian companies exhibit consid-erable organizational variety and diversity. This reflects the differing functions that these activities play in the marketing and technology strategies of the companies concerned as well as their differing indus-trial and technological trajectories.

Design and product development activities may take place in ded-icated design centres which may be stand-alone (such as DWTC and NETC); attached to a headquarters function (for example, Samsung Electronics); or located alongside a production site (evident in Nissan's original design unit which was located at its Sunderland manufacturing plant). The product design and development activities may be a green-field development, but they may be brownfield sites that have been acquired (such as DWTC). The product design and development activities undertaken at these sites range from sophisticated product design for complex global products to 're-badging' and the adaptation to local market needs of products designed and developed in the parent country.

In each case, the UK product design and development activities are part of a wider international network of innovative activities bound together through the use of advanced information and communication technologies (ICTs) to achieve a particular technology and marketing strategy. For instance, DWTC can be seen in the context of Daewoo Motor Company's wider industrial design strategy which is focused on gaining access to local market and design knowledge to design cars for the European market. As well as its acquisition of the DWTC, this industrial design strategy has seen the company develop a collaborative research relationship with the University of Metz in France. The company also had plans to set up industrial design centres in Paris (UN, 1995). For Samsung Electronics, the establishment of its European Design Centre in London was part of an effort to shift its design and marketing strategy for Europe from a country-by-country approach to one focused on Europe as a whole. The objective was to understand the European market, create appropriate product design strategies and identify market opportunities. This is a strategy orientated more towards accessing market rather than technological knowledge. Indeed, if NETC and DWTC might be characterized as home-base-augmenting activities then Samsung Electronics' European Design Centre appears to be rather closer to being a home-base-exploiting site.

The approach to product design and development adopted by Nissan has parallels with that employed by a number of other Japanese automotive companies. As Angel and Savage (1996) point out, in the context of the USA, a number of Japanese automotive companies are developing innovative capabilities according to a strategy of 'global localization', with their US subsidiaries assuming increasing responsibility for product design and development for US markets as well as local production. Sony Corporation provides perhaps the best example of global localization with marketing, product planning and industrial design functions together with R&D, production and final assembly located in each of Sony's major regional markets – the USA, Japan and Europe. Sanderson and Uzumeria (1995) argue that one of the key reasons for the success of Sony products like the Walkman in foreign markets has been the company's ability to interpret the preferences of regional markets and communicate this to its design and engineering operations in Japan. The Industrial Design Centres in Japan, New Jersey and Milan are crucial to the understanding of customer requirements and new product opportunities latent in Sony's technology. In contrast, as Sanderson and Uzumeria point out, none of Sony's major competitors locates their industrial design staffs outside Japan.[4]

Local versus Global in International Companies

The evolution from home-based exporter to international company presents a number of important organizational and strategic challenges, not least how to resolve the tension between the desire to manage a company globally while remaining sensitive to local market needs. In experiencing such tensions, these East Asian companies appear to be little different from European and US companies – although, of course, the internationalization of their innovative activities has been a relatively recent phenomenon. Consequently, it is of no surprise to see evidence in the case studies that the firms are still grappling with the issue.

The desire of Samsung's headquarters to develop a global image for the company has, in the view of one former UK design manager, caused conflicts with its desire to achieve a localized market-specific design focus. Nissan is seeking to manage the tension between sensitivity to local customer requirements and the need for global scale production to reduce manufacturing costs through its 'integrated development' strategy. The company has sought to develop, through the early involvement in the design process of its local production centres, a concept and common platform that can satisfy the requirements of its three main markets (Japan, North America and Europe).[5] By developing a common platform with standardized component layout, systems and components, Nissan are seeking to reduce costs, duplication and infrastructure. Despite some convergence, it remains the case that customers in the major markets of Japan, USA and Europe still have quite different tastes and different driving environments in which they use their cars. By sourcing component designs locally, Nissan are seeking to satisfy these differing customer expectations. In global design and development, the company has to design to achieve high unit volumes by standardizing the design strategies, and sharing components across platforms, or through supplier commonality.

PROXIMITY AND CO-LOCATION IN INNOVATION AND DESIGN: THE UK IN EUROPE

In each of these cases, the decision to establish a product design and development activity in the UK can be characterized as having been driven by a desire to get closer to the customer in locally differentiated markets and/or access some set of capabilities that the company perceived to be embedded in the UK national innovation system.

With regard to proximity to the market, in each case the market in question was Europe rather than the UK, and this raises a number of interesting questions. Not least, if user and customer requirements and preferences differ within a regional market then, in the European context, how might a design centre located in one part of Europe capture knowledge of user requirements and customer preferences in other parts of Europe? Why might it be expected to do this any more successfully than if all design activity was concentrated in the home country?

These questions have certainly emerged as important for Samsung Electronics. One of Samsung's main reasons for establishing a European Design Centre in the UK was to adapt products to European market needs. Once established in Britain, two problems quickly emerged. First, it became clear to the company that there was not one single 'European consumer' but instead that consumer tastes varied considerably between countries. To obtain knowledge of each country, the design centre found that it needed to study consumer preferences, methods of distribution and the like on a country-by-country basis. Secondly, there is a growing perception on the part of the parent company that the UK, despite having many benefits, is not a sufficiently 'European' location. Instead it is seen as being somewhere between the USA and Europe (a 'Euram' location – in Europe but not wholly part of it and constantly aspiring to many US developments). UK tastes and requirements for consumer and durable goods are also subtly different to those in other parts of Europe and, in particular, southern Europe. In the background are broader concerns amongst some East Asian companies regarding the UK's political and economic position in Europe – for example, not being in the first wave of the Euro currency launch.

It is also worth noting that while the internationalization of product design and development activities in East Asian companies may be characterized as a parallel process to the internationalization of their production activities, this does not mean that both activities are always co-located on the same site or even in the same country (Howells, 1990). It may well be the case, as Ferdows (1997) argues, that the pressure to transfer ideas from development to production ever more quickly is pushing companies to co-locate production and development in the same organizational and geographical units. However, locational attractiveness may differ between functions, and it might equally be the case that the advantages of co-location may be outweighed by the economies of scale and scope that come from concentrating activities on a small number of sites. What does seem clear is that even where both production and design and development are located in the same country (as is the case with Samsung), the design and development activities may as likely be linked with production activities in other parts of the company as with those in the same country. This is equally the case with regard to R&D activity and, at least as far as the three case study companies are concerned, it does not appear necessary for product design and development to be co-located with R&D. Nissan's R&D is centred in Japan and the USA. R&D for consumer goods in Samsung Electronics is focused in South Korea. This provides further empirical support for the work of Walsh and her colleagues (1992), who have emphasized that design can be an important part of R&D, it can also be a separate activity. As such, design activities are more widespread throughout industry and do not necessarily need to be co-located with R&D activities.

The Transfer of Management Practices and Technological Knowledge

The cases also raise issues about the transfer of management practices and technological knowledge both *within* multinational companies and *between* such companies and the host economy.

Clearly, an important issue in the internationalization of product design and development is the management of *knowledge flows and technology transfer* across geographical boundaries within the firm. There is great play made by commentators of the potential of ICTs to facilitate the development of virtual project teams and ease the internal transfer of management information and codified technological knowledge (OECD, 1992; Howells, 1995). However, if such systems are to work effectively they require much more than hardware. Take Nissan's experience as an example. Nissan has developed a tripolar network between Japan, the USA and Europe. At the moment, NETC has stronger communication links with Japan than with the USA but it is expected that data-sharing will become greater as globalization continues. Developments in ICTs mean that they can now work simultaneously on the same database. Indeed, the fact that Europe and Japan are in different time zones actually helps the process because engineers can work while the Japanese are sleeping and leave new designs for them to review when the Europeans leave for home. However, Nissan recognizes that it has to operate as a global product design and development team if it wishes to achieve a truly global product design and development effort. Sharing the same practices, the same terminology and the same design sequence across the design and development centres is regarded as critically important so that staff can feel that they are in the same company, irrespective of where they are physically located in the world. The design and development function has had to work hard to achieve this, not least because automotive business practices in Japan have historically been very different to those in Europe and the USA. A key element in effective communication is the establishment of good person-to-person relationships and seminars of Nissan engineers from around the world are held to promote relationship-building. Local engineers visit Japan to carry out specific tasks and long- and short-stay engineers and managers from NTC Japan work in NETC. Japanese staff are cycled through NETC every four years to promote technology transfer. As a result, Japanese engineers get a taste of Europe and Europe gets technology transfer. This mirrors the practice at Samsung Electronics where the design centre has a number of Korean designers-in-residence.

What about the transfer of managerial practices and technological knowledge between the companies and the UK national innovation system? Certainly, in each case, the companies have made efforts to develop formal and informal linkages with aspects of the UK national innovation system. Daewoo has sought to develop the formation of relationships with the university sector. NETC has developed a dense network of relationships with suppliers, universities, industrial and professional associations and national and European policy makers. Samsung's design centre has gained access to specialist knowledge through the use of design consultancies and relationships with higher education institutes. The formal relationships developed by the product design and development functions have been supplemented by a range of informal relationships. Talented European engineers, designers and the like have been recruited to work in the centres. In the case of Daewoo, the acquisition of IAD provided access to an established team of technical staff and such staff bring with them their own personal networks of informal relationships which can be exploited in the product design and development process.

Do these case studies represent examples of the 'hollowing out' of embedded scientific knowledge? Are they, as critics have traditionally argued, part of a strategy on the part of East Asian firms to acquire foreign technology which will be commercialized with little benefit to the host economy? Such arguments, while prominent in the 1970s and early 1980s, have been less common in recent years but the cases suggest that the situation is more complex and nuanced than the 'hollowing out' thesis might suggest. Certainly, in the case of Samsung Electronics' design centre, the dominant flow of technological knowledge appears to be to South Korea and the designs produced may be manufactured in either Europe or South Korea for the European market. The case of DWTC is a little different. At first glance this might be thought to be a clear case of the 'hollowing out' of UK innovative capacity. Daewoo has no UK motor manufacturing capacity and the dominant flow of technological knowledge and management practice appears to be out of the UK. However, the story is more subtle than this and that suggested by interpretations of direct foreign investment (DFI) theory (Erdilek and Wolf, 1997). Daewoo has made significant investments in DWTC and considerably expanded the workforce.

Arguably, the intervention of the South Korean company has sustained capabilities that, with IAD in receivership, might otherwise have been lost to the UK economy. The case of NETC is rather different again and emphasizes the fact that FDI in product design and development activities can provide opportunities for learning and the establishment of new local skills for the host economy as well as the company. NETC demonstrates the positive effects that such inward investment can have. What started as a centre primarily concerned with the localization of components is now diffusing the best of Japanese design and development practice into the UK automotive components industry. Turner, Ray and Hayward (1997) note that similar effects can be seen as a result of the diffusion of management practices from Japanese engineering companies (bearing manufacturer NSK–RHP is an example) and Japanese electronics companies.

CONCLUSIONS

This chapter has focused on the internationalization of the product design and development activities of multinational enterprises and has looked in particular at some East Asian companies with a presence in the UK. It has been noted that notions of economic and cultural globalization have become common currency but, in important respects, it remains the case that technological activity and market requirements continue to be locationally differentiated. Accordingly, the internationalization of the innovative activities of East Asian companies can be seen to be driven, on the one hand, by a desire to get closer to the customer in locally differentiated markets and, on the other, by a desire to access technological capabilities specific to particular national innovation systems.

The three case studies have served to highlight a number of key issues:

- First, they show that the product design and development activities of East Asian companies located in the UK exhibit considerable organizational variety and diversity, reflecting the different marketing and technology strategies adopted by the companies.
- Second, the study reveals that the locational configuration and co-ordination of design units appears to be significantly different from R&D laboratories. The location of design capability does not necessarily correspond with R&D capability.

- Third, the studies reveal that the firms are responding to the tension between globalization and localization in rather different ways. Common challenges do not yield similar strategic reactions by firms.
- Fourth, geographical proximity to sources of technological capabilities and local market knowledge is still important to companies but this raises interesting locational questions, not least in the context of the UK's perceived relationship to the European market.
- Finally, issues related to the transfer of management practices and technological knowledge within multinational enterprises and between such companies and the host economy have been highlighted and posited within the wider context of the discussion relating to the national systems of innovation approach.

Clearly, the financial crisis that struck Asia in 1998 has major implications for the strategy and organization of the region's companies. Our study was completed prior to the Asian financial crisis and it is too early to tell what it may mean for the product design and development activities of such companies. Will the fact that the location of research, design and development activities tends to be relatively price-insensitive protect these foreign investments? Should we expect 'home-base-augmenting' activities to become more important as companies seek to use favourable exchange rates to increase exports to Europe? What does the financial weakness of many East Asian companies mean for the prospects for new investments in design and development activities in the future?

Notes

* The support of the Design Council under its Co-Partnership Research Programme is gratefully acknowledged. We would particularly like to acknowledge the contribution to the project made by our colleague Silvia Massini. In addition, we would like to thank Ray Barrell of the NIESR and Louis Turner of the UK–Japan High Technology Industry Forum for their extremely useful comments during an interim review of the study by the Design Council. Needless to say, all errors, omissions and opinions are the responsibility of the authors.

1. There are a variety of meanings attached to this term. Bartlett and Ghoshal (1989), for instance, use it to signify one particular type of company operating in international markets. The term 'multinational enterprise' is used here to describe any company that operates production, marketing or innovative activities beyond its own national borders.

2. The percentage of R&D expenditure conducted in the USA accounted for by foreign-owned companies rose from 4.8 per cent in 1977 to 9.3 per cent in 1983 and to 15.8 per cent in 1990 (Dunning and Narula, 1994). However, a survey conducted by Dunning in 1982 found that major multinational enterprises on average undertook only 12 per cent of their R&D outside their home country, compared with 30 per cent of production (Dunning, 1994).
3. Although survey material from other case study firms will be used to support the analysis above.
4. We have also surveyed Hitachi as part of the wider study, and it had industrial design units located at both Munich and Milan.
5. With the failure of the 'world car' concept of developing a standard car manufactured globally, Nissan's emphasis on the early involvement of local production centres in design and development is seen by them to be one of two generic routes open to volume car manufacturers. The alternative is the approach adopted by Ford, with the manufacture of small cars in Europe and large cars in the USA.

References

Allen, T.J. (1977) *Managing the Flow of Technology*, Cambridge, MA, MIT Press.

Angel D.P. and Savage, L.A. (1996) 'Global Localisation? Japanese Research and Development Laboratories in the USA', *Environment and Planning A*, 28, 819–33.

Bartlett, C.A. and Ghoshal, S. (1989) *Managing across Borders: the Transitional Solution*, London, Hutchinson Business Books.

Behrman, J.N. and Fischer, W.A. (1980) *Overseas R&D Activities of Transnational Corporations*, Cambridge, MA, Oeleschlager, Gunn & Hain.

Carlsson, B. (ed.) (1995) *Technological Systems and Economic Performance*, Dordrecht, Kluwer Academic.

Chenais, F. (1992) 'National Systems of Innovation, Foreign Direct Investment and the Operations of Multinational Enterprises', in B.-A. Lundvall (ed.), *National Systems of Innovations*, London, Pinter, 192–229.

Cho, N. (1997) 'How Samsung Organized for Innovation', *Long Range Planning*, 29(6), 783–96.

Crook, C. (1994) *Computers and the Collaborative Experience of Learning*, London, Routledge.

De Meyer, A. (1993) 'Management of an International Network of Industrial R&D Laboratories', *R&D Management*, 23, 109–20.

Dunning, J.H. (1994) 'Multinational Enterprises and the Globalization of Innovatory Capacity', *Research Policy*, 23, 67–88.

Dunning, J.H. and Narula, S. (1994) 'The R&D Activities of Foreign Firms in the US', *Discussion Paper in International Investment and Business Studies* 189, Department of Economics, University of Reading.

Erdilek, A. and Wolf, M.A. (1997) 'Technology Origins of Foreign-owned Firms in Ohio', *Technovation*, 17(2), 63–72.

Ferdows, K. (1997) 'Making the Most of Foreign Factories', *Harvard Business Review*, March–April, 73–88.

Gibbs, D.C. *et al.* (1985) *The Location of Research and Development in Great Britain*, Centre for Urban and Regional Development Studies, Newcastle-upon-Tyne, University of Newcastle-upon-Tyne.

Hood, N. and Young, S. (1982) 'US Multinational R&D: Corporate Strategies and Policy Implications for the UK', *Multinational Business*, 2, 10–23.

Howells, J. (1990) 'The Internationalisation of R&D and the Development of Global Research Networks', *Regional Studies*, 24, 495–512.

Howells, J. (1995) 'Going Global: the Use of ICT Networks in Research and Development', *Research Policy*, 24, 169–84.

Howells, J. (1998) 'International Innovation and Technology Transfer within Multinational Firms', in J. Grieve Smith and J. Michie (eds), *Globalization, Growth and Governance*, Oxford, Oxford University Press, 50–69.

Howells, J. and Wood, M. (1993) *The Globalisation of Production and Technology*, Chichester, Belhaven Press/Wiley.

Japan External Trade Organisation (JETRO) (1996) *The 12th Survey of European Operations of Japanese Companies in the Manufacturing Sector*, London, JETRO.

Lorenz, C. (1995) 'Global Webs still Spun from Home', *Financial Times*, 18 August.

Lundvall, B.-A. (1992) 'User–Producer relationships, National Systems of Innovation and Internationalisation', in B.-A. Lundvall (ed.), *National Systems of Innovations*, London, Pinter, 45–67.

Macdonald, S. (1995) 'Too Close for Comfort? Implications for Strategy and Change Arising from Getting too Close to the Customer', *California Management Review*, 37(4), 8–27.

Nakamura, Y. (1997) 'Global Design and Development in the European Automotive Industry', The IMechE 1997 James Clayton Memorial Lecture, London, 12 February.

Patel, P. (1995) 'Localised Production of Technology for Global Markets', *Cambridge Journal of Economics*, 19, 141–53.

Pearce, R.D. (1989) *The Internationalisation of Research and Development by Multinational Enterprises*, Basingstoke, Macmillan.

Reich, R. (1991) 'Who is Them?', *Harvard Business Review*, March–April, 77–88.

Sanderson, S. and Uzumeria, M. (1995) 'Managing Product Families: The Case of the Sony Walkman', *Research Policy*, 24, 761–82.

Scherer, F.M. (1970) *Industrial Market Structure and Economic Performance*, Chicago, Rand McNally.

Taggart, J.H. (1997) 'R&D Complexity in UK Subsidiaries of Manufacturing Multinational Corporations', *Technovation*, 17(2), 73–82.

Turner, L, Ray, D. and Hayward, T. (1997) *The British Research of Japanese Companies*, London, Insight Japan.

United Nations (UN) (1995) *1995 World Investment Report – Transnational Corporations and Competitiveness*, New York and Geneva, United Nations.

Von Hippel, E. (1989) *Sources of Innovation*, Boston, MA, MIT Press.

Walker, W. (1993) 'National Innovation Systems: Britain', in R. Nelson, (ed.), *National Innovation Systems: A Comparative Analysis*, Oxford, Oxford University Press, 158–191.

Walsh, V., Roy, R., Bruce, M. and Potter, S. (1992) *Winning by Design*, Oxford, Blackwell.

Part 3
West into East

11 Adoption of East Asian Management Practices: Experiences of Some 'Best-Practice' Organizations in the UK

Vas Prabhu and Marilyn Riley

INTRODUCTION

The past 20 years has seen a steady growth in the adoption of East Asian management practices by UK-based companies, many of who are now regarded as exemplars of best practice. What has led to this widespread adoption, and how they have gone about adopting such practices, has been the focus of a survey of the UK's best organizations. From the late 80s to the mid 90s over 240 companies were selected from winners and short-listed candidates for major UK awards such as the Best Factory Awards, the European Quality Awards, and those listed in the 'Inside UK Enterprise (IUKE)' host-company scheme. Based on a 44 per cent response rate to a postal questionnaire, the data represent a national distribution of varying company sizes and sectors. The findings are reported in four sections: Main Drivers; Preparation for Adoption; Adopted Practices and Current Management Styles; Achievements and Sustainability. The implications of these results for business and education are raised through a summary of the challenges still facing the UK's best organizations, especially with respect to employee, process and systems management.

The more recent interest in East Asian management practices (EAMPs) in the West began in the mid-1970s when large international American businesses, such as Xerox, found their markets being wiped out by Japanese businesses that were able to produce high-quality products at a very competitive price. Naturally their success was attributed to their working practices and everyone was keen to find out what they had done and how to emulate them. The presence of initially Japanese companies and latterly other East Asian companies in Europe and the USA accelerated this interest and know-how, especially as these companies not only transplanted their management and operating practices to their manufacturing sites here, but they also expected their local suppliers to conform to them as well. The Single European Market (SEM) was the main attraction for East Asian businesses, 40 per cent of whom established themselves in the UK and formed the focus of intense interest from both industrialists, government bodies, consultants and academics throughout the 1980s and 1990s.

In particular, the chapter addresses the following questions: Why did they adopt EAMPs and what were they hoping to achieve? How much preparation work and prior thought went into the implementation process? What practices have they adopted and what impact has that had on their management styles? What have they achieved and is it likely to continue? Finally what are the challenges ahead for these and other UK businesses?

CONTEXTUAL BACKGROUND TO THE ADOPTION OF EAMPs

Before looking at the results of this survey, it is worth reflecting on how the EAMPs have taken root in the West. Most of the early stages of this learning, during the 1970s and the 1980s, took place in 'waves' of 'knowledge transfer'. The changes themselves came, as Schonberger (1990) puts it, as 'earthquakes' or momentous new ideas that reshaped the way we think about and run our businesses. They indeed affected whole industries around the world. The first of these focused on 'quality' during the late 1970s, followed by 'JIT' in the early 1980s and subsequently in the mid-1980s by people-related practices such as team working and ownership, continuous improvement and employee involvement. These practices were associated with 'cellular' organizations, simplified material flows and 'process-based' functions. Eventually these spread to other functional areas such as design, marketing and costing with techniques such as concurrent engineering, customer care programmes and activity-based accounting (ABC).

As became evident, these individual practices were not alternative solutions for raising competitiveness as was originally felt, but were all necessary ingredients towards becoming competitive, so integrating philosophies were being put forward. For example, in the UK there was TQM, representing this new wave of manufacturing and more recently it was known as 'becoming world class' (Morton, 1994) or as the 'inclusive approach' as described in the RSA study (RSA, 1996). In the USA it became known initially as 'world class manufacturing' (Schonberger, 1986) and subsequently as 'lean production' and 'lean thinking', as described by Womack, Jones and Roos (1990). Models, which everyone could emulate, were developed to provide this integrating philosophy, such as the European Framework for Quality Management (EFQM) model in Europe and the Baldrige model in the USA.

In the UK, in particular, there was tremendous impetus given to the adoption of such practices by government departments – for example, the DTI through their 'best-practice' initiatives and 'learning by emulating' networks such as the IUKE visit programmes and the vast number of publications available free of charge to all interested parties. Even a collection of 'best-practice' attributes associated with successful companies were identified in reports such as the Winning report (DTI/CBI, 1994), and the Manufacturing Winners report (DTI/TECs/DOEG, 1995).

With this growing interest in best practice, it was inevitable that measuring the extent of its usage would follow. Essentially the approach taken was to compare or 'benchmark' existing practices and performance in a company with best-known standards drawn from empirical evidence accumulated within 'winning' organizations. An example of this was the annual UK Best Factory Award, commenced in 1988, which after several years of data-gathering resulted in the publication of best-practice statistics, as in Wheatley, Szwejczewski and New (1996). Other large-scale benchmarking studies on best practice include those undertaken by IBM UK Ltd/London Business School (Hanson *et al.*, 1996).

THE SURVEY BACKGROUND

Through a postal survey undertaken in Summer 1996, the Newcastle Business School gained major insights into the strategies for business improvement employed by some of the best organizations in the UK. These organizations were selected from the winners and short-listed candidates for the major awards offered in the UK over the past eight years. The majority of them were either finalists in the Management Today/Cranfield University Best-Practice awards or DTI-recommended demonstrator sites for best practice in their IUKE initiative. Others were selected for their success in gaining the European Quality Award (EQA), based on the EFQM model, or regional derivatives of the EQA – i.e. the British Quality Award, Scottish Quality Award, etc. A database of 240 such companies formed the sample frame for this study.

This bias towards best-practice organizations was deliberate, as the main purpose of the survey was to learn from the experiences of companies that had been successful in implementing change and improving their performance. The respondents gave graphic descriptions of their journey to gaining recognition for their achievements and from these responses we have discovered how the UK's best organizations are achieving success by employing a variety of methods in all areas of planning, training and implementation of change.

The main objective of this survey was to identify the methods adopted by 'successful' companies in implementing their business-improvement programmes and to find out if there was any consensus in their approaches and practices. The questions were therefore focused on their reasons for change and the degree to which they were successful in achieving their goals. In particular, attention was given to their planning processes, the underpinning training that was undertaken, the variety of practices selected and the extent to which their outcomes were monitored. From a rigorous and thorough analysis of the data, this chapter presents the key findings and experiences of winning organizations and also puts forward a number of challenges still facing them.

SAMPLE FRAME AND SAMPLING DISTRIBUTION

In total 241 organizations were considered to have implemented successful strategies for best practice, and this sample represents a majority of the UK population of organizations that are implementing successful strategies. Five of these organizations were used for the pilot study and the remaining 236 organizations were used for the main survey. Table 11.1 illustrates the industrial sector distribution of the sample frame and the responding sample. Table 11.2 illustrates the geographical regions covered by the survey. As shown, all geographical regions are represented.

Table 11.1　Sectoral distribution of 'best-practice' organizations

Industry sector	Sample frame (*n* = 236) (per cent)	Sampling Distribution (*n* = 88) (per cent)
Manufacturing	72	70
Service	25	23
Public Sector	3	6
Education	1	1

Table 11.2　Regional distribution of 'best-practice' organizations

Geographical region	Sample frame (*n* = 236) (per cent)	Sampling distribution (*n* = 88) (per cent)
East and Northern	32	40
Midlands	21	17
Southern England	28	21
Wales	8	7
Scotland	9	13
Northern Ireland	3	3

WHY DID THEY EMBARK ON THEIR EAMP?
WHAT WERE THEIR MAIN DRIVERS?

The most popular reason, given by 59 per cent of the sample, was their desire to increase profits, sales and market share. Many others had expressed similar intentions by identifying the enablers that would assist them in their quest, such as understanding customer needs (44 per cent), improving their staff attitudes (39 per cent) and improving their staff development (19 per cent); 36 per cent wanted to increase competitiveness and 22 per cent wanted to improve the quality of the service/product.

Improving profitability as the motive was strongest amongst manufacturing organizations and those who were members of a larger group; nearly 70 per cent in each category said so. Service sector organizations, in contrast, identified the 'softer' issues of improving employee attitudes as the main driving force for their EAMPs.

Further, an analysis of the aims of the organizations' strategies clearly illustrates the synergy between the drivers, the 'driving' and the 'road map', as the long-term aims for the EAMPs clearly reflect the original desires for improvements in profitability and market share.

They also show the recognition of *enabling factors* and include improvements in employee attitudes and staff training, thus suggesting a thorough initial review and planning process.

HOW MUCH PREPARATION WORK AND PRIOR THOUGHT WENT INTO THE ADOPTION PROCESS?

What Sources of Information were Reviewed During the Planning Process?

As an initial step in the introduction of the EAMP planning process companies reviewed many different sources of information (see Figure 11.1) including the work of the quality gurus, consultants, published case studies and visits to other organizations. Most influential on the strategy design of their EAMPs was visits to other companies: 70 per cent of organizations did this, with one in five using the DTI's IUKE scheme.

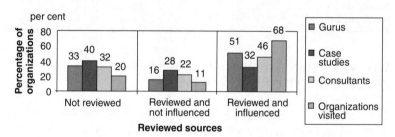

Figure 11.1　Sources of information initially reviewed by organizations

Organizations who are part of a larger group report corporate influence from the parent company to be lower than might be expected, with many preferring to select their own sources of information independently, clearly considering their needs to be unique. Nearly four in 10 organizations took the lead in their organization to begin improvements and a further third were at the forefront of change when the whole organization introduced their EAMPs. The rest had seen some illustrations of EAMPs in other parts of their organization.

In-company Involvement in the Planning Process

Most organizations still take a 'top-down' approach to planning, with only 25 per cent of companies reporting that they involved employees

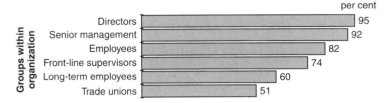

Figure 11.2   Co-operation from groups within organizations

other than management in this process; 16 per cent involved board members, senior management and junior management whilst the majority (51 per cent) involved only board members and senior management. 8 per cent of companies still only involved, in the main, board members.

Eighty two per cent of the organizations have retained this same group to continue reviewing the strategy for the EAMP, and regular reviews of their plans and strategy demonstrate a willingness to continue learning and adaptability to change, with six out of 10 organizations reviewing their strategy more frequently than annually.

The co-operation and enthusiasm stated by the organizations was overwhelming (Figure 11.2). One hundred per cent of organizations agreed that the enthusiasm of the management was crucial to gaining the support of the employees and over 90 per cent reported that there senior management and board had shown the high degree of co-operation necessary; 80 per cent reported high levels of active co-operation from staff throughout their organization. Some reluctance to participation and change is also reported, in particular long-term employees and some trade unions were cited.

Identification and Implementation of Training Needs

Management development and training for all employees has played a very significant and essential part in the implementation of EAMPs. In particular, the existing levels of in-house expertise amongst the best-practice organizations has been critical to this process. Some of the key features of this activity are summarized below.

Even though *external consultants* were used by a significant proportion of companies, they were mainly restricted to establishing the development needs of senior and middle managers. Thirty per cent of companies used them for identifying senior management needs while only 16 per cent of them brought external consultants in to assess their middle management requirements. The vast majority of companies, nearly two-thirds, however, relied on their own expertise for identifying their managers' development needs.

The reliance on external consultants was considerably lower when it came to identifying the training requirements for front-line supervisors and operators; less than 8 per cent did so. However, almost twice as many companies (14 per cent) used both internal and external consultants to determine their training needs for supervisors and middle managers. With regard to the actual training of the staff, external consultants alone delivered the training mainly for senior managers in 37 per cent of the companies and for middle managers in 22 per cent. Another approximately 15 per cent of companies used both internal trainers and external consultants for their management and supervisory training. The training at the operator level was overwhelmingly done in-house (93 per cent of companies), with the rest doing it jointly with external consultants.

A very large proportion of respondents was unable to provide information on the amount of training initially (44 per cent) or their current commitments (49 per cent). For the remainder, the average figures for each level are summarized in Figure 11.3, illustrating the decrease in training days for the board, middle and senior management, and the increase for operators, front-line supervisors and new recruits.

The findings illustrate that these organizations have undertaken a great volume of training across all levels of staff, with middle management being the major target for training, with the greatest volume of training being given to that layer of staff. Additionally, the organizations have introduced a variety of training skills through their training, with equal priority being given to both 'hard' and 'soft' skills (see Figures 11.4, 11.5).

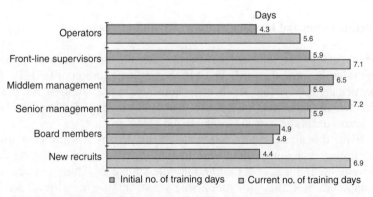

Figure 11.3   Training days

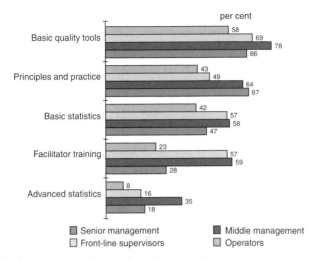

Figure 11.4   Formal 'hard-issues' training given to staff

Figure 11.5   Formal 'soft-issues' training given to staff

As far as *operators* were concerned, two-thirds of organizations have trained them in job skills and slightly fewer have taught them basic quality tools and team activity skills. Around 40 per cent of organizations have taught this level of staff the principles and practice of quality and organizational skills. Encouragingly, eight out of 10 organizations have trained their *front-line supervisors* in team, leadership and communication skills, with a further two-thirds training this level of staff in basic quality tools, statistics and facilitator skills and half of the organizations teaching principles and practice, organisational and job skills.

Middle management have received a tremendous amount of training in the key areas where new management styles and modern techniques are being developed. Four out of five organizations have trained their middle management in team, leadership, communication skills and basic quality tools. Three in five have trained them in principles and practice of quality, basic statistics and facilitator and organizational skills. *Senior management* training was pursued with equal vigour, with nearly nine in 10 organizations giving training in leadership skills, stressing the importance and willingness to learn the modern, emerging styles of leadership and the shift from older management styles. Over two-thirds have had team, organization and communication skills, and principles and practice and quality tools training.

The vast majority (86 per cent) of the companies uses a wide and varied set of monitoring methods with informal feedback from trainees the most common method (62 per cent). Formal evaluation soon after training is done by approximately six out of 10 organizations (58 per cent), though a much smaller proportion (just under one in three) assess the impact several months later (27 per cent). Only one in five organizations (23 per cent) use 'tests' for monitoring. Informal feedback from the trainees and their supervisors also provides the basis for monitoring training effectiveness in 58 per cent of the companies.

However, there is slight concern that the training is not as effective as it could possibly be. Sixty five per cent of organizations feel that their employees have fully absorbed the skills taught during their training programme and 50 per cent have agreed that that long-term employees found it difficult to learn new skills. Management, to implement skills training to its full potential, should address these issues.

WHAT PRACTICES HAVE THEY ADOPTED AND WHAT ARE THE CONSEQUENCES FOR CURRENT MANAGEMENT STYLES?

Systems/Process Changes

Figure 11.6 illustrates the *earliest* implementation date and the *latest* date that the organizations introduced each EAMP/techniques. The

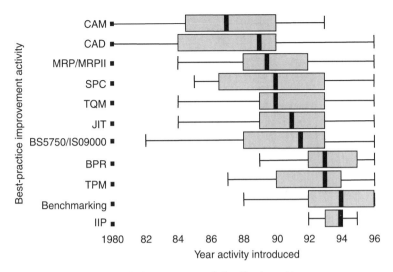

Figure 11.6   Chronological sequence and distribution of improvement activities

average year of introduction is shown by the bold, vertical bar and the shaded region illustrates the 50 per cent of organizations around the mean.

The results illustrate the adoption and popularity of a range of manufacturing and improvement techniques through the 1980s and 1990s. CAM, CAD and MRPI/MRPII, around 1987–90, followed by the major uptake of quality-related techniques, such as SPC, TQM, JIT and BS5750/ISO9000 around 1990–2, with the new techniques of BPR, TPM, benchmarking and IIP from 1993 onwards. As can be seen, many of the practices are still being actively implemented, although the introduction of CAM, for example, seems to have reduced in popularity by the mid 90s, and techniques such as benchmarking, BPR, investors in people (IIP), etc. are prime examples of techniques currently being introduced. Other survey data indicated that manufacturing organizations introduced all of these activities much earlier than service organizations, illustrating the lag in the uptake of improvement activities from one sector to the other.

Figure 11.7 illustrates the proportion of organizations that have *already* introduced a particular type of practice and those organizations that are *currently* introducing the practices. Over 80 per cent of organizations have already implemented BS5750/ISO9000; 70 per cent have implemented TQM; 64 per cent have implemented CAD; and

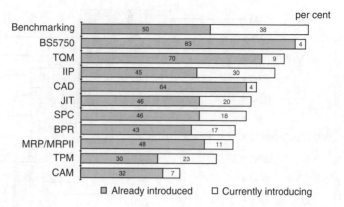

Figure 11.7   Percentage of organizations introduced/currently introducing improvement activity

50 per cent have implemented benchmarking. The most popular activities that are currently being introduced are benchmarking and IIP.

The implementation processes of the EAMPs in the 1990s reflect a more holistic approach than those started in the 1980s. The more recent EAMP programmes show widespread organizational involvement of all departments and functions. The survey revealed a focus of activity in the main production processes, warehousing and storage and personnel and training functions cascading out through all other support functions. However, attention needs to be focused on accounting and finance, IT and R&D, though one in 10 of those organizations that have not already involved R&D are currently doing so. Service sector organizations typically have lagged behind manufacturing companies in the introduction of their EAMPs and consequently these more recent programmes also reflect an holistic approach.

Management/Organization Changes

Most of the organizations experienced the changes mentioned (see Figure 11.8), as expected. Most of the changes have been correctly predicted by the organizations and have in cases exceeded the initial expectations. The major changes that were not expected include changes in organization structure, changes in staff job titles and the number of organizations that have downsized (where over one in four were totally unprepared for this consequence).

There have been far-reaching changes to the responsibilities and relationships that exist within the organizations, with management

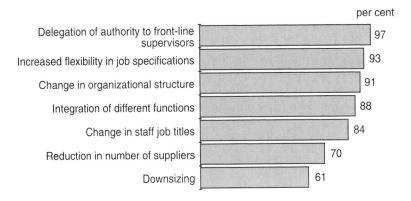

Figure 11.8 Actual and expected occurrences caused by EAMP

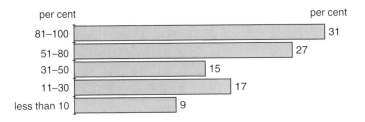

Figure 11.9 Percentage of staff involved in team activities in the organizations

being more visible around staff working areas according to 91 per cent. Front-line supervisors have been given responsibilities for the recruitment of operators nearly three-quarters stated, and operators have the responsibility to stop a key process if a fault is detected in 86 per cent of organizations. Traditional functional departments have been replaced by process-based organizations in 86 per cent of the organizations and – most surprisingly – non-financial rewards to employees who contribute to their EAMP are preferred by over 60 per cent of the organizations.

The organizations have made vast improvements in the area of team building and team working (see Figure 11.9). Nearly all of the organizations agreed that it has become common practice to use teams to implement changes. Nearly one-third of the organizations involve over 80 per cent of the workforce in team activities – and, surprisingly, eight organizations involve less than 10 per cent of employees in team work.

A variety of types of teams has been initiated, 90 per cent of the organizations having cross-functional improvement teams, 83 per cent work-based teams, 78 per cent a steering committee, just over half (56 per cent) a quality council and nearly half (46 per cent) value analysis teams. However, other survey results suggest that 34 per cent of organizations agree that long-term employees (as a sub-group of all employees) found it more difficult to work as teams.

Employee Communication/Relationship Changes

With regard to the changes made to employee internal communication methods, nearly half of the organizations (see Figure 11.10) have introduced communication changes such as email (43 per cent), steering committees (45 per cent) and newsletters (41 per cent). The current major methods of communication in best organizations are regular workforce meetings (97 per cent), notice boards (95 per cent) and newsletters (89 per cent). Awareness days (57 per cent) and quality councils (50 per cent) seem less common methods of communication.

With regard to changes to the communication of employee views to management (see Figure 11.11), the major changes have been to introduce attitude surveys (40 per cent), steering committees (36 per cent) and quality circles (30 per cent). The current major communication methods of employee view to management are through workforce meetings (91 per cent), supervisors (89 per cent), and attitude surveys (69 per cent). Only 10 per cent of the best organizations had a quality council before the introduction of their EAMP, and now the figure is nearly 40 per cent.

With regard to the changes to how customer views are communicated to the organizations, Figure 11.12 illustrates that over one in four organizations have introduced focus groups, face-to-face interviewing, telephone surveys and suggestion schemes as part of their EAMP. The major methods of communication of customer views to the organizations are market surveys (94 per cent), telephone surveys (78 per cent), and focus groups (74 per cent).

With regard to the changes in employee relations and trade unions, the responses showed that just over half of the organizations provide facilities (out of working hours) for staff to socialize. However, the rest of the organizations do not feel that it is a need that they wish to fulfill, and have no plans to adopt this. Eighty one per cent believe that there has been a positive change in staff attitudes since the EAMP was introduced. Nearly 60 per cent of the organizations feel that single status for

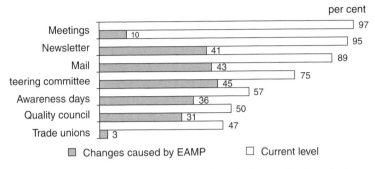

Figure 11.10   Percentage of organizations introducing mechanisms for improving employee communication, caused by their EAMP

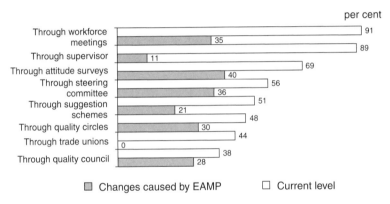

Figure 11.11   Percentage of organizations introducing mechanisms for employee communications to management

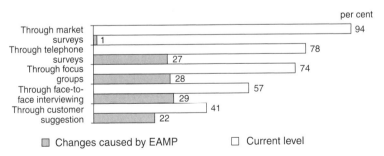

Figure 11.12   Percentage of organizations introducing mechanisms for obtaining information from customers

all employees is an integral part of their organization's culture; however, nearly 30 per cent do not feel that it is necessary, and have no plans to adopt this.

Fifty five per cent of the organizations recognized trade unions before the EAMP began, and 55 per cent of the organizations still had trade unions after their EAMP had been introduced; recognition of trade unions did not alter owing to the EAMPs in the organizations. Thirty six per cent of the organizations that have trade unions recognize only one; 22 per cent recognize two and 18 per cent recognize three. However, out of the organizations that recognize trade unions, only 28 per cent have a single-union agreement. For the award winners that have unions, only 40 per cent agreed that the unions played a crucial role in the success of the EAMP. Only 3 per cent of organizations have increased their use of trade unions to improve internal communications; there have been zero uptakes in the use of trade unions to improve organization communication methods for employees to management.

WHAT HAVE THEY ACHIEVED, IS IT LIKELY TO CONTINUE AND HOW DO WE KNOW?

A very significant proportion of the sample studied had achieved their desired goals for introducing EAMPs. For instance, 43 per cent claimed better understanding of and capacity to meet customer needs. Another 32 per cent had achieved improvements in employee attitudes. Increments in profits and reduction in costs were identified strongly by over a third of the companies (26 per cent) and reductions in waste and, further, inventory (41 per cent) and improved process lead times, were expressed by significant proportions of the companies studied (25 per cent).

As expected, the application of EAMPs and techniques such as BPR, CI, CAM, SPC, etc., was seen as a major contributory factor to the successes achieved; over one in three (34 per cent) admitted to that. A practically equal number (35 per cent) also identified improved staff attitudes as the major enabler for their successes. The emphasis given to staff training was also clearly a significant contributory factor among 28 per cent of the companies, while developing a strong customer focus and sharing these values amongst all employees was seen as the main contributory factor in a quarter (25 per cent) of the firms studied. Only 16 per cent saw reliable and measurable data as a contributory factor.

One in four organizations (25 per cent) stated that it was 'too early' to measure the benefits from their EAMP illustrating the long-term views of these organizations and confirming in some instances the time lag between the implementation of best practice and the consequential achievements. The complexity involved in changing staff attitudes was identified as an inhibitor by 22 per cent of the companies, highlighting the often-underestimated task of introducing change in practice. What did come as a surprise, was that only 9 per cent of companies identified a lack of resources as the root cause of their failure to achieve desired goals.

Improving employee attitudes, culture, etc., was still an unfulfilled goal for over a quarter of the companies sampled (26 per cent), which is a very critical factor for the long-term sustainability of such change within organizations. Other challenges that face smaller groups of companies include the ability to eliminate waste effectively (14 per cent), to realize bottom-line profits (11 per cent), to improve their supplier relationships (6 per cent) and to achieve integration with other areas of their site (5 per cent).

The organizations have shown clear moves to improve the measurement of their performance at all levels, internally and externally, and Figures 11.13–11.16 show the most popular measures used by the organizations in four areas – customer satisfaction, employee satisfaction, workflow efficiency and product/service quality. Encouragingly, 85 per cent of the organizations now have visible charts that are produced and

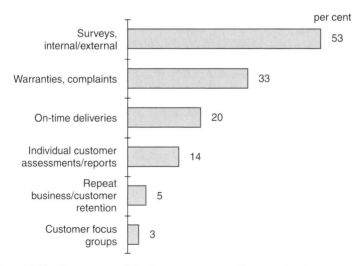

Figure 11.13   Customer satisfaction measures used by organizations

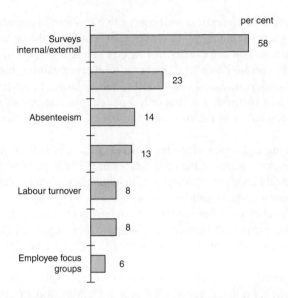

Figure 11.14   Workflow efficiency measures used by organizations

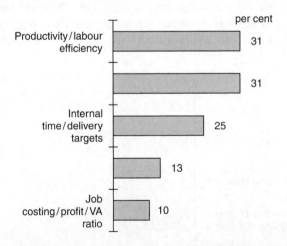

Figure 11.15   Employee satisfaction/morale measures used by organzations
Note: VA = Value added.

maintained by staff in all work areas to illustrate their performance: 83 per cent immediately feed results from monitoring back to the operators. Over 60 per cent of the organizations share information concerning better work practices with other organizations and over 60 per cent

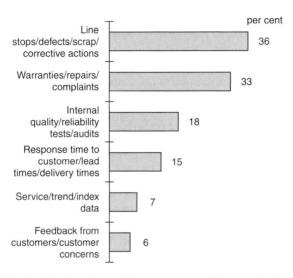

Figure 11.16   Product/service quality measures used by organizations

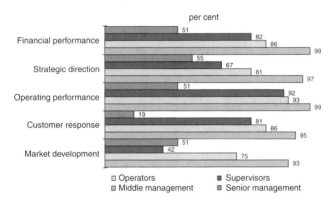

Figure 11.17   Knowledge of employee groups

of the organizations carry out benchmarking. The organizations have also established formal self-assessment methods, with nearly 90 per cent of the organizations using a formal self-assessment method, 53 per cent using BS5750/ISO9000 and 34 per cent using the European Quality Award (EQA) criteria.

The organizations have also shown clear moves towards promoting an informed workforce. Nearly 100 per cent of the organizations stated that senior management had knowledge of financial performance, strategic direction, operating performance, customer response and market development (Figure 11.17.) Surprisingly, only around half of the best organizations allowed the operators to have knowledge of these measures, with the figure falling to less than one in five organizations letting their operators know the customer response.

WHAT CHALLENGES LIE AHEAD FOR THESE AND OTHER UK BUSINESSES?

The study has clearly shown the degree to which best practice has been implemented in our sample of UK organizations. A lot has been achieved in terms of successful outcomes, as has been summarized in the report so far. However, even in these 'award-winning' organizations a number of challenges, identified by themselves, need to be addressed. Further attention to processes and practices are required to attain sustained improvements through EAMPs. These challenges are further improvements to processes and practices that are still required to fully attain the desired outcomes of the EAMPs, and can be best considered under a number of sub-headings:

- Organizations need to *manage people* more effectively. Employee attitudes is still seen as a major issue; this points to the need for more effective management of the people processes to produce more visible positive results. Significant proportions of organizations claim that they have identified a lack of support and reluctance for their improvements from long-term employees and from trade unions.
- Employee *training* should be given the utmost importance. Although there is a high volume of training in these organizations, the emphasis given to staff training as a goal in the strategy has reduced through the 1980s and 1990s. In raising the priority and volume of training, organizations need to become more aware of the current level of training that is being given to staff – nearly half of the organizations did not know how many days' training their staff had already received or their current allocation. Management need to monitor closely the type and level of training being given in order to identify gaps in their employees' skills and knowledge. This gap analysis will ensure that management are aware of the full potential, physically and mentally, of their staff and any skill areas that need addressing. When training has been given, management should ensure that the

knowledge and skills are effectively retained by staff as a significant proportion of organizations do not believe that their staff have fully absorbed the skills taught during their training. Management should be aware that half of organizations believe that long-term employees find it difficult to learn new skills. These difficulties need to be identified and confronted more effectively by management.

- Management need to create and facilitate more *teams* within the organization. A significant proportion of the organizations have identified that it has become policy to use teams to implement changes, yet a significant proportion do not have all of their workforce involved in some team activity. As with all issues, management seriously need to take into account the *sub-groups* operating within their workforce who have ingrained attitudes and established work practices – over a third of organizations stated that long-term employees found it difficult to work as teams.

- Management should ensure that employees have full *knowledge* of the organization's position on all scales and their contribution and influence to the improvements in those areas. With appropriate measurement systems and increased sharing of information, employees will be able to visualize the direct fruits of their labours. In organizations where trade unions are recognized, there has not been a substantial increase in their use to improve communication methods on the organizations.

- A contributory factor to a low level of improvement in *employee attitudes* may be the lack of involvement and consideration of employee views in the strategy design, resulting in a mainly 'top-down', senior management-driven strategy. With increased staff involvement in the strategy design process, organizations may realize an improvement in staff attitudes and a strategy that fully reflects the range of views in the organization. Management need to anticipate more clearly the possible changes that will occur through their improvements as, for a significant proportion, downsizing came as a surprise: this major employee-related consequence should have been predicted and prepared for more accurately. Management need to realize the time lag between their actions and the outcomes, as some felt that it was 'too early to measure' their successes.

References

CBI (1997) *Fit for the Future: How Competitive is UK Manufacturing?*, London, CBI.

DTI/CBI (1994) *Competitiveness – How the Best UK Companies are Winning*, London, DTI/CBI.

DTI/TECs/DoEG (1995) *Manufacturing Winners – Creating a World-Class manufacturing base in the UK*, London, DTI/TECs/DoEG.

Hanson, P., Voss, C.A., Blackmon, K. and Claxton, T. (1996) *Made in Europe 2: An Anglo-German Design Study*, Warwick and London, IBM UK Ltd/London Business School.

Morton, C. (1994) *Becoming World Class*, Basingstoke, Macmillan.

Royal Society for Arts, (RSA) (1996) *Tomorrow's Company: The Role of Business in a Changing World*, Aldershot, Gower.

Schonberger, R.J. (1990) *Building a Chain of Customers*, London, Hutchinson Business Books.

Schonberger, R. J. (1986) *World Class Manufacturing: The Lessons of Simplicity Applied*, New York, Free Press.

Wheatley, M., Szwejczewski, M. and New, C.C. (1996) *The Making of Britain's Best Factories*, London, *Management Today* in association with Business Intelligence.

Womack, J.P., Jones, D.T. and Roos, D. (1990) *The Machine that Changed the World*, Oxford, Maxwell Macmillan.

12 The Impact of British Direct Investment in China since the 'Open Door Policy'*

Kevin A. Lawler and Marcus C.H. Ling

INTRODUCTION

In 1979, China opened its economy to foreign direct investment (FDI). Investors from Hong Kong, Taiwan and the USA have led the list, with European investors contributing less than 10 per cent of the overall FDI. The British government has increasingly recognized the shift in the dynamism of the world economy from the Atlantic to the Pacific and its benefits for the West. A growing number of British enterprises are confident that the twenty-first century will be an Asian century: recent data show that Britain is China's most important partner in terms of FDI within the European Union. This chapter examines the issue of British direct investment (BDI) in China from the British perspective. It seeks to investigate the success of China's 'open door policy' and the part of UK corporations within it. By recounting organizational experiences, it hopes to provide some indications of best practice to be adopted in formulating and implementing strategies for penetrating the Chinese market.

THE CHINESE INITIATIVE TO ATTRACT FOREIGN INVESTMENT

The Chinese government has long been aware of the fact that China had technologically fallen far behind the developed countries, perhaps by as much as between 10 to 30 years. Absorption of FDI, especially, was seen as a desirable solution to the lack of funds of investment and the low level of technology. In fact, China had been isolated from advanced technology for so long that its industry had little chance of reaching world levels without inviting in foreign manufacturers.

Opening up to Western investment was nevertheless perceived as a radical move, even though China was familiar with operating joint ventures with foreign countries. In the 1950s, China had set up state-owned joint companies with the Soviet Union, but tensions between the two countries heightened, followed by the withdrawal of Soviet aid in the 1960s.

The primary objectives in opening China up to foreign investment are to bring in foreign capital, advanced technology, management skills and urban construction, and generally to catch up with the developed countries. Preference is given to foreign projects that are consistent with the long-term development plans of the Chinese national economy, and priorities have been assigned in the following areas:

- machinery and electronic products
- export-oriented products
- import substitutes
- communication, energy and transportation sectors
- agriculture, particularly machinery and cultivation chemicals.

In 1995, the Chinese government formulated a series of new policies. Under the new policies, foreign trade, retailing sale, financial services, civil aviation, real estate, information services and so on, have been partly opened to foreign investment. Other fields opened to foreign investment under the new policies are leasing, accounting, advertising, consulting, engineering, industrial designing, schools and training centres. The Law on Joint Ventures Using Chinese and Foreign Investment was announced in 1979. But it was brief and vague, with only 14 articles. However Chinese officials emphasized the need to fill in the gaps in the Law with contractual clauses to give greater flexibility, which would appeal to foreign investors.

Under the joint ventures system, the Chinese partners normally supply land, plant, labour, infrastructure and some machinery, as well as materials. Foreign partners are expected to provide technology, capital, marketing and management expertise, and possibly some raw materials. The major developments which have occurred since the inception of the 'Open Door Policy' are shown in Table 12.1. One of the most significant of these developments was the establishment of the SEZs, designed as political, cultural, educational and technological centres. The main features of the policies applied within the SEZs are:

Table 12.1   The Chronology Of China's 'Open Door Policy', 1979–89

Year	Event
1979–	'Open door' policy announced and Law on Joint Ventures
1980–	China joined World Bank and IMF
1980–	Special Economic Zones (SEZs) established (initially four)
1982–	Debt crisis enhanced the attractiveness of foreign capital
1983–	Joint venture regulation – permission granted to sell products in the domestic market (as opposed to exporting entire output) if 'urgently needed'
1984–	Patents legislation
	14 coastal sites opened
	Licence Import regulations and foreign exchange retention rules
1985–	Nominal tariff rates reduced on exports
	Tightened access to imports
	Three Open Economic Zones established
1986–	Joint venture foreign exchange balance provisions and provisions for the encouragement of foreign investment – collectively covering remittance of funds, tax and other incentives and the hiring and firing of workers
	The 13th Communist Party Conference proclaimed the need for China to join the world economy through the utilization of foreign capital, technology and raw materials
	Law on Enterprises Operating Exclusively with foreign capital – introduced with more relaxed controls
	Technical Economic Development Areas established in 12 coastal cities
1987–	Application to join GATT
1988–	Austerity programme to reduce inflation – firmer control over credit creation and tax reforms
	Bankruptcy Laws introduced
	Restrictions on economic relations with other countries loosened
1989–	The Tian-an-men Square incident followed by a credit squeeze and devaluation

- 15 per cent corporation taxes and a tax holiday
- cheap land and services (relative to Hong Kong)
- low labour costs (although higher than elsewhere in China)
- greater freedom in labour management
- zero or low customs duties
- simplified entry/exit and other formalities
- increased access to imports and the internal Chinese market.

Administrative features included the setting up of the China International Trust and Investment Corporation (CITIC), and the Ministry of Foreign and Economic Relations and Trade (MOFERT). These constitute the approval body for foreign and Chinese enterprises, respectively. Foreign businesses considering a joint venture in China are required to contribute a minimum of 25 per cent of the necessary total investment.

FOREIGN DIRECT INVESTMENT

China's strategy behind its 'open door policy' to attract FDI to the country has proved extremely successful. From 1979 to 1994 the total pledged investment was $275 billion, and actual investment reached $85.1 billion. In 1994 alone, materialized foreign investment was $34 billion, which represents about half of all FDI to developing countries world-wide; the contractual commitment of foreign investment was $81 billion (Figure 12.1). More than 210 000 foreign-founded ventures were approved from 1979 to the end of September 1994 (Figure 12.2). China is second only to the USA in attracting foreign investment. The top countries and regions investing in China are Hong Kong, Taiwan, the US, Japan, Singapore, the UK, Germany, Thailand, France and Canada (Figure 12.3).

Although this immense inflow of foreign investment capital was, not surprisingly, dominated by ethnic Chinese investors from Hong Kong and Taiwan, as well as the economic giants Japan and the USA, Britain is still number 6 in the top 10 investors' list, which is quite impressive amongst EU countries. As the largest investor among EU countries (Figure 12.4), Britain is ahead of Germany, France and Italy with pledged investment and utilized amounting to US$3013 million. In 1993 alone, contractual British investment in China were US$1990 million in total.

In 1992, the Commission of the European Communities suggested that, between 1986 and 1992 only 10 per cent of the FDI to Asia came from the European Union.[1] Britain contributed only a small share of FDI in China over this period. Compared with the total direct investment of US$110 billion in China in the period between 1979 and 1993, companies from Britain committed themselves to a total of 616 direct investment projects with pledged investment and utilized investments amounting to US$3013 million, contributing only 3.5 per cent of total actual investment in China.

The relatively small stake by British investors being held in Sino–foreign projects is surprising as Britain is, according to figures for 1993,

Value (US$ million)

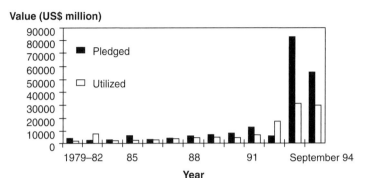

Figure 12.1   Pledged and utilized foreign investment in China 1979–September 1994
Source: *Almanac of China's Foreign Economic Relations and Trade (CFERT)*, *Financial Times*, November 1994; Agency France Press English Wire, 8 July 1994.

No. of projects

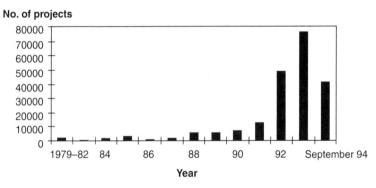

Figure 12.2   FDI projects, 1979–September 1994
Source: *Almanac of China's Foreign Economic Relations and Trade (CFERT)*, *Financial Times*, November1994; Agency France Press English Wire, 8 July 1994.

the fifth biggest provider of FDI world-wide, accounting for some US$11 billion. Furthermore, given that China was receiving the second biggest share of all FDI in 1993 (US$26 billion), the under representation of BDI in China becomes obvious. However, since 1993 a sharp increase in the willingness of the UK economy to invest in China can be identified, together with increased capital inflow from Germany, Singapore and South Korea. At the same time, investment from Hong Kong and Taiwan has been decreasing.

Pledged investment US$ millions

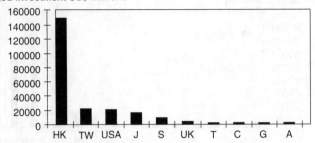

Figure 12.3   The 10 main investors in China, 1978–93
Note: HK – Hong Kong; TW – Taiwan; J – Japan; S – Singapore; T – Thailand;
C – Canada; G – Germany; A – Australia.
Source: Foreign Investment Administration, *Almanac of CFERT.*

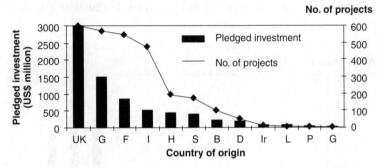

Figure 12.4   Investment from EU countries, 1979–93
Note: G – Germany; F – France; H – Holland; S – Spain; B – Belgium;
D – Denmark; Ir – Ireland; L – Luxembourg; P – Portugal; G – Greece.
Source: Foreign Investment Administration, *Almance of CFERT.*

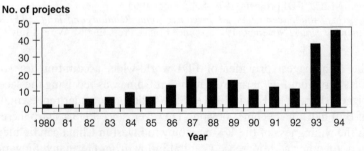

Figure 12.5   British FDI projects, by year, 1980–94
Source: Foreign Investment Administration, *Almanac of CFERT.*

It should be mentioned that there is a discrepancy between pledged and actual investment. According to figures released by MOFERT, for example, for the period 1978–85 actual investment was estimated at only US$460 million. Alternative figures published by the World Bank indicate that of US$720 million pledged up to June 1985, only US$350 million had actually been invested.[2] Compared with that of other countries and regions, however, the discrepancy is relatively small, and it has been narrowing since 1990.

It is also worth mentioning that the lack of reliable and comprehensive statistical and market information in China has created a host of problems. As Pomfret (1991) has commented, in China there is 'no strong tradition of reporting economic statistics' (Wilpert and Scharpf, 1990: 70). The data available probably understate the true situation.

THE INVESTMENT PATTERN SINCE 1986

The years 1986 and 1987 saw the first surge in the number of FDI projects as a result of the introduction of policies to encourage FDI in productive sectors, especially those involving advanced technology. The actual number of projects decreased during the period 1990–2 owing to the after-effects of 1989 Tian-an-men Square incident, but the level of investment in these three years was still higher than the pre-1986–7 era. With the restoration and consolidation of investment confidence by Deng's tour to the South in spring 1992, British investment jumped dramatically in 1993, with investment numbers almost double those of 1987. Project numbers rose further in 1994 (Figure 12.5). The strong British interest in the China market and its confidence in the future prospect of that market is also illustrated by our survey. Among the 125 British firms responding to the survey, over a third planned to invest in China within the next couple of years, while the rest said they had already invested in China

It has been suggested – elsewhere – that China's coastal areas were the first regions targeted for the country's economic development. Up to 1992 they absorbed more than 80 per cent of the total world-wide inward FDI to China. Only 9.5 per cent of all FDI in China was located in China's inland provinces.[3] While foreign investors generally emphasize the south and southeast coastal provinces of Guangdong, Jiangsu, Fujian, Shandong and Shanghai, the majority of British companies have approached the urban centres of industry, such as Beijing and Shanghai, as locations for their joint ventures. The examination of the

Table 12.2   Regional distribution of BDI in China, January 1994

Location	Companies' representatives and JVs		Sino–British JVs		Total No.	
	No.	per cent	No.	per cent	No.	per cent
Shanghai	65	24.53	30	26.09	95	25.00
Beijing	154	58.11	21	18.26	175	46.05
Rest	46	17.36	64	55.65	110	28.95
Total	265	100	115	100	380	100

Note: JV = Joint venture.
Sources: *Almanac of China's Foreign Economic Relations and Trade (CFERT)*, *Financial Times*, November 1994; Agency France Press English Wire, 8 July 1994.

current version of the investment guide of the *China Mirror* supports the above observation. Up to January 1994, 25 per cent of all Britain funded companies' representatives and Sino–Britain joint ventures (JVs) in China were located in Shanghai, and more than 46 per cent of them were located in Beijing.[4] The remaining 29 per cent of all British investment projects were located in the Chinese coastal and inland provinces. The number of projects in Shanghai and Beijing are shown in Table 12.2.

As far as industrial distribution is concerned, most of the JVs established in China are found to be engaged in the exploitation of natural fuels, labour-intensive manufacturing or tourism, as well as infrastructure projects, including highways, railways and port developments. In addition, foreign investors engage in textile, medicine, food, motorcycle and electronics industries, automotive, chemical, machinery and coal industries. This study also found that manufacturing, as well as estate and services, were the industries which received the most foreign investment and that the proportion to manufacturing dropped slightly in 1992, whereas estate and services increased by 40 per cent. This chapter further suggests a considerable increase in the establishment of high-tech projects by UK multinational companies seeking long-term commitments in China. Foreign investors are increasingly interested in infrastructure projects such as power stations, motorways and railways, and this trend will intensify.

The reason for this has been found in China's priority for new investment to improve its poor infrastructure. In 1995, for instance, new incentive guidelines attempted to direct investment towards high-tech and infrastructure projects. Thus, the proportion of telecommunications and power-generating industries is likely, to increase rapidly within the first decade of the twenty-first century, as the Asia Pacific region is likely to spend more on telephones and power than any other region in the world.

In general, the investment pattern by industry roughly corresponds to the economy's exporting structure.[5] The majority of British investors, primarily multinationals, represent industries such as mechanical engineering (27 per cent), textiles (23 per cent), electronics (9 per cent) and chemicals and pharmaceuticals (9 per cent), industries which face a structural and cost crisis in Britain.[6]

Foreign-funded ventures in China contribute considerably to the export volume of the Chinese economy. In 1994, for instance, the 10 000 foreign-funded enterprises operating in China generated exports worth some US$87.65 billion, 30.7 per cent more than the previous year, thereby accounting for 37 per cent of China's total exports (34.3 per cent in 1993). In 1991, they accounted for only US$12.1 billion (16.7 per cent), an increase of 54 per cent compared with the previous year (12.6 per cent).[7]

However, the growth rate of 54 per cent was distinctly higher than the overall growth rate of all Chinese exports, by 15.8 per cent. Foreign-funded ventures, which contribute primarily to the increase of Chinese exports, can be found in textiles, chemicals and electronics, all of which are heavily represented by BDI. In 1993, 111 of the total 616 Sino–British ventures (18 per cent) exported more than 80 per cent of their output from mainland China.[8]

THE UK INVESTORS' EXPERIENCE

The response of Western businesses generally to the opportunities presented by the Chinese incentives has not been as enthusiastic as the host country initially hoped, a fact which is now openly acknowledged. What success has been recorded is largely a result of China's low labour costs, huge and underdeveloped domestic market, abundant material reserves – and, not least, the overall enthusiasm displayed by the Chinese themselves.

Investors have encountered many problems such as infrastructure deficiencies, obtaining a share of the domestic market, getting assistance from the relevant authorities and overcoming the managerial style differences involved. Moreover, there is no doubt that the political power struggle in China shakes confidence among investors, plus the fact that, given the length of time China was cut off from international markets, UK investors feel that there has been a severe underestimation of 'how much they would have to improve their infrastructure, upgrade cadre training, and fundamentally alter their way of thinking to be competitive with other countries' (*Far Eastern Economic Review*, 1993: 44).

CASE STUDIES

The special UK experience can be illustrated by case studies. In the case of all but one, this investment has taken the form of joint ventures. The exception is Cherry Valley, which operates a compensation trade arrangement.

Cable & Wireless

Cable & Wireless (C&W) has a long-established association with China going back to the early part of the twentieth century, and currently has two equity JVs operating there. The Huaying Nanhai Oil Telecommunication Service Company Limited is a £5 million, 15-year contract providing off-shore domestic and international telecommunication services for oil and oil-field support companies engaged in development of the South China Sea oil-field. However, the reduction in the scale of oil exploitation activities in the area has now made the company relatively insignificant.

C&W's other project is the Shenda Telephone Company Ltd which provides local and international telephone services in the Shenzhen SEZ, which borders Hong Kong. C&W holds 49 per cent of the equity, with the balance being in the hands of the public sector Shenzhen Telecommunications Development Company. C&W was considered a suitable partner by the Chinese because of its strong presence in Hong Kong, and its positive attitude towards helping the Chinese authorities. In the early stages of the project, C&W imported engineering expertise from its Hong Kong subsidiary, while Chinese were sent to Hong Kong for training. C&W, being a service-based company rather than a manufacturer, helped the Chinese design the specifications with tenders from France, Japan and the USA. In return, the Chinese authorities supplied free land use and a tax holiday.

The tariff for telephone calls is set according to the international rate. Since China receives more calls than it makes, and since most of the transactions are paid for in US dollars, the Chinese side can earn foreign exchange to repay its share of the equipment costs. The return on investment is around 15–20 per cent, which C&W considers unsatisfactory. The company's expenditure to date (including loans to their Chinese partner) has been substantial, around US$50 million, which it is anxious to recoup eventually. The company has also found Chinese investment procedures lengthy and bureaucratic. It was found very difficult to arrive at a common goal through negotiations, especially with the large number of people that had to 'pass' a project in order for it to be approved. The most useful technique was found to be to get everybody together, but cultural differences made this very difficult to arrange. Problems have reduced over the years with increasing experience, but C&W still wants to see more improvements relating to screening and approval. Furthermore, the laws on investment are brief and vague, and more clarification is needed.

The Tootal Group

Tootal has been operating in forms of trade other than direct investment in Shanghai since 1949. It is currently involved in two JVs and a management contract in China. Both JVs are spinning mills and are situated in the coastal area.

The decision to go into China was a strategic move. In order to supply the area, to fight off competitors and to complement and reinforce the group's other manufacturing bases nearby, the establishment of manufacturing bases in China seemed only logical, given the existing long-term relationship with the Chinese and the very attractive offering that was provided by the host country. The equity shareholdings were agreed through discussions and resulted in Tootal owning 42.5 per cent of the equity in both the JVs established. This was provided in the form of capital (in foreign currency) and high-tech equipment brought in from Switzerland, Germany and Britain.

The export oriented nature of Tootal's operations suits China's ultimate goal of generating foreign exchange, and it has accordingly guaranteed both the supply of raw materials and an uninterrupted supply of power. Tootal has found penetration of the local market difficult, and recently concentration has been upon greater value added products. The Chinese foreign balance requirement has done little to help Tootal's two ventures, since equipment is paid for in foreign exchange; a policy of tight cash control has had to be enforced. Trust built up among the partners has helped the businesses to run smoothly, and understanding the Chinese philosophy of 'always placing personal qualities above rules and regulations' (Wilpert and Scharpf, 1990: 73), has helped formulate the right tactics.

Pilkington

Pilkington was one of five partners who set up the Shanghai Yaohua Pilkington Glass Company Limited in March 1983. The JV was to be 100 per cent equity-funded, with the three Chinese partners taking 75 per cent, and Pilkington taking half the remaining 25 per cent. Eventually, funding was 40 per cent equity and a 60 per cent loan from the Bank of China.

The project was initiated by the Chinese side, who wanted to update their huge glass industry. They had concluded the best way to do this was to set up an operation under licence from Pilkington. The first meeting was held in June 1980, but 16 rounds of negotiations ensued before the company was formally established in December 1980, mainly owing to State Planning Commission (SPC) delays.

Other problems encountered were:

- clearance of the chosen site was a major source of delay, with resettlement of people living on the site taking an unexpectedly long time
- rent for the land was high given that vacant possession was not immediately available
- ground conditions were much worse than expected from interpretation of the geological surveys; piles were needed to strengthen the site and a diaphragm wall required for excavation
- while local engineers and workers were competent, project management was inefficient
- most raw materials had to be transported by water
- the quality and volume of soda ash available locally was inadequate, and materials had to be imported
- labour quality was low and required extensive training (85 managers and operators were sent to the UK for eight weeks before production began)
- own-power generators were required because of the risk of interruption in electricity supply to what is essentially a continuous process.

The increase in total investment (from a budgeted 165.2 million 286 Renminbi to an eventual 432 million) made the original projected 15 per cent return on investment unrealistic, and the proposed export levels were not enough to cover the loans; royalties and dividends remittable increased to 50 per cent of production (due also to the poor state of the Chinese domestic economy, leading to low local sales while there was high demand abroad).

Since the third year of production the operation has been in profit, and Pilkington's existence shows that trust, firm commitment and good working relations is very important in making a successful operation. Indeed, the Chinese side is so proud of the venture that a tour of the plant has become a virtual 'must' for every visiting foreign dignitary.

Cherry Valley Farms

Cherry Valley, based in Lincoln, is considered to be the leading duck-breeding operation in the world in terms of technology and stock. Cherry Valley supplies parent breeding stock and technology as well as marketing expertise, and then deducts its share of the profits from the earnings, with the balance going to the Chinese. The Chinese side is happy with this arrangement, since they earn foreign currency from the export sales. Equipment for the process, such as incubators and cold stores, can be obtained both locally and from abroad, although the latter is often preferred because both the local equipment and technical information is generally in short supply.

The quality of feed is sometimes not as high as Cherry Valley would like, and must be supplemented through the use of vitamins and prompt rectification to prevent serious illness developing in the stock. In addition to the supply of technology, Cherry Valley also provides in-house training either in the UK or in China. Many problems are associated with this, since it is known that some trainees are looking for perks in the UK rather than training. The language barrier poses a serious problem, and this has been solved by employing a part-time translator in Chinese. Qualified trainees are subsequently sent back to China to train other Chinese in turn.

Serious problems were also created by transportation and power supply difficulties. Quick and efficient transport is essential to the transportation of livestock, while a small, but constant, supply of power is required for the incubators and cold stores, and the east coast does suffer from power disruptions from time to time.

Cherry Valley ensures that at any one time there is at least one UK representative in China. Cherry Valley is very confident about China, although the rate of growth is not the same as before the Tian-an-men Square Incident (UK personnel were repatriated within 2 weeks of 10 June 1989). The company has great pride in technology and does not like to sell it separately, it considers this part of its recipe for success.

McVitie's Cakes

Part of United Biscuits holdings, McVitie's joint venture set up in Shekou was the group's first contract with the Chinese, and is its latest addition to reinforce its Asian markets (following co-operative projects in Taiwan, Singapore and Malaysia). The joint venture, United Biscuits Guangjin (China) Ltd is owned 80 per cent by McVitie's, and was set up to produce a limited range of products to keep production costs low.

All raw materials are sourced domestically and at local prices. However, the quality and variety of materials is limited, which means the quality of products is restricted to Asian standards, which does not permit export to the West.

The start-up time for production to reach an acceptable level of efficiency was 'normal'. However, a lot of teething troubles were both expected and encountered, relating mainly to organization and management. Approximately half the products are for export to Hong Kong, with the rest being sold domestically, and while there have been no difficulties experienced with the Hong Kong market, problems have arisen with the Chinese market mainly due to the poor sales distribution system. For example, purchases by wholesalers tend to be erratic, making planning difficult. McVitie's response has been to adopt a posture of very rapid response to sudden orders and yet simultaneously to attempt to keep stocks to a minimum. Prices for products exported to Hong Kong are set according to the market price in order to make them competitive. For locally consumed products, the price is usually set according to what the market will bear.

The plant is labour-intensive, and the cost of production is reduced greatly by using existing imported technology and the extremely low local wages. The venture uses a UK manager at the top level and Chinese manager elsewhere. The UK manager is there simply to organize and assist in the running of the business, and most of the decisions are made by the Chinese team. McVitie's believes this use of Chinese management will encourage true commitment and minimize communication problems.

SUMMARY OF FINDINGS

A number of clues for commercial success in China emerge from the company case studies. The form of enterprise appears significant, with the JV being particularly favoured.[9] It is preferred by China and, from the foreign partner's point of view, this makes it easier to obtain assistance from the Chinese authorities.

All the operations examined comprised an element of technology transfer from the foreign partners. In the case of the transfer of 'soft' technology, owing to the shortage of skilled labour, training is invariably necessary, depending upon the degree of sophistication of the 'hard' technology involved. Since it is expensive to either send a group of UK instructors to China, or Chinese workers to the UK, an appropriate technique appears to be to train a small group of Chinese who are then used to train their fellows.

Every operation that involves obtaining raw materials locally has experienced difficulties in one or a combination of the following areas[10]: quality, volume, delivery and variety. The only successful solution to this problem so far identified is to import the necessary materials from abroad. Local conditions have made it difficult to bring products up to the companies' normal quality standards. In part this is due to the quality of local raw materials, but it is also explained by the fact that the Chinese have not previously been exposed to such high quality standards.

All the enterprises have had to handle their foreign exchange balances carefully, and while, so far, major problems have not arisen, this is only because it has been possible to sell at least part of the output for hard currencies which can subsequently be used to cover external expenditures (the Renminbi remaining inconvertible).

The use of Chinese management seems to be the norm in every case. This is beneficial to the operation in terms of managing the human resource to greatest economic benefit. Trust is perceived as very important in running the businesses, and the use of Chinese in the management decision making process is seen as the best way to avoid conflict between work practices and management styles. This approach also exploits every potential for the benefit of the organization and avoids many of the problems which have been experienced by expatriates, in terms of adapting to a way of living, and having to cope with the cultural differences, of a foreign country.

Almost all the operations examined had experienced infrastructure problems to varying degrees. While in developed countries energy, transport and housing are taken for granted, no such assumption should be made about China, even within the relative favoured environment of the SEZs. The most common problems encountered have been inadequate transportation and power cuts. These problems had been foreseen in most cases and their effects minimized by locating plants near their markets and installing own-generators.

A further common problem has been delays in bringing production on stream. This is attributed (variously) to poor organization, local project management deficiencies and the very high degree of bureaucracy associated with the Communist system. As an illustration of this problem, it has been reported that it took one company 2 years and 173 stamps of approval to import a single piece of machinery.[11] While no easy solution has been found to the bureaucracy problem, any prospective investor would be well advised to carry out a thorough investigation of the structure of Chinese officialdom if some of the more protracted potential delays are to be avoided. The art of cultivating a personal relationship with those in power, known as *guanxi*, is essential, and potential investors are well advised to develop this skill.

CONCLUSIONS

China's 'open door policy' still brings great opportunities for foreign investors to penetrate the Chinese and the extended Asian market. Britain's role as a China investor is steadily growing. Despite the problems British companies face when establishing projects in China, investing in this country remains an essential tool for penetrating the vast Chinese market as long as other means of doing business with China such as exporting, licensing and other co-operative forms are not available.

Difficulty has, nevertheless, been experienced in introducing radical change into an economy cut off for so long from commercial and technological developments occurring elsewhere. Although a vast number of foreign investors bringing in substantial foreign capital has been as fruitful as anticipated, most investors have experienced numerous problems related to the inadequate investment environment, complicated procedures and the difficulty of negotiating with the Chinese.

British investors also face cultural dissimilarities which result in difficulties in managing production, personnel and marketing issues.[12] Although it is the Chinese who benefit from British–Chinese business relations, especially in terms of trade, it should always be recognized that whoever wants to succeed in the Chinese market must be willing to understand the Chinese way of living, must be patient and must focus on the future.

Not all companies have experienced the difficulties mentioned, and experience suggests that once the initial hurdles have been overcome, the majority of JV investments seem to operate reasonably successfully.[13]

The attitude of the Chinese government itself has been crucial in providing an impetus to overcome the problems imposed by an inconvertible currency, exchange control regulations and a general management ethos seriously out of line with twenty-first-century requirements. Mere investment incentives and policy changes of themselves would have been insufficient to achieve even the limited success that has occurred. While many problems remain, corporations have been able to develop strategies which enhance their possibility of success. A study of the problems those corporations have encountered, and the responses they have developed, provide useful clues to success for those wishing to invest in China.

Notes

*We sincerely thank the European Economic Community (EEC) for their financial support. We also express our appreciation to the Ministry of Foreign Economic Relations and Trade (MOFERT) of the People's Republic of China, for their help in providing useful information.

1. CEC (1994)
2. World Bank (1988)
3. Vogel (1989)
4. Far Eastern Economic Review (1993)
5. Pomfret (1991)
6. Wilpert and Scharf (1990)
7. Yang (1990)
8. Walker and Done (1994)
9. Swain (1991)
10. Stavi and Gang (1988)
11. Walker (1994)
12. Islam (1994)
13. *Financial Times* (1995)

References

Commission of European Communities (1994) 'Towards a New Asia Strategy', Brussels, 13 July. CEC (1994). The report was proposed by Sir Leon Brittan, the European Commissioner for External Trade Relations, as a through review of the European Union's Asia policy, as stated in the *Financial Times* (9 November 1994).

Far Eastern Economic Review (1993) 'Switching into High Gear', *Far Eastern Economic Review*, 30 September, 44.

Financial Times (1995) 'Bayer in China Venture', *Financial Times*, 9 March, 9.

Islam, S. (1994) 'Wake-up Call', *Far Eastern Economic Review*, 4 August, 18–19.

Pomfret, R. (1991) *Investing in China: Ten Years of the 'Open Door' Policy*, Hemel Hempstead, Harvester Wheatsheaf, 103.

Stavis, B. and Gang, Y. (1988) 'A Survey of Shanghai Joint Ventures', *China Business Review*, March–April, 46–8.

Swain, J. (1991) 'Shanghai Surprise', *Sunday Times Magazine*, Business World Supplement, 10 November, 38.

Vogel, E.F. (1989) *One Step Ahead in China: Guangdong Under Reform*, Cambridge, MA, Harvard University Press, 125.

Walker, T. (1994) 'Ready for China to Westernise', *Financial Times*, 19 July, 18.

Walker, T. and Done, K. (1994) 'Chinese Roads Paved with Gold', *Financial Times*, 23 November, 18.

Wilpert, B. and Scharpf, S. Y. (1990) 'Tercultural Management-Joint Ventures in the People's Republic of China', *Journal of Psychology*, 2, 67–79.

World Bank (1988) *China: External Trade and Capital*, Washington, DC, World Bank, 54.

Yang, L. P. (1990) 'Business in China – Current Information Sources', *Asia Pacific Journal of Management*, 7, 137–45.

13 German Exports: Past Development and Future Prospects – Distribution Policy as a Competitive Strategic Component of Mittelstand Firms in the ASEAN Countries

Hans Schmengler and Jürgen Krause

INTRODUCTION

From 1986 to 1988 as well as in 1990 Germany was the largest exporter in the world. The Germans exported 6.8 per cent more than the USA and 47.2 per cent more than Japan as the third largest export nation.[1] Since then, Germany has fallen back continuously. The Statistical Federal Agency (1995) reported that Germany's export' volume in 1993 for example (US$364.6 billion), was considerably below the volume of the USA (US$473.3 billion) and only marginally above that of Japan (US$362.7 billion).[2] Within Europe however, Germany had still an outstanding position as far as its world trade is concerned. Germany, in 1993, exported almost twice as much as Great Britain or Italy and approximately the same amount as China, Hong Kong, Taiwan, South Korea and Singapore together. Since then export development has again been positive, with Germany being ranked clearly second in the world (US$ 523.8 billion) in 1995. Germany reduced the distance to the USA (US$584.7 billion) and increased its lead over Japan (US$443.3 billion).[3]

Although the export volume, according to the International Monetary Fund (IMF),[4] has developed negatively in Germany in 1996, in 1997 exports strongly increased again.

This recent positive development, however, is not due to a dramatic enhancement of activities in high-growth world regions such as East Asia or high-growth industry sectors. This development is the result of a weakening of German currency (whereas in 1994 1 US dollar cost ≈ 1.40 DM, by 1998 1 US dollar cost ≈ 1.80 DM). As a consequence, the international competitiveness of German products in terms of price has increased dramatically. This has in particular validity for German products on international markets (within Asian markets but also beyond them) competing directly with low-cost products manufactured by a growing number of Asian competitors. However, the 1998 devaluation of many Asian countries' currency will have again negative impacts on the price competitiveness of the majority of firms from the highly industrialized nations. This of course, will then also result in a decrease of these states' export volume. However, the overall slightly negative development of Germany's exports since the mid-1980s has been for mainly two reasons:

(1) Analysing German exports as well as German foreign direct investment (FDI), it appears that the majority of activities are taking part within the *European Union.* In 1996 as well as in 1997 Germany exported 56 per cent of its total exports into the partner countries of the Union.[4] All these highly developed European countries are in similar stages of the world trade cycle. Thus, negative impacts of recession, for example, are very strong for firms operating predominantly in these countries. Long-term growth regions such as Asia – in particular, China (Hong Kong), South Korea, Taiwan, Singapore, Malaysia and Indonesia, although at the present in a phase of economic recovery after years of over-speculation – have been largely neglected in the past. However, within the beginning of the 1990s the interest into these countries was extended, and has resulted in slightly increased direct investments and export volume. This viewpoint is confirmed by analysing German export figures in 1996 and 1997. In 1996 Germany exported only 2.9 per cent of its total to the Association of Asian Nations (ASEAN), 2.7 per cent to Japan and 7.8 per cent to the USA.[5] Within the first half of 1997 Germany's export proportion to the ASEAN countries comprised 9.4 per cent, to Japan 2.4 per cent and to the USA 9.1 per cent.[6]

(2) The strong position of Germany as one of the world's leading exporters is mainly made up by the *mechanical engineering, electrical engineering, basic chemical and vehicle sector.* These four sectors constitute more than 70 per cent of German exports.[7] In the mechanical and electrical engineering sector in particular companies belong mainly to the small and medium sized (SME) sector.[8] Here

firms were present very early on the world market and contributed considerably to the favourable German trade surplus.[9] However, owing to the low degree of innovative potential in these sectors, markets are maturing and international competition is growing. Simultaneously Germany's economy is quite weak in high-growth sectors based on innovative future technologies such as biotechnology, medicine technique or information technology (IT). Annual growth rates within these sectors are between 10 and 30 per cent. The German proportion within these industries on the world market, however, can be evaluated to be rather unimportant, with approximately 4–8 per cent. The same is valid also for another growth industry, the service sector. Taylor and Hahn (1990), for example, analysed strategic profiles and leadership styles in high-growth German and British mid-sized firms. They noted that the majority of the British companies were in services, including business services, publishing, retail and wholesale distribution and brewing; only 25 per cent of the British companies in the sample were in manufacturing. On the contrary – not surprisingly – the majority of the German sample were manufacturers of products such as special machinery, tools, and custom castings.[10] Thus, besides the energy and environmental technology sector German companies do not possess any distinctive market shares in emerging high-growth industries.[11] As a consequence the majority of German Mittelstand firms – based in the traditional industry sectors – will have to rely increasingly on the high-growth emerging markets such as East Asia, South America and also Eastern Europe. These markets will gain in the future much more importance for the German Mittelstand firms than may generally be assumed at present.

SPECIFICATIONS OF THE STRATEGIC-PERFORMANCE RELATIONSHIP

The long-term prosperity of any nation depends largely on the international competitiveness of its firms. Thus, one of the most important questions regarding the maintenance of any nation's international competitiveness is concerned with the most favourable strategic profile to be adopted by SMEs. A scientific investigation of this topic requires the consideration of contingency theory which can be understood as a counter to the one-way best approaches of the former.[12] Contingency theory suggests that we should not search for final, ideal solutions for complex topics but generate various solutions which are based on the actual environmental factors surrounding the firm.

As outlined above, the East Asian countries possess growing importance for the German Mittelstand firms mainly based in the manufacturing and construction sector. Taking this into account, this chapter focuses on the investigation of a key competitive strategic factor – the distribution policy – of Mittelstand construction firms operating in the ASEAN countries. Taking contingency theory into consideration again, research results possess particular validity for firms operating in this trading area and belonging to the manufacturing/construction industry sector. Owing to the limited sample size, research results should be interpreted with caution. Further research investigations will have to prove if the obtained results maintain validity under similar and differing environmental settings and parameters.

The selection of appropriate markets and segments, but also the adoption of an optimal distribution/implantation strategy, belongs to the 'core strategies' within an international business approach. That means that to operate with a maximum degree of efficiency and effectiveness, the company has to search for ideal forms to distribute its products on international markets. This strategic component is of fundamental importance for Mittelstand firms, owing to the fact that these firms build on a highly intensive form of customized marketing, closely integrating distribution and communication policy elements. Within this context a large number of successful operating Mittelstand firms use special – and for these companies important – communication channels such as international trade fairs and exhibitions as well as specialized journals; other communication-mix elements are deliberating neglected. This strategic orientation can be explained by the fact that German Mittelstand firms compete highly successfully with technologically sophisticated customized products on international markets.[13] Other than firms in the consumer goods market which deal at first hand with the emotional dimension of their products and brands, German Mittelstand firms belonging to the capital goods market are focused on communicating a vast amount of technical information and details. Personal selling and intensive customer relations are therefore highly important.[14]

EMPIRICAL STUDY

The Education and Development Centre for International Marketing of the Fachhochschule Bochum has conducted an empirical study concerning distribution policy appropriate for a Mittelstand firm belonging to the construction sector and operating in the ASEAN countries. Which implantation strategy fits best with the Mittelstand firm specifications outlined above was investigated. The research result should help to answer the question if successful SME engagement in the ASEAN countries requires intensive forms of international involvement – such as FDI – or can be founded exclusively on exporting. The investigation relates to the example of a Mittelstand firm producing world-wide packaging plants for the cement, lime, gypsum and chemical industry. All customers of this company located in the ASEAN countries – 54 cement producers – were interviewed by mailed questionnaires. The response rate was 61.11 per cent. Up to now the investigated construction firm serves its (potential) customers within the ASEAN countries exclusively by independent travelling salesmen in co-operation with a few field representatives of the parent house. The aim of the investigation is to elucidate if – considering market strategic factors – alternative forms of distribution lead to differing degrees of customer satisfaction and, thus, to higher firm performance. The following distribution policy options have to be taken into consideration.

- *Franchising* is a contractual systematized distribution of products or services. In return for payments, the franchisee provides the franchiser with know-how, the brand name as well as the usage of the product or service. Within the capital goods market only the main parts of the after-sales service should be implemented by franchisees. The advantage of this form of distribution is that a fast penetration of the ASEAN countries can be realized. As a disadvantage it has to be mentioned that the franchisees cannot be controlled carefully and, thus, sub-optimal solutions may be accepted.
- *Joint ventures* are a capital- and contractual-based co-operation usually between a foreign and a local firm. The advantage of this approach is that the foreign firm can quickly and conveniently acquire the necessary knowledge about the culture, the country and political background as well as economic conditions. The disadvantage is that different cultures and interests between the co-operation partners cause quite often severe problems, resulting in only a marginal proportion of the founded joint ventures surviving in the long term.
- The foundation of a firm-owned *subsidiary* avoids the disadvantage of a joint venture (JV) but enables the firm simultaneously to keep very close customer relations, which is of fundamental importance

for Mittelstand firms, as already outlined. Beyond that, the permanent presence in the customers' vicinity can result in improvements of company image and familiarity. This may result in higher sales volumes and amortize the high start-up investments, but the high running fixed costs of a subsidiary have to be investigated in advance.

EMPRICAL RESULTS

General and Service Orientated Customer Expectations

Customers within the ASEAN countries expect product-specific know-how, competence, decision autonomy and fast as well as punctual reaction to enquiries. Country- and culture-specific knowledge, as well as the ability to communicate in the native language of the customer, are presumed. Beyond that, the offering firm should be present at trade fairs within the ASEAN countries. The expectations of the customers in the ASEAN countries are summarized in Figure 13.1.

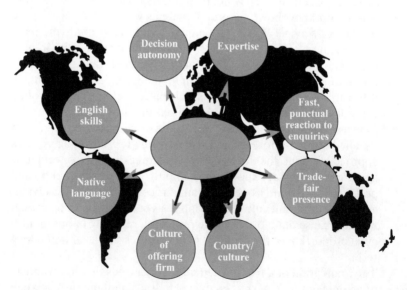

Figure 13.1   Customer expectations

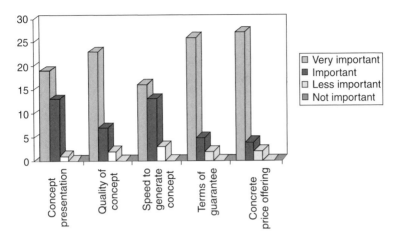

Figure 13.2 Relevant factors within the offering and negotiation phase

Two-thirds of the interviewed customers evaluate the following criteria as 'very important'. Customers expect the drawing up of a feasibility study (including details of implementation and testing for economic and technical viability), definite financial offers, timetables and appropriate information.[15] Individual financial resources of customers have to be taken into consideration and the demonstration of relevant experience, for example a reference plant, as a general requirement. The time required to develop a final concept is mentioned as 'very important' by half of those interviewed. Almost 10 per cent, however, evaluate this aspect to be of 'less importance'. Comparing this statement to the other relevant factors of the offering and negotiation phase – shown in Figure 13.2 – one can conclude that other relevant factors are valued higher than the speed with which offers are drawn up. Of particular importance for the customers are guaranteed services and definite price offers, which are classified as 'very important' by 80 per cent of those interviewed. But the presentation and the quality of a concept are also evaluated as 'important' or 'very important'.

To reduce the costs almost all customers evaluate the local production and the integration of suppliers based within the ASEAN countries as 'important' or 'very important'. This is also valid for the possibility to control an eventual local production of parts and the actual building of the plant: customers see their interests maintained after the actual contracting phase is completed. However, of highest importance within the project implementation phase is sound product documentation. This has to provide exact information about the individual components of the plant and at what time each component will be installed, and in what order. More than 80 per cent of the customers evaluate this criterion as 'very important', and 15 per cent as 'important'.

Of a similar high importance for customers are an obliging attitude and concessions. If, for example, additional activities arise which are not contractually determined, the customers in the ASEAN countries expect generous behaviour by their business partner. Beyond this, speed as well as high-quality services within the guarantee period are seen as 'very important' by 97 per cent of those interviewed. The majority of customers (almost 90 per cent) demand that this level of quality service is also maintained after the guarantee period. Almost 95 per cent of those asked are also interested in advice about the potential to modernize or upgrade their plant in the future. In spite of the long life cycle of the product, the customers want to be continuously informed about actual technical standards to maintain their competitiveness. 6 per cent evaluate this service – as shown in Figure 13.3 – as 'less important'. These customer demands include that the provider should maintain his partnership after the installation of the plant and extend the guarantee period, for example, if it is necessary.

Level of Customer Satisfaction and Preferred Distribution Policy

Next to the investigation of general and service orientated customer expectations, the study has also focused on the level of customer satisfaction with the actual distribution policy of the construction firm and emerging stimulation for improvements. At the present, 94 per cent of customers work together with the firm via local, self-employed and independent representatives and 6 per cent work together with employees of the parent firm. The analysis has clearly revealed that the majority of customers (85 per cent) is absolutely satisfied with the actual distribution policy of the firm. Beyond that, when asked for the most preferred form of co-operation with the offering firm, 78 per cent of customers confirmed a preference for local, independent representatives. Nineteen per cent, however, would like to work together with employees of the parent house and only 3 per cent declared that they would prefer the co-operation with employees of a subsidiary. These circumstances are summarized in Figure 13.4.

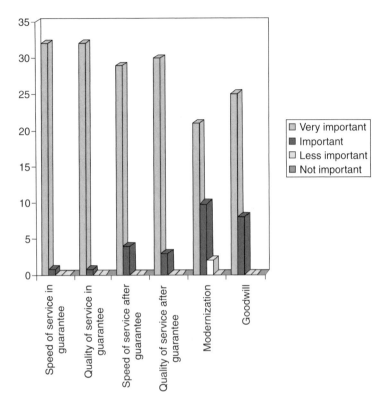

Figure 13.3   Relevant factors within the after-sales phase

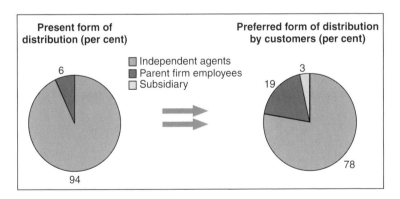

Figure 13.4   Present form of distribution and that preferred by customers for construction firms in ASEAN countries, per cent

CONCLUSION AND MARKET STRATEGIC CONSEQUENCES

Summarizing the results regarding general customer expectations as well as the relevant factors in the pre- and after-sales phase, it can be realized that almost all the criteria investigated are evaluated – as 'very important'. That means that the customers have extraordinary high requirements regarding the distribution and communication policy of the offering firms and do not place an order before they are convinced about performance and services.

The high level of customer satisfaction regarding the actual distribution and communication policy of the construction firms investigated (85 per cent absolutely satisfied) reveals the high performance level of the approach adopted. This has in particular to take the high expectations of the customers in ASEAN countries into account. Beyond this, the analysis shows that the customers in general do not wish that the construction firms investigated should change their actual distribution policy. Taking these results as well as the disadvantages of the alternative distribution forms into consideration, DFI in the form of a company-owned subsidiary does not seems a viable distribution alternative. Thus, at least in the construction industry within the ASEAN countries, direct exporting in line with independent agents has to be shown to represent a viable long-term success related distribution form. However, the measurement of the satisfaction degree of the customers within the ASEAN countries has revealed that a minority (13 per cent) wishes a closer co-operation with representatives of the parent house. This means that although the distribution of products via representatives is basically the approach demanded, the actual distribution form of the construction firm selected still possesses potential for optimization, including:

(1) development of a comprehensive network of sales representatives to meet all customers' desires in an optimal time-frame
(2) more competence for the representatives to increase flexibility and decrease response time
(3) development of strategies and benchmarks for independent representatives
(4) intensive education of representatives in financial and technical issues
(5) periodical representative meetings in the parent house as well as in the ASEAN countries to exchange experiences, expectations, problems and strategies

(6) provision of responsibility for stock of spare parts to representatives, increasing speed and quality of repair and maintenance works
(7) more intensive presence in trade fairs in ASEAN countries
(8) provision of representatives with notebooks and laptops to improve
flexibility, speed of problem-solution and direct communication
with customers.

An innovative integration of distribution and communication policy
elements should also take latest developments within the computer
industry into account. In this regard a general presence on the internet as
well as the exchange of firm data via an intranet or a fax databank is
required. Electronic prospectuses can then be sent within the offering
phase to customers in the form of CD-ROMs. Beyond this virtual reality
or CAD-illustrations can be used within the offering and negotiation
phase to provide customers with concrete plans and offerings and
subsequently discuss these via telephone conferences. Within the guarantee period plants can be monitored via modems. This enables the
parent house directly to diagnose and eventually analyze occurring
defects and failures. In interviews, 80 per cent of those asked evaluated
the general adoption of latest computer technology within the field
service in the capital goods market as positive. However, only 30 per cent
welcomed the use of computers within the contract negotiation phase.[16]
Taking these results into consideration it becomes obvious that personal
contacts should still possess priority within supplier and customer relations. Innovative computer communication technology should, however,
be used as an additional tool to support and confirm customer relations.

The empirical investigation within this study has revealed that a
change within the status quo of the construction firm's distribution policy
would not lead to higher customer satisfaction and, thus, firm performance.
As a consequence it can be concluded that to penetrate ASEAN countries
successfully – in spite of expectation to the contrary –[17] company-owned
subsidiaries are not absolutely necessary for Mittelstand firms based
in the construction sector. The neglect of subsidiaries and the exclusive
reliance on sales representatives, however, requires that firms are able
to guarantee the provision of long-term high-quality services by the
sales representatives. Therefore:

(1) representatives have to possess high decision autonomy
(2) close connections between independent representatives and the
parent house have to be developed (with common development of
strategies)

(3)   high-quality services have to be provided for customers; focus has to be addressed to personal contacts which are supported by innovative communication technologies.

A large number of Mittelstand firms do not operate so far – in spite of existing internal and external potential – on international markets. This can mainly be explained by the lack of financial and managerial resources. However, the results generated within this study suggest that the ASEAN countries can also be penetrated successfully without relying on highly expensive forms of distribution. Thus, many Mittelstand firms in the construction industry should reconsider their international policy and should give up their reluctance towards operating in ASEAN countries. If further investigations show that these research results can be transferred to other industry sectors, too, Mittelstand firms in general should enhance their exporting activities globally. This has in particular validity for high-growth nations such as Eastern Europe or South America but has some validity for other regions as well. This does not mean, however, that in general Mittelstand firms should renounce FDI, but that the relevant economic parameters should be critically examined. This has in particular validity also for the production side. Here experiences have shown that the envisaged cost reduction owing to lower direct and indirect labour costs as well as owing to lower tax rates cannot be achieved. Beyond this, quite often qualitative requirements cannot be met by the foreign production plants.[18] This, however, should not lead to the situation that Mittelstand firms withdraw from existing or planned co-operation with foreign suppliers. On the contrary, to reduce costs and thereby to maintain competitiveness, long-lasting co-operation – guaranteeing quality standards and punctual delivery times – have to be established. The empirical investigation has shown that the integration of local suppliers is explicitly demanded by the ASEAN country customers. To protect the existing know-how as well as innovative and sophisticated products, core-competencies should, however, be implemented by the parent house or company-owned subsidiaries.

GENERAL ECONOMIC IMPACTS

To meet with the negative development of German exports (adjusted by the weakening of the German currency) and the reduction of Germany's international competitiveness, Mittelstand firms have permanently to adapt to international customer requirements. Beyond this economic policy has to provide adequate target-group locational parameters.

If in the long-term locational parameters can be created which prevent the unnecessary transfer of domestic German capital to foreign countries, the reservations about a German location as well as about German long-term prosperity are unnecessary. This can be explained by the fact that the processing of innovative operations within Germany as well as the settlement of foreign capital in the immediate vicinity of these operations leads to a development of related firm clusters. These clusters secure the permanent evolution of sophisticated technology, which again guarantees the generation of internationally highly-competitive products.[19] The high growth potential of the newly industrialized nations in line with increasing customer heterogeneity of the highly industrialized nations creates favourable opportunities for the global export of high-quality, sophisticated products manufactured by SMEs. As a consequence, the future, too, should be characterized by vast increases of export volume caused by internationally exporting SMEs. A focus in this regard can be expected within the emerging markets with long-term high-growth potential, such as in particular-East Asia but also South America, Eastern to Europe and countries of the former Soviet Union (FSU).

Notes

1. Simon (1992) 115–23.
2. Backhaus Büschken and Voeth (1996).
3. *Statistisches Bundesamt* (1997).
4. *Statistisches Bundesamt* (1997).
5. *Statistisches Bundesamt* (1997).
6. Fricke and Klusmann (1997)
7. Anon (1994).
8. Zeitel (1990).
9. Simon (1992), 15.
10. Taylor and Hahn (1990).
11. Backhaus, Büschken and Voeth (1996), 11.
12. Donaldson (1995).
13. Simon (1996).
14. Muzyka, Breuninger and Rossell (1997).
15. Backhaus (1990).
16. Flory (1995).
17. Hirn (1997) see Simon.
18. Sommer (1997).
19. Porter (1990).

References

Anon. (1994) *Süddeutsche Zeitung*, 8 September, 38.

Backhaus, K., Büschken, J. and Voeth, M. (1996) *Internationales Marketing*, Stuttgart, Schäffer-Poeschel, 9.

Backhaus, K. (1990) *Investitionsgütermarketing*, a.a.O., S.437

Donaldson, L. (1995) *Contingency Theory: History of Management Thought*, Aldershot, Dartmouth Publishing Company Limited 11.

Flory, M. (1995) *Computergestützter Vertrieb von Investitionsgütern*, Wiesbaden, DU Verlag, 282.

Fricke, T. and Klusmann, S. (1997) 'Weltweit gefragt', *Manager Magazine*, 27 (12), 234–43.

Hirn, W. (1997) 'Raus in die Welt', *Manager Magazine*, October 97, 140–48.

Muzyka, D., Breuninger, H. and Rossell, G. (1997) 'The Secret of New Growth in Old German "Mittelstand" Companies', *European Management Journal*, 15(2) 147–57.

Porter, M. E. (1990) 'The Competitive Advantage of Nations', New York, *Free Press 1990*.

Simon, H. (1992) 'Lessons from Germany's Midsize Giants', *Harvard Business Review*, 70 (2), March–April, 115–23.

Simon, H. (1996) *Die heimlichen Gewinner: Die Erfolgsstrategien unbekannter Weltmarktführer*, Frankfurt and New York, Campus Verlag.

Sommer, C. (1997) 'Stille Reserven', *Manager Magazine*, April 1997, 104–16.

Statistisches Bundesamt (1997) *Deutschland als Handelspartner* http:/www. statistik-bund.de/basis/d/bd.18htm.

Taylor, B. and Hahn, D (1990) *Strategy and Leadership in Growth Companies*, in; D. Hahn, and B. Taylor (eds), *Strategische Unternehmensplanung und Strategische Unternehmensführung: Stand und Entwicklungstendenzen*, 6th rev. edn, Heidelberg, Physica.

Zeitel, G. (1990), *Volkswirtschaftliche Bedeutung von Klein- und Mittelbetrieben*, in H.C. Pfohl (ed.), *Betriebswirtschaftslehre der Klein- und Mittelbetriebe: größenspezifische Probleme und Möglichkeiten zu ihrer Lösung*, 2nd rev. edn, Berlin, Schmidt 36.

14 Experiences of JV Companies in China: Management and Operational Issues

Bob Ritchie, Lee Zhuang and
Tim Whitworth

INTRODUCTION

China as the recipient of unprecedented levels of foreign investment
has seen the establishment of 300 000 Sino–foreign joint ventures (JVs).
As China is still an industrializing and developing nation many of these
JVs have experienced management and operational problems. A number
of these are common to other developing and industrializing nations;
however, specific cultural differences and China's late entrance into the
world market has meant that some of the problems are peculiar to China.
The underlying theme of this chapter is to explore and analyse these
management and operational problems that Sino–foreign JV companies
have experienced in China. The research has primarily focused upon
Western investors in China as these companies tend to experience problems which are often related to a lack of understanding of the Chinese
business environment and the Asian culture. The results presented from
a qualitative empirical study into JVs of this type are integrated into the
wider body of evidence in the literature concerning partnership and JV
arrangements in developing countries.

This study concentrates on two key dimensions of the JV relationship
– the supply-chain management issues and the human resource management (HRM) issues. Supply-chain management in this context is primarily associated with logistics including the sourcing and transportation of
raw material inputs and the ultimate distribution of the finished products
for domestic consumption and for export. The HRM concerns addressed
include recruitment, management training and employee retention, with
specific attention given to the employment of local labour or expatriate
labour. The research builds on previous studies in this field involving

other Western organizations within China as a whole and draws on the experiences of 15 JV companies operating in Guangdong Province who were part of the empirical research study.

OPERATIONAL CHALLENGES FACING JVs

A study undertaken by the Euro–China Business Association (ECBA) on behalf of the European Union revealed a number of significant operational issues facing investors in China. (See Table 14.1)

Table 14.1   Factors inhibiting investing in China: percentage of companies surveyed citing factors as being prohibitive or 'serious'

Factor	per cent
Lack of transparency in rules and laws	72
Intellectual property violations	53
Differing rules in different parts of China	49
Corruption	41
Foreign exchange balance requirements	39
Distribution and marketing difficulties	35
Local content requirements	33
Restrictions on exporting from China	32
Retention of staff	26
Restrictions of recruiting local staff	24
Restrictions on expatriate staff	20

Sample: 102 companies.
Source: *China–Britain Trade Review*, April 1997, 16.

The issues relating to the operations of these businesses covering distribution, HRM, recruitment and training are addressed in the current chapter. The first section deals with the distribution difficulties encountered by organizations which represented an inhibiting factor identified by some 35 per cent of the organizations surveyed (See Table 14.1) and a similar proportion of the 15 companies included in the present study. The second section analyses the three key HRM factors identified – the recruitment and retention of staff, staff training and development and the restrictions on the recruitment of both local and expatriate staff. The issues associated with the legal infrastructure and their impact on the JV organization (i.e. lack of transparency in rules and laws, intellectual property violations and corruption) have been addressed in an associated paper (Ritchie *et al.*, 1999). The other set of important issues are addressed in a further paper (Ritchie, Zhuang and Whitworth, 1999), addressing the issues associated with the divergence of strategic planning and policies.

DISTRIBUTION ISSUES

Distribution is proving to be a major operational hindrance for Sino–foreign JV companies who need not only to accommodate the generally underdeveloped transport infrastructure but also the inefficiencies inherent in the structure that does operate. The distribution infrastructure has not expanded fast enough to accommodate the increasing amount of goods marketed by multinationals and local businesses seeking to penetrate new markets within China. Traditional road, rail and air channels have been undercapitalized and are consequently congested. The Chinese government's transport agencies still to a large extent 'operate under the assumption – deeply ingrained during decades of central planning – that consumers will buy what is stocked' (*Business China*, 30 October 1995).

The transport agencies still lack the concept of modern management and operations in a market economy and the need to provide an efficient and continuous method of ensuring goods reach their intended market.

China's road infrastructure is quite underdeveloped – only 24 000 km of the 1.2 million km (i.e. 0.2 per cent) of roads are classified as highways. The actual paved roads, per head of population, is only one-thirtieth the American average and half the Indian (Wilson, 1997). Moreover the congestion looks set to increase further with the number of vehicles expected to rise to 12 million by the year 2000 (Wilson, 1997). In Guangdong Province, and more particularly in the Pearl River Delta, where the primary research was conducted, the road infrastructure has shown significant improvement. This has been funded from the local profits gained from the high proportion of Sino–foreign JV companies which are situated in Southern Guangdong. The rail network, like the road system, is grossly overburdened, though many large capital improvements are in hand to improve the infrastructure with new high-speed lines between Beijing and Shanghai and a new line to Hong Kong from Beijing expected to alleviate some of the problems.

There do not appear to be any generic solutions to the distribution and supply-chain issues encountered. Experience gained in operating within China tends to enable the organization to find solutions to the problems encountered. The following cases illustrate some of the potential solutions applied in this particular context.

(1) *Nabisco* had invested in a second JV at Chongqing, an inland city. It suffered severe problems in importing the necessary ingredients to this remote area of South West China. The ingredients had to be flown in owing to the inconsistent and unreliable road network. Furthermore it experienced problems in guaranteeing a regular supply of local flour and the local outward distribution chain was somewhat fragmented. Nabisco sought to overcome these problems by selling a percentage of its stake in the JV to the local Commerce Bureau in the hope that enhanced local ownership would encourage the local organizations to find solutions. However, despite trying to rectify the distribution–supply problems the JV had to admit defeat and transfer production to Suzhou which had an advanced distribution network already in place. (*Business China*, 21 July 1997).

(2) *IBM* re-invested in China after suffering great losses in the early 1980s which led to the company pulling out. One of its primary reasons for pulling out initially was the failure of its customer service network owing to problems experienced in distribution. The company sought to rectify these previous distribution and service difficulties by entering into a JV alliance with the Ministry of Railways. The partnership has proved most fruitful for IBM as it has sited many of its new service centres in rail terminals. IBM has been able to achieve competitive advantage through its ability to ship computer parts via the rail network within 24 hours. In contrast, competitors must book cargo space three weeks in advance, not having the advantage of such a preferential arrangement. The result of this affiliation is that sales rose by 50 per cent annually from 1994 to 1997 to more than $500 million and a rapid expansion of service centres is planned (*Business Week*, 26 May 1997).

(3) *United Biscuits* maintains that overcoming the numerous hurdles in the distribution and supply chain was the company's biggest challenge. Since the deregulation of distribution the various distributors are 'learning if slowly how to operate effectively in a market economy' (*Business China*, 30 October 1995). United Biscuits opened six storage depots in major cities and is now helping local distributors with the marketing and selling of their products. They have also formed an informal conglomerate of multinationals to

discuss and provide solutions as all local multinationals in the Yangtze River Delta perceive poor distribution as a common enemy (*Business China*, 30 October 1995).

(4) *Proctor and Gamble*, after experiencing sporadic problems with local wholesalers and distributors, established its own transport and supply chain. To ensure that stores stock Proctor and Gamble products the company offers them discounts for payments received within seven days of shipment (Clifford and Roberts, 1997). Similarly, both Coca Cola and Pepsi have followed Proctor and Gamble's lead. The two soft drink companies have both abandoned 'third-party bureaucratic wholesales' and now conduct the distribution drive themselves (Wilson, 1997: 136). Pepsi feel that distribution requires direct management to ensure that it succeeds in achieving its continued expansion in China (*Business China*, 19 February 1997).

HUMAN RESOURCES

The ECBA study (See Table 14.1) found that HRM problems and issues were within the top 10 factors identified by more than 25 per cent of the businesses in the sample. A study conducted by *The Economist* Intelligence Unit on multinational companies in China: *Winners and Losers* (1997) also found that managerial skill shortages coupled with difficulties in overcoming language and culture obstacles were the major hindrances to increasing productivity in JV companies. Other barriers in order of importance were not selling enough, resistance to change and overmanning.

The increasing number of foreign-funded enterprises in China is creating operational problems in the area of human resources and staff management. In a survey of 96 Sino–foreign JVs, conducted by the Hong Kong Institute of Human Resource Management, with the Chinese State Council's International Technology and Economy Institute of Development Research Centre, it found that there were problems with the following:

- General poor quality of management
- Unmet needs for training and staff development and the development of a suitable training policy
- High staff turnover and retention problems (*Business China*, 3 March 1997).

In the empirical survey of businesses conducted in Guangdong Province a similar trend was found. Over half of the businesses contacted in the exploratory survey of problems found that:

- 53 of companies interviewed suffered from a lack of sufficiently trained managers
- in response to this, 93 of companies had initiated training schemes
- 66 of companies surveyed experienced a high level of management turnover.

The effects of these human resource problems resulted in companies suffering operational difficulties, caused by problems in recruiting the correct calibre of staff, the extra expenses associated with retraining and cultural realignment, problems of retaining and securing expatriate staff and difficulties relating to handling industrial disputes.

Recruitment

JVs were initially established by the recruitment of the local partner's staff. In the immediate years after the beginning of the 'open door policy' this was not a major problem, with the great majority of industries establishing production in China merely requiring unskilled manual labour. However, as China has now attracted a broad spectrum of industries, JVs' need trained management and workers. The major problem is that China suffers from a major skill shortage which has been intensified by China's recent historical background: the Cultural Revolution interfered with the education of those Chinese citizens born between 1950 and 1965:

> Due to the Cultural Revolution, these people did not receive a proper education. Instead some of the older ones became soldiers of the red guards. After the end of the revolution they had too much learning to catch up on. Over 40 per cent of this segment aged 30–44 are blue collar workers compared with only 16 per cent aged 18 to 29 years old. (Ariga and Yasue 1997)

Another major problem associated with recruitment is that existing staff who may have initially been inherited by the Sino–foreign JVs are hard to remove. Consequently many such JVs suffer from overstaffing. Gillette's joint venture with the Shanghai Razor Blade Factory has been hampered by 'chronic overmanning': over half of its 1000-strong workforce is viewed by the company as surplus to requirements (*Business China*, 19 August 1996). Yet in common with many other JVs Gillette has problems in reducing or rebalancing this workforce. Local government resistance and the workers' expectations of long tenure 'under the so-called iron rice bowl system' (Wilson, 1997, 143) are the primary reasons for this situation. This modern-day form of paternalism and expectation that a job is for life emanates from the Communist state planning era. However, staff redundancy and recruitment will become necessary as technology and management needs increase.

Recruitment Solutions

There are a number of approaches to solving the issues associated with recruiting appropriate staff. Each of these carry particular strengths and weaknesses which are briefly summarized below.

(1) *Direct advertising*   There is a mixed response from JVs to the use of direct advertising (Wilson, 1997). Newspaper advertisements are expensive, 'the cost of placing of full page advertisement in a national newspaper can be as much as US$20 000' (Wilson, 1997: 143). Furthermore it is advisable to set a very clear job description as many thousands of résumés may arrive with only a handful of suitably qualified applicants.

(2) *Recruitment agencies*   Recruitment agencies, either government or privately run, are a way of obtaining qualified staff. Local labour bureaux are a good and effective way of recruiting blue-collar workers. These bureaux can overcome the difficulties that many Sino–joint ventures suffer by being able to obtain the necessary work papers needed to transfer from company to company or to restricted towns such as Shanghai or Shenzhen.

(3) *Personnel exchange centres*   Personnel exchange centres are run at a provincial level and specialize in supplying technical and graduate staff. Philips has made use of this avenue to overcome its problems in effective recruitment (Wilson, 1997: 144).

(4) *Universities*   One of the best ways to ensure that competent staff are recruited is to establish links with universities. Ford has developed business links with Qinghia and Xiamen Universities where students work on actual business projects with distinctive objectives (*China Business and Investment*, March 1997). However, some universities require a payment, usually the repayment of fees, when a Chinese graduate joins a foreign firm. At Fudan

University in Shanghai the cost to a foreign firm recruiting a PhD student can be 21 000 RMB.

(5) *Service companies*   The Foreign Enterprise Service Corporation has provided a useful service in acting as a recruitment agent for JVs. However, it owns the employee and a service charge must be paid for each one. This form of recruitment can cause industrial unrest, with disparities in earnings.

(6) *Headhunters*   Foreign JVs have found it hard to recruit expatriate staff to China, and it is even harder to persuade them to stay on for an extended period. Proctor and Gamble grant 18-month contracts to its foreign staff in Guangdong and the majority are not renewed. The shortage of qualified local managers and expatriates willing to work in China has led to the formation of foreign and domestically owned executive search companies. Poaching is a major problem in China: at United Biscuit's Hangzhou factory the British company has experienced problems with the poaching of staff. To combat this, the company introduced increased training to develop a company ethos.

Training

The lack of sufficiently trained staff in China has prompted many Sino–foreign JV companies to initiate their own training schemes. This is due in part to 'China's gap in business education that has now become a huge canyon due to the demand created by a surge of private enterprises in the last eight years. Even state industries have begun to see the need for managers with business degrees' (*China Business and Investment*, March 1997). Siemens has found that Chinese employees often need training in the methods and skills of general management and international business practice (Wilson, 1997).

Increased competition in China has prompted many Sino–foreign JVs to teach functional skills such as sales and marketing and accounting. Marketing and selling were less of a priority as there was an insatiable appetite to purchase foreign or JV products; latterly, increased competition in certain sectors has meant that companies' strategies have had to be adjusted somewhat, to face the increased challenge from rural producers.

Cross-cultural Training

The misunderstandings that arise from differences between Chinese and Western culture have also generated an expanding niche for cross-cultural training. China is a collectivist nation while Western nations are more individualistic. Therefore a consensus of understanding both methods of behaviour must be gained (Hoecklin, 1992). Whirlpool, the American electrical appliance manufacturer, sends all its management team for a week's cross-cultural training programme in Colorado (Wilson, 1997).

Other Forms of Training

Most companies use in-house training. However, care must be taken to ensure effective translation of language and the correct interpretation of the specific cultural barriers that international training schemes may not transcend. United Biscuits has expanded its Shekou human resources department into a fully fledged training centre using expatriates to train the local trainers (*Business China*, 30 October 1995).

Many companies send Chinese staff to their company headquarters. Companies such as Henkel send their technical staff to Germany to teach them in areas of technical operation (*Business China*, 11 December 1995). This not only strengthens employees' technical knowledge, it also creates a closer bond and understanding of company culture (Wilson, 1997).

Another aim of such training is to teach Chinese management about the need for enforcement of quality control practices amongst the workforce. Avoiding the loss of one's 'face' or maintaining other people's self-respect is a fundamental part of Chinese society and culture. Therefore care must be taken in overcoming this obstacle when enforcement needs to take place; Chinese management must learn to take constructive criticism and advice without becoming offended. By visiting a foreign headquarters these managers can gain a better assessment of company philosophy and discover the need for effective enforcement.

Problems Associated with Overseas Training and Solutions

Full training abroad may last up to five years. This can cause some problems in itself:

- On return to China, employees are more vulnerable to being poached by competitors. To prevent such an occurrence binding contracts need to be established and also the promise of rapid promotion if successful. The Hong Kong Bank has suffered problems in maintaining staff loyalty owing to China's weak legal system (Wilson, 1997).

- Long periods abroad leave Chinese employees out of touch with conditions and expectations in China. Short-term training overseas with the prospect of further study overseas and a good promotional structure creates more responsive employees (*Business China*, 11 December 1995).

Educational Training

Another method of ensuring a well-trained future management team is to sponsor employees or trainees through an MBA course. Cable and Wireless has initiated a scholarship programme to train students in finance, marketing and communications (Revvid, 1994). The Chinese government has also acknowledged the great skill shortage by establishing many MBA courses across China. The China Business Administration Training Centre in Beijing is a JV between the Chinese government and the European Community (*Beijing Review*, 8–14 April 1996). These projects have laid the foundations to supply Chinese and foreign JVs with trained staff who reflect the skills needed in a market economy.

Salaries

The investment boom in China coupled with the huge skilled labour shortage has led to a rapid increase in salaries. Foreign JVs must compete against price inflation and general wage rises in order to keep their staff. These increases have been further exacerbated by increased demands for pension and medical expenses contributions. Prosperous areas such as Shenzhen are now becoming costly cities to produce goods in, which is why many companies are moving inland to areas offering relocation and tax holidays with significantly cheaper labour costs. Watson and Wyatt (in Wilson, 1997) found average salary increases for foreign company staff in 1994 in Beijing, Shanghai and Guangzhou to be as presented in Table 14.2.

Skills shortages can lead to situations which are unusual in the West. Secretaries can command higher salaries than accountants or architects owing to the demand for proficiency in English (Wilson, 1997).

Difficulties Related to Expatriate Workers

China's rapid growth of investment has led to an increase in demand for expatriate staff to work in China. However, these demands have

Table 14.2   Average salary increases for foreign company staff, July 1994–January 1999

	Jul. 1994–Jun. 1995 (per cent)	Feb. 1995–Jan. 1996 (per cent)	Feb. 1996–Jan. 1997 (per cent)
Non-management			
Beijing	27.7	24.6	20.0
Shanghai	28.0	25.3	19.9
Guangzhou	25.0	22.9	19.8
Management			
Beijing	26.7	19.1	19.9
Shanghai	27.1	16.7	19.8
Guangzhou	25.1	17.2	20.1

Source: Investing in China, 1997.

been affected by the Chinese government's wish to cut the number of foreign workers in favour of local staff. This has meant that when selecting expatriate staff extreme care should be taken to recruit members of staff that can adapt to the significant differences in the working and cultural environment.

A study conducted by the Manchester University Business School for the European Union suggests that expatriate workers are ill prepared to cope with the demands of their posting. The study, entitled 'Euro Expats in China', sought the views of 65 expatriates representing 50 companies in China. Respondents came from all sectors of the economy. Over two-thirds of those companies interviewed were about to increase the number of expatriates used in China. The survey found that managers were generally ill prepared for China with just over a third receiving little in the way of preparation at all. Recruits also lacked the essential basics of cross-cultural courses which tend to create a strong company philosophy. Respondents also noted a number of key challenges, one being dealing with the Chinese business environment. Another was coping with family difficulties settling in China. To overcome these complications expatriate workers needed to have excellent interpersonal skills to bridge the cultural gap (*China–Britain Trade Review*, July 1997).

Sino–foreign JVs that employ foreign executives have difficulties in attracting and keeping staff in China. To overcome this obstacle many such expatriates merely live in China during the week and spend weekends in Hong Kong. This is indeed quite a popular choice: a survey of 60 companies in 1995 found that some 31 per cent of chief executives and managing directors and 44 per cent of divisional managers were commuting in this way (Perrin in Wilson, 1997). At the San Miguel Brewery in Guangdong Province the chief executive of the brewery commutes to Manila in the Philippines each weekend (Whitworth in Wilson, 1997). Another problem is maintaining continuity in management as expatriate postings generally only stay in their position for two or three years. Before recruiting expatriates notice must be taken of the significant costs involved in maintaining and employing new expatriate staff. In addition to the basic salary there are a plethora of other costs to bear in mind:

* The payment of incentives/bonus
* Tax equalization to the level of home country
* Basic salary
* Profit-sharing
* Hardship payments
* Completion bonus
* Home leave, rest and relaxation
* Allowances (e.g. cost of living, foreign service premium, housing, meals, transportation, laundry, education, relocation and moving)
* Housing foreign staff (*Investing in China 1997*).

Housing

Large international cities such as Guangzhou, Shanghai and Beijing usually have international-standard accommodation, although this can be costly. Cadbury in Beijing pays over US$8000 per month in rent for an apartment for its Australian management team (*Business China*, 20 January 1997). San Miguel have constructed purpose-built houses in the grounds of their brewery near Foshan in Guangdong province. These large capital outlays make the selection of the right calibre of expatriate staff essential.

Prior to the 'open door policy' China's workers had been housed on site in their '*dan wei*' or work unit. The legacy of this system of providing worker housing has been inherited by many JV companies, especially those who have taken over state enterprises. The provision of worker housing can cause escalating costs for the JV, in terms of maintenance and complying with the increasing number of social regulations. Proctor and Gamble's joint venture in Guangzhou decided not to provide worker housing owing to the increased costs and the difficulties it creates when workers retire (Whitworth, 1997).

In order to attract new workers it may be necessary to provide housing assistance, as on joining a foreign JV workers may lose their subsidized state housing (Wilson, 1997). When providing housing for the work-force, some firms consider the workers are more productive and loyal. Wangles gas appliance factory in Guangdong province provides housing for its 2500-strong workforce. Furthermore, it has encouraged a strong works social programme with a choir, orchestra and sports facilities. This JV sees the encouragement of such an active works schedule as merely reinforcing the collectivist cultural society in China (Whitworth, 1996).

A final solution is to increase salaries to enable Chinese workers to rent housing. 'Housing is a deductible expense for tax purposes' (Wilson, 1997: 155).

Trade Unions

JVs are not obliged to reject unionization. However, some local author-ities guarantee no social unrest in a bid to attract foreign investment and prohibit unions from entering some JVs (Wilson, 1997).

On the whole there have been very few operational problems caused by trade unions. In China they are usually non-confrontational and rep-resent workers in areas of welfare. Representation and interference is also receding, with any activities restricted to lunch breaks or after work. This trend is set to continue as the government recognizes that foreign firms require freedom to operate.

Staff Retention

Turnover of staff is a major problem for JV companies. A survey con-ducted by Watson and Wyatt (in Wilson, 1997) found that companies reported a 16 per cent annual turnover of staff. According to other findings, rather than being due to poor management the high turnover reflects the skill shortage in China, particularly in the technological industries. Staff are often enticed by the prospect of better pay and overseas training.

Volkswagen found that after training its managers in Shanghai, the majority of those trained then left to take enticing jobs elsewhere (*Business China*, 11 November 1996).

Solutions to Staff Retention

Shangri La Hotels had an enormous problem in staff retention when it first entered China. Their Shenzhen hotel experienced an 89 per cent turnover of staff in one single year (Wilson, 1997). In order to counteract this operating difficulty Shangri La Hotels introduced a strategy, whose main elements were:

- First it decided to re-educate staff in language and etiquette skills
- It then decided to draw on local school labour by investing in new school facilities and teaching resources in return for teachers educating potential workers in English and basic business practice
- From this pool, the best recruits were then taken for on-the-job (OJT) training including computer applications. To further encourage them to join the company these pupils were given a short complimentary stay in the Shenzhen Shangri La Hotel
- After joining the hotel, new adjacent accommodation blocks were constructed for the workers, with sports facilities
- The result was that staff turnover was reduced to single figures
- The company had not just improved salaries; rather it had improved the worker's lifestyles and encouraged them to make the same commitment to the company as they had displayed to their staff (Wilson, 1997).

CONCLUSIONS AND RECOMMENDATIONS

A general conclusion one can draw from this study is that the problems illustrated in the Guangdong Province report tend to be commonly experienced by most sectors of industry in most parts of China. This merely reflects the fact that China is still very much a developing nation. The rate of foreign investment has surpassed government attempts to put in place a suitably framed business environment in which business can prosper. Indeed, future investment is being targeted and encouraged to improve the infrastructure in China under 'Build, operate and transfer schemes' (Ridding in Wilson 1997).

There seems to be a general consensus amongst investors that the government of the People's Republic of China (PRC) are now responding with purpose to the deficiencies in the distribution system. There are great variances in interpretation between Western and Asian viewpoints reflecting differences in cultural perceptions. These cultural barriers are only gradually being dismantled as Chinese authorities understand the operation of international business. International pressure can therefore be seen to have had a profound effect on China's responsiveness in relation to HRM issues. This pressure, and the subsequent realization that current levels of growth cannot be sustained indefinitely, has forced China's authorities to act and enforce its newly created regulations: many of the HRM problems emanate from China's developing status.

Infrastructure problems hamper distribution and, therefore, consultation with established foreign investors in China seems to be a crucial factor in formulating solutions.

Gaining experience in the Chinese market seems to provide a significant learning curve for any investors wishing to enter it. China is still very much underdeveloped and it appears in the future that foreign enterprises will often have to take the lead or study Chinese business solutions in overcoming obstacles in operation.

There is some evidence that the Chinese government may seek to control foreign domination by further regulating particular sectors of the economy to prohibit foreign domination. The effect of the liberalization of the retail sector has profoundly affected local businesses who are unable to compete against Western marketing methods.

JV companies must be aware of rapid changes in policy which seem to be prevalent in developing states and at the national level.

Perhaps the most interesting aspect of the operational problems that affect JVs is their ever-changing nature. These problems not surprisingly mirror China's development. In 1985, introducing consumers to Western marketing and overcoming seemingly insurmountable distribution and supply chains were the most dominant issue of the day. As China's economy matures so the operational problems will become more mundane and not so profoundly affected by environmental considerations.

References

Ariga, M, and Yasue, M. (1997) 'China's Generation III: Viable target segment and implications for marketing communications' *Marketing and Research Today.*

Business China (1995/1996/1997) EIU *China–Britain Trade Review* (1997), 'Euro Expatriates Ill Prepared for Postings in China.' April, 16.

Business Week (1997), 26 May.

China Business and Investment (1997), XVIII 5, March.

China Hand (1997) *Complete Guide to Doing Business in China*, London Economic Intelligence Unit.

Hoecklin, L. (1992) *Managing Cultural Differences: Strategies or Competitive Advantage,* London, EIU.

Investing in China (1997).

Ritchie, R.L., Lovatt, C.J., Zhuang, L. and Whitworth, T. (1999) 'Experiences of Joint Venture Companies in China: Legal Issues', *Cyprus International Journal of Management*, vol. 4, no. 1.

Revvid, J. (1994) *Doing Business with China,* London, Kogan Page, 605.

Wilson, D. (ed.) (1997) *Investing in China*, London, *Financial Times* Publication, Pearson Professional.

Part 4

China

15 Strategic Development in China's Changing State and Non-State Enterprises*

David H. Brown and Hantang Qi

INTRODUCTION

One of the remarkable and largely unpredicted features of China's economic progress over the last 20 years has been the relative performance of the state and non-state sectors.[1] In 1997, state-owned enterprises (SOEs) totalled some 305 000 (all sector categories), employed approximately 110 million people, accounted for three-quarters of China's industrial capital, and yet contributed just 30 per cent of GNP. In contrast, non-state enterprises have moved from a support role in 1984 to a pivotal one in the economy and in the eyes of the government today. Their contribution to GNP is now over 70 per cent (*China Statistical Yearbook 1997*). It is the case, of course, that both the state and non-state sectors of the economy will remain crucial if China's economic goals laid out at the 1997 15th National Congress of the Communist Party are to be achieved. In particular, the continued growth of the non-state sector will be vital to absorb the 20–30 million underemployed workers in the state sector. The aim of this chapter is to look behind the economic performance of the sectors to the strategic processes within selected organizations of both types and to assess how well placed they are to meet the expectations of their government over the next 5 years. However, locating organizations within state and non-state categories can be complex and hence we commence with some of the definitional issues.

STATE AND NON-STATE ENTERPRISES

The simplest taxonomy for the Chinese economy, namely state-owned and non-state-(owned) enterprises, although widely adopted by

273

journalists, officials and academics alike, can be unhelpful on three counts. First, the distinction that is drawn on the basis of implied ownership is problematic. Both kinds of enterprises can be publicly owned. In SOEs capital is owned by the whole society, but in reality this is vested in government departments and units at national and provincial levels. In the majority of the non-state-(owned) sector property rights *collectively* reside with community members on the basis of residency, but again real control lies elsewhere – in this case with the relevant community authorities, typically at village (*cun*) or township (*xiang*) levels in rural areas and at sub-district (*jiedao*) or district (*qu*) levels in urban areas. In essence, therefore, it is the degree of governmental autonomy that better distinguishes these two components of the economy. Even today, after the contract-responsibility reforms, it remains the case that for SOEs autonomy is low, especially with respect to significant investment, key appointments or the ability to contract formal joint ventures (JVs) with overseas companies.

A second problem with the simple taxonomy is the position of the privately owned sector. In many analyses, including some government statistics, the non-state sector subsumes the privately owned sector, but in others not. At the beginning of the reform this hardly mattered but by 1992 individual or privately owned industrial and commercial enterprises were generating some 14 per cent of GDP (Zhu and Liu, 1996: 10). And in a period of rapid growth from 1992 to 1996 numbers employed in this sector, both urban and rural, rose from 2 to 12 million (Yatsko and Forney, 1998). This growing importance is set to continue as privately owned enterprises develop the capacity to purchase small and medium sized (SME) SOEs, under the different joint stock schemes that are being introduced.

A third and final problem of the simple classification is that while it facilitates high-level economic analysis it propagates a simplistic, and possibly homogeneous, view of the non-state sector which is misleading. This sector, including the privately owned enterprises, is markedly heterogeneous. Not surprisingly, therefore, the strategic issues in this sector mirror both this variety and the rate at which the sector is changing.

There are many ways in which China's industrial and commercial enterprises can be classified – by size, location, strategic importance, ownership structure, industry sector, and so on. However, Table 15.1 summarizes the position using the conventional taxonomy, but amplifies this to underline the variety embedded within. An alternative and complementary classification is suggested by Nee (1992). He uses

Table 15.1 Classification for China's industrial and commercial enterprises, 1978–95

Type	Characteristics	Comments
State-owned (SOEs) *Low governmental autonomy*	Relatively small in number (about 305 000) but large or medium sized in assets. Includes virtually all primary industries, heavy manufacturing, defense, aerospace, transport and communications. A major recipient of foreign direct investment, mainly in the form of JVs. State 'control' via industrial and specialist ministries and local (provincial and county) bureaux; management of enterprises achieved through the Director Responsibility System. Parallel political governance exercised by the CPC.	Sector has been under reform since 1978 but particularly from 1987 onwards. Increasingly joint stock arrangement and divestment will dilute state involvement and many will revert to non-state enterprises. In 1997 renewed efforts signaled at the CPC 15th National Congress to stem the losses incurred by a minimum of 40 per cent of all SOEs. Enterprises 'non-marketized' in Nee's (1992) classification but strong pressure to become 'marketized'.
Non-state-(owned) (a) Collectives *Relatively high governmental autonomy*	Consists of district (*qu*), sub-district (*jiedao*), township (*xiang*), and village (*cun*) enterprises (urban and rural) and farmers' co-operatives. Enterprises can be large (5000 employees) but typically very much smaller. Control is via local or community authorities; political governance is via the local CPC. The linkage between the enterprise and the local authority can be very close, affecting both policy and operational decisions.	A rapidly growing sector with growth rates of 20–30 per cent up to 1995. Complex ownership arrangements are common. Many enterprises have domestic JVs with SOEs and a growing number with foreign partners. Growth has been 'bottom-up' and there are likely to be 30 million enterprises (collectives plus privately owned) by the year 2000. *Important to note:* 1. Collectives and privately owned enterprises are frequently combined and referred to simply as 'non-state enterprises'.

Table 15.1 (*cont'd*)

Type	Characteristics	Comments
		Enterprises are 'marketized' in Nee's (1992) classification.
(b) Privately owned *High governmental autonomy*	Consists of individuals and small businesses typically of Eight people or less (*getihu*), registered private enterprises, limited liability companies and foreign funded firms (even though the partner is frequently an SOE). Management is within the enterprise but patronage from supervisory authorities is widespread and is given in return for licence fees, and so on. No direct political governance but the tax authorities and the so-called non-governmental associations (*minjian xiehui*) for example, the Private Enterprise Association – seek to exercise a degree of influence.	By far the fastest growth sector, but from a small base – growth rates have been as high as 60 per cent per annum, but failure rates also high. Limited liability companies are becoming a common form. Enterprises are 'private' in Nee's (1992) classification.
		2. Registered collective enterprises are often in reality private enterprises and can be large. Their false registration affords them economic, political and social benefits. The practice is widespread and is colloquially known as putting on the 'red hat' (*dai hong mao*).

Source: Authors' data.

transaction type and industrial property rights to identify three types of enterprises: 'non-marketized', in which state involvement remains high in areas such as production volumes, distribution, pricing and financing; 'marketized', in which the market largely determines production and price but links with authorities for access to raw materials, distribution, and finance are common; and, finally, 'private', in which the enterprise is purely market-based. Given the emphasis on 'market solutions' in the context of enterprise reform, Nee's market-based categories are included in Table 15.1.

Economic Emergence

The relative neglect of the non-state enterprises and the dominance of the state sector are long-standing; this theme is developed in Zhu and Liu (1996). The concept of 'all the land in the world belongs to the King' can be traced back to the Shang Dynasty (17–11 BC). Since then virtually all dynasties up to the end of the Qing Dynasty (1911) favoured feudal, state centralized arrangements. Even after 1949 little changed, indeed it can be argued that the position of the non-state sector further deteriorated. The ideological position that socialism necessitated public ownership of the means of production meant that 'state-owned enterprises must be managed by the state'. Priorities set by the state at that time concentrated on the development of heavy and military industries. Policies of nationalization and collectivization meant that by the mid-1950s the non-state individual economy was eliminated, even barbers' shops and public baths were nationalized. Against this setting it is hardly surprising that culturally SOEs were viewed as respectable while non-state individually based enterprises were disreputable (Zhu and Liu, 1996: 5, 17, 21–2).

The cultural and economic rehabilitation of the non-state sector has its origins in Deng Xiaoping's reforms of 1978. Much was written in the late 1980s and onwards about the various outcomes, anticipated or otherwise, of implementing the reforms (for example, Warner, 1987). However, a review of this typical literature reveals how relatively little of the analysis concerned the rurally based non-state enterprise sector. At the commencement of the reforms this sector consisted of about 1.52 million commune- and brigade-run enterprises, operating mainly in the 'five small industries': fertilizer, agricultural machinery, cement, energy and iron and steel. The reforms – and in particular the household contract responsibility system (*jiating lianchan chengbao zerenzhi*) – gave increased autonomy and incentives in the form of loans, tax benefits and technology inputs. The sector developed rapidly and in 1984 was redefined to include individual enterprises and farm co-operatives and renamed township enterprises (TVEs), bringing the whole number of enterprises to 6.1 million. Helped by the opening of the coastal cities, rapid growth continued to 1988, was temporarily depressed for the next two years following the aftermath of Tian-an-men Square, and by the end of 1992 totalled 20.8 million enterprises, employing 105.8 million people (*China Statistical Yearbook 1996*). This underlines how small scale many of these businesses are, with an average work force of about five employees.

The legitimacy of this sector was further reinforced by the keynote speech of Deng Xiaoping during his inspection of south China in 1992 (Zhu and Liu, 1996; Liu *et al.*, 1996). A snapshot of the structure of the economy in 1992 (see Table 15.2) reveals the extent of the growth of the non-state sector. Only in the area of transportation are the SOEs dominant and in the industrial sector, for the first time, the non-state sector exceeded the state-owned sector in output value. In other ways, too, the performance of the sector was impressive. From virtually nothing in 1984 by 1992 TVEs were contributing, directly or with co-operative JVs (foreign and domestic), some 20 per cent of total exports (see Liu *et al.*, 1996, for further detailed analysis).

Table 15.2   The emerging dominance of the non-state sector, 1992
(percentage of GDP)

	Agri-culture	Industry	Con-struction	Transport	Commerce	Total
Total	16.27	66.38	9.30	3.23	4.82	100
SOEs	2.81	48.10	43.40	81.50	41.30	41.29
Non-state enterprises *	97.19	51.90	56.60	18.50	58.70	58.71

Note: * Includes urban collectives, TVEs and privately - owned enterprises.
Sources: Adapted from Zhu and Liu (1996); *China Statistical Yearbook 1992*.

From 1992 to 1997 the sector continued to develop more rapidly than the state-owned sector, but not without complications. A number of trends can be identified, each with strategic implications:

(1)   Within the non-state sector the growth of privately owned enterprises, including foreign JVs and limited liability companies, has been particularly significant. For the first time in 1993 this trend

was seen in all provinces, but it remains the case that the 17 major coastal cities/areas have benefited most. For example, in Guangdong the registered capital of private enterprises increased sevenfold in a single year, 1993. For China generally the increase that year was more than double. For organizations, however, operating in the purely market environment remains high-risk. An estimated 40 per cent of private enterprises fail or are on the edge of survival, 40 per cent make small profits and only 20 per cent make large profits (Zhu and Liu, 1996: 26). Survival is a strategic issue.

(2) The registration of enterprises as 'collective' or 'private' is suspect. Possibly up to 50 per cent of private enterprises are registered as collectives and the trend is well established. Privately owned enterprises can face tax disadvantages and greater difficulties in raw material acquisition and product distribution. The situation is further exaggerated by the fledgling property rights now being developed, seemingly sometimes on an ad hoc basis. Cross-ownership between collectives and private firms involving working shareholders, outside investors and the enterprise itself as a shareholder is common and complex, but is underpinned by inadequate law. Given the increasing importance of the private sector as a vehicle for economic growth the framework within which it operates – both legal and industrial/commercial – gives real cause for concern. A related observation is the limited use of the concept 'private organization', interpreted in a Western sense, for understanding the Chinese situation. (This is an area developed in detail by Boisot and Child, 1996, in their analysis of emerging economic forms in China.) In the context of this chapter the point is not unimportant when considering strategic implications at the organizational level.

(3) Arguably the most important trend is the declining growth rate for the non-state sector. From an original growth rate of 20 per cent or more up to 1995 this dropped to 17.79 per cent in 1996 and 11 per cent in 1997. The decline reflects a more difficult environment for enterprises and the prospect of difficult strategic choices.

Notwithstanding the above trends, the case remains that together collective and private enterprises account for more than 71 per cent of industrial output. In contrast, the position for SOEs is increasingly problematic. Over 40 per cent are loss-making and the reforms intended to be implemented within the Ninth Five-Year Plan (1996–2000) were drastic. Of the 305 000 SOEs only 16 000 are likely to survive as formally state owned and many of these will be converted to stockholding companies. The intention is for the remainder to fend for themselves (*China Daily*, 1998). For both state and non-state enterprises, therefore, the future strategic challenges will be severe and we now look at the strategy formulation processes that are in place for two typical organizations.

STRATEGY IN ACTION – ILLUSTRATIVE CASES

To explore this core issue of strategic thinking in China's varied enterprises we draw below on two empirical investigations. The first was a major comparative study into strategic investment decision making and human resource management (HRM) between large SOEs in China and equivalent companies in the UK. This work has been reported on elsewhere (Brown and Porter, 1996; Easterby-Smith and Gao, 1996). From this original investigation, we have selected a petrochemical company and extended the research. Our account traces the company's strategic development up to 1998 and identifies, at least in part, the strategic processes underlying this development by detailed reference to an example of a major investment decision.

Our second case concerns the strategic development of an enterprise in the non-state-(owned) sector manufacturing building materials, mainly cement. This work is ongoing and forms part of a larger study by the authors into this sector. In both cases we set the scene, without interpretation, as a basis for discussion later in the chapter.

Case A: The State-owned Sino–Oil Company[2]

Sino-Oil is controlled by the state-owned China National Petrochemicals Corporation which, as a very large and nationally important corporation, enjoys ministry-level status. Situated in Southwest Beijing, Sino-Oil is China's largest petrochemical complex. It is highly regarded and has been designated as *shihua gongye de yimian hongqi* (a 'red flag' in the petrochemical industry). For day-to-day business Sino-Oil is an independent legal entity, responsible for its own accounts and for its own profits. In the area of planning, however, the situation is more complex. For major personnel matters, production allocation (planned quota of inputs and outputs) and investment approval the company is subordinate to the corporation. The links between the two are very close but nevertheless it is the corporation that approves Sino-Oil's annual plan and long-term development strategy.

The administrative structure of Sino-Oil comprises a headquarters, with some 46 functional departments, and below this the operating plants themselves, further sub-divided into workshops and work groups. In addition there are two companies – a sales company dealing with customers and a service company. The latter is a collectively owned enterprise which provides subsidized foodstuffs (from fish and chicken farms) to the company employees as well as alternative employment for their dependants. Parallel to the management hierarchy there co-exists the party system. The party committee includes the enterprise director and deputy directors, the chief accountant, engineer and economist and the party secretary. The committee reports through to the Beijing municipal party committee.

The company employs some 45000 workers of whom 23000 are support staff (catering, hotels, medical services, schools, transport and others) and 22000 production-related. In total, the refinery complex processes 7 million tons of crude oil per year into fuel and chemical products and measured by turnover is China's sixth largest company.

Sino-Oil's development took place over several stages. The first stage was from 1966 to 1972 when the State Council decided to build a modern 2.5 million-ton capacity petrochemical plant to serve Beijing and northern China. The next stage from 1973 to 1978 was the introduction of ethylene production and related technologies. Again, this was sanctioned by the State Council and the 300000-ton plant utilized Japanese technology. The third stage lasted until 1992. The priorities during this period were to improve poor infrastructures, develop social facilities and improve or renovate the existing production facilities by adopting advanced technology and improved management. It was during this stage that the company faced key decisions on ethylene production.

In 1985 it was clear to the company that demand for ethylene-based chemicals warranted increased production, but there were more pressing priorities. In 1989, the project proposal was revisited. This time, however, the condition of the existing plant had become a safety issue and there was added urgency. The proposal for a renovated ethylene plant with an increased capacity of 20 per cent was embedded in the annual plan produced by the company's Programme Department. Early indications were that, both within the company and the national corporation, the proposals were not ambitious enough and in the view of the company's management 'would not keep Sino-Oil on top'. What followed was a reworking of the project within a network of actors – the national corporation (which allocated the crude oil feedstock), the municipal authorities (for water, energy, environmental and land approvals), 'external' state consultants (for economic and market analyses) and the banks. All this was co-ordinated by the Programme Department and within six months a revised proposal for a 50 per cent larger plant was ready. The strategic arguments used by Sino-Oil for the project were: a demonstrated national demand for ethylene; an opportunity to gain experience of the new technology for the benefit of other companies; and a chance to exploit the flexibility of the Sino-Oil plant to generate superior ethylene yields compared with other plants. The formal proposal for the project, costing US$45 million, was championed by the General Director and approved via the national corporation, the State Planning Commission and finally the State Council in 1991. The plant was commissioned in 1993.

The final stage of development, 1992 to date, follows directly from the 14th CPC National Congress in 1992, which initiated the corporatization project. Sino-Oil has become the Sino-Oil Petrochemical Group and now has 32 subsidiaries largely through an aggressive acquisition programme. The company now has assets of US$5.4 billion and a product range from basic fuels to specialty chemicals, synthetic rubber and advanced plastics. Already listed on the Shenzhen stock exchange it has now received a listing in Hong Kong. Its goal is to compete internationally and to do this it believes it has to be large (*Business Week*, 1997).

Case B: The Township-based Jiangsu Cement Industrial Group Company

By 1997 the Jiangsu Cement Industrial Group Company had 4000 employees, produced 1.7 million tons of cement annually, and had profits exceeding 10 per cent of total sales. Within Jiangsu Province it had become the number one enterprise within the building materials sector for generating profit and taxes.

In 1974 the Jinshan Cement Plant was set up by Jinshan Township near the historic and cultural city of Suzhou in Jiangsu Province with an annual production of less than 10 000 tons. Over the next 22 years it developed to become the Jiangsu Cement Industrial Group Company, a province-class conglomerate. The transformation of this company from such an inauspicious start occurred in three distinct stages, or 'great leaps forward', as the company prefers to call its development. Each stage is characterized by a major investment programme and together they provide an insight into the strategic processes within the company and the way in which it is likely to cope with the future strategic agenda.

The 'first leap forward' was from 1974 to 1986. Development started slowly and it took four years to acquire a second kiln to raise the output to 20 000 tons per year. In 1979 Sun Jinnan, the local Party secretary in Fenghuang Village, Jinshan Township, was appointed Plant Director. On taking office he soon established that local demand for cement exceeded supply and he set down plans to double the plant's capacity with a new rotary kiln. Entirely from self-raised funds the US$400 000 investment was completed in 1983 and increased the plant's capacity to 50 000 tons. Within the next three years a further US$1.3 million investment, with 50 per cent from government and bank loans, enabled the company to raise production with a fourth kiln to 200 000 tons per year and become a leading cement production business in Suzhou district. The company was officially designated a medium-sized township enterprise and its name changed to the Mudu Cement Plant, reflecting a change in local administration.

The 'second leap forward' was from 1986 to 1993 and took plant capacity to 700 000 tons in two stages. Proximity to the rapidly developing Shanghai meant that demand for cement was enormous. Mudu's first investment was with the active financial support of the Shanghai Municipal Construction Bureau, who was interested in continuity of cement supply. A 250 000-ton plant costing US$4 million was planned and building started in 1989. Almost immediately national construction was slowed down by government edict, known in China as a macro-adjustment (*hongguan tiaokong*); the price of cement fell by half and Mudu laid off a third of its labour force. During the next difficult 12 months Sun Jinnan, by now the General Manager, changed project by upgrading the technology to match that of the leading SOEs and at the same time to increase quality and energy efficiency. In 1990 construction of the plant restarted and was successfully completed in 1991. Just a year later, despite a second 'macro-adjustment' (*hongguan tiaokong*), leading to depressed cement sales, Mudu invested in a second energy-efficient kiln costing US$6.5 million and by 1993 had achieved the 'number one ranking' of township enterprises in this sector.

The 'final leap forward' brings the company almost to the present day. In 1992 on his southern inspection tour, Deng Xiaoping delivered his second rallying speech for a further deepening of the economic reforms. Government authorities at all levels responded by encouraging enterprises 'to take an enormous leap forward' and Jiangsu provincial authorities saw the Mudu Cement Plant as a prime candidate to become a nationally renowned cement corporation. With growing confidence in 1993 Mudu planned and commenced construction of a 1 million-ton cement complex, using waste heat to generate 33 000 kilowatts of electricity for the southern part of Jiangsu province; the total project cost was US$60 million. In the same year the Jiangsu Cement Industrial Group Company was established with Mudu Cement Plant as its core, and with Sun Jinnan as Chairman of the Board and General Manager and chief fund-raiser.

Over the next few years the Group merged the Mudu Power Plant and Suzhou Seamless Steel Tube Factory, both loss-making; established JVs with Hong Kong and Taiwan partners in the areas of cement production and tile manufacture; invested in further JVs with a consortium of Swiss, New Zealand and Singaporean companies; and established companies for trading, including export sales, and for real estate development. A final initiative has been to establish a trading company in Miami, USA – seen to be useful for 'tours of investigation abroad'!

INTERPRETING THE CASES

From these two cases, what evidence is there that these and similar organizations are ready to cope with the new reform agenda? Although broad generalizations would be unwise the particular enterprises we selected are very relevant to the debate. As one of the favoured state enterprises for strategic development (one of the 'top 1000') the Sino-Oil group aims to transform itself into a cost-efficient, profitable world-ranking corporation. Similarly, the Jiangsu Cement Group Company is exactly the kind of non-state enterprise that President Jiang Zemin (1997) is relying on to repeat its historic growth and provide the future employment opportunities so necessary for the reform of the SOEs to proceed meaningfully.

To explore the question posed above our approach is first to identify a relevant theory framework and then to apply this in the context of the two cases.

Devising a Relevant Theoretical Framework

A characteristic of the field of strategy and strategic management is the plurality of approaches for thinking about and tackling what is in essence a complex and creative process. However this chapter is not the place for an exhaustive comparison of contributions for the purpose of establishing the most appropriate framework. Indeed, in our view such a quest would be unhelpful. Given that the context is China and that the theoretical contributions derive from Western experiences of organizations and markets, considerable caution is needed. Our preference, therefore, has been to devise the simplest frameworks that we believe are sufficiently robust and insightful in understanding the strategic processes within the enterprises.

We start with the analysis of strategic processes. Our proposed framework is based on three analytical perspectives: Outside-In, Inside-Out, and Networks.

Outside-In is the perspective that largely informs 'conventional' strategic analysis and tends towards prescription. From the starting point of a statement of purpose (mission or objectives) the approach puts emphasis on a thorough assessment of the *external environment*, including competitors, to determine opportunities and risks. Taking into account organizational capabilities and internal values strategic alternatives are then identified, selected and implemented. The notion of *environmental fit* is central to this perspective. Concepts such as 'gap' analysis and 'strategic group' analysis enable the organization to position itself with respect to markets and competitors. Indeed, the strategy may be couched in positional language, for example 'moving from *A* to *B* by doing *X* and *Y*'.

Inside-Out is essentially a resource-based perspective. The underlying notion is that an organization's competitive position can be better sustained by exploiting its *core competencies*. Prahalad and Hamel (1990), in an influential article, defined these in terms of the organization's collective learning, especially the co-ordination and integration of production and technology skills. Kay (1993), in an extended analysis, developed the resource approach using the idea of *distinctive capabilities* – architecture, reputation, innovation and strategic assets. This approach has emerged relatively recently in the context of increasingly difficult markets, including globalization effects. It is demanding both in terms of the organization's self-knowledge and in the requirement for managerial creativity to translate these internal, resource-based strengths into market advantage.

Networks, our third perspective, is an approach to the strategy process which places a premium on understanding, managing and influencing the set of *actor–resource relationships* within which the organization transacts its business. (There is a correspondence here with 'architecture' which is one of Kay's four distinctive capabilities.) Exchange relationships between actors in the network is the basis of establishing trust and leads to *resource interdependence*, which can further strengthen the relationship. Quite separately, and in the China context, the importance of networks and *guanxi* (helpful relationships) to an organization's development is understood – for example, the significance of clientelist networks and patron–client linkages is convincingly argued by Wank (1996). A further extensive treatment of the uniqueness of Chinese style management, as embodied in the Chinese network form, is Li (1998).

The Strategy Development Process: Some Conclusions

The application of this framework to the two cases is shown in Table 15.3 and contains detailed analysis. Examination of Table 15.3 exhibits marked similarities. The major conclusion is that in both companies the dominant strategic process combines outside-in with a network perspective, and the influence of a resource-based approach is low. But there are important differences. In Sino-Oil the separation of the investment planning from line management was (and remains) a distinctive characteristic; in the Jiangsu company the activities of 'planning and doing' resided in the General Manager for all key strategic decisions. The network factor was also different. Although important to Sino-Oil its significance for Jiangsu is hard to overestimate. Although it can be argued that the shortage of cement and related products effectively constituted a munificent market environment it is not a sufficient explanation for the company's success since other companies in the same sector have done noticeably less well. The efficacy of Sun Jinnan's network was necessary to realize that potential.

In terms of the strategic readiness of the two companies to meet the expectations within the Ninth Five-Year Plan, there will be difficulties. In the case of the state-owned Sino-Oil there are two fundamental problems. Firstly, the dominant strategic process is environmental-and position-driven, which blurs the responsibility for strategic intent and strategy formulation. When the environment was relatively stable this was possible; but in the turbulent situation which exists (in both international and domestic markets), this is unwieldy. Secondly, once a relative monothematic business Sino-Oil has embraced commercial versatility in its quest to become a conglomerate. Size, measured in assets and sales, has become a strategic end in itself. This stance ignores well established experience that economies of scale are regularly overestimated and that managing merged businesses or alliances is demanding and increased profitability by no means certain.

For the Jiangsu Group our conclusion is that its historic growth will be difficult to maintain as the overall economy slows to a target growth of 7–8 per cent. A second factor is that the company's other businesses

Table 15.3   Characterizing the strategic processes

	Outside-In	Inside-Out	Network
Sino-Oil Company (State)	'Outside' is viewed as (1) contributing to China's national requirements, hence no real domestic competition; (2) competing with international corporations, especially on chemicals. The evidence of an 'Outside-In' perspective is strong; close links between the national corporation, which sets production levels, and the company; very formal planning and approval systems for new investments; and large staff resources for planning at 'ministry' and company levels. Industry 'position' is a dominant factor in strategic intent (for example the 'top 500' goal and the recent corporatization).	No evidence of conscious organizational learning as a means of driving competitive advantage. In terms of distinctive capabilities the most significant is the strategic asset of crude oil quota. Reputation is good but is not commercially significant in the domestic market. Innovation is important but not distinctive since technical advances are shared by domestic producers. No evidence that the recent diversification is based on distinctive, or even historic, capabilities.	Relatively stable network of inputs, production and distribution. Managing network relationships as a means of securing approval for the development of the company is longstanding and effectively institutionalized. For this reason the efficacy of the network linkages, especially between the national corporation and the company is high. Horizontal linkages (*hengxiang lianxi*) likely to have been influential in diversification activities.

Table 15.3   *(cont'd)*

	Outside-In	Inside-Out	Network
Jiangsu Cement Industrial Group (Non-state)	Very much in evidence. The continuing expansion of the cement market and lack of local competition have driven strategy. The pace of investment (plant expansion) is largely decided and engineered by the General Manager. No sophisticated analysis – increasing production by ×2 or ×3 was the 'rule of thumb'. Consideration of alternative strategies limited to technical options. 'Position' very important – initially to be number one at township and then at provincial levels. Strategic intent is to achieve parity with the large SOEs – again a positional statement.	Some evidence that internal capabilities, especially quality, could offer the company advantage by reinforcing reputation. The company's brand had export certification, which obviated the need for third party inspection. Otherwise no conscious attempt to achieve market innovation or advantage based on existing resources.	Extremely important and network relationships pervade every element of strategic development. Firstly, in securing access to inputs, especially energy. Secondly, by reducing the commercial risk – the link with the authorities effectively underwrote a large part of the increased production. Thirdly, by accelerating the project approval. (To gain the necessary permits for building in Suzhou, for example environmental protection permit, the city authorities needed to be highly co-operative.) And fourthly, the financing of the strategic development was achieved through a network of investors, private and public, with cross guarantors. Many of the relationships in this network are personal to the Chairman.

are more speculative. To develop these requires competent commercial, technical and managerial staff which township enterprises, with their residency and ownership constraints, have found difficult to acquire, and although this is changing it remains a factor.

While extrapolating from the particular to the general needs to be done with due caution we believe that both these organizations exhibit strategy formulation practices shared by many other enterprises. The lack of awareness of the importance of a capability perspective in strategy development will create problems – either failure or lower than anticipated profits. In conclusion, this analysis suggests that the next stage of enterprise growth will be more difficult and that the scope of the enterprise transformation envisaged in China's Ninth Five-Year Plan is unlikely to be achieved.

Notes

* We are most grateful to the ESRC, the Chinese National Science Foundation and the British Council for the research into SOEs, and to the British Council for its further support of the non-state enterprise research. Chen Zhihong, a research fellow in Shanghai Academy of Social Sciences, Li Meikun, secretary to Mayor of Suzhou City and Zhu Jiwei, section chief of the people's government of Wuxian City, accompanied one of the authors during the whole field-work in the Jiangsu Cement Industrial Company: they deserve special thanks.

1. In contrast to the SOE sector, for which detailed national statistics and management structures and procedures are readily available, the non-state sector is less accessible. Details are fragmented at the village, township and provincial level and assembling a valid, up-to-date picture is not straightforward. Frequently, sources contradict each other, or categories of statistic overlap, and care is needed. The contributions of Liu *et al.* (1996) and Zhu and Liu (1996) were particularly helpful and are recommended; they were complemented by other secondary sources, by discussions with non-state enterprise managers (not just from the case example dealt with in the chapter), from the relevant supervisory bureaux, and the *China Statistical Yearbooks*.

2. Sino-Oil is a code name given to the company and used in other writings on the project.

References

Boisot, M. and Child, J. (1996) 'From Fiefs to Clans and Network Capitalism: Explaining China's Emerging Economic Order', *Administrative Science Quarterly*, 41; 600–28.

Brown, D.H. and Porter, R. (1996) 'An Introduction to Management Issues in China', in D. H. Brown and R. Porter (eds), *Management Issues in China: Vol. 1, Domestic Enterprises*, London, Routledge.

Business Week (1997) 'Can China Reform Its Economy?', 29 September: 38–44.

China Daily (1998) 'State Sector to be Revitalized', 14 January.

China Statistical Yearbook 1992/1996/1997.

Easterby-Smith, M. and Gao Junshan (1996) 'Vision, Mechanism and Logic: Understanding the Strategic Investment Decision Making Process', in D.H. Brown and R. Porter (eds), *Management Issues in China: Vol. 1, Domestic Enterprises*, London, Routledge 106–25.

Jiang Zemin (1997) 'Hold High the Great Banner of Deng Xiaoping Theory for an All-Round Advancement of the Cause of Building Socialism with Chinese Characteristics to the 21st Century', Report to the 15th National Congress of the Communist Party of China, 12 September, printed in full in *China Daily*, 23 September.

Kay, J. (1993) *Foundations of Corporate Success: How Business Strategies Add Value*, New York, Oxford University Press.

Li, Peter Ping (1998) 'Towards a Geocentric Framework of Organizational Form: A Holistic, Dynamic and Paradoxical Approach', *Organization Studies*, 19(5), 829–61.

Liu Hong, Campbell, N., Lu Zheng and Wang Yanzhong (1996) 'An International Perspective on China's Township Enterprises', in D.H. Brown and R. Porter (eds), *Management Issues in China: Vol. 1, Domestic Enterprises*, London, Routledge.

Nee, V. (1992) 'Organizational Dynamics of Market Transition: Hybrid Forms, Property Rights, and Mixed Economy in China', *Administrative Science Quarterly*, 37, 1–27.

Prahalad, C.K. and Hamel, G. (1990) 'The Core Competence of the Corporation', *Harvard Business Review*, May–June, 79–91.

Wank, D.L. (1996) 'The Institutional Process of Market Clientelism: *Guanxi* and Private Business in a South China City', *The China Quarterly*, 147, September, 820–38.

Warner, M. (1987) (ed.) *Management Reforms in China*, London, Frances Pinter.

Yatsko, P. and Forney, M. (1998) 'Demand Crunch', *Far Eastern Economic Review*, 15 January, 44–7.

Zhu Huayou and Liu Changhui (1996) Chapters in S. Gao and F. Chi, (eds), *The Development of China's Nongovernmentally and Privately Operated Economy*, Beijing, Foreign Language Press.

16 China Reconstructs: The Transformation of Management in Two Telecommunications- Technology Producers

Xiaobai Shen

INTRODUCTION

There is a widespread perception that China will become a leading player in the world economy in the twenty-first century, underpinned by its recent experiences of sustained and rapid growth in many areas of mass production. China is keen to accelerate this process, to move into more advanced technology areas and to compete with Western and Asian economies. A major challenge it needs to tackle is to improve the quality of management – and, in particular, to improve the performance of the many state-owned firms that continue to be the mainstay of the Chinese economy. This chapter explores attempts to transform management practices, in the course of China's economic transition. It focuses upon China's attempts to acquire advanced technological compet- encies in the strategically important area of production of public digital switching systems (PDSS) – the technology at the heart of modern tele- communications. It presents two contrasted cases – one a joint production venture with a Western firm and the other an indigenous development in a state-owned firm.

Many (including the Chinese government) have looked to professional business training as the source of management improvement. However, opinions remain divided. After a detailed study of the infrastructure of Chinese management training, its achievements and shortcomings in comparison with other countries, even Warner still doubted whether the idea of business schools could be transplanted from the West to the East (Warner, 1992). As John Child has noted: 'the benefits of even the best training can be nullified if the management philosophy and climate of the enterprise is not receptive to personal development and initiative' (Child, 1992: xii).

The broader social and economic context is possibly the more influential in relation to Chinese managers. The case studies in this chapter provide ample evidence of this point. This chapter addresses the problems inherited from the old socialist central planning system which had produced a generation of Chinese managers who lacked modern management skills. It examines how the changing elements of the system in China's transition have contributed positively and/or negatively to the transformation of Chinese management.

PROBLEMS OF CHINA'S ECONOMIC SYSTEM

China's economic transition has now got to the stage that to sustain and further strengthen national economic growth it is increasingly necessary to improve industrial productivity and the effectiveness of management. In this context, the lack of qualified managers is seen a major constraint on the industrial reform needed to improve productivity and also to build more efficient market-oriented system.

For over 15 years, China's 'open door policy' towards foreign trade and technologies, and the progressive introduction of market mechanisms into the economy, has given rise to enormous changes in the industrial system. Foreign capital investment, technologies and managerial methods have been pouring into the country, and most (if not all) people's view of the world has been greatly widened and changed. Given the consensus about the lack of qualified managers, the question arises as to how existing management, a key section of manpower, operates; how it is changing in the context of the economic transition; and what are the obstacles to management learning modern methods.

This chapter is particularly concerned with the issues involved in achieving advanced technological capacities. As technology comes to play an increasingly important role in China's economy, it has come to be seen as essential in business management. It poses new issues, in terms of the ability of managers to make use of technological resources. This involves a range of difficult decisions and choices about how to acquire and implement technological knowledge and capacities in order to innovate successfully and meet business demands in terms of product price and quality arising from a market that is increasingly exposed to global competition. However, this chapter argues that these capabilities cannot be built up merely through professional business training. Instead it emphasizes the processes of learning taking place among existing Chinese enterprises and how the broader social and economic context provides an environment and incentives for such learning.

Problems Inherited from China's System of Central Planning

A number of articles have examined and analysed the weaknesses and difficulties which beset the economies of (current and former) socialist states under the system of central planning (see Zhou, 1982; White, 1988; Brus and Laski 1989, and other Chinese economists). In particular, the central planning mechanism and controlled economies were not able to provide a close and sustained linkage between producers and customers or between R&D and industrial organizations (i.e. technology suppliers and users) and failed to generate incentives for technological changes and improvements in technique. In this context, the output targets of manufacturing firms were set on a continuing 'ratchet principle', that impelled them to seek increased output without concern for cost, quality or customer satisfaction. Industries had little incentive to innovate technology and improve product quality. In turn, customers had only limited scope to impose their requirements because of shortages and a lack of choice in what was essentially a supply-driven system. They found that they had little option except to accept what was produced. All these factors resulted in low product quality, low productivity and a waste of technological resources. Such a system in China had fostered the generation of Chinese managers who are now considered to lack the range of capabilities which are needed for market oriented business operation. More important, perhaps, is the fact that it also fostered a whole generation of people – not only product designers and producers, but also users, including not only managers but also workers and others involved in the process – whose perception of the importance of technology, quality, etc. was underdeveloped.

Any visitor to China today could not fail to notice the profound and widespread changes that have taken place since the start of the economic reforms and the 'open door policy', particularly regarding the importance attached in people's minds to making profits. The business environment has been changing constantly and substantially. However, problems have arisen because the established socialist centrally planned system is still in the process of transforming itself into a more market oriented system. Reform is uneven and incomplete. As a result, markets are extremely imperfect. In this context, many of the most successful commercial players may well be opportunists, largely unconstrained by moral or ethical issues, who have useful connections with government and industry decision makers, and who have obtained access to scarce resources and seek to maximize their gains. These are not necessarily the best and most experienced business managers. Even the best Western managers might prove unable to make Chinese companies prosper under these circumstances. During the twilight of the old economic and legislative systems, and the development of the new market oriented one, neither system is complete or perfect. There are business rules, however, and at the same time, no rules. To a great extent managers are forced to learn, if they want to be successful, and to learn how to make use of such an environment and get more out of it. In such circumstances, the lessons may be far removed from the formal principles of professional business education. For example, managers have to learn how to side-step regulations that stand in their way; expediency may force them to adopt measures which in other contexts might be seen as corruption, whether, at the bottom of their hearts, they approve of this or not.

The key issue, then, for Chinese management concerns how well they can learn to deal with this turbulent context. This chapter takes as its focus one of the most obdurate problems facing China's economy today concerning the increasing importance of product quality. As China opens up its economy, its producers come under pressure to respond to the higher quality standards of Western products. These pressures may be particularly acute, for example, as Chinese consumers become aware of, and have the opportunity to purchase imported, higher-quality Western products, or where Western technologies require more stringent controls and finer tolerances than have been traditional in lower-technology Chinese products. However, as already noted, poor-quality production was widely entrenched in the old centrally planned system.

The detailed case studies, summarized below, provide an opportunity to examine the detailed learning processes in the enterprise and their relationship with the relevant elements in the broader social and economic context. The case studies show how people's perception of quality has been changing and how managers have been learning to manage their resources and business operation in the transition.

THE CASE OF A STATE-OWNED COMPANY – LTEF

The Luoyang Telephone Equipment Factory (LTEF) is a fairly typical state owned enterprise (SOE), in terms of the institutional structure, incentives and methods of operation. The establishment of LTEF dates back to 1972 and the government's 'self-reliance' policy, prior to economic reform, that the country must build up its own telecommunications industry. LTEF was a new factory, built from scratch. The factory came into operation in 1980, producing cross-bar public telephone switches with a maximum capacity of 200 000 lines per year. LTEF was one of 28 manufacturing enterprises run by the Post and Telecommunications Industrial Corporation (PTIC), the manufacturing and procurement organization of the Ministry of Posts and Telecommunications (MPT).

Like many state-owned factories that were located away from the coastal area during the 'cold war' in order to avoid the imperialists' attacks, LTEF was situated in the middle of China, in Henan province. The factory lies in the remote outskirts of the city of Luoyang. This created inconvenience in transport between the city and the factory. Because of this, when the factory was set up, it decided to establish its own social welfare facilities for its employees working in the factory – providing houses nearby; kindergartens and schools for their children; a hospital, a post office and telecommunications service; buses to and from the city to the factory seven or eight times per day; restaurants and canteens, guest houses, a bathhouse, a travel agent and all kinds of other services. As staff described vividly: 'Here we have everything except for a crematorium.'

The factory employed a large number of staff which was owing partly to labour-intensive production and partly to the socialist ideology that was supposed to provide everyone with a job. By 1992, the number of employees was over 2700. The whole community, including the families of its staff, was estimated as around 7000. People's jobs were permanent. The director of the firm played a role as head of a community, and accordingly the managers of each department and section took care of their staff to a large extent. For instance, if someone was ill, the company would be obliged to send him/her to hospital and pay the expenses. If someone's family experienced disaster, his/her boss should, on behalf of the group, offer help and express their sympathy. Similarly, if a member of staff could not find a partner, the trade union of the factory would possibly play the role of a match maker.

All raw materials were supplied to LTEF, and its products sold, at fixed prices by arrangement of the state. All the chief officials regarded as important to the firm, such as the director, major department managers, chief engineer and accountant, etc., were appointed by the MPT. The recruitment of graduates the factory received every year from universities and technical schools (most of which were run by the MPT), was organized according to the state plan. Prior to the economic reforms, a factory like the LTEF would be a 'plan-taker' (White, 1988: 155) immune to any problems from the imbalance between input and output.

Soon after LTEF established its production and social facilities, its social and economic environment and the underlying socialist doctrine begun to change. In the first five years of the economic reform, it remained untouched within MPT's protection. But it sensed the insecurity of its position owing to one event. At the beginning of the 1980s, MPT offered the newly equipped LTEF factory to its foreign partner BTM[1] to establish a joint production venture. The offer was turned down and the foreign partner chose another cross-bar manufacturer in Shanghai as its base. This made the LTEF feel sour. However, at that time, the economic reform was merely a gentle breeze for the firm, and it did not exert much pressure.

By 1984, the central focus of economic reform had gradually shifted to the reorganization of the industrial sector, involving provision of greater autonomy to firms and reduction of government protection. In other words, firms had to organize their resources fully or partly and sell their products in markets.

This made LTEF face both internal and external pressures. Financial constraints became stringent – how to sustain the unduly large workforce – and, more urgently, how to feed about 3000 staff. The existing institutional establishment – once well suited for the central planning system – did not provide the structure and incentives for high productivity. What had previously been seen as advantageous under the socialist systems – the significant community function of the firm – became a heavy burden. The opening up of the public switching technology market favoured foreign advanced microelectronic-based systems rather than the older Chinese cross-bar technology even though the price of the former was augmented as a result of disadvantageous international pricing and import tariffs. Orders for cross-bar products decreased sharply.

LTEF bid twice to be included in joint ventures (JVs) with foreign firms, but without success (partly because its location was not attractive to overseas investors). After this it turned to a military R&D institute – the Centre for Information Technology (CIT) – to develop a Chinese public digital switching system, HJD-04.[2] Their effort was very successful, and a Chinese system was delivered from laboratory to workshop at the end of 1991.

Reform to Survive

Efficient production capability was the key to turn the new technology from a blueprint to a product which could succeed in the market.
The situation had reached a point where the firm could not move on
without restructuring its entire organization, to address productivity
and the requirements for producing the new technology. However, this
was the most thorny problem for a state-owned firm like LTEF.
Restructuring would touch every member of staff and their individual
vested interests. The stakes were so high that managers of the firm
would have avoided getting involved in these issues if this had been at
all possible.

Instructions for reform eventually came from above. These were
applied all over the country, although the speed and incidence of their
application varied from place to place. At this stage, the major target
was an administrative innovation in firms to shake off the rigid system,
popularly known as 'smash the big iron rice bowl', it was based on a
belief that employees of enterprises from shopfloor workers to the
director of the firm lacked motivation to work hard. The new system
to be built, described as the 'responsibility system', was based on a
contractual arrangement,[3] which also defines the respective roles of the
enterprise director, party secretary and the other chief managers. However, because the rules of the new arrangement, and the dogma of
'socialist market mechanism' underlying it, were not explicit, people's
understanding of the responsibility system varied considerably.

At LTEF, the most urgent problem was not the rigid administration
system, but the unduly large workforce especially since the new technology required much less labour. As it was a relatively new firm, and
staff were newly enrolled and young on average, people's performances
were not that bad. However, the production of the new HJD-04 exchange
was capital-intensive, requiring only 800–900 people, compared to the
total workforce in the firm of 2700. LTEF therefore faced a dilemma:
to follow 'socialist' principles the firm had to be concerned with the
basic needs of the majority; to respond to 'market pressures' it must
cut off its community roles and become more efficient. Solving this
problem became critical for the firm, and this became a key matter of
concern for the director in charge. As he noted

> The market economy is the market economy, no matter whether one
> calls it socialist or capitalist. What I care about is that I have been
> living with people here for so many years I can't see them jobless. If

we just kick workers out after they have served this country for so many years, where is justice and humanity? We are trying to find a way for them to make a living. Otherwise we would rather wait for a solution from central government. (Director of LTEF, 22 April 1993)

This was a common reaction in state-owned firms all over the country, especially from those who, like the director of LTEF, had lived together with staff in the same living quarters for many years. However, as the financial pressure on the firm intensified, some measures had to be taken.

LTEF eventually established an internal labour market. Surplus labour was allowed to stay at home on 70 per cent of their salary. A bureau was set up to organize the internal labour market and meanwhile seek new jobs for them – e.g. to find some products which were in demand at the time for them to make; to arrange for them to work temporarily or long term in other companies which needed spare labour; to train them technically in order to return to workshops with different skills, etc. This move also had the positive result that each department of LTEF could choose better labour from the internal labour market. The internal labour market did not solve the fundamental problem of the unduly large workforce, but it created great scope for engineering a dynamic system. Its positive side was that it created a buffer that reduced the immediate pressure on LTEF. As it was accepted by the majority of the staff, it did not produce any danger of unrest and instability – a matter which was a major concern of the administration of the firm.

Simultaneously, the firm reorganized its management institutions and operating systems, and introduced new incentives. In the last quarter of 1992 when the internal reform was unfolded, LTEF adapted the 'responsibility system' to introduce what it described as the 'optimum constituting system'. Under this new company constitution, posts became selective, with appointments made on only a one-year contract; and the performance of an individual in his/her post was annually assessed. The role of each post was defined more clearly than ever before, especially that of the managers of each department. They had more scope to make decisions, and took on more responsibilities, compared to the previous tradition of collective decision-making. The biggest change was with the Department of Production. It became more autonomous and had its own internal accounting system which gave a great scope for the department to fully use its income as a means to motivate workers to improve both quantity and quality of production.

A new salary structure was introduced, described as 'performance oriented salary'. Under this system, the salary was broken down into two parts: basic pay and performance-related pay. The basic pay depended upon how long the employee had worked in the company or in other SOEs, and on what qualifications he/she had, etc. The performance-related pay was based on performance, in so far as the employee's working hours and output met the standards set by the firm, and the output exceeded the quota. Alternatively, good group and departmental performance would lead to bonuses in the individual's salary. The sum of these two parts is then weighted by a measure of the quality of individual's work.[4] In this way, control over workers was intensified through a set of detailed regulations and disciplines. In addition, because of the great size of the labour force, there were many to choose from for each post. Thus, for people with posts, the workers standing-by were a pressure on them – an 'internal' reserve army of labour!

All these changes focused upon improving the productivity of the system. Material incentives were seen as an important means of motivating every cell of the system to achieve the firm's aims. At the same time, efficient production organization was put on the firm's agenda. This reform, more or less, achieved its purposes. Workers on the shopfloor were working harder than before. When the firm needed, they worked in their lunch breaks and in the evenings. So did the engineers, especially young and unmarried engineers. Since they lived alone in the dormitory of the firm (just 5 minutes walk from the workshop), they often came back to work in evenings.[5]

In spite of these achievements, the state-owned firm could not yet get rid of all its social burdens. LTEF remained less productive than private and JV companies. Moreover government tariff policy also favoured JVs.[6] As a result the disparity between a state-owned firm and a private and/or JV firm was large. As one department manager said: 'We are competing with these companies on an unequal basis. As such, we will never catch them up' (Manager of the Planning Department, 23 April 1993).

Apart from these developments, the nature of the state-owned firm had not changed much. All of the social welfare facilities were still there; without them staff could not live. For instance, if the firm cancelled the bus, people living in town would have to walk for hours to get to the factory. The firm's role in taking care of staff well-being had not changed much either. According to the Director, when a newly employed worker was seriously ill, the firm spent several tens of thousands of Chinese yuan on his medical expenses. As he explained: 'Tell me, how could I just kick him out even though we are very tight in finance? We are a socialist country after all!' (Director of the LTEF, 22 April 1993).

When I was interviewing the manager of the Department of Production, somebody came in urging him to leave: he apologized to me that, as a head of the department, he must act on behalf of the whole department and go to visit a member of staff whose mother had just died. At that time (April 1993), the firm was laying pipes in its living quarters to install a central heating system to improve the staff's living conditions. The former head of the Directorial Office of PTIC viewed this situation in a broader sense. He said:

> We state-owned enterprises were and are still undertaking the role as a backbone of this country. Now, the other companies can select people who are relatively young and healthy, and can escape from paying pensions, providing medical care or child care and the other expenditures. But it is us who are looking after possibly their parents, spouse and children. Everybody knows the ideal structure of a family is that father works for joint ventures and mother works for state companies, so their dependants can still be in the welfare scheme. Without us, this society would have already lost its balance. (The former head of the Directorial Office of the PTIC, 6 April 1993)

Learning in the More Market Oriented System

Since economic reforms, state control over raw materials had been gradually liberalized. A state-owned firm, like the LTEF, was ultimately bound to lose its privileges of getting low-price supplies. However, the firm remained dependent on the state, and in particular on MPT, until it found that the state price for a number of materials was much higher than that in the freely negotiated market. This discovery provoked an important change in managers' attitudes in LTEF. Their immediate reaction was that they sold spare copper materials bought in at a low state-regulated price on the negotiated market at a much higher price without the state's permission. More importantly, through this, the firm's management learned that it had to rely on itself.

To produce HJD-04 technology, a large number of components needed to be imported from overseas. However, LTEF did not have direct access to overseas companies. Components had to be purchased through various means: usually through certain domestic trading companies which in turn purchased the goods from trading companies in Hong Kong. And the companies in Hong Kong might have ordered the components through some other intermediaries. As a result, LTEF found it difficult to know who the real suppliers were; more seriously, the quality of components differed to a large extent, and the timing of the shipping-in of the goods was often off schedule. LTEF had a number of frustrating experiences which gradually taught its business team how to deal with these problems – e.g. to find alternative suppliers, to make more practical plans in provision, etc.

Despite its severe problem of surplus labour, LTEF was at the same time short of qualified technicians and engineers for the new-technology production. The market economy had resulted in large disparities between private, JV companies and state-owned companies with the ability to provide increased rewards for such manpower, so that LTEF, which could not provide high wages and bonuses, lost its attractiveness as an employer.

In the past, people, once assigned to work in the firm, could leave only with the firm's permission, unless the transfer was ordered from a higher level. Now because political control upon private and JV companies had been loosened, they accepted new employees who had professional qualifications without the official 'leaving certificates' that had formerly been required. Skilled workers and qualified engineers could quit and leave the firm for a better-paid job in a JV or private company locally, or even in the Special Economic Development Zones. LTEF had not experienced much of a problem with people leaving, because once people were settled – e.g. when their children were in school or kindergarten and their spouses were working in the same community – it was not easy for them to leave. However, there was an urgent need for the firm to recruit new manpower and then make them stay.

As a state-owned firm, LTEF was clearly not a favoured choice for graduates, especially because of its geographical location. The manager of LTEF Personnel Department said of these difficulties:

> In the past, according to the state quota, graduates were assigned to our factory annually. They came but hadn't got enough to do. We often felt there were too many graduates and only a few suitable posts for them. Now, things have changed. My boss has been constantly pressing me to get some new graduates. It's not easy. We are not Shanghai Bell which has got privileges. Well, as long as we are determined to do it and are not stingy with money, we will make it. I have

been travelling around attending 'human resource exchanging meetings'.[7] We are not attractive, indeed. We can't get the best students, but it doesn't matter. I always tell them the truth: our living conditions are not that good, but our HJD-04 is good, it's a Chinese system; the mastery of this technology is like having personal property [as the skills are in great demand]. We need those who are willing to work on the technology. We have got some contracts done this year [1993]. This year, our budget for this recruitment is about 100 000 yuan, with it we can get 40 graduates. You know, we have to pay for it. Well, it is understandable that universities need money too. (Head of Personnel Department, 23 April 1993)

On the one hand, the firm was actively recruiting manpower from external resources. On the other, it was running a retraining programme – by sending people to study in universities, notably to CIT to be trained directly in its laboratory; and by inviting experienced and knowledgeable engineers within the firm, and experts from the CIT, to give lectures in the classroom or teach practically in the field. As the director of LTEF understood: 'Now, we see that competition means a race in technology rather than only in the market. After all this is a competition for manpower' (Director of the LTEF, 22 April 1993).

Also the firm had been trying its best to attract key staff to settle down in the community, by providing them with the best living and working conditions that the firm could afford. The new incentives were: higher salary, better housing and, moreover, job satisfaction.

People in LTEF learned gradually that there is a profound difference between a centrally planned socialist system and a market mechanism. 'Efficiency' and 'high productivity' are essential for a market oriented system, and are closely linked to the profitability of a firm. Under central planning, high productivity was hardly a major consideration. Now, two key factors affected the firm's manufacturing operation. The first stemmed from the changes in telecommunications switching technology. Cross-bar switches were based on electro-mechanical technologies, whereas digital switches like HJD-04 were based on microelectronics. For the firm, it was a fundamental change not only in production technology, but also in production organization. Hence, the second problem was how to control production quality effectively in this new situation.

Since LTEF lost the protection of the state and was pushed into the market, it had to compete with foreign companies, JVs as well as the other HJD-04 producers. The new HJD-04 production was put in a competitive environment in which advanced foreign systems had already set high quality standards. This situation made the firm's management realize the vital importance of quality.

'No quality, no quantity' became an almost everyday phrase spoken by people in the firm from the director to shopfloor workers; it was discussed on programmes made by the in-house wired-broadcaster everyday; and mentioned by every manager I interviewed. It was not a phrase from propaganda; rather, it was a lesson learned from their experiences in markets. Without quality, there would be no market, and the firm would not survive. That was the reality they were facing. Hence gaining high product quality had become the major task of the firm.

Recognition of importance of quality control is one thing, to materialize it is another. In the past, people also paid attention to product quality, but because the production was not the only undertaking of the firm, quality control was often left behind while the other tasks took precedence. Quality control was addressed by a series of disconnected mass movements like other political tasks. After each campaign, quality would remain high for sometime and then deteriorate until another campaign was needed. From its recent experiences, the firm learned that quality control needed a set of well designed methods and that these methods needed to be implemented over the whole production process. At the beginning of 1993, after the institutional reform of the firm, the Department of Quality was set up and a knowledgeable person[8] was made head of the department. Compared to the previous quality control organization, which involved several small teams working in individual departments, the new department had more power.

The first target of the new department was to improve the quality of imported components. As mentioned above, the firm had no direct access to international markets, with the result that these components' quality was unpredictable. For this, the firm increased its investment on testing equipment within the factory. At the same time, some components were sent out of the province to two electronic R&D institutes which had appropriate test apparatus, as the firm lacked qualified labour and necessary equipment at that time.

The implementation of quality control methods in the process of production was more difficult, given the shortage of expertise, manpower and the means of production needed. For instance, in the workshop, many work procedures were done manually. Women workers sat in lines, soldering components on printed-circuit boards by hand. Under these conditions, the quality of production varied depending on individual workers, their experience, attitude towards their job – and, possibly, upon the time of day and on how workers felt. In addition, uneven availability of components often made things worse. When one lot of imported components was rejected by the LTEF owing to poor quality and needed to be returned to the supplier, the time delay was severe. As a result, the workshop sometimes ran out of components while, at other times, too many piled up. As a consequence, workers had nothing to do on some days and on other days had to work over 8 hours to catch up. The stress and fatigue of such long hours meant that quality became uneven on these occasions. Apart from that, even though some quality problems appeared, as long as they were not too serious, workers as well as their managers would not like to stop work, because their salary was also linked with the quantity of their work, according to the new salary system.

The problems of quality control must be understood in the context of the 30-year history of Chinese socialism, in which people had got used to Mao's idea that: 'Ants can move Mount Taishan,' and 'The more people and the higher inspiration, the better the thing will be.' Along with a system of non-market competition, this left the industries of the country with underdeveloped production organization, including adequate production means, technical design of the production process and production management. In LTEF, when HJD-04 production was started the assembly procedure had to be completed manually. The practice taught the firm that (as was described by the new manager of the Department of Quality):

> The HJD-04 production is technology-intensive. Its quality is not visible and tangible. You just can't expect such a technology to be made by hand and be of a good quality. This is in complete contrast with the traditional idea: 'The more people and the high inspiration' can't do any good to product quality. We've got to have an automated production process. In assembling components, anti-electrostatic measures are necessary. The fewer the people involved, the better the quality of production. Besides, while the degree of integration of printed-circuit board gets higher, soldering on it by hand becomes more and more impossible. Automation is the only and best solution, whether we like it or not. (Head of the Department of Quality, 27 April 1993)

The manager of the Department of Technology was still worrying about the management of the whole production process. He realized that the firm's capability of technical design for the production process was weak. The final documentation of technical design for the whole assembly procedure had not been completed by April 1993. Shopfloor workers were not used to strictly following documented instructions. Taylorism was never fully applied in socialist China; instead, workers were usually encouraged to complete a piece of work in their own way as long as they could complete their job. For example, 10 different workers might drill a hole in a piece of work in 10 different ways, rather than following a standardized procedure. Obviously, this could not meet the standards of mass production of the HJD-04 system. As the manager pointed out:

> In the past, technical design of production used to be considered less important than the design of product itself. This was common all over the country. As a consequence, innovations of production technology used to be considered less significant and, worse, technologists working on the production process were easily ignored. Because of this, we now lack technologists and expertise on production organisation. We have to learn gradually. It takes time; it's not easy. (Head of the Department of Technology, 27 April 1993)

The internal institutional reform transformed the Department of Technology. The department laid down new operating rules for workers and tightened the procedures in the workshop. In order to speed up the improvement of production organization, the firm raised the salaries for all in this department, and allowed the department to recruit technologists from different sources, as many as were needed. 'I have been working in the area since the 1960s, for me, the change is remarkable,' noted the head of the Department of Technology.

By contrast, the head of the Department of Quality, who was not satisfied, could not help complaining:

> Till now, many of our managers are still sticking to the old idea that quality control is only the responsibility of our department. Each department for different reasons tries to cover up quality problems rather than put the problems on the table and track down the sources so us to root them out. We lack co-operation between departments and sections. Apart from this, pressures come from PTIC which asked us to produce 25000 lines this year [1993]. When production 'quantity' becomes critical, 'quality' can only be left behind. You know, we have got too many problems, and new machines have not arrived yet. (Head of the Department of Quality, 27 April 1993)

'Product quality' can only be the result of a successful process made up of the combination of every piece of qualified work done by each worker. The experience of LTEF shows that this capability takes time to build up with respect to expertise of quality control and know-how of production organization, as well as qualified workers, technicians and engineers.

The firm had been strengthening its technological capability with regard to production, installation and maintaining capability. Between October 1992, when HJD-04 technology was put into production, and April 1993, about 80 000 lines and 10 systems had been produced and installed.

THE CASE OF A JV – SHANGHAI BELL

Shanghai Bell Telephone Equipment Manufacturing Company Ltd is a Sino–Belgian JV enterprise between the Chinese MPT's Post & Telecommunications Industrial Corporation (PTIC), and Bell Telephone Manufacturing Company of Belgium (BTM). BTM's equity share amounted to 32 per cent of the total, with a further contribution of 8 per cent from the Belgian government's Fund for Development Cooperation, and the PTIC held the remaining 60 per cent. In July 1983, the JV contract was signed in Beijing. This involved the transfer of the technology needed to produce BTM's System 12 exchanges (designed originally by ITT). The Shanghai Bell factory was designed to produce 300000 lines of exchanges a year, and construction of the factory began in 1984. Before Shanghai Bell production reached full speed, however, a series of financial and technical problems arose which almost pushed the JV to bankruptcy. Substantial subsidies from MPT and other supportive measures helped the company out of the crisis. Since 1988, the first profitable year, Shanghai Bell's production has been rapidly increasing. It is now the largest local manufacturer and supplier of exchange equipment in China. Its capacity had increased to 4500 000 lines in 1994 after the new plant was completed in May 1994 in Pudong (East Consulting Ltd., 1995).

Privileges

As a joint production venture, Shanghai Bell was allowed to pay much less tax than domestic companies.[9] Shanghai Bell was free of tax for the first couple of years, and tax charges were deducted by 50 per cent in the following few years. After this, as it was classified as a high-tech company, tax reductions were still applied.[10] In addition, the state granted a licence for Shanghai Bell to import components at a low tariff rate. Shanghai Bell was given the right to purchase components directly from overseas and, moreover, allowed to collect a certain portion of its payments from Chinese customers in foreign currencies.[11] A JV like Shanghai Bell was also given management autonomy to decide internal organizational structures and material rewards.

MPT gave considerable attention to Shanghai Bell's creation, resource allocation and the market for System 12. From the outset, it set up a dedicated bureau in Shanghai to co-ordinate with local government on the building of Shanghai Bell's factory. To ensure its domestic market, MPT decreed in an internal circular[12] that System-12 was one of the principal switching systems for use in the Chinese tele-communications networks. MPT also endeavoured to obtain funds and loans required by Shanghai Bell from relevant government departments.

In terms of human resources, at the end of 1983 MPT brought together a group of highly skilled staff from MPT's R&D institutes, universities and factories across the country to Shanghai Bell to set up the plant. Among them were many experienced senior engineers and knowledgeable professors in the telecommunications field. They played a crucial role in building up the company in the early stages. In October 1985, when the first production assembly was to be put into operation in Shanghai Bell, MPT again took the role in recruiting capable graduates and experienced young engineers all over the country to join the workforce. Many of them later became departmental directors and section managers and formed the technical nucleus of the company.[13]

As a JV located in Shanghai, Shanghai Bell had received substantial support from the Shanghai municipal government. In particular, in the early stage of constructing the JV, the Shanghai municipal government helped the company in obtaining the necessary resources within its territory, from electric power supply to new workforce recruitment. As Shanghai Bell was regarded as a source of advanced technologies for the region, it was even better treated than its state-owned counterparts by the government. In May 1991, with a Shanghai government nomina-tion, Shanghai Bell was conferred the title of a top 10 JV company in China. In June of the same year, the Shanghai municipal government awarded the Shanghai Bell's Belgian director the 'Magnolia Medal' – a high honour conferred by the city.

Quality Control is also a Problem

With the increasing technological capability of the Chinese engineer and rapid expansion of production, managerial problems came to the fore. Quality control in the process of production became the main issue. In 1989 the first year of full-scale production, the Department of Productivity and Quality Management was set up, with a Belgian quality control specialist in charge.[14] He set up routines in the production process in line with world-class standards including motivation, examination in each section, regular reporting, record analysis and internal and external auditing. As with BTM, the target of production quality control in Shanghai Bell was to reach the level of ISO (International Standard Organisation) 9001.[15] A year later, a young Chinese engineer took over the position. However, the level of quality control was not attainable in the short term, reaching the world standard takes time. A Belgian manager had a vivid explanation.

> You should not expect there will be a overnight change. Quality is, first of all, the people's perception. Look! [standing by his office's window, he pointed through the window, to the area – one of the poorest housing areas in Shanghai, where Shanghai Bell's workshops are located] People are living in an environment like this. How can you expect them to have a good sense of quality?! (Director of the Engineering Department, 2 February 1993)

The young director of the Department of Productivity and Quality Management described the current situation:

> Workers are still not aware enough about the importance of quality. There are two major problems: first, quality of production is often ignored when quantity of production becomes urgent; second, understanding of the importance of quality has not penetrated much beyond management circles. Quality incidence changes in cycles. After managers stress the importance of quality, then workers begin to pay more attention and quality becomes good. However, it usually declines bit by bit along the way until, when it reaches 'red line', the managers have to 'sound the alarm' again. (Director of the Department of Productivity & Quality Management, 9 November 1992)

Under the Chinese government policy of import substitution in the early stage of economic reforms, Shanghai Bell was compelled to pursue the targets for domestic supply of imported components set up by the central government. The target for Shanghai Bell was to gradually increase the proportion of components that were locally produced from 20 per cent to 70 per cent by 1993. At the same time, it was granted licences for imported components at a low tariff against its achievement of this target.

To Shanghai Bell, the task of domestication was not negligible; nor were the costs involved. As a manager in the Operation Department described, 'the cost of importing 1 500 000 line components is about 120 million RMB. If the tariff could be reduced to 10 per cent, it is a big deal for Shanghai Bell.' The Chinese General Manager of Shanghai Bell expresses the extremely pragmatic stance of the company:

> The government has its view for the entire country, similarly we have ours. We are seeking profit for the company. However, the government policy changes, we will pursue our own goals. When government is pushing us to adopt import substitution, well, we will do it, as long as the interests of the company are not compromised. We have our own programme. Eventually, we need to establish a large local supplier network to strengthen our position. (Chinese General Manager of Shanghai Bell, 1 February 1999)

Shanghai Bell co-operated with the local government and actively engaged in the project of import substitution. The first problem it encountered was again quality. In the late 1980s, China already possessed more than 100 electronic component assembly lines, but none of these could meet Shanghai Bell's standards. For exchange uses, components have to be functionally very stable and durable. To meet this criteria required, first of all, co-operation of local producers to improve their quality of products. It was a common phenomenon that sample products were usually fine, but the quality of mass-produced products was often much lower. The head of the Domestication Division described the confrontation between Shanghai Bell and local producers, saying:

> No matter whether high-tech or low-tech products, we have often had battles with local producers about quality, which often ended up with unpleasant feelings on both sides. They thought we were unreasonable and hypocritical, and went to the municipal office to complain that we did not like to use local products. The quality problem can be

traced back to our socialist tradition: no market, no competition; users could buy only whatever producers made, and producers took this for granted. We understood the problems of local producers. However, we could not accept their products. We have our standards, which we have learned from BTM. Local producers have to face the challenge too. (Head of the Domestication Division, 28 February 1993, Shanghai)

To take one, typical, example: on one occasion Shanghai Bell needed to buy a lot of screws, a commonly used product. It sent an order to a local screw producer and attached to the order the technical specifications they required for the screws. However, when the order was delivered to Shanghai Bell, many unexpected problems were found. For example, the thread of the screw was not deep enough; the surface finish was not smooth enough, etc. Shanghai Bell insisted on returning this batch of products, since these defects would reduce the screws' endurance and, further, influence the exchange's quality. The manager of the local producer was astonished and did not understand this, as for this company, this batch of products was all up to their own internal standards, and had certificates of inspection. Besides, the company had been producing screws for ages, and they had never come across such a complaint.

Another example was when Shanghai Bell went to find a local producer for a component – a Light-Emitting Diode (LED). After having checked all the technical features, the engineer from Shanghai Bell found that the angle of the light beam was not wide enough and asked the local producer to make a modification from 75 degrees to 120 degrees. He explained that, as the LED was used on the front panel of the exchange, a wider angle could make it more visible for operators. Although the engineers at the local company still believed that Shanghai Bell was being pernickety, and that the change was unnecessary, they eventually agreed to make it. However, that was not the end of the story. After the angle was modified, another problem was found: the brightness of individual LEDs varied, which meant that, when they were fitted, on a same panel, some would look brighter and some dimmer. This again caused friction between two sides. The producer argued that this was too tiny an imperfection to be a problem, whereas the Shanghai Bell side persisted with its standard.

To solve the problem, Shanghai Bell invited managers of local producers to visit the Shanghai Bell's production workshop, to see how their components were fitted into the system through the assembly line and were functioning in the switching system. To ensure the local production quality in the longer term, Shanghai Bell established a programme with each local component producer for periodically inspecting the production process and examining products, as well as random checks. This programme sought to track down the source of quality problems and finally helped the local producer to solve them.

During the course of domesticating production of System 12 components, local companies' awareness of product quality gradually developed and production capabilities were strengthened, although quality problems were still occurring from time to time, as these could not just disappear overnight. Even the most successful import substitution project – the Shanghai–Belling JV project to manufacture large-scale integrated chips (LSI) for System 12 – still had a reject rate of end-products of 60 per cent, lagging behind the producers in industrialized countries. But, compared to a reject rate at as high as 98 per cent in the early production stage, it still represented big progress.

Managing Resources

With the expansion in production capacity by Shanghai Bell, more human resources were required. Learning lessons from state-owned companies, it had a policy for dealing with shortage of manual workers by 'borrowing' labour where possible in preference to recruiting, in order to avoid creating a future situation where it had a surplus of labour on its books which would require employment and provision of long-term welfare facilities. It 'borrowed' large numbers of labourers from other companies which were economically stagnant and were keen to reduce the burden of their surplus labour. By the end of 1992, among 1313 enlisted employees in Shanghai Bell, over 300 were temporarily transferred from the other factories and institutes.[16] Most of them were low-skilled workers. They were happy with the move. They received the basic salary from their original companies, which was a relatively small portion of their income, in comparison to the bonus that Shanghai Bell gave them. Although their average income was less than that of Shanghai Bell's employees, it was still much more than what they had previously received.

Shanghai Bell also managed to get many highly skilled external 'workers' working for the company. They were all engineers sent by customers to Shanghai Bell. By agreement between Shanghai Bell and its customers, after their six month training courses, these engineers would continue their further practice in Shanghai Bell for 18 months to two years. As a result, given their previous experience in the field and their newly acquired knowledge about System 12, they were very capable indeed. They played an important role in helping Shanghai Bell to install and maintain System 12 in the field. The benefits of this arrangement were mutual, and most of these engineers were happy to work for Shanghai Bell. On the one hand, with their salary from their own company plus the portion Shanghai Bell provided on top, their income became much higher than usual and, on the other, working with Shanghai Bell, they could acquire new expertise.

As the production capacity expanded rapidly, Shanghai Bell hired several MPT engineering teams to carry out installation works in their neighbouring areas which they were familiar with. It also used engineers who had been technically trained in Shanghai Bell to cover a relatively difficult job in installation – software testing. This measure proved to be economical as well as effective.

In terms of R&D, Shanghai Bell co-operated with local universities and research institutes. In installation and maintenance, it sought help from MPT engineering teams and experienced engineers in local Post and Telecommunications Agencies (PTAs). It hired local professionals to provide other logistic services, such as providing food and medical service to its staff, rather than establish its own hospitals and canteens. Through this policy, Shanghai Bell's employment only increased by 54 per cent, from 855 in 1989 to 1313 in 1992, compared to a 317 per cent increase in its production capacity during the same time.

A JV like Shanghai Bell attracted enormous government attention. Its managers, and in particular Chinese managers, who understood the importance of this connection, had learned how to utilize the government's concern. While the Belgian managers found the government intervention irritating, Chinese managers seemed to be more relaxed about it. For example, Shanghai Bell's annual production volume was usually decided jointly by BTM and the Chinese government through their representatives on Shanghai Bell's Board of Directors. In 1992, soon after the time for both sides to work out the production volume for 1993 and the Board of Directors had decided that it was to be 1 500 000 lines, a new message came through from the Chinese government indicating that production volume should increase greatly. The SPC proposed a number as high as 2 200 000 lines, and MPT pushed this even further and made the figure 2 700 000 lines. The Belgian side was irritated, and also thought this aim was incredible. However, Shanghai Bell's Chinese top managers reacted differently. They went to find out the reasons for this recommendation and decided that fulfilling it would be also good for Shanghai Bell. First, from the Chinese government's point of view it had already become inevitable to open its domestic PDSS market to the USA. To ensure Shanghai Bell's position in the market, the government wanted Shanghai Bell to expand its market share as far and as quickly as possible. This coincided with Shanghai Bell's interests in long-term development. Second, now that the SPC had given this quota, it gave Shanghai Bell the possibility of getting a low import tariff for the components needed to produce 2 200 000 lines. Shanghai Bell therefore accepted this figure – and, moreover, reached this level of production in 1993.

Apart from taking advantage of the Chinese government's support, Shanghai Bell was also able to use fully its technical resources overseas. By 1993, many System 12 components could be purchased locally. Nevertheless, Shanghai Bell still continued to import a portion, in order to keep its links open to technological changes in the world, even though this irritated the Customs Office. As the Deputy Manager of the Department of Engineering explained:

I have to say that, in terms of technology, the core technology of System 12 is still not in our hands. The future of System 12 depends more or less on technological development in the industrialized world. We do not want to drive foreign suppliers away. Rather we want to be kept informed of their product changes, to keep the pace with the world. (Deputy Manager of the Engineering Department, 30 February 1993)

Mixed Style of Management

At the outset, the management style in Shanghai Bell was to copy BTM. Later Shanghai Bell gradually developed its own style, which was considered to be a hybrid between Chinese and Western methods. At the very beginning, some young Chinese managers were sent to BTM and other management schools in China and abroad to learn modern management theories and methods. However, very soon, practice proved that it was impossible to apply many Western methods to the Chinese environment. Inevitably, the outcome of adapting Western management methods to the Chinese environment was a mixture of both. Western methods dealt with question of productivity and efficiency whereas the Chinese way dealt with incentives of staff.

The primary objective of the company was market growth and achieving profits. Shanghai Bell's management had been concentrating on this target, with the result that it had achieved a high level of productivity. In 1992, the production output was 1 380 000 lines, with only 800 workers. Although there were political organizations in the company, such as the Communist Party, trade unions, the Youth League and Women's Association, their importance had already given way to productivity: their organizational activities took place only after work, and they took up only the smallest fraction of the company's agenda, compared to state-owned companies, where the Party's activities were always given high priority.

Material incentives were explicitly adopted, as already noted. In comparison with state-owned companies, Shanghai Bell offered much higher salaries, although the salary level was still far from the highest in the Shanghai area. As an early established JV, Shanghai Bell was allowed to raise the salary level for its employees only by up to 30 per cent above the average of state-owned companies. This was set by the government in order not to cause unrest among workers in state-owned companies, especially in MPT's companies. Over time, as more and more joint ventures and private companies were set up and started to compete with each other in offering high salaries, the average salary increased rapidly. Shanghai Bell, as a large company, was simply not able to follow the pace. In 1992 it raised its general salary levels, but very soon the other companies caught up and overtook it.

To compensate for this, Shanghai Bell provided employees with housing;[17] it spent 50 per cent of the company's total welfare expenditure on housing for staff. By the end of 1992, about 10 per cent of its employees lived in company flats, provided for key persons such as department managers and senior engineers, fully furnished, and some even equipped with all household electrical appliances. For ordinary Shanghai residents, it was paradise and could not be better. One department manager, a flat-holder said: 'I won't expect any better than this, and I think that our company's offer is the best in the whole Shanghai area, although our salary is a bit low' (Deputy Director of the Engineering Department, 30 February 1993). A condition attached to this offer was that, if a worker left Shanghai Bell, they should leave the flat as well.[18]

Chinese management traditions tended to treat the company as if it were a family. Its administration system was fairly hierarchical, but the relationship between the upper and the lower levels was not necessarily very formal. The authority of a director of the company could be very parent-like. Even a manual labourer at the lowest level was encouraged to approach directors or higher level managers of the company for help with personal problems, even bypassing intermediate management. In this respect, Shanghai Bell still kept the old tradition. A department manager explained:

> People still turn to us for help when problems occur with their family, things like that a child was ill or couples had a row, etc., although these are now not considered to be our responsibilities according to the job specification. However, we have got used to it. The company takes care of them, and they take care of the company. (Deputy Director of the Engineering Department, 30 January 1993)

The Chinese General Manager of Shanghai Bell believed the combination of Chinese and Western management methods was necessary:

> Working for a foreign company will make you feel that you are only working for a company which belongs to strangers. But in our company you still feel you are working with people who belong to your 'family', having a feeling of being a part and sharing with them. When a member of staff has got a problem, he or she can approach me directly, either with or without an appointment, in working or non-working time, as long as I have got time. This is Chinese culture. Although Western management provides us with efficiency in production organization, we still need staff who are devoted to hard work. The fact that we, Shanghai Bell, could achieve such a production expansion, has to be attributed to the combination of Chinese and Western management. (Chinese General Manager, Li Dalai, 1 February 1993)

Belgian managers were very sympathetic to their Chinese counterparts, believing that they must be exhausted dealing endlessly with problems, such as wages, housing and so on, which they themselves could not have stood. They were happy with the division of management responsibilities, whether explicit or implicit, that the Belgian managers would concentrate on production and leave personnel issues altogether to Chinese managers.

ANALYSIS AND CONCLUSIONS

As we have seen in both cases, the state of management in production, resource allocation and marketing is still relatively poor, especially in state-owned firms. This backwardness stemmed from the old centrally planned system, relating to the weak institutional links between actors involved the process and the lack of incentives for improvement. When technology users were accustomed to having little choice but to accept what suppliers produced, their sense of quality was suppressed. Similarly there was little opportunity for consumer demands for better products to be heard by technology designers and producers. Likewise, when all the resources – including human, material and finance as well as the allocation of products – were administratively arranged through specified state agents, producers were mainly 'plan-takers'. Without needing to face competitive challenges, producers had little motive to pursue improvements in technology or productivity. The two case studies provide some rather typical illustrations. For instance, were it not for the efforts of Shanghai Bell as a customer, the local screw producer would have never realized that its production quality needed to be improved – let alone that it might need to meet the specifications of particular customers or market segments. In such an environment, it was not surprising that Chinese managers had little experience or skill in dealing with all these formerly unimportant aspects.

This situation has begun to change since the economic reforms and the progressive introduction of market mechanisms. The changing environment places enormous pressures on manufacturing enterprises and compels them to improve their capabilities in a number of areas, including the effective management of production, marketing, resource allocation, etc. The market mechanism provides incentives to build better links between a wide range of players, within and beyond the enterprise, including managers, engineers, shopfloor work forces, customers, etc. and to involve them in the learning process about production improvement.

In the LTEF case, confronted by intense pressure, the firm has been learning to build up its basic capabilities for dealing with the business issues which arise in a more market oriented system. Unlike Shanghai Bell, it could not just start again from scratch, but had to transform a deeply rooted culture and methods of operating. The process was painstaking, as LTEF was not in a position simply to shake off all of the traditions and social burdens inherited from the past. Management learned to motivate staff to work harder in the new environment by reforming the administrative system, setting up an internal labour market, etc.; to manage production and quality more efficiently and effectively; to have greater autonomy in allocating human, financial and material resources on its own; and to 'marketize' its products by providing better-quality products, services (and even adopt arguably corrupt measures) to win customers. It was primarily signals through the market mechanism which motivated LTEF to improve its understanding of customers' requirements of 'quality'. The market (and the availability of Western technology) established criteria for indigenous producers like LTEF to achieve.

Similarly, in an increasingly market oriented context, Chinese managers in Shanghai Bell had to learn quickly to segregate the company's own business interests from those of the Chinese government. Though on the one hand it resorted to technical, financial and political support from the central government, MPT and the Shanghai municipal government, on the other it rejected certain kinds of interference from them which would conflict with its best interests. Shanghai Bell learned to take advantage of its position as a newly established JV. It developed pragmatic policies and measures, and articulated its domestic and overseas strengths. Its learning of Western managerial methods was not a simple copying of BTM: rather, it developed a hybrid style of management between Western and Chinese methods through which it achieved high productivity. In marketing and resource allocation, local managers articulated Shanghai Bell's natural connections both domestic and overseas, and established specific measures and policies in customer training, staff recruitment, technical collaboration, etc. to maximize the company's profits. Moreover, to ensure the quality of locally produced components on which the quality of System 12 relied, Shanghai Bell persuaded all its local suppliers – e.g. for LEDs, resistors and even the screws used on the switches – to improve their production management. This can be considered as a common phenomenon in the new environment. We thus see the market mechanism as providing an incentive to not only motivate awareness of production improvement, but also to promote the wider diffusion of such awareness.

The Chinese managers in both LTEF and Shanghai Bell have been learning how to manage in a changing context. However, the case studies indicate that this learning, by individuals or institutions, was significantly shaped by the broader social, economic and political environment of China's transition. Imperfections in the evolving market system can also produce negative outcomes and result in distorted learning. For example, under the pressure of market competition, LTEF even adopted some measures that could be seen as corrupt – moves which have to be seen in the light of incomplete development of the still newly established legislative system, together with the lack of a legal tradition in China to test and implement the law and weaknesses in the internal administration and culture of firms.

The process of building up management capabilities at firm level proved to be uneven and unstable, heavily dependent on the contingencies of the particular setting and historical inheritance of individual companies. The two case studies show that internal management within firm varies in different types of firms. Compared to state-owned firms, Shanghai Bell is a new company without the social burdens from which a company like LTEF has suffered. This reminds us that the obstacles to management learning and its outcomes in these two companies are very different, operating within different restraints. In a company like LTEF it was almost impossible for managers to lay off surplus employees and operate with no concern for their fate. As a result, they sought to set up an internal labour market which ameliorated, but did not fundamentally solve, the problem of surplus labour.

A crucial point shown by the two cases is that the improvement of management is not just an issue of management itself. Rather, it is a question of improving the entire system, which demands not only institutional restructuring, but also a wider change in workplace practice and cultures necessitating the mass involvement of the workforce in learning about technology, quality, production skills, marketing, etc. This learning process needs to cover a wide range of individuals and institutions. The scale of learning required is perhaps much larger than might generally be expected, and goes beyond the employees to include others in the supply chain. For instance, without knowledgeable customers who are accustomed to exercising their rights, and without a mechanism which is able to convey customers' needs to producers, the firm's management would have little incentive to improve their products. Similarly, without capable engineers, shopfloor workers, salesmen, etc., management policies would have little impact within the enterprise. One implication of this need to have such mass involvement in learning processes is that change may take far longer than has been anticipated. If there is an 'Asian miracle' in China (ignoring for the moment the setbacks of the 90s) we should not expect China to suddenly make a quantum leap. Rather, it would be more realistic to pin expectations on the ability of the Chinese to intensify the learning processes by promoting a social and economic environment that will encourage such developments.

Professional management training alone will not be able to achieve this transformation. What professional training can achieve is widening managers' perspectives and providing general management knowledge and methods, as well as a general awareness of comparative modern management practice in other societies. Thus, management training might provide tools for managers actively involved in the improvement of business practices.

Another point which should not be overlooked is that, in the case of China's transition, the business environment has been changing constantly. It is not possible to find a single 'best-practice' model of management which could be expected to lead to business successes within this diverse and changing context. Diverse firms, with different products, in different circumstances and with different historical backgrounds, face very different obstacles for building up management and firm capabilities. They need to consider a variety of possible strategies and experiments and learn with these. In addition, it should not be forgotten that the basic concepts and methods of modern management are largely based on the experience of industrialized economic systems, modelled in particular on Western lines. These share certain commonly recognized and often taken-for-granted features in terms of the development of market mechanisms, legislative systems, rules of ethical business conduct, etc. As a result, the substantive relevance of much management training can be of only limited practical use in the very different context of China's transition.

We can conclude that a key feature, if China is to overcome these barriers to efficient management, is a more supportive social and economic environment. In turn, to build up a more efficient and less corrupt and bureaucratic business environment requires change at various levels including a wide range of individuals (or institutions) within the system, including managers. To follow the metaphor, if professional management training may enable local managers to 'take the horse to water', we should look to the broad social and economic context if we want to 'make it drink'.

Notes

1. Bell Telephone Manufacturing Company of ITT, now owned by Alcatel.
2. CIT was the computer R&D laboratory for the People's Liberation Army. The economic reforms led it to seek income from commercial developments to make up for reduced state funding, and it decided to move into the area of telecommunications switching, with a radical new modular design, incorporating cheap standard microprocessors and development tools that were readily available on the world market. It sought to link up with an exchange producer who knew about the particular demands of China's telecommunications systems and had contacts in the market.

3. This kind of contract varied from firm to firm. Usually, workers signed contracts with the head of their departments, heads of departments signed with the director of the firm and the director with his boss at higher-level organizations, accordingly.
4. The formula for counting is Total salary = (Basic salary + Performance + oriented salary) x Quality as weighted variable from 0–1.
5. According to my personal interview with three engineers and technicians, all of them had graduated from university and left their home town and come to work in this factory. One had got married living in the dormitory, the other two were single.
6. For attracting foreign investment in Chinese industry, the government issued several tariff bills: 'Regulations for the Implementation of the Law of the People's Republic of China on Joint Ventures Using Chinese and Foreign Investment', promulgated by the State Council on 20 September 1983, indicated that, 'A joint venture can apply for reduction or exemption of industrial and commercial consolidated tax for a certain period of time' (Shanghai Municipal Foreign Trade Committee 1985a: 223–56); 'Some Provisions of the People's Republic of China Concerning the Reduction of or Exemption from Income Tax in the Absorption of Foreign Funds', 21 September 1982, indicated that, 'A newly-established joint venture, jointly operated for a period of more than 10 years, with the approval of tax authorities upon an application filed by the enterprise, may be exempted from income tax in the first profit-making year, and allowed a 50 per cent reduction in the second and third years' (Shanghai Municipal Foreign Trade Committee, 1985b: 386–391). Along with that, many coastal cities and districts added some more radical local policies to give joint ventures more privileges.
7. These were organized to let companies and students get to know each other.
8. According to my interview, he had been involved in quality control work since 1973 and was sent to study on production management at a college during that time.
9. According to The Law of the People's Republic of China on Joint Ventures Using Chinese and Foreign Investment, Article 7, 'a joint venture equipped with up-to-date technology by world standards may apply for a reduction of or exemption from income tax for the first two to three profit-making years'. This law was adopted on 1 July 1979 at the Second Session of the Fifth National People's Congress, and promulgated on 8 July 1979, (Shanghai Municipal Foreign Trade and Economic Committee, 1985).
10. Interview with the deputy manager of Department of Operational Finance at PTIC.
11. Domestic enterprises did not have such rights.
12. Interview with the vice chief engineer in Shanghai Local Telecommunications Administration, and confirmed in other interviews in Shanghai Bell. I did not see the internal circular. However, there is the State Council No. 56 dispatch in 1989 which indicated clearly, 'it is requested for all purchasing of foreign switching systems to use the ones which have already been selected by the government', (The Telecommunications Administration Bureau at Zhejiang Provincial Posts and Telecommunications Administration, 1992: 93).

13. Many of the young managers I interviewed in Shanghai Bell belonged to this batch of recruits, which was arranged by MPT.
14. According to the director of the Productivity & Quality Management. 'He is a very experienced manager. Apart from building up a quality control system in Shanghai Bell, he also introduced his knowledge to other local companies and had a very good relationship with Shanghai Quality Management Association' (Director of Productivity & Quality Management, 9 November 1992).
15. Most detailed material about production quality control was provided by the manager of the Department of Productivity Quality Management in the interview of 9 November 92.
16. Interview with the Manager of Personnel Planning & Education at the personnel & Administration Department, 3 November 1992.
17. Housing in Shanghai was extremely scarce, as vividly described by a popular saying that here: 'It is easier to find a wife than a flat'.
18. The Manager of Personnel Planning & Education at the Personnel & Administration Department, Shanghai Bell, provided me with the details about the material incentives which Shanghai Bell provided to its staff.

References

Brus, W. and Laski, K. (1989) *From Marx to the Market: Socialism in Search of an Economic System*, Oxford, Clarendon Press.
Child, J. (1992) 'Foreword', in M. Warner, *How Chinese Managers Learn – Management and Industrial Training in China*, London, Macmillan, xi–xiii.
East Consulting Ltd (1995) *Telecommunications in China: Entering the Market of the Decade*, London, Financial Times, Telecoms and Media Publishing.
Shanghai Municipal Foreign Trade and Economic Committee (1985a) 'Regulations for the Implementation of the Law of the People's Republic of China on Joint Ventures Using Chinese and Foreign Investment', *Shanghai Overseas Investment Utilization Manual*, Shanghai, Shanghai Translation Publishing House, July 1985 edn, 223–56.
Shanghai Municipal Foreign Trade and Economic Committee (1985b) 'Some Provisions of the People's Republic of China Concerning the Reduction of or Exemption from Income Tax in the Absorption of Foreign Funds', *Shanghai Overseas Investment Utilization Manual*, Shanghai, Shanghai Translation Publishing House, July 1985 edn, 386–91.
Shanghai Municipal Foreign Trade and Economic Committee (1985c) 'The Law of the People's Republic of China on Joint Venture Using Chinese and Foreign Investment', *Overseas Investment Utilization Manual*, Shanghai, Shanghai Translation Publishing House, July 1985 edn, 217–22.
The Telecommunications Administration Bureau at Zhejiang Provincial Posts and Telecommunications Administration 'Dispatches of the Application Management of Digital Switching Systems Installation in the Public Telecommunications Network', *Selected Dispatches and Documents on Telecommunications*, August 1992 edn, (Internal Circular), 93–4.
Warner, M. (1992) *How Chinese Managers Learn – Management and Industrial Training in China*, London, Macmillan.

White, G. (1988) 'State and Market in China's Socialist Industrialisation', in G. White (ed.), *Developmental States in East Asia*, Basingstoke, Macmillan, 153–92.

Zhou, Shulian (1982) 'The Market Mechanism in a Planned Economy', in Lin Wei and A. Chao (eds), *China's Economic Systems: Essays in Honour of Ota Sik*, Basingstoke, Macmillan, 186–92.

17 Clusters, Industrial Districts and the Competitiveness of Chinese Industries

Hua Li, Frank McDonald and Giovanna Vertova

INTRODUCTION

The role of geography and institutional factors has received little attention from orthodox economics because economic analysis tends to focus on the characteristics of the competitive environment with little regard for the location of economic activity. However, a number of economists have given a greater emphasis to the nature and performance of local economies within nations (Porter, 1990; Krugman, 1991, 1995; Ottaviano and Puga, 1998). Economic geographers have also pointed out the importance of geographical factors in influencing the costs and benefits associated with location (Amin and Thrift, 1994; Dicken, 1998). It has been argued that geographical proximity facilitates gains in efficiency and flexibility that individual producers, who operate in isolation, can rarely attain (Porter, 1990). These gains may help developing countries to attain international competitiveness (Nadvi and Schmitz, 1994). This chapter examines the phenomenon of geographical concentration of firms (clusters and industrial districts) and assesses their importance for the competitiveness of two Chinese regions – Beijing and Shanghai.

This chapter merges the theoretical tradition of Marshall (1890) on industrial districts with the new socioeconomic models (Pyke, Becattini and Sengenberger, 1990; Sengenberger and Pyke, 1991). The central difference between Marshall and his modern followers is the relative importance given to networks that are composed of individuals and private and public organizations. The influences of the community, the family, social relationships and rules of behaviour are key determinants for the formation of the modern industrial district. However, Marshall's analysis of industrial districts concentrates on the external economies of scale that arise from geographical concentrations of firms. This chapter clarifies the differences between clusters, Marshallian industrial districts and modern industrial districts, and assesses the importance of geographical concentrations of firms for national and international competitiveness in the context of two Chinese regions.

CLUSTERS AND INDUSTRIAL DISTRICTS

A 'cluster' is conceptually different from an 'industrial district', although the two terms are often used interchangeably. Schmitz defines clusters as 'A group of producers making the same or similar things in close vicinity to each other' (Schmitz, 1992: 65). Therefore, a cluster is identified as a sectoral and geographical concentration of firms within the same industry. Clusters have two defining characteristics: geographical concentration and sectoral specialization. The conditions that encourage firms to cluster in a particular geographical area are not fully understood. Nevertheless, four factors can be identified as being strongly connected to the clustering process.

Geographical Factors

Location theory suggests that transport costs prohibit geographical concentration of production. However, firms can benefit from geographical concentration when economies of scale are available. Consequently, transport costs and other locational costs must be assessed in relation to the economies of scale that are available from reducing the number of production sites. In cases where economies of scale are large relative to transport costs geographical concentration of production sites becomes attractive (Krugman, 1991, 1995). Geographical proximity of firms can also lead to external economies of scale because of such factors as the existence of a pool of skilled labour and a constellation of firms able to supply appropriate materials and services that are required in the production process.

Historical Events

Firms often cluster as the result of some historical event such as the development of computer science in Stanford University that had a strong influence in the establishment of Silicon Valley in California

(Saxenian, 1985). The development of many clusters has been influenced by historical events (Porter, 1990). Moreover, once a cluster is created, it is then maintained by its historical path-dependence and by the possibility to become locked-in into a certain pattern of specialization (Antonelli, 1997).

Institutions

Institutional frameworks provide the legal, political and social structure that defines the rules of human interaction. Some institutional frameworks are conducive to low transaction costs (North, 1990), thus encouraging the concentration of firms in certain locations where business activities are less costly owing to lower transaction costs.

Technology

The development of clusters has often been influenced by the evolution of new technologies within geographical areas. Silicon Valley is a modern example of this process. However, Marshall also found that technological developments were an important factor in the origin and expansion of clusters in nineteenth-century Britain. Technological developments were often important to help to overcome common problems or to develop markets. Geographical proximity appeared to stimulate technological development owing to the benefits arising from regular business and social interaction between entrepreneurs. The importance of technological developments in the evolution of Sheffield as a major centre for steel production provides a good example of the type of phenomenon that Marshall observed (Tweedale, 1995).

The formation of clusters is strongly influenced by these factors. Any one of them may be sufficient to begin the process of geographical concentration. A combination of these factors is likely to provide strong incentives to locate in clusters, and the combination of the various economies that are available from the establishment of clusters leads firms to reap what are often called 'agglomeration economies' (Bellandi, 1989).

According to Brusco 'A district comprises a cluster of firms producing something which is homogeneous in one way or another, positioning themselves differently on the market. Thus, the district could be defined as being a cluster, plus a peculiar relationship among firms' (Brusco, 1990: 14). The main difference between a cluster and an industrial district is therefore the presence of networks. An industrial district develops from a simple cluster when networks are involved.

Networks involve relationships that are neither purely market transactions nor hierarchies, but are also embedded in social and cultural conditions. Networks emerge, as co-ordinating mechanisms, when the creation and diffusion of information incurs substantial costs. Networks can be defined as 'a set of high-trust relationships which either directly or indirectly link together everyone in a social group' (Casson, 1997: 4). Therefore, the basic element of networks is a relationship of mutual trust between individual and organizations.

Two different sets of networks can be identified – business networks and socioeconomic networks. These networks lead to the creation of different types of industrial districts.

BUSINESS NETWORKS

Business networks are composed of a family of firms that are linked together for the purpose of effectively undertaking business operations. According to Brusco (1990), an industrial district is composed of three different kinds of firms that form business networks in a given geographical area. 'Final firms' are those producing for the final market, 'stage firms' are those involved in only one stage of production, and 'others' are all those working in a different industry to that one which defines the district but, nevertheless, belong to the same vertically integrated sector as the final firms. Following this categorization, three kinds of business networks can be identified in an industrial district:

- *Horizontal networks* that are based on close inter-firm relations among 'final firms' supported by the common provision of technical, business, financial and other services.
- *Vertical networks*, networks of 'final firms' and 'stage firms' linked by backward and forwards vertical integration – the so-called 'supply chain'.
- *Other networks*, such as links among firms and institutions for the support of the activities of 'final firms' – relationships with universities, R&D agencies and government bodies, for example.

SOCIO-ECONOMIC NETWORKS

When firms want to expand their business, important economic decisions must be taken and the more information that is available, the better. Firms need reliable and low-cost information on prices, sources of inputs with the correct qualities, access to financial resources and to appropriate technology. In these circumstances it is important whom the manager knows and, especially, it is crucial to know the right people. Extended families, churches, educational organizations, local government authorities, local political parties and trade unions can be involved in these networks of people and groups (Becattini, 1990). Such networks embody a homogeneous system of values that creates trust among the members of the network based on a strong 'sense of belonging'. The creation of trust-based networks provides the basis for socioeconomic networks to reduce the time, effort and uncertainty associated with gathering and processing information. Furthermore, it is likely that these socioeconomic networks are more likely to occur in countries that have difficulties in institutionalizing trust through national institutional frameworks (North, 1990). Therefore, people may be encouraged to form local socioeconomic networks to compensate for the inadequacies of their national institutional frameworks. However, socioeconomic networks may not emerge if national institutional frameworks can deliver acceptable means of establishing trust.

The type of industrial district created depends upon the kinds of networks firms are able to develop. The clustering process can be seen as the primary force that drives firms to concentrate in certain areas. It is easy to assume that clustered firms operating in the same industry will engage in some kind of business networks from the very beginning. However, the development of socioeconomic networks has historical and institutional roots and, therefore, can take a long time to emerge.

According to this evolutionary process, a cluster precedes an industrial district, but does not necessarily lead to it unless some kind of network is created. Figure 17.1 shows the three determinants of clusters and the development towards industrial districts when networks are created. Clusters involved only in business networks of small firms in a geographical area can be classified as Industrial Districts Type I (ID1). This kind of district is very similar to Marshall's concept of an industrial district. The majority of industrial districts will be ID1, where business networks are predominant because the primary characteristic of industrial districts is business activity. Therefore, business links between firms in clusters are nearly inevitable. Clusters that have both business and socioeconomic networks can be classified as Industrial District Type II (ID2). Figure 17.1 shows the development of these two different kinds of networks. Industrial districts may expand over time as more and more networks are created among an increasing number of

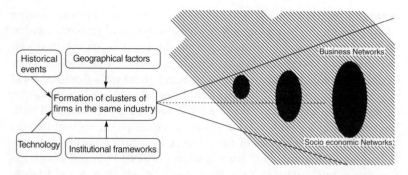

Figure 17.1   The development of clusters and Industrial Districts

agents. In cases where institutional frameworks limit the development of high-trust business networks, socioeconomic networks are likely to emerge as industrial districts evolve.

The major characteristics of industrial districts are: the presence of firms operating within the same industry, a distinguishable market supplied from the industrial district, a pool of human resources with relevant skills, the sharing of technical knowledge and a locally-based financing system. When these are combined with a local community with a 'sense of belonging' based on a shared system of values that is networked into the business networks, ID2 will develop. The balance between competition and co-operation is an important feature in industrial districts (You, 1994). Competition among firms in industrial districts is a very strong feature, particularly for those firms producing similar products or operating at the same stage of the productive process. However, co-operation is at least as important as competition in the organization of an industrial district. Collaboration can occur among firms in order to develop the most appropriate technical specification and design for their products, or in order to ensure a collective provision of skilled labour. This kind of co-operation takes the form of 'good neighbourliness', such as lending of tools, passing on of advice and helping in emergencies. (Sengenberger and Pyke, 1991).

SOCIOECONOMIC NETWORKS AND CHINESE BUSINESSES

Italian industrial districts are typical examples of ID2. Identifying ID2 in countries other than Italy has been a controversial matter. It has been suggested that this kind of industrial district is less likely to be found in developing countries, especially in East Asia, owing to the lack of an established industrial culture and to the insufficient development of local networks (Park, 1996). On the other hand, it has been argued that the Chinese family business model (in Chinese businesses based outside of the People's Republic of China) relies on social networks owing to the inability of Chinese society to institutionalize trust (Kao, 1993). Moreover, social networks, such as family and personal relationship, have been found to be the key to understanding the success of the emerging entrepreneurial class in China, after the reform process started in 1979 (Ping, 1997; see also Chapter 16 in this volume). Evidence that a type of industrial district structure is developing in rural China has also been found, but these industrial districts are less geographically concentrated than, for example, the typical Italian case (Christerson and Lever-Tracy, 1997).

The important role that personal relationships play in Chinese organizations has been identified by both sociologists and organizational theorists (Jacobs, 1980; King, 1991; Lockett, 1988). The term *guanxi* is often used to describe the role of personal relationships as a means of overcoming a lack of trust that pervades Chinese society. *Guanxi* refers to a system of reciprocal bonds based on personal relationships (Redding, Norman and Schlander, 1993). *Guanxi* is usually based on family relationships (including the extended family) and on relationships founded on shared experiences – for example, school and university friends (Tsui and Farh, 1997). Many aspects of social interaction in China are based on the *guanxi* system.

The *guanxi* system that operates in local communities in China has many similarities to the socioeconomic networks of the type that are found in ID2. Since the economic reform of 1979 there has been a large increase in private sector enterprise in China, of which about one-third is based in townships and villages (Ping, 1997). Personal relationships based on *guanxi* play an important role for private enterprises in providing finance and in helping to find appropriate materials and labour (Ping, 1997). The nature of Chinese institutional frameworks leads to some handicaps that limit the development of private enterprises in China. However, the *guanxi* system provides a means of establishing trust-based networks that help private enterprises to overcome the obstacles that result from the institutional frameworks. As many of the new private enterprises are located in townships and villages these networks have characteristics similar to what would be found in ID2. The literature on the development of Chinese private enterprises indicates that something similar to ID2 are developing in China as a result of the liberalization that followed from the 1979 economic reforms.

However, the continuing influence of old state planning ideas is also evident in the development of clusters in China. The Beijing New-Tech Experimental Zone (BEZ) in the Zhong'guancun district in the Beijing region is an example of how the development of an industrial district in China can be strongly influenced by government (Wang and Wang, 1998). The BEZ was created as a result of the encouragement of the state government to develop high-tech firms in China. This policy attracted many high-tech multinationals to Zhong'guancun and has also stimulated Chinese firms to develop in the district. The BEZ has many of the characteristics of an ID1. The firms and supporting agencies in the BEZ are centred on the production of electronic products. However, government support for the BEZ has been focused on large firms. This has led to problems in developing local networks that can help small and medium sized enterprises (SMEs) in Zhong'guancun to prosper. The main limiting factor to the development of SMEs in the BEZ has been the encouragement by the state government and the local Beijing government of large vertically integrated firms. The tendency to adopt such an approach stems from the legacy of state planning that emphasized vertical integration as a solution to problems of co-ordinating economic activity. However, this approach has limited the development of smaller and perhaps more dynamic firms. Solutions to this problem have been proposed that call for an extension of locally-based networks that would move the BEZ towards an industrial district that would be similar to the concept of an ID2 (Wang, 1997). The case of the BEZ indicates the importance of institutional factors in the development of industrial districts in China and highlights the strong influence that the old ideas of state planning still exert on Chinese business activity.

COMPETITIVENESS AND GEOGRAPHICAL PROXIMITY

The new international economics emphasizes the role of geography as a key determinant for the trading and economic performance of nation's industries and as a way to enhance international competitiveness. The new international trade theory indicates that intra-industry trade, in particular, is generated by economies of scale and first-mover advantages that often lead to clusters (Krugman, 1991, 1995). Porter explains national export success as the result of self-reinforcing industrial districts and first-mover advantages (Porter, 1990). In many industries geographical proximity of firms permits them to reap external and internal economies of scale that allows them to gain competitive advantages that are not available to firms that are not geographically concentrated. The importance that geographical proximity has on international competitiveness is witnessed by the fact that regions with successful industrial districts performed particularly well in the global economic crisis of the 1970s and the 1980s (Harrison, 1992). Silicon Valley and the Italian region of Emilia-Romagna are typical examples (see Saxenian, 1985 for Silicon Valley, Capecchi, 1990 for Emilia-Romagna). Firms within clusters that lead to economies of scale and other advantages, therefore, obtain economic advantages by geographical proximity that could otherwise not be achieved.

Competitiveness may be achieved through the development of clusters or industrial districts that enable firms to gain three possible benefits:

- First-mover advantages that arise from cost advantages owing to high set-up costs that allow producers to retain competitive advantage even if some other producers could potentially manufacture the same goods or services more cheaply. Thus, a pattern of specialization established by historical accident may persist even when new producers could have lower costs.
- Reductions in production costs that emerge from the reductions in transaction costs that firms in clusters or in industrial districts enjoy. These transaction cost benefits allow firms to reap external economies of scale that can grant them lower production costs than other competitors that are not located in a cluster or in industrial district.
- Quality advantages, an important part of the competitive environment in those markets that have strong elements of non-price competition. In such environments, firms that provide the right quality of products and services are the most competitive. In these conditions firms need to obtain suitable labour and technology in order to supply what the market requires. Proximity to other firms, organizations and people who can help to procure such inputs will convey advantages that are not easily available to firms located in isolation.

Therefore, clusters and industrial districts can lead to competitiveness through reduction in costs and the ability to increase the quality of

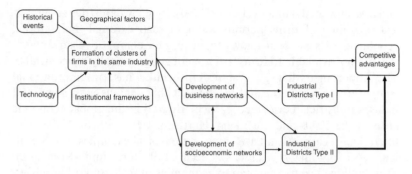

Figure 17.2   Competitive advantages from the development of Clusters and
Industrial Districts

output. These benefits are likely to be different according to the ability
of clusters and industrial districts to reduce the transaction costs of
their operations. In societies where institutional frameworks are not
effective in reducing transaction costs, the development of ID2 may
provide an alternative means of reducing these costs. Figure 17.2 shows
that firms in an industrial district can reduce their costs more than
simple clustered firms. Firms that become integrated into business
networks create a ID1 that allows them to reap agglomeration economies not available to firms that form only a cluster. The extension of
these networks to include socioeconomic factors leads to the creation
of ID2, which in turn reap even further agglomeration economies.
Therefore, in these circumstances ID2 obtain higher agglomeration
economies and quality advantages than ID1, which, in turn, can reap
more than a simple cluster of firms.

A taxonomy of clusters according to the different kind of competitiveness that they are able to enhance can be derived from the work of
Porter (1990). Using this framework three different kinds of clusters
can be identified:

- *'Porter case'*   When the clustering process results in domestic competitiveness that directly leads to international competitiveness. In
  this case, domestic firms have comparative advantages over other
  domestic firms and also in international markets. Most of the typical
  Italian industrial districts belong to this category.
- *'Reverse Porter case'*   When the clustering process leads to international competitiveness, but not domestic competitiveness. In this
  case, domestic firms achieve competitiveness over international

firms, but not over other domestic firms. This may arise from the characteristics of demand. In the domestic market, demand for high-quality products may be constrained by low incomes and, therefore, high-quality and expensive products cannot easily be sold in domestic markets. However, high-quality products may satisfy conditions for export markets and, therefore, are more easily sold abroad. In these circumstances clusters are likely to be focused on the export rather than the domestic market.

- *'Domestic case'* When the clustering process leads only to domestic competitiveness, without leading to international competitiveness. In this case, domestic firms have comparative advantages only over other domestic firms but not in international markets.

AN OVERVIEW OF BEIJING AND SHANGHAI

Since Deng Xiaoping set China on the path to liberalization in 1978, Chinese GDP has grown on average by 9 per cent a year, income per head by 6 per cent a year and Chinese share of world GDP has doubled to 10 per cent. Moreover, China's exports grew at an annual average rate of 15.8 per cent during the period 1979–1996, which was the highest growth rate in the Asia Pacific Region (Central Statistical Office, *Statistical Yearbook for China*). Furthermore, in terms of population and geographical size, China is the largest developing country undergoing economic transition from a socialist central planning system to a market economy. China's economic reforms and 'open door policy' has changed the orientation of the country's industrialization and brought dramatic changes in the Chinese economy. The 'open door policy' gave foreign investors special beneficial treatment in order to attract FDI (Lan, 1996; Sun, 1998). Since 1979, FDI in China has increased rapidly and, by August 1997, the country had approved 266 900 foreign-invested enterprises. China is now the largest recipient of FDI in the developing world (Child and Stewart, 1997).

However, this export orientated strategy of the Chinese government laid greater stress on urban coastal regions, thus increasing the dualism of the Chinese economy. Following the promulgation of the first Joint Venture Law in 1979 the government set up four Special Economic Zones (SEZs) where special economic policies were pursued to utilize FDI. Most of these zones were in the east of the country. In April 1984, the Chinese government announced that 14 coastal cities would open to FDI, thus expanding the 'open door policy' from the SEZs to other regions. A gradual simplification of the joint venture (JV) approval process occurred after 1986 with greater autonomy in decision making at the local level. Provinces and cities were allowed to provide their own incentives in addition to those already granted by the central government. These incentives included exemption of local tax, lower land use fees and lower charges for using public utilities. Furthermore, almost all of the open coastal cities set up Economic and Technical Development Zones designed for high-technology industrial projects. In these zones, extra tax breaks were offered in addition to other incentives. The high concentration of FDI in the coastal regions was regarded as a problem by the Chinese government and this led to attempts to encourage the inland provinces to open up to foreign investors. However, this policy was not successful. The coastal regions have advantages over the inland regions in terms of economic conditions and investment environment; the coastal regions and major economic centres, such as Shanghai and Beijing, were therefore more developed than the inland regions in terms of economic structure, industrial infrastructure, public utilities and cultural facilities. These location-specific advantages have accounted for a particular geographical distribution of FDI (Dunning, 1977). Moreover, in term of transaction cost theory (Williamson, 1975), the advanced facilities help the investors to reduce information and other relevant costs by improving efficiency.

A country with such a big disparity between the coastal areas and the inland regions is very likely to develop clusters because certain locations are more attractive than others for business activities. Moreover, this clustering process may be helped and supported by the 'open door policy'. It is, therefore, more likely to find clusters in the coastal region than in the inland areas of China and that is why the Shanghai and Beijing regions were selected for study. Moreover, in 1994, these two regions enjoyed higher *per capita* annual incomes than most other comparable units of population within China (Child and Stewart, 1997).

Beijing, the capital of China, is an ancient city with a long history of political and cultural events. The Beijing area boasts a great number of universities and colleges, scientific research institutes, cultural and mass media units and facilities, where talented and qualified persons are gathered. As China's international standing is rising, Beijing is playing a more and more important role in its relations and co-operation with the world. Moreover, since the 1979 reforms there have been considerable economic developments within the city. City construction has developed rapidly and top priority has been given to the city's infrastructure, including energy and water supply and transport. By working hard over the past three decades, Beijing has changed from an economically backward city into a fairly prosperous one. Yet, the city remains very much a city of officials rather than a commercial centre, and draws its importance from the administrative functions associated with being a capital city. Despite the presence of a few heavy industrial complexes, such as the Capital Iron and Steel Company, Beijing is primarily characterized by light industry including a significant high-technology electronic sector. In 1994, the gross industrial output value of the city reached almost 19 000 million US$. Foreign trade is developing slowly and, in 1994, Beijing exported around 2000 million US$ (Central Statistical Office, *Statistical Yearbook for Beijing*).

Shanghai is China's largest city and is also the centre of many types of economic activity. Like Beijing it also has a large number of universities and other research institutions. After opening as a port city in 1843, Shanghai soon became the centre of finance and commerce in East Asia. Expansion of foreign concessions and further development, under Japanese and then Nationalist rule, led to expansion from a small, walled settlement to an urban centre and Shanghai became a centre for finance and trade in the Far East. By the 1920s, Shanghai had become one of the main manufacturing centres in China, notable for its number of spinning and weaving mills, many foreign-owned, especially by Japanese firms. This historical experience gave Shanghai a strong infrastructure, industrial base, skilled labour force, as well as a prime location as the gateway to inland China. Before the Second World War, the city was by any standards the most important city in Asia and its nickname of the 'Paris of the East' reflected its cosmopolitan sophistication. After 1949 the development of centralized planning and increasing emphasis on heavy industry, regional self-sufficiency and minimal reliance on foreign trade, changed the character of China, and especially of Shanghai. However, since the economic reforms Shanghai has begun to return to its former role as a centre of finance, trade, culture, science, technology and a major port. In 1994, its gross industrial output value reached almost 50 000 million US$. Exports in 1994 were around 3000 million US$ (Central Statistical Office, *Statistical Yearbook for Shanghai*).

ANALYSIS OF THE DATA

From the theoretical framework of this chapter four hypotheses about clusters were derived, three of which were tested by use of published data for the regions of Beijing and Shanghai:

- clusters exist in the regions of Beijing and Shanghai
- some clusters lead to domestic competitiveness
- some clusters lead to domestic and international competitiveness
- transaction costs vary according to whether firms are just clustered or belong to an industrial district.

The analysis of the published data allows only the first three hypotheses to be tested. The fourth hypothesis is left to a future research programme that will be based on the study of networks. The survey of the literature (see Socioeconomic Networks and Chinese Businesses, p. 328) suggests that both business and socioeconomic networks provide important competitive advantages in successful Chinese businesses. Furthermore, the literature survey suggests that industrial districts resembling ID2 probably exist in China and that they grant transaction cost advantages to those firms located within industrial districts. The first three hypotheses were tested using published data to assess whether clusters existed and whether they led to domestic and/or international competitiveness. All data was collected from the *Statistical Yearbook for China Shanghai, Beijing* and from the UN *International Trade Statistics Yearbook*. The data refer only to 1994, thus providing only a snapshot picture of these two regions.

Some problems of classification occurred because of differences in the classification of production and exports. All data for the two regions and for total Chinese production are expressed in national currency and are classified according to Chinese classification systems. By contrast, the data on Chinese exports was taken from the UN *International Trade Statistics Yearbook*, classified according to the Standard International Trade Classification (SITC, revision 2). In order to compare total Chinese shares with the shares of the two regions, the two classifications had to be matched. This matching created problems in the case of Beijing, because Chinese export data for Beijing are very aggregated and the match with the SITC data could not go beyond the first digit. However, in the case of Shanghai it was possible to match Chinese data with the 2-digit level of the SITC. These limitations mean that the data calculated for Shanghai are likely to be more accurate than those for Beijing. Finally, the data for the two Chinese regions was converted into US$ by applying the exchange rate published in the IMF *International Financial Statistics Yearbook*.

The data on industrial production revealed that 8.3 per cent of total Chinese production comes from Shanghai and 3.1 per cent comes from Beijing. The difference between the two regions shows that

Shanghai is a more industrial region than Beijing, thus increasing the probability of finding more clusters in the Shanghai region. An industry is identified as a 'cluster' when its market share is higher than the total market share of the region under investigation. Therefore, an industry is deemed to be clustered in the Shanghai region when its market share is higher than 8.3 per cent and the Beijing region when its market share is higher than 3.1 per cent.

Export data was used as a proxy of the international competitiveness of the two regions. Exports are not the only measure of competitive advantage for international business, other measures can be used – for example, FDI, international licensing and strategic alliances. However, export data are easily available and widely accepted as a measure of international competitiveness. The published Chinese export data revealed that 20.4 per cent of the total production of goods in China is exported. This indicates that China is a relatively open economy, given the size of the Chinese economy. Only 2.7 per cent of total Chinese exports come from the region of Shanghai and only 1.6 per cent from the Beijing region. The low contribution of two regions to total Chinese exports results from the large size of the Chinese economy. However, relative to these region's shares of total population of China, this contribution is very significant. An industry is identified as an 'export oriented cluster' when its market share is higher than the total export share of the region under investigation. Therefore, an export oriented cluster in the Shanghai region must have an export share higher than 2.7 per cent and in the Beijing region must have an export share higher than 1.6 per cent. Table 17.1 shows the taxonomy used to identify different kinds of clusters in the regions of Shanghai and Beijing. Figure 17.3 and 17.4 show the results for each of the two regions.

The most remarkable result is that there are very few 'Porter cases' in both regions. It can be therefore suggested that the evolution of competitiveness from domestic to international developed by Porter (1990) may not always be applicable to developing countries. In Shanghai, 'plastics and rubber products' (which includes tyres and other products connected to the transport industry) is a strong 'Porter case' and 'transport equipment' is a weak 'Porter case'. Both these Porter cases are related to the transport industry and may be explained by government intervention in strategic industries, such as missiles and aircraft production. Shanghai's laboratories were commissioned with the task of building some of China's ballistic missiles and transport aircraft. In the process, Shanghai added a military wing to its industrial complex by contributing to the production of satellite launchers and the development

Table 17.1   Taxonomy of clusters, Shanghai and Beijing

	Shanghai (per cent)		Beijing (per cent)	
Strong 'Porter caise'	Production > 8.3	Exports > than double 2.7 (5.4)	Production > 3.1	Exports > than double 1.6 (3.7)
Weak 'Porter case'	Production > 8.3	Export > 2.7 but less than 5.4	Production > 3.1	Exports > 1.6 but less than 3.7
Strong 'Reverse Porter' case	Production < 8.3	Exports > than double of 2.7	Production < 3.1	Exports > than double 1.6
Weak 'Reverse Porter' case	Production < 8.3	Exports > 27 but less than 5.4	Production < 3.1	Exports > 1.6 but less than 3.7
Strong 'Domestic case'	Production > than double 8.3 (16.6)	Exports < 2.7	Production > than double 3.1 (6.2)	Exports < 1.6
Weak 'Domestic case'	Production > 8.3 but less than 16.6	Exports < 2.7	Production > 3.1 but less than 6.2	Exports < 1.6

Source: Authors' elaboration on *Statistical Yearbooks for China, Shanghai, Beijing.*

of aircraft (Yusuf and Wu, 1997). This result shows that, when government intervention has a strong goal such as military production, the support given to such production can enable the achievement of some degree of international competitiveness. In Beijing, 'miscellaneous products' is the only 'Porter case', but the export share is so low that 'miscellaneous products' could nearly be classified as a 'domestic case'. 'Miscellaneous products' includes stationery goods such as pens, pencils and paper for office use. Beijing, as the capital of China, has high concentration of bureaucracy and, therefore, a strong demand for stationery products of this type.

The second important result is the number of 'Reverse Porter' cases found in both regions. In Shanghai, 'raw hides, leather and furs' and 'textile materials and products' are two strong 'Reverse Porter cases'. In Beijing, 'textile, rubber and metal products' and 'chemicals and related products' are two weak 'Reverse Porter cases'. Except for

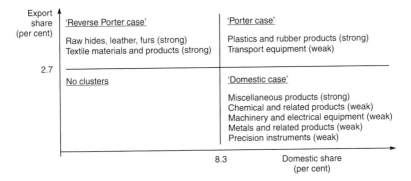

Figure 17.3   Clusters, Shanghai

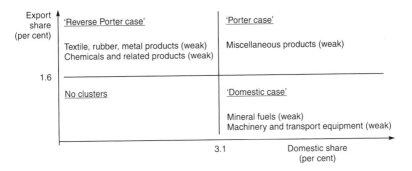

Figure 17.4   Clusters, Beijing

chemicals and related products, in both regions, 'Reverse Porter cases' occurred in traditional industries.

Both regions have some strong domestic cases. In Shanghai, they are in 'miscellaneous products', while all the others are weak 'domestic cases'. In Beijing, weak 'domestic cases' are in 'mineral fuels' and 'machinery and transport equipment'. The presence of the 'domestic case' of 'mineral fuels' is related to the presence of that particular natural resource in the Beijing region. The existence of a 'domestic case' in 'machinery and transport equipment' can be explained by the lack of government support for this industry in Beijing. However, this industry was helped in Shanghai and this may have helped it to become competitive on international markets.

By comparing the two regions, it is noticeable that 'Porter cases' in the Shanghai region are related to industries that are more technologically advanced than in the Beijing region. This suggests that Shanghai has more technologically advanced production facilities than Beijing and can, therefore, more easily achieve competitiveness in industrial products in international markets. This advantage probably arose from strong government support received by those industries that were 'Porter cases' in Shanghai. 'Reverse Porter cases' occur in both regions, mainly in traditional industries. This probably is related to the structure of the demand that led to high-quality, but expensive, products for export markets that could not easily be sold in the domestic market. The existence of strong 'domestic cases' suggests that agglomeration economies and quality benefits have, in some cases been sufficient to generate domestic but not international competitiveness.

CONCLUSIONS

The results of the analysis of published data support the hypothesis that clusters do exist in the Shanghai and Beijing regions. Moreover, the data indicate that clusters may have helped in promoting domestic and international competitiveness. However, the results indicate that the impact of clusters in these two Chinese regions does not always lead to the result that would be expected from an analysis based on the framework developed by Porter (1990). In particular, some clusters are primarily export-related, while others are domestically orientated. In only a very few cases do clusters appear to follow the classical 'Porter case' – that is, to have both domestic and international competitive advantages.

These conclusions lead to some suggestions for policy prescriptions. The theoretical framework of this chapter suggests that clusters emerge from the influences of geographical factors, historical events and institutional frameworks and are therefore path-dependent. Consequently, it is not possible to copy the development of clusters outside their own environment. Policy makers should keep in mind that the development of clusters is constrained by past historical events, by specific institutional factors and by particular geographical conditions and therefore the particular form of existing clusters may not be able to be transplanted from one geographical area to another.

The presence of 'Reverse Porter cases' in the two Chinese regions indicates that developing countries might benefit from developing an export oriented strategy, rather than concentrating on national championship, at least in some industries. The main factors involved in identifying which industries might fall into this category are the characteristics of domestic and international demand with respect to the quality of products. More effort and resources are used in industries that achieved international competitiveness than on domestic industries. However, if the 'Reverse Porter case' arises from the need to meet higher-quality demand and characteristics for export markets, the expertise gain may prove useful as the development process leads to the growth of domestic income with a subsequent domestic demand for higher-quality products.

Future research agendas might include the study of clusters and industrial districts in other areas of China. Moreover, research can be directed towards the analysis of industries where clusters or industrial districts have had major effects on international competitiveness to determine the characteristics of these industries. The examination of the relative importance of geographically concentrated business and socio-economic networks as means to enhance domestic and international competitiveness can be the objects of further research.

The main finding of this chapter is that historical, sociological, institutional and geographical factors play an important role in the development of clusters and industrial districts and these geographical concentrations of firms appear to be important sources of competitive advantage in some industries. Nevertheless, the evidence from the Shanghai and Beijing regions suggests that geographical concentrations need not always generate the type of competitive advantage that Porter attributes to clusters.

References

Amin, A. and Thrift, N. (eds) (1994) *Globalisation, Institutions, and Regional Development in Europe*, Oxford, Oxford University Press.

Antonelli, C. (1997) 'The Economics of Path-dependence in Industrial Organization', *International Journal of Industrial Organization*, 15, 643–75.

Becattini, G. (1990) 'The Marshallian Industrial District as a Socio-economic Notion', in F. Pyke, G. Becattini, and W. Sengenberger (eds), *Industrial Districts and Inter-firm Co-operation in Italy*, Geneva, International Institute for Labour Studies.

Bellandi, M. (1989) 'The Industrial District in Marshall', in E. Goodman, J. Bamford and P. Saynor (eds), *Small Firms and Industrial Districts in Italy*, London, Routledge.

Brusco, S. (1990) 'The Idea of the Industrial District: Its Genesis', in F. Pyke, G. Becattini and W. Sengenberger (eds), *Industrial Districts and Inter-firm Co-operation in Italy*, Geneva, International Institute for Labour Studies.

Capecchi, V. (1990) 'A History of Flexible Specialisation and Industrial Districts in Emilia-Romagna', in F. Pyke, G. Becattini and W. Sengenberger (eds), *Industrial Districts and Inter-firm Co-operation in Italy*, Geneva, International Institute for Labour Studies.

Casson, M. (1997) 'Entrepreneurial Networks: A Theoretical Perspective', *Discussion Paper in Economics and Management*, 371, University of Reading.

Central Statistical Office (1994, 1996, 1997) *Statistical Yearbook for China, Shanghai*, Beijing.

Child, J. and Stewart, S. (1997) 'Regional Differences in China and their Implications for Sino–Foreign Joint Ventures', *Journal of General Management*, 23, 65–86.

Christerson, B and Lever-Tracy, C. (1997) 'The Third China? Emerging Industrial Districts in Rural China', *International Journal of Regional Research*, 21, 569–88.

Dicken, P. (1998) *Global Shift. Transforming the World Economy*, London, Paul Chapman.

Dunning, J. H. (1977) 'Trade, Location of Economic Activity, and the Multinational Enterprises: A Search for an Eclectic Approach', in B. Ohlin, P.O. Hesselborn and P.M. Wijkman (eds), *The International Allocation of Economic Activity*, New York, Holmes & Meier.

Harrison, B. (1992) 'Industrial Districts: Old Wine in New Bottles?', *Regional Studies*, 26, 469–83.

International Monetary Fund (IMF) (1997) *International Financial Statistics Yearbook*, New York, IMF.

Jacobs, J. (1980) 'The Concept of Guanxi and Local Politics in a Rural Chinese Setting', in S. Greenblatt, R. Wilson and A. Wilson (eds), *Social Interaction in Chinese Society*, New York, Praeger.

Kao, J. (1993) 'The Worldwide Web of Chinese Business', *Harvard Business Review*, March–April, 24–6.

King, A. (1991) 'Kuan-hsi and Network Building: A Sociological Interpretation', *Daedalus* 120, 63–84.

Krugman, P. (1991) *Geography and Trade*, Cambridge, MA, MIT Press.

Krugman, P. (1995) *Development, Geography and Economic Theory*, Cambridge, MA, MIT Press.

Lan, P. (1996) *Technology Transfer to China through Foreign Direct Investment*, Aldershot, Ashgate.

Lockett, M. (1988) 'Cultural Problems in Chinese Management: A Preliminary Study', *American Sociological Review*, 28, 55–69.

Marshall, A. (1890) *Principles of Economics*, London, Macmillan.

Nadvi, K. and Schmitz, H. (1994) 'Industrial Clusters in Less Developed Countries: Review of Experiences and Research Agenda', *Discussion Paper*, 339, University of Sussex, Institute of Development Studies.

North, D. (1990) *Institutions, Institutional Change and Economic Performance*, Cambridge, Cambridge University Press.

Ottaviano, G. and Puga, D. (1998) 'Agglomeration in the Global Economy: A Survey of the "New Economic Geography"', *World Economy*, 21, 707–31.

Park, S.O. (1996) 'Network and Embeddedness in the Dynamics of New Industrial Districts', *Progress in Human Geography*, 20, 476–93.

Ping, H. (1997) 'New Private Entrepreneurs in China: Family Relations and Social Connections', in M. Rutten and C. Updhya (eds), *Small Business Entrepreneurs in Asia and Europe. Towards a Comparative Perspective*, New Delhi, Sage.

Porter, M. (1990) *The Competitive Advantage of Nations*, London, Macmillan.

Pyke, F., Becattini, G. and Sengenberger, W. (eds) (1990) *Industrial Districts and Inter-firm Co-operation in Italy*, Geneva, International Institute for Labour Studies.

Redding, G., Norman, A. and Schlander, A. (1993) 'The Nature of Individual Attachment to the Organization: A Review of East Asia Variations', in M. Dunnette and L. Hough (eds), *Handbook of Industrial and Organizational Psychology*, Palo Alto, CA, Consulting Psychology Press.

Saxenian, A. (1985) 'The Genesis of Silicon Valley', in P. Hall and A. Markusen (eds), *Silicon Landscapes*, Boston, MA, Allen & Unwin.

Schmitz, H. (1992) 'On the Clustering of Small Firms', *IDS Bulletin*, 23 (1), 64–69.

Sengenberger, W. and Pyke, F. (1991) 'Small Firm Industrial Districts and Local Economic Regeneration: Research and Policy Issues', *Labour and Society*, 16, 1–24.

Sun, H. (1998) *Foreign Investment and Economic Development in China: 1979–1996*, Aldershot, Ashgate.

Tsui, A. and Farh, J. (1997) 'Where Guanxi Matters: Relational Demography and Guanxi in the Chinese Context', *Work and Occupations*, 24, 56–79.

Tweedale, G. (1995) *Steel City*, Oxford, Oxford University Press.

United Nations(UN) (1997) *International Trade Statistics Yearbook*, New York, UN.

Wang, J. (1997) 'Guanyu Zhong' guancun xin jishu quyu fazhan wenti de shenceng sikao', in Jing Tihua (ed.), *Beijing jingji xingshi fenxi yu yuc*, Beijing, Capital Normal University Press.

Wang, J. and Wang J. (1998) 'An Analysis of New-tech Agglomeration in Beijing: A New Industrial District in the Making?', *Environment and Planning*, 30, 681–701.

Williamson, O.E. (1975) *Markets and Hierarchies: Analysis and Antitrust Implications*, New York, Free Press.

You, J.-I. (1994) 'Competition and Co-operation: Towards Understanding Industrial Districts', *Review of Political Economy*, 6, 259–78.

Yusuf, S. and Wu, W. (1997) *The Dynamics of Urban Growth in Three Chinese Cities*, Oxford, Oxford University Press.

Part 5
South East Asia

18 Indigenous Supply-Chain Development: Case Study Evidence from Singapore's Electronics Cluster

Ross Brown

INTRODUCTION

Backward linkages to indigenous suppliers of materials have tradition-ally been considered one of the main ways in which foreign direct investment (FDI) develops host economies (Hirschman, 1958). Hend-erson and Appelbaum (1992) claim that FDI is significant for economic transformation only when it stimulates local firm production linkages and/or results in shifts to higher value-added forms of production within multinational enterprises (MNEs). In addition, increasing competition for scarce inward investment projects is driving policy-makers to take greater account of the long term economic spin-offs generated by inward investment such as local linkages (Young, Hood and Peters, 1994).

According to Porter's (1990) influential work on the competitive advantage of nations, dynamic industrial clusters typically feature dense localized interrelationships between industrial buyers or end-users and other firms in local supply chains or *filières*. On the other hand, regional economists and economic geographers have generally discovered limited linkages and weak local supply chains in less dynamic sectoral clusters (see Turok, 1993). One of the key features delineating leading-edge clusters from branch plant clusters is thought to be the higher levels of foreign ownership in the latter cluster type (see Birkinshaw and Hood, 1997).

Beginning in the late 1960s, Singapore attracted various layers of FDI as the country developed from a low-cost production platform to a higher-value added manufacturing centre (see Toh, 1993). In Singapore, the electronics industry is now the largest sector within manufacturing industry, accounting for 42 per cent of gross manufacturing value added (EDB, 1994). Within the manufacturing sector as a whole, the electronics sector accounts for about half of total output and a third of total employment. In 1996, the industry employed 128 590 people and growth was 9 per cent. Such has been the impact of FDI that Singapore has become a centre of excellence in the manufacture of the 3.5-in Winchester hard disk drives (HDDs) and has been dubbed 'Winchester City' in recognition of the importance this sector plays in the country's economy (Yuan and Low, 1990).

During the 1970s researchers analysing the electronics industry in Singapore discovered low levels of local linkages (Pang and Lim, 1977). Over the subsequent decade, higher levels of linkages were detected in the electronics industry, with case study evidence suggesting moderately high levels of local sourcing by foreign-owned firms (Lim and Pang, 1982). More recently, studies show that foreign firms are successfully stimulating local suppliers, generating a substantial number of spin-offs as employees of MNEs became successful entrepreneurs, often becoming suppliers to their former employees (Lim and Pang, 1991). Some claim that Singapore has developed to such an extent that its electronics industry is the 'Southeast Asian "star" when it comes to linkage formation' (Henderson, 1994: 275–6). Detailed empirical analysis of linkages in Singapore paints a more cautious picture of linkage development on the island (Perry and Hui, 1998). Perry and Hui found that foreign-owned companies in Singapore gave a low priority to localized linkages and that global sourcing was increasingly being used as a strategy by MNEs.

This chapter examines linkages between foreign-owned companies and local suppliers in Singapore's electronics cluster. In contrast to studies on the aggregate level of local linkage formation, it focuses on the inherent *quality* of linkage formation in Singapore by examining the structure and development of local suppliers using a case study approach. It is useful to look beyond the sheer numbers of linkages and look at their intrinsic quality, especially as this relates to the long-term economic health of a region (Turok, 1993). The empirical material used within this chapter draws upon in-depth interviews with a sample of foreign-owned electronics manufacturers and local suppliers in Singapore (see Brown, 1996).

The structure of the chapter is as follows. We begin with a discussion of previous empirical and conceptual linkage studies. This allows contextualization of the factors underpinning linkage development while enabling different types of linkages to be categorized. Following this, the chapter assesses the nature of Singapore's electronics supply base, focusing on three key sub-sectors. Case studies are used to illustrate the qualitative nature of supply-chain development in Singapore. A preliminary classification of alternative linkage scenarios in Singapore is presented, and the final section provides some brief concluding remarks.

UNDERSTANDING LINKAGE DEVELOPMENT

Many early linkage studies in the 1960s and 1970s took a highly reductionist approach towards assessing linkages between foreign investors and local suppliers, often utilizing quantitative research techniques (see Hoare, 1985). This approach has been heavily criticized for two reasons. First, quantitative analysis fails to uncover the *causal factors* underpinning linkage development. Second, such an approach fails to take into consideration the *all-round quality* of the linkages (i.e. local suppliers) which develop when foreign firms locate in a region or country. More recent linkage studies frequently focus upon the nature of MNE production, the type of inputs purchased by MNEs, the degree of plant-level marketing/R&D and the capabilities of local suppliers (see Turok, 1993; Brown, 1998).

Glasmeier's (1988) case study analysis of branch plants in different locations in the USA is a good example of this new approach. The study focused on the linkages and spin-off activities of Motorola in Phoenix, Harris Corporation in Melbourne (Florida) and Rolm in Austin. This afforded a chance to investigate, in some depth, the dynamics of plant-level autonomy and purchasing responsibility. Glasmeier's study discovered that neither Motorola nor Harris had fostered the development of significant, backward-linked supplier firms. The overall figures for local sourcing for Motorola and Harris were 5 per cent and 1 per cent, respectively. Even very low-value added items were not sourced locally by Motorola. Glasmeier remarked that for Motorola 'less than 25 per cent of local demand for packing materials, boxes and shipping crates, was satisfied locally' (1988: 293).

One of the main reasons for Motorola's lack of linkages was the parent organization's policy of consolidating purchases across the company as a whole. In this vein, she asserts that branch plant support for industrial complex development is inversely related to the strength of the linkages to the parent-headquarters' location. Meanwhile, having adopted a policy of internalizing production, the Harris Corporation had effectively precluded meaningful supplier relationships from arising. The reason the Harris Corporation had a high degree of vertical integration was the highly customized nature of the communication systems they manufactured. According to Glasmeier (1988), inter-industry linkage development is closely associated with the product type and organizational structure of the firms' studied.

The final case study differs markedly from the other two corporations. Rolm's products were highly customized and its plant highly vertically integrated. One of the reasons behind Rolm's predilection for this latter point was the desire for flexibility of output (Glasmeier, 1988). Although no figures are given for the level of inputs sourced locally, it is thought to be significantly higher than the other two organizations because its products were thought to be 'component-rich' and produced in volumes that enabled substantial linkages (Glasmeier, 1988). Nevertheless, Rolm procured the majority of its products from Silicon Valley for two main reasons: first, Silicon Valley is the location of the parent-company headquarters; and Austin's component supply industry is insufficiently developed. However, Glasmeier maintained that the prospects for local sourcing are increasing owing to the company's policy of developing local suppliers.

Clarke and Beaney (1993) examined the agglomeration and linkage effects engendered by the Scottish data processing sector. They also looked at the relationship between plant-level characteristics and local linkage levels. Overall, they discovered weak local linkage formation and poor spin-off rates in this sector of Scotland's electronics industry. They asserted that high-value components continue to be world-sourced with local sourcing weak in sub-assemblies and other peripherals such as keyboards, monitors, disk drives and power supplies. Nevertheless, they conceded that recent inward investment in the component and peripheral sector had augmented the agglomeration effects of the industry.

Unlike others who see the co-location of R&D and production as positively correlated to higher levels of local linkage (e.g. Young, Hood and Dunlop, 1988), Clarke and Beaney discovered that, despite evidence pointing towards increasing R&D intensity in Scottish plants, there was little evidence suggesting a concomitant increase in Scottish sourcing. Similarly, they conclude that the operation of JIT is 'designed around the perceived capabilities and cost structure of suppliers in different parts of the world' (1993: 226). Owing to increasing cost pressures generated by shorter product life cycles, especially in very cost-competitive markets such as personal computers, they claim that the MNEs are not willing to accept a premium for local sourcing.

The behaviour of individual branch-plant operations also plays a significant part in the levels of local sourcing they undertake. However, Clarke and Beaney claim that there is a 'danger in overemphasising plant or subsidiary status as a factor in regional development' (1993: 217). In fact, the financially driven semi-autonomous nature of some decentralized corporations could actually hinder the survival of some subsidiaries (Clarke and Beaney, 1993). Their analysis of the Scottish electronics industry provides some insight into the contingent nature of the processes underlying the creation of upstream linkages.

As we can see, organizational change, in the shape of vertical disintegration, has important implications for regional development. Processes of externalization may not be translated into improved levels of local sourcing if the types of activities being externalized do not coincide with the industrial structure of a particular region (Mair, 1993). Turok (1993), for example, discovered that, although vertical disintegration was increasing in the Scottish electronics industry (revealed in the falling quantities of value added done in-house by electronics MNEs), local input linkages were actually decreasing. One of the main reasons behind this trend is that intensifying cost pressures coupled with short product life cycles force MNEs to undertake more long-distance sourcing in low-cost economies.

From the perspective of local suppliers, some have noted that the main benefits of this new procurement environment fall disproportionately on well equipped medium-sized enterprises (Dicken, Forsgren and Malmberg, 1994), with most smaller suppliers condemned to a role of 'uncertain dependency' (Rainnie, 1991: 374). Even well resourced suppliers are finding the implementation of new supply systems precarious (Morris and Imrie, 1992). Morris and Imrie found that price continued to be an important factor in supplier negotiations irrespective of the rhetoric about 'quality' and 'delivery'. Haphazard implementation of JIT systems inevitably saw suppliers bearing the brunt of reduced inventory on behalf of large firms (Rainnie, 1991; Morris and Imrie, 1992; Turok, 1993).

On the basis of the available empirical evidence, there seems to be a delineation between two alternative linkage scenarios: developmental and dependent (see Turok, 1993). Turok claims that the former situation is characterized by a scenario whereby vertical disintegration of large corporations and decentralization of decision making powers demand more collaborative relationships between individual plants and their suppliers (see Table 18.1). Alternatively, dependent relations merely expose local economies to volatile world markets and make

Table 18.1   A summary of alternative linkage scenarios

	Developmental	Dependent
Nature of local linkages	Collaborative, mutual learning Based on technology and trust Emphasis on added value	Unequal trading relationships Conventiona sub-contracting Emphasis on cost-saving
Duration of linkages	Long-term partnerships	Short-term contracts
Nature of relationships	High level interaction to accelerate product development and increase responsiveness to volatile markets	Price-cutting and short-ter convenience for MNEs
Large companies ties to the locality	Deeply embedded High investment in decentralized, Multi-functional operations	Weakly embedded Branch plans restricted to final assembly operations
Benefits for local firms	Markets for local firms to develop and produce their own products Transfer of technology and expertise strengthens local firms	Markets for local firms to make standard, low-tech components Sub-contracti means restricted independent growth capac
Quality of jobs	Diverse, including high-skilled, high-income	Many low-skilled, low-paic temporary and casual
Prospects for the local economy	Self-sustaining growth through cumulative expansion of the industrial cluster	Vulnerable to external forces and corporate decisions

Source: Based on Turok (1993).

them vulnerable to the harsh forces of international competition where linkages are driven more by cost-cutting than by co-operation. The former scenario conforms to the 'flexible specialization' (autonomy) model while the other relates to the 'flexible firm' (dependency) framework (Turok, 1993). According to Curran and Blackburn (1991), the differences between these two variants of economic restructuring rest-primarily on the degree of power and autonomy which suppliers and sub-contractors are able to obtain.

That said, the autonomy–dependency dichotomy reveals little about the locational implications of these alternative models. Vertical disin-tegration may be happening but that may not, by itself, lead to greater localized linkages. The overall spatiality of sub-contracting is open to 'considerable supposition as to whether subcontracting necessarily demands geographic concentration' (Walker, 1988: 391). For example, those who found sub-contracting to accord with the autonomous or developmental model were predominantly conducting their work in dynamic industrial clusters such as Silicon Valley (see e.g. Scott, 1992). Research undertaken on linkage relationships in countries and regions dominated by foreign-owned MNEs tends to paint a less favourable picture. Singapore's electronics cluster, therefore, is an interesting case study owing to its dynamic growth rate yet almost complete reliance on foreign ownership (see Brown, 1998).

LOCAL SUPPLIERS IN SINGAPORE

In recent years, the electronics sector in Singapore has been supported by about 1500 companies providing a wide variety of components and services (Chia, 1995). In turn, these suppliers form a wide variety of relationships with local and non-local end users.[1] For this reason, three different types of suppliers are analysed: component manufacturers, contract manufacturers and HDD suppliers. The first category of firms manufacture basic-supply items such as sheet metal enclosures, printed circuit board (PCBs) and plastic injection mouldings. The second group of suppliers mostly undertake PCB assembly (PCBA) as their core business activity. The third group are high-value added suppliers manufacturing HDDs which are modular storage products used mostly, but not exclusively, for the PC industry. Each sub-sector is now examined in greater depth using case studies to illustrate the firm-specific nature of each sector.

The Component Manufacturing Sector

Most firms in this supply area are locally-owned sheet metal companies, plastic moulders and PCB manufacturers, although some specialist and foreign-owned firms have developed in this industry grouping. The ownership of suppliers is a mixture of local and foreign-owned. Foreign-owned suppliers tend to be bigger and better resourced; this seemed especially the case when specialist and expensive capital equipment was necessary. For example, in the PCB sector local firms comprise 71 per cent of total establishments yet account for only 14 per cent of total value added. Although suppliers in this sub-sector most often conform to the traditional dependent pattern of localized linkage formation, some suppliers have developed beyond this simple pattern.

A Case Study of Supplier Dependency: Meiki Plastic Industries

Meiki Plastic Industries (MPI) was established about 25 years ago. MPI are a well established, locally-owned company making a range of plastic injection mouldings (PIMs). In addition to this, the firm also offers customers various mould/tool making services such as tool and die, jig and fixture. The mould making aspect of the business employs 15 people. In addition to the 130 people employed in their Singapore facility, MPI employ another 80 people in Malaysia. The latter plant is geared towards the needs of MNEs located in Malaysia; it was not established whether the two plants have different production processes. The company are heavily concentrated in the consumer electronics industry and specialize in the production of small PIM parts for colour televisions (CTVs), video recorders (VCRs) and other domestic appliances such as irons. This focus is attributable to their machinery (40–280 tonnage presses) which can manufacture only smaller parts (CTV cabinets require much larger tonnage presses).

Meiki's largest customers are Philips and Toshiba, accounting for 90 per cent of the firm's output (70 and 20 per cent, respectively). They also do some work for Siemans–Nixdorf (i.e. PIMs) and Sanyo–Showa (i.e mould making). Meiki do not engage in any substantial export activity. MPI are heavily reliant upon Philips and supply three separate divisions of Philips with tuner controls, CTV lenses, and iron casings to the Dutch MNE. Owing to the diverse nature of their supply activities with Philips, Meiki's susceptibility to sectoral downturns may not be so great as it first seems. The relationship with Philips has been developing since about 1980. MPI are still, however, used primarily as a capacity spillover supplier owing to the fact that Philips also make plastics parts in-house. Philips use their own tool making capability and give the mould to MPI once they transfer production to an external supplier. The small nature of the parts supplied by MPI did not seem to warrant close proximity on a JIT supply basis.

With some business occurring on very short lead times basis, flexibility and responsiveness are seen as important qualities that customers expect from MPI. No real design capability is expected from the company, and they seem to be used as a traditional capacity supplier by most customers. Unsurprisingly, price was the most important factor when seeking new business. Although the importance of price varies between customers, most customers sought annual price reductions of about 10 per cent. For example, Philips were not thought to be as price-sensitive as Toshiba. Given their overwhelming reliance upon Philips, it was unsurprising the company wished to widen its market focus. One factor thought likely to prevent capital investment was the lack of guaranteed orders which would be necessary to justify such investment. The firm seem unaware of the programmes run by the Economic Development Board (of Singapore) (EDB) which could help fund speculative capital investment. In any case, the company has no desire to expand beyond its current size. MPI seems to conform to the traditional dependent supplier model espoused earlier, with little growth potential, relying on a precarious linkage with one large albeit diversified MNE for the majority of its business.

The Contract Manufacturing Sector

All firms within this sectoral grouping have PCBA as their core business activity. This industry sub-sector employs nearly 14 000 people and constitutes a sizeable proportion of the supply base (EDB, 1994). The importance of this supply sector goes beyond these substantial employment figures. For example, some PCBA firms also undertake original equipment manufacture (OEM) supply arrangements for MNEs which often involves PCBA suppliers assembling complete products for end-users. Some firms within this sector have used their sub-contract skills to upgrade and become more integrated, often undertaking OEM arrangements with customers. These so-called 'latecomer firms' use OEM arrangements with MNEs to overcome market barriers to entry while gaining process and product technology (see Hobday, 1995). Although foreign-owned suppliers feature strongly in this sub-sector, some local suppliers have grown and developed rapidly (see the VM case study below).

A Case Study of Supplier Upgrading: Venture Manufacturing Ltd

Venture Manufacturing (VM) have been in business since 1984. The Venture group as a whole have two plants in Singapore, one in the USA, a plant in China and two further plants in Malaysia. The company also have sales offices in California and London. The main manufacturing plant in Singapore (SMT) is based at Ang Mo Kio, but in addition to this, VM own Multitech Systems which is a fully-owned subsidiary of the Venture group. Together VM employ 850 people in Singapore and

900 people in its overseas subsidiaries. Their core business activity is PCBA, a service they provide to a wide range of firms in the electronics industry. On a more limited scale, the firm undertake full OEM production for customers. Modems, thermal printers, electronic mice, bar-code readers and digitizers have all been fully assembled by VM. Unlike some firms undertaking OEM agreements with MNEs, VM can procure the necessary materials for manufacture. The company also have a small design capability (five employees) that can help firms with manufacturability issues. Only 10–15 per cent of their business is done with MNEs based in Singapore.

The company are currently expanding at a very rapid pace. VM experienced a compound annual growth rate of 60 per cent between 1989 and 1996. Given that they have 18 surface-mount assembly lines, finance does not appear a major hindrance to their expansion plans. In fact, Venture have just issued a rights issue in order to fund their latest bout of expansion which will entail a new plant in Shanghai. The firm's public status would seem to alleviate the need for recourse to banks as a source of finance. Public policy has benefited VM when they adopt new automated production processes by offering new investment allowances. Interestingly, they claimed that the EDB were more concerned with the MNEs than local suppliers.

VM are a good example of a rapidly developing firm (they claim to be one of the fastest growing groups in Asia) which is progressing owing to market expansion outwith the local electronics industry. Likewise, the firm realize that the provision of additional services (design and materials procurement) enables them to become a higher-value supplier. For example, in 1993 they increased their technical and engineering staff by more than 20 per cent. The level of investment in SMT at their Ang Mo Kio operation would indicate that local production as well as headquarter activities remain secure in Singapore.

The HDD Sector

During the early 1980s nearly all the major HDD firms (Seagate, Conner, Western Digital and Maxtor) established manufacturing capacity in Singapore. In sectoral terms, the HDD sector is perhaps the most important sub-sector in Singapore's electronics industry. Primarily, this sector differs from the previous two in that it is almost entirely foreign-owned. For example, the HDD sector in Singapore accounted for 42 per cent of world rigid disk drive production in 1996 (EBD, 1997). Employing over 25 000 people, the sector comprises 22 per cent of total value added in the electronics industry (EDB, 1994). Current growth in this sector is being driven by the needs for storage-intensive PC software and the need for storage in a host of other applications. The industry is moving towards the manufacture of higher-end HDDs with storage capacities in excess of 1000 megabytes (EDB, 1994). The existence of this sub-sector also has very important linkage effects for the Singapore economy. Most of the PC firms in Singapore source some of their HDDs locally (Apple, Compaq and Hewlett-Packard). For example, Apple claimed that once disk drives are subtracted from their local material spend, their local sourcing figure falls by 50 per cent. Having this supply sector reduces the need for large quantities of imported disk drives, and it also makes the electronics cluster a better integrated sectoral unit.

A Case Study of Second-Wave FDI: Conner Peripherals

Conner's Singapore plant opened in 1987. The company manufacture a wide array of HDD products and tape drive products in Singapore. The plant employs 3000 people, some of which are short-term contract staff. In contrast to the other Conner plants in Asia (i.e. Penang and China), the Singapore plant manufactures slightly more sophisticated products. The Conner plant in Penang supplies some MNEs in Singapore with lower-end HDDs. The Singapore plant lies somewhere between the plants in the USA and Conner's other offshore operations in terms of the technical sophistication of the products manufactured. Although no basic research is conducted in Singapore, the plant does perform some important development work. Collaboration between Conner and its customers on design work remains rooted in the USA, however.

The decision to locate in Singapore may have reflected the close relationship between Conner and Compaq (Compaq used to own part of Conner), however local linkages with Compaq in Singapore account for only 10 per cent of their output. Within Singapore, the plant's main customers are: Compaq, Apple, IPC and Wearnes. Interestingly, the latter two firms are locally-owned PC manufacturers. It also deals with independent distribution agents. The plant is now globally oriented, with very extensive linkage patterns – for example, it supplies Compaq at three manufacturing plants world-wide: Erskine, Houston and Singapore. A similar situation exists with Apple who are supplied in Ireland and the USA.

The negotiations with customers are not conducted at the Singapore plant level. On a day-to-day basis, most dealings with customers in Singapore related to inventory management. This emphasizes the truncated nature of the subsidiary's autonomy. Obviously, the lack of negotiations on price preclude a full assessment of the nature of the relationship in Singapore. However, the plant felt that quality was the most important factor governing the relationship between Conner and their main local customers, Apple and Compaq. Meanwhile, independent distributors were seen as more price-driven. Compaq used to single source Conner on all their HDD requirements, but now Compaq has three HDD suppliers. The reason given for this was the inability of Conner to meet the steep rises in demand expected by Compaq. Material shortages encountered by Conner was seen as the main barrier which caused this situation. An indication of a close relationship existing between the firms, despite this problem, was the decision by Conner to set up a plant in China close to a neighbouring Compaq facility.

The main factors inhibiting the plant's development in Singapore, other than material shortages, was the spatial and labour constraints in Singapore. The use of cheap foreign labour was seen as one solution but this was being discouraged by the government's levy on foreign workers. Nonetheless, there are some signs that Conner are moving their Singapore operation towards a more advanced design-intensive facility concentrating on higher-end HDDs (i.e. fast, high-capacity 3.5-in drives for performance workstations and servers) while pushing lower-end production (low-priced 3.5-in drives for entry-level desktop systems) to Malaysia. Conner's Singapore subsidiary is now its worldwide centre for manufacturing and has been used to transfer technology to other plants (see Hobday, 1994).

Classifying Linkages in Singapore

Singapore's suppliers portray a disparate level of all-round strategic competence and technological capability. Even within the small sample of case studies examined during the research, considerable variation arose. It would appear that a specialized supplier can expect a more equitable relationship in a sub-contracting relationship than a simple low-cost capacity sub-contractor. If suppliers wish to avoid a purely cost-driven adversarial supply system, their activities will have to be based on more specialized functions and services that cede better bargaining positions.

Owing to this, not all supply relations fall into the simple dependent and developmental categories. Indeed, other research on linkages in Singapore reveals how many contracting relationships exist in an 'uneasy middle ground' somewhere between these two extremes (Perry and Hui, 1998: 1606). For this reason, it would be unwise to label supply linkages in Singapore as being either 'dependent' or 'developmental.' However, it is important that some type of classification of linkages in Singapore is undertaken in order to differentiate the quality and structure of local linkages. On the basis of the available empirical evidence, there seems to be an delineation between three linkage scenarios which are now outlined.

Convenience Linkages

Convenience linkages are primarily driven by the short-term needs of the buyer. Usually entailing minimal co-operation between buyer and supplier, the MNE is very much in command in this relationship. This owes much to the fact that they are buying something which they possibly make in-house, but require additional capacity on a cyclical basis. Alternatively, components formerly made in-house are now externalized to reduce cost. This type of linkage provides employment in the supply base but does little to aid the technology transfer process. Owing to relatively low barriers to entry, suppliers are often locally owned and price pressure is often acute. The ease of entry often leads to low margins and poor profitability for many suppliers. The ready availability of these components, coupled with the ease with which buyers can switch between suppliers, means that MNEs classify these suppliers as non-strategic items. Given that need for regular supplies of these low-value, high-weight items, spatial proximity between buyer and supplier often leads to localized linkages in this supply area. This type of linkage is common throughout the component (metalwork, plastics, PCBs) manufacturing sector in Singapore, as the Meiki case study illustrates.

Interactive Linkages

The second linkage scenario requires more involvement than the first on behalf of MNEs. In this instance, MNEs often invest time and money bringing these suppliers up to their required level of competency in order to make the most of these linkage relationships. Additionally, MNEs often use suppliers for more than their manufacturing capabilities. Although this may not involve vast levels of product design interaction, some collaboration on process technology can take place. MNEs can switch between suppliers, but such interchangeability is restricted owing to the closer nature of the relationships between the two firms. Owing to this, linkages are more durable than in the first instance. This type of relationship is often associated with links between buyers and the contract manufacturing sector, but also takes place between MNEs and large component manufacturers. Buyers which engage in this type of linkage are those which may have slightly above average levels of decision making autonomy. Spatial proximity between buyers and suppliers is sought where possible, but will not ensure local linkage formation. A good example of this linkage relationship would be the relationship VM have with their customers in Singapore.

Autonomous Linkages

Autonomous linkages are driven by a fundamentally different set of power relations than the first two scenarios. In this type of relationship, suppliers bring a range of technical and managerial skills which sometimes surpass those of the buyer and suppliers generally have their own substantive design capabilities. The high level of supplier competency enables them to avoid price-driven relationships with buyers. Components which feature this type of linkage would be semiconductors, disk drives and display devices such as monitors. Such sectors are regulated by oligopolistic market rules which include very high barriers to entry, prohibitive start-up costs and imperfect competition. Linkages in this sector are dominated by large US and Japanese MNEs. Unlike the spot market relationship in the first category, the supplier's position regarding the buyer is greatly enhanced, not least because these components are not manufactured by the buyer and may be designed specifically for one customer. An example of this linkage would be the relationship between Apple and Conner in Singapore. Although both Apple and Conner are located in Singapore, owing to the high value–weight ratio of these components, spatial proximity between buyers and suppliers is not imperative.

CONCLUSIONS

Backward material linkages between MNEs and local suppliers within Singapore's electronics industry have boosted output and value added within the electronics industry as a whole. Linkages have also worked to the advantage of the local economy through the exposure of local firms to world-class manufacturing techniques. However, not all links between suppliers and MNEs can be treated uniformly in terms of their long-term economic development potential.

Although the above classification system is insufficiently broad to incorporate all types of linkages, it does provide a useful system for categorizing linkages according to their key internal dynamics and spatial manifestations. It also allows some form of assessment regarding the long-term development potential of any given linkage. This enables some analytical coherence to be given to their inherent diversity. For example, it helps illustrate how suppliers with certain attributes will be more able to progress away from the most basic form of linkage relationship which is dictated by buyer convenience to a situation which is more mutually beneficial. It also shows how suppliers can manoeuvre themselves into a more equitable bargaining position by upgrading the all-round nature of their supply activities.

Notwithstanding this, the somewhat indeterminate nature of linkage formation must not be forgotten. Although MNEs with high levels of autonomy are better equipped to engage in complex supplier relationships, especially the ability to instigate genuine technology transfer, MNEs with high levels of autonomy do not always embark upon high-quality linkages. Even though Philips could be deemed a high-quality plant in Singapore, they still utilize low-quality linkages for some of their components – as illustrated by the case study of Meiki Plastics.

As we saw, some of the best equipped and most competent suppliers examined in Singapore were HDD manufacturers. However, these were not judged to be the most important in terms of linkage development. Owing to the truncated nature of decision making functions within foreign-owned HDD firms in Singapore, opportunities for close interactive linkages with customers are limited. Higher-quality linkages were deemed to be those which saw close co-operation between buyers and suppliers which could in turn lead to MNEs assisting suppliers with technical issues. Such linkages were also thought to be more durable and likely to lead to higher levels of technology transfer between buyer and supplier. As reported by the author elsewhere, this type of relationship is most prevalent in the contract manufacturing sector, especially suppliers undertaking OEM arrangements with customers (see Brown, 1998).

Plainly, then, market forces seem to work in favour of linkages in some areas but not in others. Put simply, as components become less bulky and supplier-specific, the need for local sourcing seems to reduce. Conversely, global sourcing increases as buyers move away from traditional component suppliers towards more rounded holistic suppliers, commonly found in higher-value components such as LCD displays and HDDs. Essentially this suggests that, unhindered, convenience linkages will tend to be the most prevalent linkages generated by FDI.

The policy implications of the research are inevitably largely location-specific. Hitherto, policy makers in Singapore have concentrated on developing the internal production processes of local suppliers while filling gaps in the local supply chain through second-wave FDI (Brown, 1998). Policy efforts will have to be stepped up in order somehow to capture the higher-value areas in the supply chain and to enhance the bargaining position of local suppliers *vis-à-vis* MNEs. Following the economic crisis sweeping Asia, however, the Singapore government is currently reviewing its economic development strategy for the next few years. In 1997, the Prime Minister, Goh Chok Tong, established a Committee on Singapore's Competitiveness to review the country's growth prospects, strengths and weaknesses. One of the key recommendations arising from this was the need to forge stronger partnerships between MNEs and local suppliers. The government realizes that, left unaided, MNEs may not automatically generate high-quality local linkages with local suppliers. Given the tendency towards global sourcing in the electronics industry, it is imperative that Singapore continues and develops further its pro-active supplier development policies and encourages the development of strong global suppliers who can act as strategic partners to foreign-owned MNEs.

At a more general level, what can economic development practitioners learn from local linkage formation in Singapore? Possibly the most important lesson from this case study is the fact that sectoral clusters dominated by foreign-owned firms do not automatically generate durable, high-quality linkages, thereby reducing the scope for self-sustaining economic development. In order to maximize the benefits of foreign-owned firms, cluster strategies have to ensure that MNEs work with and develop indigenous industry. It is therefore important for policy makers to upgrade the quality of local supply relationships by making MNEs actively work with local companies to foster a climate which encourages technology transfer between buyers and suppliers. Research has shown that pro-active supplier development policies can play a vital role in aiding this process (see Brown, 1998). Cluster-based economic development policies which fail to address these issues run the risk of perpetuating the problems associated with weakly embedded branch plant regions.

Note

1. The empirical material used within this chapter draws upon an in-depth interview-based study of seven foreign-owned electronics manufacturers and 12 local suppliers in Singapore (see Brown, 1996). Funding for the research was provided by Scottish Enterprise National and I would like to acknowledge their support. Thanks are also due to John Bachtler for his comments on an earlier version of this chapter. The usual disclaimer applies.

Amtek Engineering are a good example of a component manufacturing firm which has interactive linkages with MNEs. Amtek is a sheet metal fabrication company who have grown in tandem with the electronics industry in Singapore. In fact, the company has been described as a 'showcase of MNC-linked local entrepreneurship' (Yuan and Low, 1990: 91). Amtek are now a major MNE in their own right, having expanded into other geographic and sectoral markets. As well as having a large number of customers in Singapore, Amtek also work closely in conjunction with their customers on design-related issues. Amtek and their subsidiary companies employ over 28 000 people world-wide and in excess of 800 people in Singapore. The company has expanded rapidly during recent years, becoming a publicly limited company in 1987. The company's turnover grew from S$103 million in 1993 to S$288 million in 1997.

References

Birkinshaw, J. and Hood, N. (1997) *Foreign Investment and Industry Cluster Development: The Characteristics of Subsidiary Companies in Different Types of National Industry Clusters*, Stockholm School of Economics and Strathclyde University, mimeo.

Brown, R. (1996) 'Foreign Direct Investment and Regional Economic Development: Backward Electronics Linkages in Scotland and Singapore', Unpublished PhD thesis, Glasgow, University of Strathclyde.

Brown, R. (1998) 'Electronics Foreign Direct Investment in Singapore: A Study of Local Linkages in "Winchester City"', *European Business Review*, 98, 196–210.

Chia, S.Y. (1995) 'The International Procurement and Sales Behaviour of Multinational Enterprises', in E.K.Y. Chen, and P. Drysdale (eds), *Corporate Links and Foreign Direct Investment in Asia and the Pacific*, Sydney, HarperCollins.

Clarke, T. and Beaney, P. (1993) 'Between Autonomy and Dependence: Corporate Strategy, Plant Status and Local Agglomeration in the Scottish Electronics Industry', *Environment and Planning A*, 25, 213–32.

Curran, J. and Blackburn, R. (1991) 'Changes in the Context of Enterprise – Some Socio-economic and Environmental Factors Facing Small Firms in the 90s', in J. Curran and R.A. Blackburn (eds), *Paths of Enterprise: The Future of the Small Business*, London, Routledge.

Dicken, P., Forsgren, M. and Malmberg, A. (1994) 'The Local Embeddedness of Transnational Corporations', in A. Amin and N. Thrift, *Globalization, Institutions, and Regional Development in Europe*, Oxford, Oxford University Press.

Economic Development Board (EDB) (1994) *Sectoral Briefing: Singapore's Electronics Industry*, Singapore, Economic Development Board.

Economic Development Board (EDB) (1997) *Sectoral Briefing: Singapore's Electronics Industry*, Singapore, Economic Development Board.

Glasmeier, A. (1988) 'Factors Governing the Development of High-tech Industry Agglomeration: A Tale of Three Cities', *Regional Studies*, 22, 287–301.

Henderson J. (1994) 'Electronics Industries and The Developing World: Uneven Contributions and Uncertain Prospects', in L. Sklair (ed.), *Capitalism and Development*, London, Routledge.

Henderson, J. and Appelbaum, R.P. (1992) 'Situating the State in the East Asian Development Process', in J. Henderson and R.P. Appelbaum (eds), *States' Development in the Asian Pacific Rim*, Newbury Park, CA, Sage.

Hirschman, A.O. (1958) *The Strategy of Economic Development*, New Haven, Yale University Press.

Hoare A.G. (1985) 'Industrial Linkage Studies', in M. Pacione (ed.), *Progress in Industrial Geography*, London: Croom Helm.

Hobday, M. (1994) 'Technological Learning in Singapore: A Test Case of Leapfrogging', *Journal of Development Studies*, 30, 831–58.

Hobday, M. (1995) 'East Asian Latecomer Firms: Learning The Technology of Electronics', *World Development*, 23, 1171–93.

Lim, L.Y.C. and Pang, E.F. (1982) 'Vertical Linkages and Multinational Enterprises in Developing Countries', *World Development*, 10, 585–95.

Lim L.Y.C. and Pang E.F. (1991) *Foreign Direct Investment and Industrialisation: In Malaysia, Singapore, Taiwan and Thailand*, Paris, OECD Development Centre.

Mair, A. (1993) 'New Growth Poles? Just-in-time Manufacturing and Local Economic Development', *Regional Studies*, 27, 207–22.

Morris, J. and Imrie, R. (1992) *Transforming Buyer–Supplier Relations: Japanese-Style Industrial Practices in a Western Context*, London, Macmillan.

Pang E.F. and Lim L. (1977) *The Electronics Industry in Singapore: Structure, Technology and Linkages*, Singapore, Economic Research Centre.

Perry, M. and Hui, T.B. (1998) 'Global Manufacturing and Local Linkage in Singapore', *Environment and Planning A*, 30, 1603–24.

Porter, M. (1990) *The Competitive Advantage of Nations*, New York, Free Press.

Rainnie, A. F. (1991) 'Flexibility and Small Firms: Prospects for the 1990's, *Working Paper*, 1991/2, Hatfield Polytechnic Business School.

Scott, A.J. (1992) 'The Role of Large Producers in Industrial Districts: A Case of High Technology Systems Houses in Southern California', *Regional Studies*, 26, 265–75.

Toh, M.H. (1993) 'Partnership with Multinational Corporations', in L. Low, M.H., Toh, T.W., Soon, K.Y., Tan and Hughes H. (eds), *Challenge and Response*, Singapore, Times Academic Press.

Turok, I. (1993) 'Inward Investment and Local Linkages: How Deeply Embedded is "Silicon Glen"?', *Regional Studies*, 27, 401–17.

Walker, R. (1988) 'The Geographical Organisation of Production Systems', *Environment and Planning D*, 6, 377–408.

Young S., Hood, N. and Dunlop, S. (1988) 'Global Strategies, Multinational Subsidiary Roles and Economic Impact in Scotland', *Regional Studies*, 22, 487–88.

Young, S., Hood, N. and Peters, E. (1994) 'Multinational Enterprises and Regional Economic Development', *Regional Studies*, 28, 657–77.

Yuan, L.T. (1994) *Overseas Investment: Experience of Singapore Manufacturing Companies*, Institute of Policy Studies/McGraw-Hill, Singapore.

Yuan, L.T. and Low, L. (1990) *Local Entrepreneurship in Singapore*, Singapore, Times Academic Press.

19 International Production Networks and Human Resources: The Case of the Malaysian Electronics Industry

Barry Wilkinson, Jos Gamble, John Humphrey and Jonathan Morris

INTRODUCTION

This chapter reports on one part of a study into the consumer electronics and clothing industries in the Asia Pacific region. The rationale for the research was to gain an understanding of the evolving cross-border division of manufacturing operations in the region, and the implications this has for work organization and human resources development and management. The methodology was case-study based, using interviews with managers guided by semi-structured questionnaires. Detailed studies of over 60 manufacturing plants were undertaken, the majority in Japan, Korea, Hong Kong, Malaysia and China. The plants were inter-linked through supply-chain relationships, and often ownership too.

The focus here is on electronics in Malaysia, where we studied the plants of two household-name Japanese consumer electronics assemblers, together with eight plants which supplied components and materials into them. In addition we studied four Japanese 'mother' and 'sister' plants in Japan. (We also studied a number of plants of the same 'parent' ownership in China, though these findings are not reported here.) This chapter is thus further focused because of its emphasis on Japanese electronics plants, though we will argue for the need to be careful in attributing characteristic patterns of work organization and personnel practices to 'Japanese management'.

The manufacturing plants and their links are presented diagrammatically in Figure 19.1, but before describing their activities we will

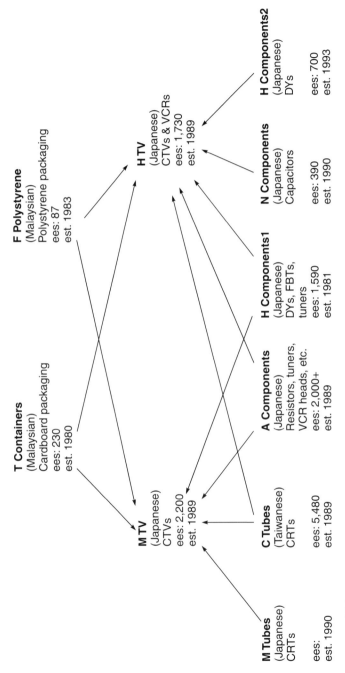

Figure 19.1

provide a description of the development of the electronics industry in Malaysia so that our plant sample can be placed in context. The chapter is organized as follows. First, we provide a brief description of the status of the electronics industry in Malaysia, and place the companies studied in this context (why are they here?). Secondly, we provide a description of what activities are undertaken, particularly in terms of products and processes (what do they do?). Thirdly, we describe shopfloor work organization (what do workers do?) and fourthly we give an account of human resources development and management (how are workers managed?). We conclude with an explanation of work organization and human resources management (HRM) in terms of the position of the Malaysian electronics industry in an international division of labour, and a discussion of the prospects for the country to move up to higher league.

WHY ARE THEY HERE?

Japanese (and American) electronics companies began to establish plants in the ASEAN countries on a significant scale in the 1970s. At the time Japanese companies were facing rising labour costs and labour scarcity at home, while ASEAN was offering cheap and plentiful labour to foreign investors as part of an attempt to industrialize. Malaysia was very successful in attracting a large share of this investment to its Free Trade Zones (FTZs – the first was set up in 1970), with an apparently stable government offering a range of tax and other incentives. At the end of the 1970s, 19 Japanese electronics subsidiaries had been established in Malaysia, compared with 16 spread across Indonesia, the Philippines and Thailand (Takayasu and Ishizaki, 1995). (Singapore had been more aggressive and quicker off the mark in its search for export oriented foreign investment, and had attracted 43 Japanese electronics subsidiaries by the end of the 1970s.) Initially the emphasis in Malaysia was on the assembly of low-value electronic components, mainly to be exported back to Japan for final assembly together with higher-value parts produced in Japan: as late as 1986, 84 per cent of the output of the Malaysian electronics sector was accounted for by electronics components.

Then in the mid-1980s came the well documented *endaka* (high-yen crisis) when the Japanese currency was forced by the major industrial powers to virtually double in value against the US$. The obvious (and of course intended) effect was to make export oriented production in

Japan all the more expensive, and this measure combined with trade sanctions (and threats of further trade sanctions) led to Japanese companies locating production facilities in North America and Europe on a much bigger scale than had been the case in the past (Morris, 1991). It also contributed to a renewed and bigger investment push in Asian, and especially ASEAN, economies. In expanding the ASEAN presence Japanese multinationals were taking further advantage of relatively cheap labour and therefore controlling production costs; at the same time they could use quotas and trade arrangements more favourable than those applying to exports from Japan (Guyton, 1995). A third important factor was the steady growth in demand for electronics goods across the East and South East Asian regions, and the perceived need to have a serious presence there.

Malaysia was well placed to take advantage of the further internationalization of production: it already had a significant electronics components base (creating a 'follow-my-leader' effect and offering economies of agglomeration); it was strategically placed geographically between Thailand, Singapore and Indonesia (which were further sources of componentry and whose closeness could enable speedy transit between plants); and the Malaysian government was continuing to woo foreign investments in the context of gradual recovery from a late 1980s' recession. Between 1985 and 1994, a further 201 Japanese electronics subsidiaries were added to the ASEAN (excluding Singapore) stock, 109 of them landing in Malaysia (Takayasu and Ishizaki, 1995).

It is worth adding a note here on the Asian Newly Industrialized Countries (ANICs) of Singapore, Taiwan, Korea and Hong Kong. During the 1970s these were the favoured locations for Japanese foreign electronics subsidiaries, but in the investment boom of the late 1980s and early 1990s those countries themselves experienced acute labour shortages and rising wage costs, and hence were often bypassed in favour of ASEAN – the ANICs (including Singapore) attracted 83 new Japanese electronics subsidiaries between 1985 and 1994 compared with ASEAN's (excluding Singapore) 201 (Takayasu and Ishizaki, 1995). Further, rapidly developing indigenous Taiwanese, Korean and Hong Kongese electronics companies were themselves becoming international players, further contributing to the growth of the electronics industry in ASEAN and elsewhere in Asia (Wilkinson, 1994).

In the late 1980s and early 1990s the investment push from Japan (and elsewhere) was in a wider range of activities. In particular there was a drive to locate final assembly and testing of goods in Malaysia, which in turn attracted more components companies (Takeuchi, 1993). By 1995 electronic components accounted for 42.9 per cent (in 1986 it was 84 per cent) of the Malaysian electronics sector's output, the rest being consumer electronics (25.2 per cent) and industrial electronics (31.9 per cent) (Ministry of International Trade and Industry, 1996).

Malaysia's export oriented industrialization strategy appeared to be working. Manufactured exports as a proportion of total exports from Malaysia were less than 40 per cent in 1986, lagging far behind the ANICs. By 1995, the figure was almost 80 per cent. Targets set in the first industrial master plan (1986–95) on GDP growth, and manufacturing value added, exports and employment, were all exceeded (Ministry of International Trade and Industry, 1996). The electronics industry was central to this development: 55 per cent of manufactured exports in 1995 were in electronics (Malaysian Industrial Development Authority, 1996). The remarkable rises in electronics industry employment, output and exports from the mid-1980s to the mid-1990s is indicated in Table 19.1.

We should also note the markets served by the Malaysian electronics industry. Around a half of all electronics exports from Malaysia are destined for the Asian region, with other ASEAN countries and Japan being the most important markets. The USA and Europe take up all but around 10 per cent of the remainder. In the consumer electronics sector, the focus of our research, 44.1 per cent of exports are to other Asian countries, including 17.4 per cent of the total to ASEAN and

Table 19.1   Malaysian electronics industry: employment, output and exports, 1986–95

Year	Employment (000)	Output (RM billion)	Exports (RM billion)
1986	57	6.5	7.1
1987	89	8.9	9.2
1988	106	12.2	13.0
1989	123	15.9	17.9
1990	144	20.3	23.1
1991	171	26.1	30.4
1992	204	32.2	34.6
1993	231	42.1	46.7
1994	278	56.4	66.4
1995	313	71.0	85.0

Sources: Malaysian Industrial Development Authority (1996); Ministry of International Trade and Industry (1996).

Table 19.2   World exports and imports of CTVs: Japan and
Malaysia, 1992–6 (US$ million)

Item	1992	1993	1994	1995	1996
Exports from Japan	2 402	2 240	2 450	2 256	2 031
Imports to Japan	393	632	1 008	1 391	1 484
Exports from Malaysia	851	1 236	1 732	2 239	2 084
Imports to Malaysia	19	33	38	28	18

Source: UNCTAD data.

13.5 per cent to Japan. The USA takes 29.6 per cent and Europe 16.1
per cent (Ministry of International Trade and Industry, 1996). Interestingly, Japan is well on its way to becoming a net importer of some
categories of electronics goods, including CTVs and VCRs, many of
which are made by Japanese companies in Asia, particularly ASEAN
(see Table 19.2).

However, this is not necessarily evidence of *kudoka*, or the 'hollowing
out' of Japanese industry, at least not yet. Rather, there is emerging
a product-to-product (e.g. camcorders v. VCRs; widescreen TV v. conventional TV) and process-to-process (e.g. key component production
v. simple assembly) division of labour across Asia, with Japan at the
highest-value end of the spectrum (Guyton, 1995; Takayasu and
Ishizaki, 1995). Together with the transfer of the capital equipment
and machinery necessary for production from Japan to Malaysia, this
undoubtedly goes a long way to explaining Japan's consistently large
and growing trade surplus with Malaysia during the 1990s – according to
data from JETRO the Japan–Malaysia trade balance favoured Japan
by US$1.2 billion in 1991, growing to US$3.6 billion in 1996.

We will now locate the manufacturing plants studied in this broad
context, which should help the reader to judge how 'representative' or
'typical' our small sample is. Two of the plants – M TV and H TV –
are important subsidiaries of their respective parent companies in
Japan, engaging in the final assembly of CTVs (and VCRs in H TV's
case). In both cases the plants were established in 1989, primarily
because of cheaper production costs. The other eight plants are important suppliers into these two assemblers (there are of course many other
suppliers to the two plants in Japan, Malaysia and elsewhere in the Asia
Pacific region). Two of these plants, established in the early 1980s, are
indigenous Malaysian owned – T containers and F Polystyrene. Both
make packaging primarily for the consumer electronics and white-goods'

industries in Malaysia. (Indigenous company participation in the networks we studied was minimal, and limited largely to packaging, metal stamping, some plastic moulding, and labels and nuts and bolts. This is generally the case in the electronics industry in Malaysia as identified by MITI.) One other plant, H Components1, was an early investor, serving assemblers around the region.

The remaining five plants were all established between 1989 and 1993: it is noteworthy that the two assemblers in the sample located in Malaysia partly because of the existing supply infrastructure; further Japanese (and other) components' manufacturers then followed such assemblers into Malaysia, or – as in the case of H Components – expanded with new plants (H Components2). (A Components also established a second plant in the early 1990s, though we were not allowed to pay a visit – the two plants between them employ over 5400 workers.)

In terms of markets, M TV produces almost solely for export, being set up specifically to serve Asia (including Japan) and Oceania (sister plants in Europe and North America serve those markets). There is a separate M TV assembly plant only a few miles away. This plant has a small capacity; it was set up back in 1966 specifically for the Malaysian market, and has continued to do so into the 1990s. M TV also maintains relatively small TV production facilities within the markets of Thailand, Taiwan and the Philippines. These are known as 'mini-M plants'. CTV production at H TV, on the other hand, constitutes less than a third of total output, destined for the Malaysian and ASEAN markets. VCR production, on the other hand, is increasingly for the world market place. The VCR world market appears to be in decline and there is a general problem of over-capacity. H TV's response has been to close its British and German plants (in 1995 and 1996). Its US plant has limited capacity, and this will not be increased. And the VCR plant in Japan – which was described to us as far more efficient than the Malaysian plant but too expensive to run – is now under threat of closure.

It is worth pointing out here that in terms of Gereffi's (1996) commodity-chain framework, CTV production represents a producer-driven rather than a buyer (retailer)-driven chain. There are signs that this may be beginning to change for some segments of the CTV market – in fact we studied one Hong Kong CTV manufacturer which produced small CTVs to specifications provided by overseas buyers (retailers who sold under their own brand names). There could be important implications of this potential shift, easily the subject of another chapter. The important point here is that the commodity chains described in this chapter were driven by the CTV assemblers.

The two packaging plants, as mentioned above, serve a range of electronics and white-goods' companies in Malaysia. The remaining component manufacturers typically serve a range of assemblers, including M TV and H TV, in Malaysia and elsewhere in the region, and to some extent each other. C Tubes is the exceptional plant in our sample, having neither a Japanese nor a Malaysian parent. This Taiwanese tube manufacturer enjoys 48 per cent of the Malaysian market for CTV picture tubes, and 52 per cent of the Malaysian market for display monitor tubes. Its CRT know-how was originally provided by Toshiba in the 1970s. Today C Tubes is one of the major players in picture tube markets in Pacific Asia and Europe.

Having attended to the question of why the plants are here (primarily reasons of cost, labour availability and market access) we will now turn attention to exactly what they do.

WHAT DO THEY DO?

Our argument is that work organization, and HRM and development, must be understood against the background of the activities carried out at the plants. Hence in this section 'what they do' (and equally importantly 'what they don't do') is described with regard to products made and production processes. We will also look at how the activities of product and process innovations, so crucial in an electronics industry facing ever-shorter product life cycles and ever-increasing cost competition, are undertaken.

Products

As described, M TV and H TV make CTVs and VCRs, and the other plants in the sample supply componentry and packaging materials into them. However, the products tend to be at the lower-value and 'standardized mature' end of the spectrum. This is clearly illustrated in the cases of H TV and M TV.

In a mature and stagnant VCR market with limited product differentiation, H TV is forced to compete primarily on price with Korean and smaller Japanese firms for world market share. H TV's CTV output, on the other, is of the smallest and simplest types. All of its CTV output is of conventional CTVs with screen sizes between 14 in and 21 in (though it does plan to introduce production of conventional 25 in CTVs). The sister VCR plant in Japan, as mentioned earlier, may soon close, leaving the great bulk of a stagnant world VCR market to be served from Malaysia. The mother CTV plant, on the other hand, has reduced its conventional CTV output, allowing H TV to serve South East Asian markets (European and North American sister plants serve those markets) but focused instead on innovative and high-value added high-definition TVs (HDTV), together with widescreen TVs and display monitors. The plant also produces projectors and CD-ROM drives.

The picture is similar at M TV. Although M TV does have the capacity to produce (conventional) CTVs of screen sizes up to 29 in, around 90 per cent of its output is of CTVs of 21 in or less. M TV has a longer-established sister plant in Japan which produces the same range of conventional 14–29 in CTVs (its output is skewed towards larger screens) and when we visited we found a plant desperately attempting to improve its labour productivity in the face of cost competition from M TV (more on this below). The future of this plant was highly uncertain. M TV also has a 'mother' plant in Japan – the CTV headquarters for the whole M group. This plant produces only small numbers of conventional CTVs, and far more widescreen and HDTVs. In sum, newer and higher-value added CTV and related products are made in Japan; standardized mature products are made in Malaysia.

Interviews with the component manufacturers confirmed that more and more componentry was being made in Malaysia (and other ASEAN countries), thereby helping the assemblers increase their local content ratios. The local manufacture of picture tubes, constituting around 40 per cent of the value of a conventional CTV, was particularly important in extending local content. However, the highest value sub-components, such as deflector yoke cores and capacitor foils, were typically imported from Japan, Taiwan or Singapore, indicating a significant process-to-process division of labour. Among the Japanese component makers, 40 per cent of sub-componentry by value imported from Japan was typical, with Singapore being the next most important non-Malaysian source. There was also some evidence of product-to-product differentiation: for instance N Components produces only one out of four types of capacitor in Malaysia; more sophisticated capacitors are manufactured in Singapore and Japan.

Processes

In the majority of the plants studied the production process consisted primarily of the mass assembly of components and sub-components, followed by testing, inspection and packaging. CRT and packaging manufacture were more akin to continuous process, with a high degree of automation, and entailing machine monitoring together with heavy loading, unloading and packaging work. In all the companies we studied mass production was under way, with relatively little product variety, and processes were highly standardized.

The international division of products and processes we have described, according to Malaysia's MITI, also applies to the production of other componentry. For instance, while Malaysia is a major producer and world exporter of semiconductors, hardly any wafer fabrication is currently undertaken in Malaysia. Rather, Malaysia's semiconductor industry is largely confined to assembly and test operations, and is almost entirely dependent on imported wafers (MITI, 1996).

Product Innovation

Both M TV and H TV undertake some design work in Malaysia. H TV employ around 30 in R&D; M TV employ around 80, including 24 graduate engineers, some of whom are Japanese expatriates. Although the significance of this work should not be understated, it is important to emphasize that they are not pushing back the frontiers of media technology. Rather, they are modifying basic chassis designs sent from Japan in order to reduce the complexity of componentry and to improve the ease of manufacture. At M TV, suggested changes to designs are constantly communicated electronically to the Japanese mother plant, which provides guidance and advice (in Japan, M TV's parent employs over 500 R&D engineers and technologists, many with PhDs, devoted to TV innovations). The resulting chassis modifications have been used in the Malaysian plant, and also in the group's 'mini-M' plants in the region, confirming the status of M TV as the most important group company in Asia outside of Japan. More fundamental research is of course carried on in Japan, and it should be pointed out that manu-facturability design work on a more complex chassis, especially for HDTV which embodies far greater componentry, remains firmly in Japan.

Among all the supplier companies studied, a total of less than 10 people engaged in any form of product design work, though two companies (A Components and M Tubes) said they were considering introducing design teams in response to the needs of companies like M TV: they explained that designers in buyer and supplier companies really need face-to-face contact.

Process Innovation

A first point to note here is that the bulk of capital equipment and machinery is imported – mostly from Japan, and in the case of C Components from Taiwan. (Rasiah, 1994, did document a degree of growth in local sourcing of production machinery in the 1980s, but we saw little evidence of this in the plants we studied, and certainly the expensive automated equipment and machinery was not made in Malaysia.) Imports of capital goods represents another way in which Malaysia is dependent on more advanced countries.

The second important point is that a huge amount of the continuous improvement activity for which Japanese firms are famous has been carried out in Japan at 'mother' and 'sister' plants prior to the export of the process. At the extreme, the Japanese parent plant may design a whole production process, fine-tune the machinery and equipment and run the process under the scrutiny of industrial engineers with select Japanese labour to establish optimum methods, standard times, maintenance regimes, etc. Of course in practice there will be some differences in the processes established overseas, not least because the levels of automation found in Japan are not likely to be wholly replicated – the economics of robot assemblers (common in electronics production in Japan) may work in Japan but not Malaysia. The principle is, however, clear: design the process in Japan; productionize and standardize in Japan; export the finely tuned production process.

We will finally add a few points on international procurement and marketing, which are quite complex activities. International procurement is complicated because even after make-or-buy and local source v. import decisions are made, for many components there is the need to secure scale economies by buying for several plants in different locations in Asia, or even across the world. Marketing can be very complex because the output of any one plant is likely to be destined for several countries, which in turn might be served by more than one Asian plant. In most of the companies we studied, sourcing and marketing activities are located in Japan, or in a Singapore regional headquarters. M TV is the exception here: recently a significant part of the international procurement activity was shifted to M TV, and strategic Asian marketing has also been added, creating a number of white-collar professional jobs. As with the arrival of chassis design modification in Malaysia, managers at the plant felt these developments represented quite a coup.

Having located our sample plants within an international division of operations and specified the activities in which they engage, we are now in a position to examine the organization of the shopfloor.

WHAT DO WORKERS DO?

In most parts of most plants there was a minute division of tasks across production lines. Work cycle times for most assembly, testing and quality checking tasks were around 20 – 30 seconds. This is the case for over half of those employed in our sample of companies. In the more highly automated plants – tubes and packaging – the work is more a case of machine minding, with lots of routine and heavy loading, unloading and packaging of finished goods ready for shipment. Work is more skilled in tubes plants than elsewhere, on-the-job (OJT) training lasting for between one and three months, depending on the precise job, with skills and abilities continuing to develop over a number of years. In component and TV assembly plants OJT training for as little as a few days precedes taking a job independently on the line. The local description of tubes' plant work is, however, 'dirty and dangerous', and Malaysian workers are difficult to recruit. More skills and training are also entailed in the automated sections of the component and CTV assembly plants. For instance, in some plant sections there is automatic insertion or mounting of components onto printed circuit boards (PCBs). Here, operators have to load magazines of components, unload finished goods and monitor the machinery. Some degree of understanding of the machinery is useful, and some operators are given minor programming skills; more technicians are employed in these areas, too.

A regimented and highly disciplined workforce has been well documented in Japanese plants in the UK and USA (Delbridge, Turnbull and Wilkinson, 1992). Discipline is similarly imposed on the workforce in Japanese electronics plants in Malaysia, for instance with regard to time-keeping, attendance and the wearing of company uniforms. Displays of production targets, output and defects are commonly used, typically at the level of work teams, and these are updated hourly, or in some cases in real time. The detailed attention to quality is reflected in most plants in an individual fault-tracing capability, though quality feedback was sometimes at the level of teams rather than individuals for fear of alienating workers. Such detailed monitoring and measurement of worker performances has also been documented in Japanese (and other) plants in the UK and elsewhere (Sewell and Wilkinson, 1992, and see Chapter 9 in this volume).

A minute division of labour and short work cycles on assembly lines can be an isolating experience, but workers are typically organized into 'teams', with a 'team leader' whose job it is to constantly seek improvements on performance against output and quality targets within specified manning levels. The targets are set by industrial engineers and production managers, and in some plants discussion about efficiency ratios in Malaysia compared with Japan were commonplace. In many cases team leaders would brief their members at the start of the shift, and they tried to encourage a 'customer' ethos – the downstream team being the upstream team's customer.

Job rotation is sometimes practised, but typically is limited to workers developing a capability in two or three different assembly tasks within a line, except for a small number who act as floats or utilities to fill in for absentees under conditions of tight manning.

What workers do routinely in their jobs, then, appears quite limited. But what about the employee involvement activities – quality circles (QCs), *kaizen* teams and the like – for which the Japanese are famous? In fact all but one of the 10 companies studied (and including the Taiwanese- and Malaysian-owned plants) had attempted at some time to introduce small-group activities, but almost all had either failed miserably or were quite limited in their spread and life span. Our data do not allow us to judge to what extent this was down to worker disinterest or recalcitrance, or to management's own lack of commitment. Some Japanese managers interviewed blamed the workers – 'they don't share the Japanese culture', 'they're not so well educated', etc. However, the fact that most of the production processes had been *kaizened* to death in Japan before being exported to Malaysia probably had something to do with it: the emphasis was on achieving levels of output and quality already established in Japan rather than being inventive. No doubt the high labour turnover in these plants (see below) was another factor constraining the investment in improvement activities.

One exception to the '*kaizen* in Japan, transfer to Malaysia' rule we came across, an exception which contradicts the 'Malaysians are not capable' view, was at A components. Here local line leaders and supervisors were involved in a *kaizen* programme based on a re-combination of assembly tasks in conjunction with re-designed production machinery organized in small 'cells'. Managers claimed big productivity and quality improvements which exceeded standards in Japan. Managers from Japan were due to visit the Malaysian plant to consider transferring the process innovation back to Japan. An expatriate Japanese manager at the plant said it was easier to make such changes in the Malaysian plant because it was more authoritarian: consensus decision making and associated company politics were obstacles in Japan.

Interestingly, M TV's sister plant in Japan was experimenting very much along the same lines as A Components, as part of a desperate attempt to ensure its survival in the face of higher costs through raising labour productivity. A document written by the sister plant's manager and circulated among staffs describes average work cycle times on some lines of 15 seconds. Experiments showed that re-combining tasks to create one-minute cycles and using the feedback of buzzers and lights to signal to operators when the end of the target cycle was imminent led to productivity improvements of between 40 and 50 per cent. The document presents this experiment as an example of a 'soft' processing technology 'that is beyond the capability of the South East Asians'.

The plants under study are, then, engaged in standardized, mature mass production, and unsurprisingly work on the shopfloor is mostly repetitive and more demanding of concentration and diligence than of skills and intelligence. Opportunities for employee involvement are highly limited. This is not necessarily to be technologically determin013i-stic; the two experiments described above should put us on our guard in that regard, however limited they were. The main point here is that standardized mature production processes have been exported from Japan with the aim of replicating Japanese levels of efficiency at lower costs. Improvements through re-design of processes are secondary to the requirement for cheap unskilled labour.

HOW ARE WORKERS MANAGED?

We would agree with the argument of Keenoy and Abdullah (1995) that HRM and development in Malaysian electronics can best be understood not simply by reference to a 'Japanese management syndrome', nor to what Abo (1995) calls 'hybrid management' – a mix of Japanese and Malaysian management styles. Rather, they are understood by locating them in relation to (1) the activities of plants within international production networks or 'commodity chains', and (2) the characteristics and situation of labour, the one commodity which talks back, within the host environment. Our focus is here is on operator levels in the work forces.

Recruitment and Selection

When M TV established in Malaysia in 1989, the country was still coming out of a late-1980s' recession; 6000 applicants applied for the first 300 jobs on offer. M TV focused on 17-year-old high-school leavers with reasonably good educational credentials, and used interviews and psychological tests to try to pick out 'team players' and those with 'potential for growth'. But the situation of labour changed rapidly as Malaysia boomed, and high selectivity could not last for very long. The response of firms has been to reduce expectations regarding educational requirements – at some firms down to basic literacy and numeracy – and to seek out labour from ever-more remote rural areas (industrialization in Malaysia has been focused around the Kelang Valley, Johor Bahru and Penang). One company (H Components1) described how they send personnel staff out to the *kampongs* (rural villages) to recruit what they can on the spot. Interviews are conducted and workers are selected, then the next day a bus is sent to collect the new recruits. H Components2 was set up, in 1993, in a rural area, specifically because of recruitment problems at H Components1. But that rural area (near Ipoh) has since increasingly industrialized, and the catchment area is now beginning to widen again.

Some plants have also become dependent on foreign labour, especially from Indonesia and Bangladesh. The packaging and tubes plants we studied have a 20–40 per cent dependency on foreigners. Interestingly, they said they actually preferred foreigners because they are more or less captive for the three years or so of their contracts – legally, they cannot job-hop, and training efforts are less likely to be wasted.

Many Japanese managers complained to us about the lack of loyalty, laziness, and rising wage bills associated with a tight labour market (some also put these characteristics down to 'Malaysian culture'). Comments that 'we'd be better off nowadays in Indonesia or Vietnam' were not uncommon, though none revealed to us any plans of relocation. Turnover was typically 3–4 per cent month, with peaks on the receipt by workers of annual bonuses; turnover rates were even higher than this among Malaysian workers (not immigrant labour) in the 'dirty and dangerous' tubes and packaging plants.

Induction and Training

A couple of weeks' induction and OJT training for operators was typical. After this, operators would take their place on the line proper.

In the tubes plants 1–3 months OJT, depending on the specific task being trained for, was used. Further training – mostly in-house – was available for those identified as having potential for promotion to line leader and supervisor, and some companies, as a part of their paternalistic provision, offered limited non-work-related educational opportunities, such as foreign language classes.

Pay and Promotion

Starting salaries for operators were typically around RM430 per calendar month for a 45-hour week, with two months' pay as an annual bonus. Peaks and troughs in demand were met by the use of overtime; temporary workers were rarely used, and would in any case be difficult to recruit in present labour market circumstances. High turnover of staff was also useful here. Output downturns could to some extent be accommodated without having to resort to layoffs simply by freezing recruitment.

Most plants gave seniority increments of around RM50 per year of service. Limited paternalistic benefits were also provided, including subsidized dormitories, free bussing, meal vouchers, medical and recreational facilities, and in one case for workers who spent several years at the plant (M TV) housing loans at favourable interest rates.

It is unlikely that paternalism is a result of 'Japanese management'. In fact the Taiwanese tube maker in our sample did at least as much on the company welfare front as any of the Japanese companies. Keenoy and Abdullah (1995) similarly reported that American electronics plants were equally paternalistic as Japanese plants. Rather, it is related to the necessity of meeting some of the basic needs of a young workforce from a rural background, often many miles from home, and to the underdevelopment of a state welfare system in Malaysia.

Promote-from-within policies were universal, partly reflecting the difficulty recruiting team leaders and supervisors from outside, partly as an attempt to bond workers to the company, and partly as a consequence of the 'no-poach' agreement between Japanese companies. The no-poach agreement did not, however, prevent job-hopping, and the attempts of companies to create stronger internal labour markets was having only limited success. Of course, success on this front in the context of a tight labour market would be likely to depend on higher wage and benefits: raising such costs would contradict the purpose of locating in Malaysia in the first place.

Industrial Relations

In seven of the 10 plants studied there was no union, just limited consultation with worker representatives via the personnel department. In fact electronics companies in Malaysia have 'pioneer' status, and union activities among them are severely restricted. As in Singapore (Deyo, 1991), this is a case of the state helping to control labour on behalf of multinational capital in a situation of dependent development. Nonetheless the Electrical Industry Workers' Union (EIWU) has been knocking on the doors of electronics companies ever since the 1970s, and has frequently disputed whether companies should be defined as 'electronic' (see Abdullah, 1992, for detailed analysis of union activity in Malaysian electronics).

One such company in our sample was H Components1, which the EIWU tried to organize following an illegal strike in 1991. The company sacked all the workers, then re-recruited most of them on condition they accept an in-house union (in-house unions are promoted by the Malaysian government as a means of establishing harmony in employee relations). In 1994 the EIWU then tried to organize H TV. This time the company went to court, which ruled that H TV was indeed an electronics company exempt from union recognition. They now plan to introduce an in-house union. H Components2 established an in-house union in 1996 to pre-empt EIWU interest. M TV is the one plant in our sample to recognize an independent union; the EIWU successfully gained recognition there in 1993. M TV has not faced any industrial action, but the union does seem to have some influence on pay and conditions (though we could not unravel this influence from labour market effects). Overall the EIWU remains relatively weak. Its membership grew from around 10 000 to 25 000 between 1986 and 1996 (EIWU, 1996) but this compares with a more rapid growth in employment in the electronics sector over the same period, and most of the representation is in the white-goods' sector.

CONCLUSIONS

Shopfloor organization and related HRM and development practices must increasingly be understood in relation to the international production networks associated with specific industries. As Gereffi (1996: 430) puts it: 'globalization diminishes the influence of national origins.' In the case of the electronics industry – or, more specifically, the consumer electronics and associated components industry – Malaysian plants occupy a particular space within the developing commodity chain. Decisions by the major players in the industry about international divisions of labour by product and process, and the location of product and process innovation, have led to the establishment of plants in Malaysia which produce mature goods which compete in world markets mainly on price; engage in relatively low-value activities, particularly mass assembly; do limited product design work; and engage only in highly limited ways in process innovation.

It is in this context that we can understand the limited demands on the skills of shopfloor workers and the emphasis on workforce discipline to achieve reasonably high productivity and therefore control costs. Independent labour organization is largely denied workers by the state in order to preserve managerial prerogatives, though workers have been given some degree of power (to 'vote with their feet' by job-hopping) by an extremely tight labour market in the 1990s. In sum, the activities undertaken in Malaysia are mature and productionized, and they are applied to a weakly organized and socially detached workforce. As Kenney and Florida (1994) found in their study of Japanese *maquiladora* plants in Mexico, the labour process requires cheap labour, does not demand involvement and high labour turnover can be tolerated so long as it does not push up labour costs.

The Malaysian government is fully aware of the limitations of the electronics industry, and has established ambitious plans to attract more and more high-value added activities, and to encourage the development of indigenous Malaysian electronics companies capable of competing in world markets with Japanese-, Korean- and Taiwanese-owned companies. Malaysia has economies of agglomeration on its side, and there are large-scale initiatives to improve the educational infrastructure and therefore the supply of well educated engineers and technologists. If successful, we would see major changes in patterns of work organization and human resources development and management. However, there are huge problems to be overcome. The generation and development of indigenous companies may be increasingly difficult precisely because of the internationalization of production networks: de-packing and modifying technology is not easy with an ever-more complex international division of activities (Morris-Suzuki, 1992). And attempts to attract higher-value investments from the multinationals, for the moment at least, appears to rub against the low-cost rationale for present investments. Further, Malaysia is adjacent to the more highly developed NIC, Singapore, with whom it may have to compete for

384   *The Malaysian Electronics Industry*

better-quality investments. Malaysia is also adjacent to Indonesia, which has much lower wages than Malaysia, and a huge reservoir of labour. Malaysia sits uncomfortably between these two, and the danger is that, agglomerations notwithstanding, rising production costs remove the rationale for an electronics industry in the country.

References

Abdullah, R.S. (1992) *Management Styles and Strategies and Employee Responses in Malaysia: A Study of Management Industrial Relations Styles of US and Japanese Multinational Companies in the Malaysian Electronics Industry*. PhD thesis, Cardiff, University of Wales.

Abo, T. (1995) *Japanese Electronics Assembly Plants in East Asian Region: A Comparative Study of 'Hybrid Factories' in East Asia, the US and Europe*, paper presented to the 12th Annual Conference of Euro–Asia Management Studies Association, SDA-BOCCONI-ISFSAO, Milan, 8–11 November.

Delbridge, R., Turnbull, P. and Wilkinson, B. (1992) 'Pushing Back the Frontiers: Management Control and Work Intensification under JIT/TQM Factory Regimes', *New Technology, Work and Employment*, 7(2), 97–106.

Deyo, F. (1991) *Beneath the Miracle: Labor Subordination in the New Asian Industrialism*, Berkeley, University of California Press.

Electrical Industry Workers' Union (1996) *Report of the Executive Council, 1993–1996*, Kuala Lumpur, EIWU.

Gereffi, G. (1996) 'Global Commodity Chains: New Forms of Coordination and Control Among Nations and Firms in International Activities', *Competition and Change*, 4, 427–39.

Guyton, L. (1995) 'Japanese FDI and the Transfer of Japanese Consumer Electronics Production to Malaysia', *Journal of Far Eastern Business*, 1(4), 63–97.

Keenoy, T. and Abdullah, R.S. (1995) 'Japanese Managerial Practices in the Malaysian Electronics Industry: Two Case Studies', *Journal of Management Studies*, 32(6), 747–66.

Kenney, M. and Florida, R. (1994) 'Japanese Maquiladors: Production Organization and Global Commodity Chains', *World Development*, 4(1), 27–44.

Malaysian Industrial Development Authority (MIDA) (1996) *Industry Brief: The Electrical and Electronics Industries in Malaysia: Status, Prospects and Opportunities*, Kuala Lumpur, MIDA.

Ministry of International Trade and Industry (MITI) (Malaysia) (1996) *The Second Industrial Master Plan 1996–2005*, Kuala Lumpur, MITI.

Morris, J. (ed.) (1991) *Japan and the Global Economy: Issues and Trends in the 1990s*, London, Routledge.

Morris-Suzuki, T. (1992) 'Re-Shaping the International Division of Labour: Japanese Manufacturing Investment in South East Asia', in J. Morris (ed.), *Japan and the Global Economy: Issues and Trends in the 1990s*, London, Routledge, 135–53.

Rasiah, R. (1994) 'Flexible Production Systems and Local Machine-Tool Subcontracting: Electronics Components Transnationals in Malaysia', *Cambridge Journal of Economics*, 18, 279–98.

Sewell, G. and Wilkinson, B. (1992) '"Someone to Watch Over Me": Surveillance, Discipline and the Just-in-Time Labour Process', *Sociology*, 26(2), 271–89.

Takayasu, K. and Ishizaki, Y. (1995) 'The Changing International Division of Labor of Japanese Electronics Industry in Asia and its Impact on the Japanese Economy', *Pacific Business and Industries*, 1, 2–41.

Takeuchi, J. (1993) 'Foreign Direct Investment in ASEAN by Small- and Medium-Sized Japanese Companies and its Effects on Local Supporting Industries', *Pacific Business and Industries*, 4, 36–57.

Wilkinson, B. (1994) *Labour and Industry in the Asia-Pacific: Lessons from the Newly-Industrialised Countries*, Berlin, de Gruyter.

20 Planning and Partners: The Growth of the Aerospace Industry in South East Asia

David Smith

INTRODUCTION

Historically, the aerospace industry has been dominated in the years since the Second World War by the USA (Piggott and Cook, 1993). In the military field this is by virtue of the size and scale of the armed forces maintained by the USA in its role as a superpower. In the commercial field this is a reflection of American success in the development of commercial jet airliners (Heppenheimer, 1995) and the size of the domestic market in the USA (Hanlon, 1996).

Europe, all too often handicapped by diverse national interests, has managed to maintain a significant presence in the aerospace industry and has latterly come to challenge US domination in certain parts of the industry. The most notable example of this European challenge is the Airbus Industrie consortium which by the mid-1990s was rivalling Boeing in terms of orders taken per year.

In the past Asia has not been a significant player in the world aerospace industry. Despite having been a major aerospace manufacturer before 1945, Japan had only a minimal role in aerospace in the immediate post-war period. In 1980, Japan's aerospace output was less than a fifth of the UK (Figure 20.1), then the leading European aerospace nation, which was itself producing on a modest scale by comparison with the USA. Elsewhere in Asia, only China could claim to be an aerospace producer, having considerable experience of building Soviet aircraft under licence. Though China had built up its aerospace manufacturing expertise during the 1950s, high-technology industries like aerospace were not accorded a high priority in the internal upheavals of the late 1960s and early 1970s and its modest progress stagnated during this period.

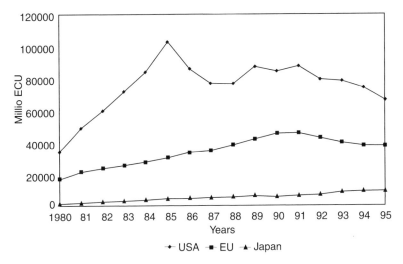

Figure 20.1   US, EU and Japan aerospace industry turnover, 1980–95
Source: European Commission (1996).

Since 1980, Asia has made very considerable progress in developing its aerospace industry. This chapter sets out to trace the development of aerospace manufacturing across South East Asia since the late 1970s. It looks not only at developments in Japan, but at the involvement of its South East Asian neighbours. The chapter also examines how development of the aerospace industry has been achieved, noting the considerable variation between both companies and countries.

THE AEROSPACE INDUSTRIES OF SOUTH EAST ASIA

Japan

The Japanese aerospace industry is the largest and most advanced in South East Asia and is dominated by four major firms, Mitsubishi, Kawasaki, Fuji and Ishikawajima-Harima (Table 20.1). The position of the industry in relation to its counterparts in neighbouring countries can be directly attributed to the Japanese government's 'critical role in fostering the development of the industry' (Todd and Simpson, 1986: 211). This has been undertaken through the Japanese Defence Agency (JDA) and the Ministry of International Trade and Industry (MITI). The former has purchased the products of the industry, while MITI,

Table 20.1   Aerospace manufacturers of South East Asia, 1997

No.	Manufacturer	Country	Turnover ($ million)
1	Mitsubishi Heavy Industries	Japan	3 166
2	Kawasaki Heavy Industries	Japan	1 732
3	Ishikawajima-Harima Heavy Industries	Japan	1 135
4	Fuji Heavy Industries	Japan	566
5	Samsung Aerospace	South Korea	480
6	Singapore Technologies	Singapore	454
7	Nissan	Japan	391
8	Japan Aircraft Manufacturing	Japan	262
9	Korean Air	South Korea	184
10	Daewoo	South Korea	114
11	Hyundai Space and Aircraft	South Korea	25

Source: Flight International.

having identified aerospace as a strategic industry, has provided financial support and facilitated collaboration.

The post-war origins of the industry lie in the military sector. The
Korean War in the early 1950s led to the revival of aerospace by creating a demand for overhaul and maintenance services in which Japanese
firms were actively encouraged to participate by the US military
authorities (Mowery and Rosenberg, 1985). The need to equip Japan's
own newly created armed forces in the mid-1950s provided the stimulus
for a move into manufacturing. This took the form of licensed production of US military aircraft. Contracts were allocated under MITI's
guidance (Todd and Simpson, 1986) to Japan's major industrial companies including Mitsubishi, Kawasaki and Fuji. Manufacturing expertise was built up in stages as licensed production developed from the
assembly of knock-down kits to the incorporation of locally made parts.
Licensed production continued over successive decades as the JDA
sought to update the country's fleet of fighter aircraft. In the 1960s, the
Lockheed F104 and McDonnell-Douglas F4 fighters were built in Japan
under licence, as was the McDonnell-Douglas F15 in the early 1980s.

The industry took a major step forward in the 1980s with a move from
licensed production to collaborative programmes. Although licensed

production had enhanced the industry's manufacturing capability, with many aircraft having a high level of local content, Japan still lacked basic design and development expertise as far as advanced combat aircraft were concerned. The FSX indigenous fighter programme, involving a joint venture with General Dynamics of the USA to produce a derivative of the F16 fighter, was designed to remedy this situation. Set up under MITI's guidance, development work started in 1988 with the first prototype flying in 1995. Although it has undoubtedly enabled the leading Japanese aerospace companies to enhance their design and development capability, this has been achieved at very high cost compared to the cost of equivalent aircraft purchased directly from the USA.

Prohibited from exporting military aircraft, the Japanese government also sought to foster civil programmes. Government support for such programmes has been less generous than for military programmes and has taken different forms. To penetrate the civil airliner market MITI initially sponsored collaboration between Japanese aerospace manufacturers (Endres, 1996). This took the form of a consortium known as Nippon Aircraft Manufacturing Company (NAMC), set up to develop a short-range turboprop airliner, the YS-11. Government involvement was not confined to establishing the consortium as it also met more than half the development costs of the programme. The YS-11 was technically successful and provided the participating firms with valuable experience, but export sales were modest, amounting to about one-third of total sales which had reached 182 when production ceased in 1973. This led both MITI and the Japanese aerospace manufacturers to seek less risky routes into the civil aircraft market, opting instead for participation as sub-contractors and risk-sharing partners.

Mitsubishi, Kawasakii, Fuji and other leading Japanese aerospace manufacturers undertook sub-contract work, often involving major sub-assemblies such as entry doors, rudders, flaps and wing ribs on major US civil airliners including the Lockheed L-1011, Mcdonnell-Douglas DC 10 and Boeing 747, 737 and 757 airliners (Todd and Simpson, 1986). At the start of the 1980s came the first risk- and-revenue-sharing partnership involving a US firm and Japanese aerospace manufacturers, when Mitsubishi, Kawasaki and Fuji took a 15 per cent stake in the development of Boeing's new wide-bodied twin jet, the 767. Once again MITI was heavily involved both in terms of setting up the consortium, Japanese Aircraft Manufacturing Company (JADC), that was to work with Boeing and in providing financial support. Although Boeing retained overall responsibility for the design of the aircraft the Japanese were actively involved for the first time in the development of a major civil airliner. A similar arrangement, though involving a 20 per cent stake, was negotiated for the development of the Boeing 777 (Sabbagh, 1996) in the 1990s. This time JADC was responsible for the development and manufacture of the majority of the fuselage panels and doors, the wing centre section, the wing-to-body fairing and the wing-in-spar ribs (Relman, 1996).

International collaboration has not been confined to commercial aircraft. As far back as 1979 MITI concluded an agreement with Britain's Rolls-Royce to develop a medium-sized jet engine, the RJ500 (Hayward, 1986). A consortium, Japanese Aero Engine Corporation (JAEC), comprising Mitsubishi, Kawasaki and Ishikawajima-Harima, was to be responsible for the Japanese share with substantial financial support from the Japanese government. Although the project was aborted, the collaborative arrangement re-emerged with JAEC joining Rolls-Royce, Pratt and Whitney of the USA, MTU of Germany and Fiat of Italy to develop the V2500 engine for the new Airbus A320 narrow-bodied jet. JAEC's stake in this major joint venture (JV) was 19.9 per cent, with Japanese companies being responsible for the development and manufacture of the engine's fan and low-pressure spool (Gunston, 1995). The V2500 went into service in 1989 and engines are currently being produced at the rate of 300 per year (Birch, 1998). The V2500 has provided the Japanese manufacturers with exposure to engine development on a major engine programme. This has enabled them to negotiate collaborative agreements with the Big Three engine manufacturers to participate in the development of a new class of ultra-high-thrust engines, such as the Rolls-Royce Trent, that came into service in the mid-1990s. These engines represent the pinnacle of jet engine technology at least within the commercial sector. Though their relative shares are small, nonetheless the involvement of Japanese aerospace manufacturers means they are important players within the engine sector.

While the USA remains the dominant aerospace nation and European countries have closed the gap a little, Japan has exhibited a much faster rate of growth over the last decade than either of these trading blocs (Figure 20.2). The rate of growth was such that by the 1990s Japan had emerged from obscurity to be an important centre for aerospace manufacturing with about 3 per cent of the world market (Hayward, 1994). Figure 20.1 shows that Japan has dramatically closed the gap between itself and the leading European aerospace nations France and Britain, having overtaken Germany during the course of the 1990s. However Japan was still heavily dependent on military work. In 1997 military work comprised 70 per cent (SJAC, 1998) of the industry's

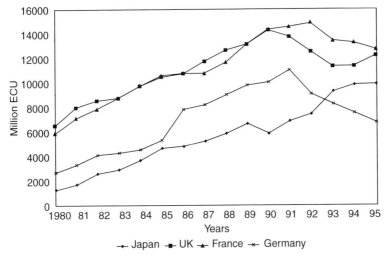

Figure 20.2   Aerospace industry turnover by country, 1980–95
Source: European Commission (1996).

output. Also it was heavily dependent on the USA. Its military work involved the development of derivatives of US designs while in civil work its main partner, Boeing, retained overall design control. In both military and civil fields Japan lacked the capability to design and develop complete aircraft. Despite this, Japan was clearly the leading aerospace nation in South East Asia.

Korea

Korea is a comparative newcomer to aerospace. Its aerospace industry originated in the 1970s when two of Korea's large industrial conglomerates or '*chaebols*' (Steers, Shin and Ungson, 1989), Samsung and Hanjin, diversified into aerospace by setting up aerospace divisions. Samsung Aerospace and Korean Air were established to manufacture US aircraft under licence as part of offset agreements linked to defence contracts.

The scale of the industry and its aerospace capability was still modest when two more chaebols, Daewoo and Hyundai, also established aerospace divisions in the 1980s. Since then expansion has been rapid though the industry is still small by comparison with its Asian neighbour, Japan, and in the early stages of development (Kim, 1996). By the mid-1990s, the Korean aerospace industry ranked fourth in Asia in employment terms. This figure understates the true size of the industry in Korea because it covers the four main manufacturers, but excludes around 100 sub-contractors. Including the aerospace-related employment of such firms places Korea at least on a par with Singapore.

The industry is still heavily dependent on military work, 70 per cent of Daewoo's turnover in 1997 (Lewis, 1998a), for instance, was derived from military contracts. However military work has progressed well beyond licence production involving the assembly of aircraft from kits of parts produced in the USA. The only complete aircraft to be designed and developed in Korea is the KTX-1 turboprop trainer developed by Daewoo and due to enter service with the Korean air force during 2000. Of greater significance, because of the advanced military jet technologies involved, is the Korean Fighter Project (KFP) to develop an indigenous fighter. This project, a joint venture between Samsung Aerospace and General Dynamics of the USA and the largest aerospace programme ever undertaken in Korea, has not only exposed Korean companies to the technologies associated with advanced military jets, it has also provided Samsung Aerospace with much-needed design and development experience.

Progression into the commercial aerospace field has been on the basis of foreign sub-contracting. Daewoo, Samsung Aerospace and Korean Air manufacture major airframe sub-assemblies for large commercial airliners such as the Boeing 747. Korean manufacturers have also turned their attention to Europe, with Daewoo contracted to supply Daimler-Benz Aerospace with fuselage sections for the Airbus A320 (Lewis, 1998a). Just as with military projects, foreign sub-contracting has relied heavily on support and assistance from the Korean government. The 1988 Aerospace Industry Development Act (*Aviation Week and Space Technology*, 1989), underpinned by a desire to bolster national security and promote high-technology industries, set the goal of putting Korea among the top five aerospace nations by 2005 (Bickers, 1998). To assist in achieving this goal, the act tightened offset requirements associated with defence procurement. Consequently Korea's substantial purchases of military aircraft from the USA have resulted in a willingness on the part of Boeing and Lockheed to sub-contract the manufacture of components and sub-assemblies to Korean manufacturers. Though the purchases have been of military aircraft the resulting offset has come to the civil sector. To facilitate such work, Korean manufacturers made major investments in new facilities – Hyundai, for instance invested $350 million in plant and tooling at Seosan, to enable it to undertake the manufacture of wings for Boeing's new 717 regional jet

(Lewis, 1998a). As is normal for Korea's *chaebols*, the funds for this came from the government via the Korean Development Bank (Steers, Shin and Ungson, 1989).

The Korean aerospace industry's progress in both military and civil sectors was badly affected by the Asian financial crisis of the late 1990s, which led to a shortfall in work as military orders were cut. With expensively upgraded manufacturing facilities, Korean manufacturers have sought to fill the gap by increasing the proportion of sub-contracting on civil programmes. This has proved difficult and a government-brokered merger of the aerospace divisions of Samsung, Daewoo and Hyundai led to a single corporate entity in October 1999. This is likely to lead to the rationalization and consolidation of each manufacturer's respective operations at Changwon, Sachon and Seosan. Although this will result in a contraction of the industry, it will strengthen it in the long term by eliminating the duplication of facilities and over-capacity that has resulted from the rapid, government-sponsored growth of the late 1980s and early 1990s.

Taiwan

The origins of the Taiwanese aerospace industry lie in the normalization of US–China relations in the 1970s which left the country to become self-sufficient in many aspects of aircraft manufacture. The importance of defence for a country like Taiwan, combined with the absence of large conglomerates as in Japan and Korea (Chowdhury and Islam, 1993), resulted in the creation of a state-owned aerospace company, the Aerospace Industry Development Corporation (AIDC). Initially under military control, the AIDC began by producing aircraft under licence. Among the aircraft produced in this way were the T-34 trainer built under licence from Beech of the USA and more than 300 Northrop F5 fighters (Shaw, 1996) which still form the mainstay of the Taiwanese airforce. Changes in the American relationship with the People's Republic of China in the 1980s led to the decision to develop the Indigenous Defence Fighter (IDF) known as the Ching-Kuo. This project was seen as the key to enhancing the national capability in aerospace and included a joint venture with Allied Signal to produce the TFE 1042 engine. Although the Ching-Kuo fighter entered service in 1993, the project proved expensive and the government cut back on the number of aircraft ordered.

AIDC currently undertakes offset work for three Western manufacturers – Lockheed, Dassault and Raytheon – in connection with military contracts and has also attempted to collaborate on commercial projects. Despite extensive negotiations with McDonnell-Douglas for a stake in the development of the MD-11 airliner no agreement was ever reached. Similarly negotiations to purchase British Aerospace's regional jet division fell through. However AIDC was able to negotiate a small stake in what has since become the Boeing 717 regional jet (Lewis, 1997a), for which it builds the empennage. Currently it also has 5 per cent stake in the Sikorski S-92 helicopter. Hanman (1997) predicted full privatization of AIDC involving a split into three separate concerns corresponding to its main production sites. However AIDC currently remains a single government owned corporation.

Indonesia

Like several of its Asian neighbours, the Indonesian government from the mid-1970s onwards focused on aerospace as part of its industrial strategy (Todd and Simpson, 1986). However, in contrast to other Asian countries, Indonesia has only one aerospace manufacturer, IPTN.

Established in 1976, IPTN has always been closely linked to the Indonesian government. Until he took over the presidency from Dr Suharto early in 1998, IPTN was run by Dr B.J. Habibie, the Minister of State for Research and Development. His political connections ensured that IPTN enjoyed a very high level of financial and political support. It required the intervention of the International Monetary Fund (IMF) to bring the financial support to an end.

In terms of industrial policy IPTN's remit was to form the basis of a viable aerospace industry. Lacking aerospace experience and expertise, IPTN began by assembling the C-212 commuter aircraft under a licence agreement from the Spanish aerospace manufacturer CASA. Starting from the assembly of knock-down kits, IPTN gradually increased the level of local content until it reached 80 per cent (Todd and Simpson, 1986). Domestic expertise was built up to the point where IPTN was able to supply CASA with wing assemblies. Indonesian-produced C-212s sold well, particularly to other Third World countries that appreciated their rugged if unsophisticated qualities. By the mid-1980s IPTN had extended its operations to include helicopter production, though it continued with a cautious policy of licence production, this time in association with Aerospatiale of France.

Since the mid-1980s IPTN has embarked on much more ambitious projects. In a joint venture with CASA it developed the CN-235, a larger commuter aircraft again suited to the needs of Asian countries with poorly developed transport infrastructures. IPTN's close connections with the Indonesian government again gave it access to very generous financial support, amounting to $1 billion in state aid in the case of the CN-235 (Hayward, 1994).

The third phase of IPTN's development was the acquisition of new technology and the application of acquired and indigenous resources to the design and manufacture of an entirely new product, the N250 turboprop regional airliner. First flown in 1995, this aircraft is due to enter service shortly. By this time IPTN had a workforce of 15 000, making it, in employment terms, the second largest aerospace industry in South East Asia. However the financial crisis that hit Asia in 1997 combined with political unrest, brought IPTN's dramatic rise to an abrupt end. Indonesia's financial rescue by the IMF was predicated on ending state aid to the company, and its survival is likely to rest on its success in negotiating some form of collaboration.

Singapore

Singapore's involvement in aerospace stems from its position as a major trading centre in South East Asia. With a large airforce to protect its position and one of the world's most profitable airlines (Singapore Airlines), the country's aerospace industry, like many others developed initially around overhaul and maintenance (O and M) work. Unlike most other Asian countries its aerospace industry has chosen to specialize in O and M work. Currently the industry has a turnover of $1.1 billion and employs 9500, placing it third among the South East Asian aerospace industries. O and M currently comprises 87 per cent of aerospace output (Lewis, 1998b).

The aerospace industry in Singapore is dominated by Singapore Technologies Aerospace, a $2 billion engineering conglomerate in which the government is a major shareholder. Singapore Technologies Aerospace capability extends to O & M work on both airframes and engines. The rapid growth of air traffic in the region (Hanlon, 1996) combined with Changi airport's location as a regional hub, has stimulated this work and several of the major engine manufacturers now use Singapore as a regional maintenance centre. Singapore Technologies Aerospace also has O & M facilities in the USA. In recent years the company has attempted to diversify into manufacturing. This has extended to the manufacture of major sub-systems, as well as refurbishment and conversion work. In the mid-1980s Singapore Technologies Aerospace began upgrading the Royal Singapore Air Force's older aircraft types and while this continues, it has lately extended to more modern fighters such as the F-16. More recently Singapore Technologies Aerospace has developed its engineering capability in the field of helicopter manufacturing with a 15 per cent stake in the European Eurocopter EC 120 programme. An attempt to move into sub-contracting on major airframe programmes proved less successful when negotiations with Airbus Industrie to build a regional jet, the AE31X, in collaboration with AVIC of China collapsed.

As the major shareholder in Singapore Technologies Aerospace, the government of Singapore has been able to play a significant role in directing the development of the country's aerospace industry, not least through direct investment. As the economy has matured the government's policy has since 1987 been one of gradual privatization and it has reduced its equity stake in a number of government-owned enterprises including Singapore Airlines and Singapore Technologies Aerospace. Today government policy is focused on the 'dual engines of growth' (Islam and Chowdhury, 1997: 206), namely financial and business services and high-technology manufacturing activities. To this end, the government is promoting Singapore as a regional and global hub for service activities such as air transport, hence the particular focus of Singapore's aerospace industry.

Malaysia

Malaysia is the newest recruit to the ranks of the South East Asian nations with an aerospace industry. This is reflected in the size of the industry and its capability. The origins of the industry are closely connected, as in Singapore, to the country's airforce, its national airline Malaysian Airline Systems (MAS) and its location. Currently the industry's capability is confined largely to O and M work. Unlike Singapore this does not extend to refurbishment and conversion work (MITI, 1996). O and M work is undertaken by MAS and AIROD, the latter being a joint venture (JV) in which the US manufacturer Lockheed has a major stake. Created in 1985 to undertake O and M work for the Malaysian air force, it diversified during the 1990s into civilian work for commercial airlines. In this it was helped by the rapid growth of civil aviation in the Asia Pacific region during the decade.

The Malaysian aerospace industry also has a limited manufacturing capability in the field of light aircraft where SME Aviation, a government-owned company, assembles the Swiss single-engine Datwyler MD3-160 trainer (Walters, 1998). SME Aviation has successfully tapped the domestic market and exported the MD3–160 to other Asian nations. Though the industry is still in its infancy with only 3240 employees in 1995 (MITI, 1996), the Malaysian government has identified aerospace as one of the broad areas targeted for development in the future. This extends to seeking to develop aerospace as a 'significant sub-sector of the national economy by the year 2000' (MITI, 1996: 305).

China

China has experience of building Russian aircraft under licence that stretches back to the 1950s (Hayward, 1994). More recently Chinese firms have accrued aerospace expertise through the development of low-budget aircraft for countries that require smaller relatively unsophisticated aircraft. Typical of such projects has been the Y-7 turboprop developed by the Xian Aircraft Corporation (XAC) from the Russian Antonov An-24 (Lewis, 1997b). Latterly China has turned to Western firms to help in enhancing its aerospace capability. China's Shanghai Aviation Industrial Corporation (SAIC) entered into a collaborative agreement with McDonnell-Douglas in the early 1980s to build MD-80 airlines for domestic use as well as supplying parts for McDonnell-Douglas' own production.

As part of China's plans to develop the aerospace industry, a new state enterprise, Aviation Industries of China (AVIC), was formed in 1993 as a consortium of aerospace organizations. AVIC is overseeing a contraction of military production in favour of civil work and is actively pursuing JVs. An example is the JV between the US aero engine manufacturer Pratt and Whitney and Chengdu Engine Company (CEC) a state-owned diversified engineering concern, established in 1996 to produce commercial aircraft engine components.

THE GROWTH OF THE AEROSPACE INDUSTRY IN SOUTH EAST ASIA

Karl Sabbagh (1996), in his study of the making of the Boeing 777, notes that the drawings, coloured to show the national origins of each part, appear to indicate that the Japanese are responsible for manufacturing about half of the aircraft. In fact the actual contribution of the Japanese is nearer 20 per cent, but nonetheless the point is made that South East Asia is now an important centre for aerospace manufacturing and is a contributor to some of the global aerospace industry's most advanced products, a situation very different from that which prevailed 20 or 30 years ago.

At the same time the larger Asian aerospace companies are major players within the global aerospace industry. Four Asian aerospace manufacturers have a turnover in excess of $1 billion per year. One firm, Mitsubishi, is now among the top 20 aerospace firms in the world and three more, Kawasaki, Ishikawajima-Harima and Samsung Aerospace, are not far behind.

The technological capability of South East Asian manufacturers is such that they are now valued contributors to major aircraft projects. They are noted both for their quality and their productivity, key features in the highly competitive aerospace market place. The extent to which they are now accepted and valued can be judged by the number of major aircraft projects, such as the Boeing 777, to which South East Asian manufacturers contribute in some form. Nor are South East Asian aerospace manufacturers confined to a single niche of the aerospace industry. They are to be found in aero engine manufacturing as well as airframe manufacturing.

Although the aerospace industry in this region has made great strides over the last decade in terms of its development, the picture of Asia as a rising star in the aerospace field is subject to a number of qualifications. First, Japan is much the biggest of the aerospace nations of South East Asia. Japan's aerospace industry employs three times the size of comparable competitors such as Singapore and Korea. (Comparison with Indonesia is unrealistic in view of that country's current economic and political problems.) Hence it would be misleading to draw conclusions about Asia on the basis of Japan's performance. Secondly, even Japan has its limitations. Japan is heavily dependent on military work; the proportion of aerospace output going to the military sector may have fallen in recent years, but at 70 per cent in the mid-1990s it is still high by comparison with the USA and Europe. Also Japan, like its neighbours, is not a prime contractor with overall design responsibility on a major aerospace programme. Moreover where it has been a prime contractor in the past, as in the case of the YS-11, it has enjoyed only limited success. Where Japan is involved in collaboration, its share is generally small. Japan has yet to participate in a JV where it is on equal terms with an established US or European aerospace manufacturer. Finally there are major differences in the types of aerospace work undertaken across South East Asia. Countries like Japan and Korea are mainstream aerospace manufacturers. From licence production involving no more than the assembly of kits, they have moved into component and sub-assembly manufacture and have acquired some design and development expertise. Singapore and Malaysia, on the other hand, have taken a different route. With major airline interests based on their location, they have chosen to specialize in O and M work. With air traffic in the Asia Pacific region growing faster than anywhere else in the world, this strategy clearly has much to commend it. However, what it means is that the aerospace industries across South East Asia are not necessarily pursuing the same pattern of development. There is considerable diversity, with Singapore and Malaysia operating in a specific niche, and assessments of aerospace in the region have clearly to take this into account.

INDUSTRIAL POLICY AND COLLABORATION

In accounting for the rapid rise of the aerospace industry in South East Asia, the two factors that stand out as being of overwhelming importance in facilitating industrial development are the role of government and the role of collaborative programmes.

Across South East Asia governments have sought aerospace as though it were the jewel in the crown of industrial development, its desirability reflecting its perceived value both in terms of support for military priorities and scope for technology transfer. Exactly how governments have pursued this particular jewel has varied. Japan, Korea, Indonesia, Malaysia and Singapore all identified aerospace as a strategic industry and incorporated it into their plans for industrialization and economic development. In the case of Japan and Korea these plans sought to encourage industrial enterprises to develop aerospace interests. The encouragement took the form of government assistance in bringing firms together to create consortia and the provision of generous financial support. The financial support ranged from funds for the construction of new plants to funding of R&D and subsidizing manufacturing. While the forms of support varied, the level of generosity did not. An alternative strategy was applied in Singapore and Malaysia where the limited scale of the industrial base resulted in state ownership, initially at least, of aerospace concerns. Underpinning both routes to aerospace development has been extensive use of military procurement. This has allowed Asian manufacturers to build up aerospace expertise even when production economies would have made the purchase of aircraft 'off the shelf' much cheaper. Unfortunately heavy dependence on military work has meant that while firms have acquired technological expertise they have not built up their commercial expertise in areas such as marketing and product support.

Just as strong support from government has been a feature of the development of aerospace industries across Asia so, in various forms, has collaboration. If the definition of 'collaboration' is extended to licensed production, then collaboration has been used throughout South East Asia. However using a narrower definition confined to risk-and-revenue-sharing partnerships and JVs, which comes much closer to collaboration among equals, then collaboration has been used more selectively. Really only Japan has been a successful proponent of this type of collaboration, through its involvement in Boeing programmes such as the 767 and the 777. Other countries have found the collaborative route more difficult. Many have developed small-scale collaborative projects, particularly in the field of helicopter production, but have been unable to realize their ambitions on major civil airliner programmes. Korea, Singapore, Taiwan and China have all tried to engage in collaboration with Western aerospace manufacturers on major airliner projects, but have failed to negotiate an enduring agreement.

Hence while close government involvement has been universal, the same cannot be said of collaboration.

CONCLUSIONS

The last 20 years has seen a transformation of aerospace manufacturing in South East Asia, in terms of both scale and proficiency. The scale of aerospace manufacturing in the region has grown dramatically: four Asian aerospace manufacturers have a turnover in excess of $1 billion per year. Not only have Asian manufacturers grown rapidly, their technological capability has also been much enhanced. Most of the major manufacturers have gone from licence production, where they did little more than assemble parts produced by the major Western manufacturers, to responsibility for the manufacture of major components and sub-assemblies. The technological capability of East Asian manufacturers is such that they are now valued contributors to major aircraft projects. They are noted both for their quality and their productivity, key features in the highly competitive aerospace marketplace.

Key factors in bringing about this growth have been government support and inter-firm collaboration. Government support has been a feature of all the countries of South East Asia and it has extended not only to generous financial support but also to political support. Indeed, few countries in the region have not sought to nurture aerospace as a major part of their economic development (Donne, 1997). A feature of the collaboration that has taken place is that alliances with major prime contractors from the West have generally been more productive than regionally-based collaboration.

Despite the rapid growth of aerospace industries in Asia, especially over the last 10 years, it is unlikely that Asian manufacturers will pose a major threat to Western manufacturers in the near future. The aerospace industry in South East Asia is still very diverse, even in Japan the aerospace industry is divided among four major firms. Although the leading aerospace producers have begun to achieve parity with equivalent firms in the West, in terms of their technological capability, none has had significant experience of overall programme leadership, with the result that they lack both systems integration and marketing and product support skills. Furthermore there is still heavy dependence on military work and little in the way of collaboration between Asian manufacturers.

References

Aviation Week and Space Technology (1989) 'Korean Aerospace Firms Seek Greater Role in World Market', 12 June, 201–6.

Bickers, C. (1998) 'Clipped Wings: South Korea's Crisis Grounds its Jet-building Plans', *Far Eastern Economic Review*, 29 January, 49.

Birch, D. (1998) 'International Thrust – V2500: Derivative Engineering at its Best', *Air International*, 54 (6), 367–9.

Chowdhury, A. and Islam, I. (1993) *The Newly Industrialising Economies of East Asia*, London, Routledge.

Donne, M. (1997) 'Risks Shared for Future Rewards', Aerospace Industry Survey, *Financial Times*, 12 June, 11.

Endres, G. (1996) 'NAMC YS-11: The Japanese Commuter', *Air International*, July, 22–7.

European Commission (1996) *The European Aerospace Industry 1996*, Brussels, European Commission.

Gunston, B. (1995) *World Encyclopaedia of Aero Engines*, 3rd edn, Sparkford, Patrick Stephens.

Hanlon, P. (1996) *Global Airlines: Competition in a Transnational Industry*, Oxford, Butterworth–Heinemann.

Hanman, B. (1997) 'Changing the Guard', *Flight International*, 152(4564), 5–11 March, 49–50

Hayward, K. (1986) *International Collaboration in Civil Aerospace*, London, Pinter.

Hayward, K. (1994) *The World Aerospace Industry: Competition and Collaboration*, London, Duckworth.

Heppenheimer, T.A. (1995) *Turbulent Skies: The History of Commercial Aviation*, New York, John Wiley.

Islam, I. and Chowdhury, A. (1997) *Asia-Pacific Economies: A Survey*, London, Routledge.

Kim, S.C. (1996) 'Cleared for Take-off', *Business Korea*, 13(10), 46–8.

Lewis, P. (1997a) 'Asians Bid for AI(R) Jet Places', *Flight International*, 151 (4566), 19–25 March, 8.

Lewis, P. (1997b) 'Time out in Asia', *Flight International*, 152(4599), 5–11 November, 38–40.

Lewis, P. (1998a) 'Compromise and Change', *Flight International*, 154(4648), 21–27 October, 42–4.

Lewis, P. (1998b) 'Singapore Support', *Flight International*, 153(4613), 18–24 February, 69–70.

MITI (1996) *The Second Industrial Master Plan (1996–2005)*, Ministry of International Trade and Industry, Kuala Lumpur.

Mowery, D. and Rosenberg, N. (1985) 'Commercial Aircraft: Cooperation and Competition Between the US and Japan', *California Management Review*, 27(4), 70–92.

Piggott, J. and Cook, M. (1993), *International Business Economics: A European Perspective,* London, Longman.

Relman, P. (1996) 'Three Sevens for Twenty-one . . . ', *Air International*, 51(6), 349–56.

Sabbagh, K. (1996) *21st Century Jet: The Making of the Boeing 777*, London, Pan.

Shaw, R. (1996) 'Taiwan – The Dawn of Modernisation', *Air International*, 50(2), 102–8.

SJAC (1998) *Aerospace Industry in Japan*, Society of Japanese Aerospace Companies Inc., Tokyo.

Steers, R.M., Shin, Y.K. and Ungson, G.R. (1989) *The Chaebol: Korea's New Industrial Might*, Cambridge, MA, Ballinger.

Todd, D. and Simpson, J. (1986) *The World Aircraft Industry*, London, Croom Helm.

Walters, B. (1998) 'Hold that Tiger', *Air International*, 54 (2), 81–5.

21 The Asian Crisis: The End of an Economic Miracle?

Hua Li and Frank McDonald

INTRODUCTION

Before the onset of the Asian crisis the high growth rates and impressive export performance of many of the South East Asian countries led some commentators to proclaim that they had discovered the secret of sustained economic growth (Wade, 1992). Countries such as Hong Kong, Singapore, Indonesia, South Korea, Malaysia and Thailand were given the title of 'Asian Tigers' because of their ability to sustain high growth and to capture an ever-expanding share of the world market for manufactured products. The 'Asian Tigers' were seen as dynamic economies following in the footsteps of Japan and destined to become major centres of economic activity. The Asian economic miracle was considered to be based on cultures that encouraged hard work and a collaborative approach to the conduct of business activities (Dore, 1987). The co-operative arrangements between governments, banks and companies enabled the mobilization of labour and capital and access to appropriate technologies and contributed to the success of the 'Asian Tigers' (World Bank, 1993).

The high growth of the Asian economies focused attention on the 'Asian way' of operating a capitalist system. In business and management circles the 'Asian way' attracted many advocates, especially for the lean production systems developed in Japan (Imai, 1986; Womack, Jones and Roos, 1990). The twenty-first century was to be the century of Asia, with economic activity centred on the Pacific Rim countries with Japan and the Asian Tigers becoming the engines of the world economy (Houseman, 1995; see also Chapter 1 in this volume). The arrival of first Japanese and then South East Asian companies in the USA and in Europe confirmed the view that the 'Asian way' contained important lessons for moribund industries in the West. The *laissez-faire* approach of Anglo–Saxon economies and the social regulation of

continental Europe were considered to be incapable of delivering competitiveness and reform of these systems was advocated based on the
adoption of the key characteristics of the Asian version of capitalism
(Channon, 1998). This attitude was expressed by the Dean of the Sloan
School of Management who wrote that the Asian form of capitalism
was superior to American capitalism (Thurow, 1992).

However, in the 1990s the Japanese economy experienced a series of
banking crises that led to low growth in the real economy. In these
crises the Japanese government clearly demonstrated that it was incapable of taking decisive action to stabilize the system. Moreover, the close
collaboration between governments, banks and companies appeared to
worsen the problems in the Japanese economy because the interdependence between agents prevented the necessary restructuring of financial
and corporate structures. In the same period old-fashioned American
capitalism was delivering high non-inflationary growth and a stream of
new high-growth industries based on new technologies. Against this
background the Asian crisis raised doubts about the superiority of the
'Asian way'.

Nevertheless, the extent of the crisis surprised even those who had
doubts about the reality of the Asian economic miracle.

> It seems safe to say that nobody anticipated anything like the current
> crisis in Asia. True, there were some Asia sceptics – including myself –
> who regarded the claims of an Asian economic miracle as overstated,
> and argued that Asia was bound to run into diminishing returns
> eventually. And some people – again including myself – raised warning
> flags a year or two before the Thai crisis, noting that the current
> account deficits of South East Asian countries were as high as or higher
> than those of Latin America, and arguing that Asian economies had
> no special immunity to financial crises. But even pessimists expected
> something along the lines of a conventional currency crisis followed
> by at most a modest downturn, and we expected the longer-term
> slowdown in growth to emerge only gradually. What we have actually
> seen is something both more complex and more drastic: collapses in
> domestic asset markets, widespread bank failures, bankruptcies on
> the part of many firms, and what looks likely to be a much more
> severe real downturn than even the most negative-minded antici-
> pated. (Krugman, 1998)

The severity of the crisis raises questions about the wisdom of Western
countries following the 'Asian way'. The Anglo–Saxon way – or, more

accurately, the 'American way' – is increasingly being seen as the best system to follow to prosper in modern capitalism. At the very least American- or Western-type regulation of financial markets is seen as essential to avoid crises of the type that afflicted the 'Asian Tigers' (see, for example, Chapter 2 in this volume). The close collaboration between governments, banks and companies has also been identified as leading to moral hazard. The close collaboration between banks and governments resulted in implicit contracts that banks would be bailed out if they encountered difficulties and the growth of interdependence of banks and companies based on high indebtedness to a small number of banks. This 'crony capitalism' limited sound financial assessment of investments and encouraged a deepening of relationships between banks and companies that led to overinvestment with many projects providing low or negative returns. However, rising demand for exports and high asset prices encouraged investment in the hope of adequate returns in the long term (Krugman, 1998). However, others have questioned laying all the blame for the crisis on deficiencies in the 'Asian way'. The crisis exposed weaknesses in the international financial system arising from the liberalization of financial markets and the consequent explosion in short-term capital flows. George Soros, a major figure in the short-run capital markets, considers that the international financial system was responsible for the Asian and other currency crises. He also regards the system as inherently unstable and potentially ruinous to the health of the world economy (Soros, 1998). Academic writers have also identified crucial weaknesses in the international financial system (Furman and Stiglitz, 1998; Krugman, 1999).

This chapter examines the Asian crisis to identify the main causes of the financial and economic meltdown and assesses if the problems of the 'Asian Tigers' are rooted in the characteristics of the 'Asian way'. On the basis of this examination an assessment is made on what managers and management and business academics can learn from the Asian crisis.

THE UNFOLDING OF THE CRISIS

The crisis began in Thailand in July 1997 when capital flight led to pressure on the currency, the baht, the markets also began selling other South East Asian currencies and Thailand, Malaysia and Indonesia experienced significant devaluations (Table 21.1). Capital flight spread to include South Korea and the Philippines. Hong Kong and Singapore

Table 21.1　Some key events in the unfolding of the Asian crisis,
July 1997–May 1998

1997	
July	Thai currency (baht) devalued by 20 per cent against the dollar and the Philippine peso by 10 per cent. Malaysia abandons the defence of its currency (ringitt) and it devalues by around 10 per cent.
August	Mahathir Mohamed, the Prime Minister of Malaysia, blames George Soros for creating the crisis by speculating against the currencies of South East Asian economies. Malaysia begins to place curbs on the operations of international money and capital markets.
October	The Hong Kong stock exchange experiences a 40 per cent reduction in equity prices, but the currency board manages to defend the parity of the *HK* dollar.
November	South Korea abandons the fight to maintain the value of the won and substantial devaluation follows. The government of Thailand resigns after civil unrest and widespread dissatisfaction over the lack of action by the government to stabilize the economic situation.
December	The South Korean government and the IMF continue to disagree over an aid package, despite large-scale bankruptcies and bad debt portfolios in the banking sector and large-scale financial problems among the 30 largest *chaebol* (large conglomerate corporations).
1998	
February	The Indonesian government estimate that 10 per cent of the workforce will be unemployed by the end of the year.
March	The eighth largest *chaebol* in South Korea (Kia Group) is put in the hands of a consortium of banks in an attempt to avoid bankruptcy.
May	Six students are killed in a protest rally in Indonesia about the handling of the crisis by the government. These pressures eventually lead to a new government in Indonesia.

also became entangled in the crisis, but they did not suffer the collapse of currencies and financial systems that afflicted many of the Asian Tigers. The crisis started in Thailand, but rapidly spread to other South East Asian countries' currencies and banking and financial services industries. The resultant financial crisis spilled over into the real economy and led to political and social upheaval (see Table 21.1). The first phase of the crisis originated in the banking system when it became clear that many Asian countries had serious current account deficits and that property and stock markets had grossly inflated prices that could not be sustained. These factors placed many Asian banks in danger of significant default on debt. Moreover, many financial institutions held significant levels of equity on their balance sheets and when share prices fell the financial position of these institutions deteriorated, thereby further undermining confidence in the system. Weaknesses in the regulation and control of the banking system also undermined confidence in the financial system of the 'Asian Tigers'.

The second phase of the crisis was triggered when foreign investors lost confidence in the ability of countries such as Thailand and Indonesia to stabilize their financial systems. The loss of confidence led to capital flight that put downward pressure on currencies. These pressures quickly led to the significant devaluation of currencies that heralded the third phase of the crisis.

As currencies devalued, banks and companies found the value of their assets (valued in local currency) plummeted while much of their debt was denominated in dollars. This worsened the financial condition of banks and companies. The deteriorating financial position spread to the real economy as plunging asset prices lowered the wealth of people and organizations, leading to a fall in consumption and investment. The collapse of confidence induced investors to withdraw assets from banks and other financial institutions, thereby creating a downward spiral of falling asset prices that further undermined financial systems. This led to more cutbacks in consumption, a halt to new investments and the cancellation of many projects. This led to the crisis spilling over into the real sector, resulting in a rise in company failures and large-scale loss of markets. These factors led to rising unemployment that further lowered consumption. This set in motion a downward spiral of falling asset prices leading to falling confidence that led to capital flight that further reduced asset prices. For a time it seemed that the 'Asian Tigers' were in free fall and the search for a means to stabilize the crisis seemed to elude governments, banks and the corporate sector.

The crisis began to stabilize when the IMF organized rescue packages and when the fall in asset prices reached the level where it became profitable to acquire real assets at a fraction of their pre-crisis value. By the end of 1998 the South East Asian countries had attained a degree of stability that stopped the downward spiral in asset prices and of the value of currencies. However, in the aftermath of the crisis the 'Asian

Tigers' were in poor shape, with high unemployment, low investment and substantial restructuring of debt that hampered the ability of companies to obtain funds for investment. These countries face the twenty-first century with very severe financial and economic problems. The crisis highlighted a number of weaknesses in the structure of the economies of the 'Asian Tigers' that took some of the shine off the Asian economic miracle.

THE IMF RESCUE PACKAGE

The IMF recognized that there were significant differences in the economic conditions in the countries of South East Asia. In Thailand, the current account deficit as a proportion of GDP was high compared to South Korea or Indonesia. Corporate debt–equity ratios (gearing ratios) also varied between the 'Asian Tigers'. The highest gearing ratios were in South Korea (600) and Thailand (300) with much lower ratios in Malaysia (170), Indonesia (200) and the Philippines (170). External debt in 1996 ranged from 50 per cent of GDP in Thailand to 33 per cent in South Korea. However, external debt as a proportion of the value of the exports of goods and services ranged from 102 per cent in South Korea to 41 per cent in Malaysia (Stone and Kochhar, 1998). The attitude of governments to the IMF's reforms also varied. Some countries (Thailand and South Korea) waited until their reserves were exhausted before they called in the IMF, while Indonesia and the Philippines sought help early in the crisis. South Korea resisted the proposed IMF package for many months and the governments of Indonesia and Thailand experienced significant difficulties in implementing the IMF reforms (Fischer, 1998).

Despite these differences in economic and political conditions, the IMF adopted a similar approach to the crisis countries. The rescue packages were based on three main planks:

- Substantially increasing *short-term interest rates* to stabilize the currencies of the 'Asian Tigers' by increasing the returns on assets denominated in these currencies
- *Reforming banking systems* by introducing internationally accepted accounting and disclosure practices and by developing effective financial regulation and supervision by governments

- *Tightening fiscal policy* to provide funds to cover the cost of financial restructuring and to help to correct current account deficits.

In the area of fiscal policy the IMF followed different approaches based on the size of government budget deficits. Countries such as Thailand that had a large fiscal deficit had to adopt a tough stance on fiscal policy whereas in Indonesia, where the government budget was considered to be under control, only minor adjustments were required (Fischer, 1998).

The approach of the IMF has been criticized as being inappropriate, inadequate and misguided. The latter objection is a type of 'moral-hazard' argument on the same lines as the controversy that surrounds the cancelling of Third World debt. To avoid reckless behaviour in the future the 'moral-hazard' argument favours no or little help. Such action provides incentives for countries and investors not to allow greed, ineptitude and corruption to lead to crisis. However, the reason for bailing out the Asian economies was that they had substantial trading, investment and financial links with the West that threatened to transfer the crisis to the USA and Europe. The argument that the rescue packages of the IMF were inadequate is based on the limited funds that the Fund provided to support the currencies of the crisis economies. This led to calls for large-scale increases in the capital base of the IMF. This approach has not gathered significant support (Fischer, 1998). However, the main opposition has been that the rescue packages have been inappropriate (Furman and Stiglitz, 1998; Griffiths-Jones, Cailloux Pfaffenzeller, 1998). The austerity packages of the IMF increased interest rates, closed banks and tightened fiscal policy with only limited help to restructure bad debt. These policies added to the problems of the crisis economies by further reducing demand and thus contributing to the downward spiral in economic activity. The critics also complain that the IMF failed to accept that weaknesses in the international financial system were at least partly to blame for the crisis. The IMF appeared to learn some lessons from the crisis and by the time of the second rescue package for South Korea in December 1997 the focus was on restructuring debt with less emphasis on increasing interest rates and tightening fiscal policy. This policy had a quick and effective impact on the South Korean currency (Radelet and Sachs, 1998). The IMF rescue packages eventually stabilized the crisis, but at a high cost in terms of company failures and subsequent depression of the real economies of the Asian economies. Furthermore, the problems caused by failings in international capital markets received little attention from the IMF.

CAUSES OF THE CRISIS

Five main theories have been advanced to explain the underlying reasons for the crisis:

1. *Overheated economies*, with large external deficits and property and stock market bubbles that sustained unrealistic expectation about the prospects for future growth
2. *Weak prudential rules and regulatory systems*, that led to high risk loan portfolios
3. *Fixed exchange rates*, that encouraged high dollar-denominated borrowing and contributed to the speculative frenzy when fundamental weaknesses in the Asian economies became evident
4. *Over-investment*, arising from 'moral-hazard' problems of implicit contracts, anticipated bailouts and strong interdependency that existed between governments, banks and companies
5. *Contagion in financial markets*, that rapidly spread the crisis across the 'Asian Tigers'.

Overheated Economies

In the 1980s the 'Asian Tigers' experienced rapid growth, high investment and strong export performance. This was accompanied by rising current account deficits and high external debt, especially short-term debt. Export growth slowed in 1996 because of real exchange rate appreciation (see below), high growth of wages in export industries, increased competition from China and Latin American countries, low growth in Japan and falling prices for products such as semiconductors, clothing, footwear and textiles (Hussain and Radelet, 1999). The large fall in the prices of semiconductors and other computer-related hardware badly affected the 'Asian Tigers' because they had invested heavily in these areas (Stone and Kochhar, 1998). When export growth slowed down, governments in the 'Asian Tigers' did not take action to dampen economic activity and investments were channelled into property and production facilities for domestic consumption. However, large investments in plant for the export market continued in areas such as computing equipment and semiconductors despite overcapacity in these markets and falling prices. Property and stock market booms were fuelled by buoyant domestic demand bolstered by high levels of investment and rising income levels. In Indonesia, for example, between 20 and 25 per cent of bank debt was allocated to property deals, with 15–20 per cent in the Philippines, Malaysia and Thailand (Ranis and Stewart, 1998). When property and equity prices collapsed banks and financial institutions were faced with a high level of bad debt that undermined their balance sheets. The combination of surging asset prices and investment in the face of falling demand for exports (the main drivers of growth in the 'Asian Tigers') could not be sustained. However, the governments of these countries failed to take appropriate macroeconomic policies to curb their booming economies. This was perhaps because they believed the rhetoric of those who claimed that the 'Asian Tigers' had learned the secret of continual growth and that they were somehow immune from the problems of balancing economic activity that afflicted the developed economies.

Weak Prudential Rules and Regulatory Systems

The Bank for International Settlements (BIS) identified a series of shortcomings in the banking systems of the 'Asian Tigers', including excessive expansion of loans, inadequate prudential rules and inappropriate regulatory systems, particularly to manage the new conditions that emerged after financial liberalization (BIS, 1997). Financial liberalization gave South East Asian banks access to a large pool of short-term capital. The banks took advantage of this new-found liberty and dramatically increased foreign borrowing. In Thailand the foreign liabilities of banks rose from 5 per cent of GDP in 1990 to 28 per cent in 1995 (Radelet and Sachs, 1998). However, not all South East Asian banks experienced such a rise in foreign borrowing. Nevertheless, in many of the 'Asian Tigers' external corporate debt rose dramatically and much of the debt was in the form of short-term capital flows (Stone and Kochhar, 1998). Failure to control the banking and financial sector led to large increases in foreign indebtedness (much of it short-term), which meant that the collapse of confidence by foreign investors led to severe problems for the sector. Moreover, poor assessment of the potential returns from investments led to a large portfolio of bad debt. These factors contributed to a lack of confidence in Asian financial systems to adjust to the new conditions brought about by financial liberalization, low export growth and rising current account deficits. When the crisis broke, the banking and financial system was in a poor state to handle the financial implications of economies that were not experiencing fast growth and ever-rising asset prices.

Fixed Exchange Rates

All of the 'Asian Tigers' fixed their exchange rates to the dollar. This encouraged large-scale borrowing (denominated in dollars) because exchange rate risk was perceived to be low. The large dollar borrowings allowed a domestic investment boom to be financed. However, real exchange rates were not fixed and they altered in response to the boom in domestic economic conditions. The foreign price of tradable goods and services was fixed because of pegged exchange rates, but the price of non-tradable goods and services, especially property and construction, rose on the back of the booming economic conditions. This forced up domestic prices and thereby increased the domestic price of exports, directly leading to higher export prices owing to the fixed exchange rate. This led to appreciation of the real exchange rate (the ratio of the price of exports to the price of imports). The over-valuation of real exchange rates was estimated to be as high as 20 per cent for Thailand, Indonesia, Malaysia and the Philippines (Radelet, and Sachs, 1999). This was a substantial decline in the competitiveness of the 'Asian Tigers' at a time when they also faced declining demand for their products on world markets. Furthermore, the commitment to defend the dollar parity of currencies led to a rapid depletion of reserves when the crisis began. This further intensified the crisis, because once reserves were depleted a devaluation became a 'one-way bet' for currency speculators. The commitment to fixed exchange rates arose from a desire to reduce exchange rate risk and thereby to promote exporting activities. Fixed exchange rates also helped to curb inflation tendencies in the 'Asian Tigers' by linking their monetary policies to the low inflation performance of the USA. However, this policy also permitted the financing of bubbles in the property and stock markets and undermined the competitiveness of the 'Asian Tigers'. Furthermore, pegged exchange rates systems encouraged strong speculative pressures when the reserves of the Asian economies were depleted.

Overinvestment

The co-operative arrangements between governments, banks and companies, combined with large-scale foreign investments, facilitated rapid capital accumulation in the 'Asian Tigers'. In the early 1990s rising investment levels accounted for about 40 per cent of GDP in South Korea, Malaysia and Thailand (IMF, 1998). Determination of the correct level of investment for a country is very difficult; empirical work has provided support for the argument that overinvestment took place in the 'Asian Tigers'. Studies indicate that accumulation of capital and labour was the most important factor in their growth while improvements in productivity were of lesser importance (Bosworth and Collins, 1996). Total factor productivity (TFP) increases played a considerably less important role in the growth of the 'Asian Tigers' than had been the case when Japan and the European economies went through their period of technological catch-up in the 1950s and 1960s (Crafts, 1998). The large levels of investment were accompanied by increasing incremental capital–output ratios (ICORs), indicating that capital accumulation was not boosting productivity sufficiently to offset diminishing returns from investments. Only in Hong Kong and Singapore was the development of more capital-intensive production methods sufficient to explain rising ICORs (IMF, 1998). In these economies rising ICORs was due to the move towards production systems that required more capital per unit of output. However, in the other 'Asian Tigers' rising ICORs indicated that productivity growth was not sufficient to justify the level of capital accumulation that was taking place. In the period 1960–90, Singapore's average rate of growth was 8.4 per cent per year, but only 4 per cent of this annual growth was due to increasing TFP. The remaining 96 per cent of growth originated from the application of capital and labour to new production processes. As most of the capital invested embodied the latest technology, the 'Asian Tigers' were able to achieve remarkable increases in output. However, very little of their growth arose from improvements in the use of capital and labour. In the same period in Mexico 42 per cent of annual average growth came from increases in TFP and in Brazil the figure was 28 per cent (Krugman, 1994). These Latin American economies were able to boost growth not only by the application of capital, labour and new technology, but also from improving the productivity of capital and labour. This implies that the 'Asian Tigers' were not efficient machines that could deliver competitiveness owing to the inherent advantages of the 'Asian way'. Blame for overinvestment has been placed on 'moral hazard' arising from implicit understandings that governments would bail out banks that ran into problems with bad debt. In these circumstances incentives are provided to undertake very risky investments on the grounds that failure will not lead to large-scale losses (Fischer, 1998; Krugman, 1998). Furthermore, the close collaboration between governments, banks and companies created interdependence between these agencies that made it difficult to take action that would harm one or more of them. In countries such as Indonesia, close family ties between leading members of the government, banks and companies further increased the interdependence and thereby made it more difficult to take action to curb overinvestment.

Contagion

The onset of the crisis in Thailand led to large-scale disinvestment and this process rapidly spread to the other 'Asian Tigers'. The shock in the Thai financial markets rapidly transmitted to other markets as financial panic set in among investors (Baig and Goldfajn, 1998). Initially, many commentators attributed the 'contagion phenomenon' to rational actions by investors who considered that all of the 'Asian Tigers' faced similar problems. Alternatively, the transactions cost of checking conditions in each of the 'Asian Tigers' was too high and therefore disinvestment was the least-cost policy to follow. The main cause of the contagion was seen to be concern about overinvestment owing to 'moral hazard' combined with overvalued currencies and inept and incompetent government policies (Fischer, 1998; Krugman, 1998). However, the extent of the crisis and its spread to include healthy economies such as Hong Kong led to a view that the financial markets had acted in panic and that a herd instinct developed that led to contagion across Asian markets (Radelet and Sachs, 1998; Griffiths-Jones, Cailloux, and Pfaffenzeller, 1998). Krugman, who had originally thought that the crisis was largely due to 'moral hazard', changed his mind and argued that contagion based on irrational herd behaviour in the markets was a major cause of its depth and extent (Krugman, 1999).

LESSONS FROM THE CRISIS

Most of the problems that have been identified as causing the Asian crisis are rooted in weaknesses in the financial sector in the 'Asian Tigers' and with problems concerning the operation of international capital markets. The main areas that call into question weaknesses in the real economy are overinvestment and low growth in TFP. The first problem is connected to financial markets because 'crony capitalism' links governments, banks and companies into a set of interdependencies that encourage reckless investments and make it difficult to stop overinvestment. There is also evidence that the 'Asian Tigers' were not good at improving TFP by making effective use of capital and labour in production processes. The main source of growth in the 'Asian Tigers' was from the accumulation of capital and labour. High levels of capital accumulation (embodied with the latest technology) resulted in large increases in output, but did not guarantee that capital and labour was used the best way possible. In this respect, there is some evidence that the Asian economic miracle is a myth and Western companies would be unwise to unreservedly adopt the 'Asian way' (Krugman, 1994).

Clearly the high growth rate of the 'Asian Tigers' was not primarily due to the discovery of new and efficient ways of organizing economic activities, but was mainly the result of large injections of capital and labour. However, many developing economies in other parts of the world also had problems with overinvestment, as measured by rising ICORs, but they did not suffer financial crisis. Therefore, it is difficult to see why the crisis had such a devastating effect among the South East Asian countries given that some of them did not have as serious problems as Thailand or Indonesia. Furthermore, close collaboration between governments, banks and companies that permits large scale-capital accumulation with low or even negative rates of return is not limited to the 'Asian Tigers'. Neither are poorly regulated financial systems, corruption and nepotism confined to South East Asian countries (Furman and Stiglitz, 1998; Radelet and Sachs, 1998). If 'crony capitalism' leading to overinvestment and imprudent lending activities was the source of the crisis it is hard to see how countries such as China, Russia and many Latin American countries were not also entangled. It is true that Russia, Argentina and Brazil suffered from currency crises in 1998–9, but these were not blamed on 'crony capitalism' or imprudent lending by banks.

In many quarters the crisis is seen to stem from problems in the banking and financial sectors in Asian countries and from large scale short-term investments from the advanced industrial countries (Griffith-Jones, Cailloux and Pfaffenzeller, 1998; Radelet and Sachs, 1998). Minford (Chapter 2 in this volume) places the blame for the crisis on poor macroeconomic management in Japan and the 'Asian Tigers' and a failure to institute prudent management of the banking sector. The first reaction of Krugman was to blame overinvestment arising from 'moral hazard' as the source of the crisis (Krugman, 1998). However, he now sees the crisis as revealing major shortcomings in the operation of international capital markets (Krugman, 1999). George Soros concluded that the Asian crisis was caused by capital flight driven by irrational and unstable capital markets (Soros, 1998). Increasingly, the crisis is being seen as primarily arising from regulatory problems in the banking and financial services industry in Asian countries and from unstable and irrational short-run capital movements (Radelet and Sachs, 1999), the latter problem emerging from the liberalization of financial markets that gave the 'Asian Tigers' access to the global capital market. In this view the solution to the crisis and the road to recovery requires reform of the banking and financial system in the 'Asian Tigers' and changing the 'international financial architecture' to curb the caprices of the global capital market.

This analysis suggests that Western companies may still have much to learn from the 'Asian way' in terms of developing more collaborative relationships in their business operations and in cultivating a team spirit among the workforce. Adoption of Asian characteristics such as building networks that engender trust and developing social norms that encourage investment in education and that promote the value of hard work may be helpful to develop competitiveness without recourse to socially divisive policies. The identification of global capital markets as irrational and unstable reinforces the view that capitalism driven solely by the pursuit of profit can be harmful for human welfare. However, the crisis revealed major shortcomings with the 'Asian way' and the social costs of the crisis resulted in substantial costs in terms of human misery and poverty (Ranis and Stewart, 1998). It is not clear if the 'Asian way' provides a good model of how to successfully operate in a modern capitalist system. Moreover, one of the key elements of the 'Asian way' was the close co-operation between governments, banks and companies; this, however, appears to lead to 'crony capitalism' with a built-in tendency to overinvest. Furthermore, the 'Asian way' seems to provide few incentives for companies to pursue strategies that improve the productivity of capital and labour by using these inputs more intelligently.

It is likely that reform of the financial systems of the 'Asian Tigers' will curb the problem of 'moral hazard' by the introduction of Western-style prudential rules and new regulatory frameworks for the financial sector. The development of such systems will undermine the ability of the 'Asian Tigers' to engage in large-scale accumulations of capital and labour. In the future it is likely that the Asian economies will have to search for growth by the intelligent use of capital and labour – in effect, the same way that the advanced industrial economies must follow to achieve growth. The Asian crisis may have created a conflict between making use of foreign capital flows and continuing the system of 'crony capitalism' that has existed in the 'Asian Tigers'. Western investors chose to deal with the uncertainties connected to investing into relatively closed 'crony-capitalism' systems in Asia by short-term capital investments that could be easily pulled out if risks became unacceptable. The costs experienced when they removed these investments when the financial crisis occurred may reduce the willingness of Western investors again to commit large capital flows to the 'Asian Tigers'. Reforms of their financial systems would make it easier for Western investors to monitor financial performance and therefore to encourage less emphasis on long-term investments with low returns. In these circumstances 'crony capitalism' will not survive in South East Asia. However, the close relationship between governments, banks and companies that characterized the 'crony capitalism' did generate benefits by mobilizing capital, labour and technology leading to significant development of economic structures.

Problems with 'crony capitalism' emerged when the 'Asian Tigers' financed substantial amounts of their investments by use of short-term capital flows from the international capital markets. At this stage, two fundamentally different financial systems became linked. Asian systems placed strong emphasis on long-term close relationship-based finance that focused on maximizing value on the assumption of high asset prices and ever-expanding growth. In contrast, international capital markets are based on arm's-length relationships that are centred on risk assessment on the basis of current and expected prices. Asian financial systems provide a good way to mobilize capital, labour and technology that enables rapid economic development to take place. However, Western systems are geared to short-term investments when it is difficult to accurately assess risk. Long-term investments are normally undertaken only when risk can be measured and risk premiums added to compensate for the uncertainty surrounding investments. Alternatively investment can take the form of direct foreign investment (DFI) that allows investors to have substantial control over investments. International capital flows are not as good as Asian systems in providing large-scale, long-term, investments in developing economies, especially when FDI is difficult to undertake.

Countries such as Thailand, Indonesia and the Philippines are less well developed than Hong Kong, Singapore or South Korea. The former countries may have much to gain from continuing a type of 'crony capitalism' that will help them reach a higher level of development. However, the more advanced economies of South East Asian need to be more focused on improving TFP and allocating investments to achieve such results. This probably requires the development of a more Western-type approach to investment and to a curbing of 'crony capitalism'. Larger use of FDI may also be a means of attracting capital and technology that is able to boost TFP.

Most of the 'Asian Tigers' (Hong Kong and Singapore may be exceptions) need to develop better macroeconomic policies to stabilize economic booms and slumps. The failure to alter economic conditions when trade and growth patterns altered was a major contributing factor to the crisis. The failure to adjust exchange rates was also an important factor. This highlights the importance of using exchange rate adjustments when economic conditions become unbalanced: slavish attachment to fixed exchange rates in the face of fundamental imbalances can be very harmful to the well-being of normal financial and economic activities.

CONCLUSIONS

The Asian crisis highlighted many deep-seated problems in the financial and economic structures of the 'Asian Tigers'. The inability of Asian governments to provide stable financial and economic environments was a significant factor that brought about the crisis and hindered the search for a solution to the downward spiral in asset prices and currencies. However, shortcomings in international capital markets also contributed: panic by Western investors spread the crisis across the countries of South East Asia. The crisis has clearly shown that the 'Asian Tigers' have not discovered the Holy Grail of high sustainable growth in the long run. The importance of good government in terms of providing good regulatory frameworks and stable macroeconomic conditions has been firmly underlined by the crisis. Deficiencies in international capital markets have also been emphasized, and the need to reform the international financial architecture has become apparent, in particular, to improve the monitoring and control of short-term capital flows into emerging countries and to develop new methods of dealing with currency and debt crises.

The Asian economic miracle has been shown to be something of a myth. The 'Asian Tigers' have not been particularly good at improving productivity, or at using capital and labour intelligently. High growth and the capture of large shares of export markets have been largely achieved by the copious application of capital and labour to new production processes. The close collaboration between governments, banks and companies facilitated rapid development. However, this process contained the seeds of its own destruction because it led to 'crony capitalism' that encouraged overinvestment and fed property and stock market bubbles. 'Crony capitalism' has advantages for countries that wish to rapidly mobilize capital, labour and technology. However, the hunger for capital that is generated by this system requires inputs from international capital markets. Unfortunately, the goals of international capital markets and 'crony capitalism' are not compatible, and conflict between them leading to crisis is a likely outcome of the clash of interests.

The need to improve TFP as the 'Asian Tigers' developed also highlighted problems with the 'Asian way'. Improvements in productivity increasingly depend not on the application of ever-larger amounts of capital and existing technologies but on developing ways of using capital and labour more intelligently. This requires close evaluation of the returns from investment and the avoidance of interdependencies that lock banks and companies into closed systems that are impervious to new ideas and techniques.

Western companies may be able to learn from the 'Asian Tigers', but the crisis may have revealed that the main lessons to be learned are practices and systems that should be avoided. What may appear to offer an easy route to high and sustainable growth may contain dangerous side-effects that can prove dangerous to the health of economic and business activities. The crisis has also revealed that once economies become developed they encounter much the same problems as those that afflict the existing advanced industrial economies. In this respect, the Asian economies may be able to learn from the crises and institutional reforms that emerged in the West in the 1920s and 1930s. The new institutional structures that emerged in the USA and Western Europe in the aftermath of the Second World War and the evolution of these systems may also provide helpful lessons to the Asian economies about the need for good institutional frameworks to manage advanced capitalist systems. The crisis has also revealed that financial liberalization and the growth of short-term capital flows have created a new and powerful force that we do not fully understand. The need to develop institutional frameworks that can channel this force towards good outcomes is now pressing.

References

Baig, T. and Goldfajn, I. (1998) 'Financial Market Contagion in the Asian Crisis', *IMF Working Paper*, WP/98/155, Washington, DC, IMF.

Bank for International Settlements (BIS) (1997) *67th Annual Report*, Basle, Bank for International Settlements.

Bosworth, P. and Collins, S. (1996) 'Economic Growth in East Asia: Accumulation Versus Assimilation', *Brookings Papers on Economic Activity*, 1, Washington, DC, Brookings Institution.

Crafts, N. (1998) 'East Asian Growth Before and After the Crisis', *IMF Working Paper*, Washington, DC, IMF.

Channon, D. (1998) 'Dinosaurs versus Dragons: Should Strategic Management Theory Redirect its Focus to the East?', in F. McDonald and R. Thorpe, *Organizational Strategy and Technological Adaptation to Global Change*, London, Macmillan.

Dore, R. (1987) Taking Japan Seriously: a Confucian Perspective on Leading Economic Issues, London, Athlone.

Fischer, S. (1998) 'The Asian Crisis: A View from the IMF' <http//www.imf.org/external/np/speeches/1998/012298>.

Furman, J. and Stiglitz, J. (1998) 'Economic Crises: Evidence and Insights from East Asia', *Brookings Papers on Economic Activity*, 2, Washington, DC, Brookings Institution.

Griffiths-Jones, S., Cailloux, J. and Pfaffenzeller, S. (1998) 'The East Asian Financial Crisis: A Reflection on its Causes, Consequences and Policy Implications', *Institute of Development Studies Discussion Paper*, 367, University of Sussex.

Houseman, G. (1995) *America and the Pacific Rim: Coming to Terms With New Realities*, New York, Rowmans & Littlefield.

Hussain, M. and Radelet, S. (1999) 'Export Competitiveness in Asia', *Asian Competitiveness Report 1999*, Geneva, World Economic Forum.

Imai, M. (1986) *Kaizen: The Key to Japan's Competitive Success*, New York, Free Press.

IMF (1998) *World Economic Outlook*, Washington DC, IMF.

Krugman, P. (1994) 'The Myth of East Asia's Miracle', *Foreign Affairs*, 73, 62–78.

Krugman, P. (1998) 'What Happened to Asia?' <http://web.mit.edu/krugman/www/distinter>.

Krugman, P. (1999) 'The Return of Depression Economics', *Foreign Affairs*, 78, 56–74.

Radelet, S. and Sachs, J. (1998) 'The East Asian Financial Crisis: Diagnosis, Remedies and Prospects', *Brookings Papers on Economic Activity*, 1, Washington, DC, Brookings Institution.

Radelet, S. and Sachs, J. (1999) 'What Have We Learned, So Far, From The Asian Financial Crisis?', *US Agency for International Development*, Washington, DC.

Ranis, G. and Stewart, F. (1998) 'The Asian Crisis and Human Development', East Asia Crisis Workshop, Institute of Development, University of Sussex <http://www.ids.ac.uk/ids/research/stewart>.

Stone, M. and Kochhar, K. (1998) 'The East Asian Crisis: Developments and Policy Lessons', *IMF Working Paper*, WP/98/128, Washington, DC, IMF.

Soros, G. (1998) 'Testimony of George Soros to the US House of Representatives: Committee on Banking and Financial Services', 15 September, Washington, DC.

Thurow, L. (1992) *Head to Head; The Coming Economic Battle Among Japan, Europe and America*, London, Nicholas Brealey.

Wade, R. (1992) 'East Asian Economic Success', *World Politics*, 44, 270–320.

Womack, J. Jones, D. and Roos, D. (1990) *The Machine that Changed the World*, New York, Rawson Associates.

World Bank (1993) *The East Asian Miracle, Economic Growth and Public Policy*, Washington, DC, World Bank.

Index

Abbreviations used in index:

EAMPs East Asian Management Practices
EU European Union
FDI foreign direct investment
JVs joint ventures
R&D research and development
SAR Special Administrative Region
SEZ Special Economic Zone (in China)
SOEs state-owned enterprises
TNCs transnational companies
UK United Kingdom
USA United States of America